Lecture Notes in Computer Science 3525

Commenced Publication in 1973
Founding and Former Series Editors:
Gerhard Goos, Juris Hartmanis, and Jan van Leeuwen

Ali E. Abdallah   Cliff B. Jones
Jeff W. Sanders (Eds.)

Communicating Sequential Processes

The First 25 Years

Symposium on the Occasion of 25 Years of CSP
London, UK, July 7-8, 2004
Revised Invited Papers

 Springer

Volume Editors

Ali E. Abdallah
London South Bank University
Faculty of BCIM
Institute for Computing Research
103 Borough Road, London, SE1 0AA, UK
E-mail: A.Abdallah@lsbu.ac.uk

Cliff B. Jones
University of Newcastle upon Tyne
School of Computing Science
Newcastle upon Tyne, NE1 7RU, UK
E-mail: cliff.jones@ncl.ac.uk

Jeff W. Sanders
Oxford University Computing Laboratory
Parks Road, Oxford OX1 3QD, UK
E-mail: Jeff.Sanders@comlab.ox.ac.uk

The cover illustration is the work of Bill Roscoe.

Library of Congress Control Number: 2005925390

CR Subject Classification (1998): D.2.4, F.3, D.1.3, D.3.1

ISSN   0302-9743
ISBN-10   3-540-25813-2 Springer Berlin Heidelberg New York
ISBN-13   978-3-540-25813-1 Springer Berlin Heidelberg New York

Springer is a part of Springer Science+Business Media

springeronline.com

© Springer-Verlag Berlin Heidelberg 2005
Printed in Germany

Typesetting: Camera-ready by author, data conversion by Scientific Publishing Services, Chennai, India
Printed on acid-free paper   SPIN: 11423348   06/3142   5 4 3 2 1 0

Preface

This volume, like the symposium CSP25 which gave rise to it, commemorates the semi-jubilee of Communicating Sequential Processes.

Tony Hoare's paper "Communicating Sequential Processes"[1] is today widely regarded as one of the most influential papers in computer science. To commemorate it, an event was organized under the auspices of BCS-FACS (the British Computer Society's Formal Aspects of Computing Science specialist group). CSP25 was one of a series of such events organized to highlight the use of formal methods, emphasize their relevance to modern computing and promote their wider application. BCS-FACS is proud that Tony Hoare presented his original ideas on CSP at one of its first meetings, in 1978.

The two-day event, 7–8 July 2004, was hosted by London South Bank University's Institute for Computing Research, Faculty of Business, Computing and Information Management. The intention was to celebrate, reflect upon and look beyond the first quarter-century of CSP's contributions to computer science. The meeting examined the impact of CSP on many areas stretching from semantics (mathematical models for understanding concurrency and communications) and logic (for reasoning about behavior), through the design of parallel programming languages (i/o, parallelism, synchronization and threads) to applications varying from distributed software and parallel computing to information security, Web services and concurrent hardware circuits. It included a panel discussion with panelists Brookes, Hoare, de Roever and Roscoe (chaired by Jeff Sanders), poster presentations by PhD students and others, featured a fire alarm (requiring evacuation in the rain!) and concluded with the presentation of a fountain pen to Prof. Sir C. A. R. Hoare.

We owe thanks to the BCS-FACS steering committee and its chairman, Jonathan P. Bowen, for their overwhelming support. Special thanks are due to Dedian Hopkin (LSBU Vice Chancellor) for opening the event in the newly built Keyworth Centre; Chris Clare (Dean), Geoff Elliot (Deputy-Dean), and Terry Fogarty (Head of the Institute for Computing Research) for providing a stimulating environment for hosting the event. Our gratitude goes to our sponsors for their generous support: Microsoft Research, Cambridge, UK; Formal Systems Europe, Limited; Handshake Solutions, Philips, Netherlands; Verified Systems International,GmbH, Germany; Formal Methods Europe (FME); and London South Bank University, Institute for Computing Research. We would like to thank the local organization team: Ali N. Haidar, Michelle Hammond, Kalpesh Kapour and Paul Boca for their hard work to ensure the smooth running of the local arrangements.

---

[1] *Communications of the ACM*, **21**(8):666–667, 1978.

We would also like to thank Bill Roscoe for his "Golden Valley"[2] painting used in the cover of this book. This was the favorite among CSP25 authors who considered several other alternatives. What's its relevance to CSP25? In the words of one of the contributing authors:

> It's a lovely scene with a prominent feature, the much-branching tree representing CSP, and the road winding off representing the 25 years so far, with the rest hidden behind the tree. (Who knows where it may still lead?)

After presentation at the symposium, the contributions were reworked by their authors and fully refereed. We are grateful to all for their timely and efficient work, particularly in the refereeing process where helpful and incisive comments were made. The resulting papers are gathered here, as they were in the workshop, into session-sized chunks, described below.

The conference website can be found at www.lsbu.ac.uk/menass/csp25 and www.bcs-facs.org

Semantic Foundations

The first paper to confront the denotational semantics of CSP with due regard to the interplay between communication and abstraction was "A Theory of Communicating Sequential Processes[3]" by Steve Brookes, Tony Hoare and Bill Roscoe. Before it, the simplistic but intuitively compelling traces model had been the basis for a semantics capable of capturing safety properties but not of capturing liveness (being too weak to capture deadlock or divergence). That paper concentrated on the communicating fragment of CSP, TCSP, based on recursively defined communicating processes evolving in parallel. The study concentrated, inevitably, on the distinction between the choice of events due to the environment choosing from a menu (external choice) and as the result of abstraction (internal, or nondeterministic, choice); in a subsequent paper[4] Brookes and Roscoe extended the denotational model to account also for divergence.

This collection begins with two papers on the semantic foundations of CSP. Brookes replaces the naive traces semantics with one based on actions and Roscoe extends the semantics of divergence and provides an appropriate definition of fixed point. Each paper responds to developments in theoretical computer science during the couple of decades since the 1984 and 1985 papers: the former by acknowledging work on action-based transition systems and the latter by acknowledging progress in our understanding of divergence and fixed points. Each paper provides stronger techniques whilst retaining the flavor of the original CSP.

---

[2] Autumn scene in the Golden Valley, Herefordshire, 2000.

[3] JACM, 31(3):560–599, 1984.

[4] "An Improved Failures Model for CSP," Proc. Seminar on Concurrency, Springer, LNCS 197, 1985.

In the cleverly titled *Retracing the Semantics of CSP* Brookes argues for a traces semantics that is at once more general than that of CSP and yet retains much of the simplicity and design elegance of the original. The only cost is re-evaluation of the notion of trace, to make it action based, and imposition of a fairness condition on processes. The result is a general formalism allowing a bisimulation-type equivalence between processes that differ only in atomicity of their actions.

In *Seeing Beyond Divergence* Roscoe shows how to refine the standard denotational model of a mild extension of TCSP to reveal traces of a process, more extended than just the minimal traces, after which it may diverge. Concentrating on possible divergence, and so ignoring 'refusals or failures' information, he constructs a model (named $\mathcal{SBD}$ as in the title of the paper) to distinguish a process's various opportunities to diverge — something TCSP has never done. To provide meaning to recursion in $\mathcal{SBD}$ Roscoe shows that neither greatest nor least fixed points would be correct and so he is forced to use a two-stage process whose result he calls a reflected fixed point.

A further contribution to fixed-point theory in CSP is provided by Mike Reed in his paper *Order, Topology and Recursion Induction in CSP* later in this volume.

Refinement and Simulation

The major difference between CSP and, for example, the process algebra CCS[5] lies in the distinction each makes between processes. Whilst processes in CSP are related by refinement (one can be replaced by the other for the purpose of implementation), those in CCS are related by the finer notion of (bi)simulation.

In July 2002 a workshop was held at Microsoft Research Ltd. Cambridge to contemplate the differences and similarities between the various process algebras, with the aim of reconciling the fundamental ideas of refinement and simulation, particularly for CSP and CCS. One outcome has been the two papers in this section. Not surprisingly, established co-authors Hoare and He have produced related treatments. Each paper uses the notion of barbed traces in a treatment of process algebra in which refinement and simulation coincide. In fact a combination of the papers, which the reader will find of quite contrasting styles, might be regarded as an extra chapter for their book[6]. Use of barbed traces might be regarded as an alternative solution to the high-level plan of Brookes.

Hardware Synthesis

From its early days CSP has been closely associated with hardware design. David May provides an entertaining account of those days in *CSP, occam and transputers*, the paper of his after-dinner speech. He makes a convincing case for

---

[5] Robin Milner, *Communication and Concurrency*, Prentice-Hall, 1989.
[6] *Unifying Theories of Programming*, Prentice-Hall, 1998.

remembering our own (collective) principles as we progress and for valuing more highly the things at which we are good; and he draws potent conclusions for industry, research and education.

At the same time as inmos, occam and CSP exploited highly-synchronized communication, asynchronous hardware design was enjoying a resurgence of popularity[7]. The appropriate modification to CSP and the revised laws (thought of as being obtained by inserting unbounded buffers along channels) was undertaken by Mark Josephs whose paper *Models for Data-Flow Sequential Processes* extends that work to a wider family of processes and more sophisticated semantic models. It provides some laws and concentrates on denotational semantics.

Philips Electronics, Eindhoven, has shown a long-standing commitment to the use of formal methods and in particular to the work on asynchronous CSP. In his monumental paper *Implementation of Handshake Components*, Ad Peeters shows how CSP underlies the techniques of the established Handshake Technology developed at Philips for the design and implementation of unclocked circuits. The interest focuses on handshaking protocols that are efficient and correct in the various paradigms for unclocked design — summarized in this self-contained article. Peeters demonstrates the remarkable extent to which process algebra successfully pervades the various levels of abstraction.

Transactions

The laws satisfied by asynchronous processes communicating lazily via streams, as treated in the previous section, for example in the article by Mark Josephs, resemble those satisfied in transaction processing: a topic at the heart of applied formal methods. In fact, in his book *Communicating Sequential Processes* Hoare introduced operators to model the interrupt, checkpoint, rollback and recovery of transaction-processing systems. In this section that topic is further explored; the main concern is to maintain atomicity in a distributed system. Some treatments have attempted to do so using event refinement, the process algebra version of the data refinement of sequential programming.

But in *A Trace Semantics for Long-Running Transactions* Michael Butler, Tony Hoare and Carla Ferreira give an elegant calculus of compensations for a restriction of CSP to achieve a similar result. They adopt a traces semantics in which an action is compensable if it can subsequently be undone atomically, and presents a compositional 'cancellation' semantics for processes with nested interruption and compensation.

In *Practical Application of CSP and FDR to Software Design* Jonathan Lawrence acknowledges the difficulty confronting transfer of research — in this case concerning CSP — to industry and presents a case study encapsulating valuable lessons. The study centers on a recent IBM project using CSP and FDR to produce a multi-threaded connection pooling mechanism connecting a transaction-processing system to a Web server. The project spanned three days

---

[7] Ivan Sutherland, "Micropipelines", CACM, 32:720–738, 1989.

and included formal specification in CSP of the required system, validation with some degree of confidence that it captured the informal requirements, expression of the design in CSP and verification of its correctness in FDR. The result was so successful that subsequent enhancements to the delivered Java code could confidently be done by hand. Lawrence highlights the value of applied MSc's which include projects providing students with an opportunity to transfer what they have learnt on the MSc to the workplace.

Concurrent Programming

The extremely active occam user group continues the application of CSP begun in the work described by May in this volume to programming-language design. In *Communicating Mobile Processes* Peter Welch and Frederick Barnes introduce occam-π as a hybrid of occam and the π-calculus introduced by Milner and studied extensively in CCS. The approach is largely pragmatic, including benchmarks and the outline of applications. It is envisaged that a semantics would be denotational, following those of CSP and influenced by the π-calculus.

In *Model-Based Design of Concurrent Programs* Jeff Magee and Jeff Kramer use Label Transition Systems (LTS), a notation based on CSP, to model concurrent systems and to study their behaviours. Their approach combines clear modelling with tools that support graphical animations and systematic generation of parallel implementations in concurrent Java. Both safety checks (essentially traces properties) and liveness checks (under assumptions concerning scheduling and choice) are achieved. They conclude that such animations are useful both to students and practitioners in overcoming resistance to formal methods.

Security

One of formal methods' huge successes in the past decade has been to reasoning about security. In terms of CSP, the success has been largely due to work by Bill Roscoe et al. and Gavin Lowe (with the Caspar tool).

In *Verifying Security Protocols: an Application of CSP* Steve Schneider and Rob Delicata provide an elegant case study showing how CSP, with the notion of a rank function, can be used to reason about an authentication protocol. After proposing a putative protocol their analysis locates a flaw and verifies the correctness of a modification. In verification, the rank function is used to show that illegitimate messages do not occur. The paper is self-contained and might be used by those familiar with CSP as an introduction to this topical area.

Over the years various models of computation have been used to formalize non-interference. Typically these floundered on non-determinism, "input/output" distinctions, input totality and so forth. In *Shedding Light on Haunted Corners of Information Security* Peter Ryan outlines how process algebras, in particular CSP, can be applied to give a formal characterization of the absence of information flows through a system. Unfortunately, Peter Ryan was unable to attend due to compelling personal reasons at the last minute. Hence, only the abstract of his talk is included in this volume.

Linking Theories

Whilst security has provided one important playing field for CSP, probability has provided another. The challenge is to express and reason about distributed probabilistic algorithms using a variant of process algebra that includes a combinator for choice, with given probability, between two processes. Unacceptable attempts abound. In *Of Probabilistic wp and CSP — and Compositionality*, Carroll Morgan starts 'afresh' from the successful work on probabilistic sequential programming and targets process algebra via the intermediary of action systems. His translation throws up healthiness conditions for probabilistic CSP and suggests a program of work that might — finally — result in a compositional probabilistic process algebra. Incidentally his discussion of (general) compositionality using the example of eye color and the Mendelian concept of allele is a gem.

In this section is included the abstract for the talk by Mike Reed *Order, Topology and Recursion Induction in CSP* that might be thought of as a contribution to semantic foundations. He presents a recursion-induction principle that produces least fixed points for functions whose least fixed points are maximal (i.e., deterministic in the failures model of CSP). The setting is a Scott domain and the results are general enough to cover existing instances of recursion induction in CSP; in topology they are strong enough to provide answers to open questions from domain theory and point-set topology.

Automated Development, Reasoning and Model Checking

As a formal method, CSP was slow to respond to the pressure for automation. Perhaps as a result, Formal Methods' tool FDR achieved immediate success; for instance it has played a crucial role in many of the papers in this volume. But it, and its scope, still progress as the papers by Michael Goldsmith and Ranko Lazić indicate.

In *Operational Semantics for Fun and Profit* Michael Goldsmith observes that a source of computation inefficiency in FDR is evaluation of the structured operational semantics of the operationally–presented target system (an evaluation that is necessary whenever a denotational property is to be determined). He proposes a *supercompilation* procedure to overcome it, if not in every case then at least in many. An unexpected benefit of supercompilation is transformation of a process to a form accessible to previously studied *watchdog* transformations that enable a refinement check to be recast in more efficient form.

The method of data independence allows a model-checking argument, concerning a process whose data type takes on a single value, to be extended to that process with arbitrary data value. In *On model Checking Data-Independent Systems with Arrays with Whole-Array Operations* Ranko Lazić, the originator of the technique of data independence in CSP, Tom Newcomb, and Bill Roscoe show how to extend it to programs using arrays indexed by one data-independent variable that have values from another. They obtain simple and natural conditions for decidability or undecidability of realistic questions concerning the use of such types.

For all its use, and all its appearance in this volume, FDR is far from being the only formalism for animating CSP. In the article by Magee and Kramer *Model-Based Design of Concurrent Programs* an alternative has already been demonstrated.

Industrial-Strength CSP

We have seen how CSP has been used to study theoretical aspects of concurrency and that it seems to offer yet further potential for doing so. We have seen how it has been used in hardware design, at both the implementation and design levels. And we have seen how its tools offer industrial-strength model checking. But what about the broader scope of software engineering?

In *Industrial-Strength CSP: Opportunities and Challenges in Model-Checking*, Sadie Creese demonstrates the use of FDR in reasoning about various aspects of high-integrity systems from industry, as seen from her perspective in the Systems Assurance Group within QinetiQ.

In the paper *Applied Formal Methods — from CSP to Executable Hybrid Specifications* Jan Peleska discusses his work at Verified Systems International and the University of Bremen. His case studies are drawn from an impressively realistic range, including an implementation of Byzantine agreement to provide a fault-tolerant component of the International Space Station, and the avionics controller of the Airbus A340. He discusses the difficulties involved in the production of large and complex systems. Hybrid methods become important and executability, in the form of tools available for prototyping, necessary to convince coworkers. But in the end formal methods, and in particular CSP, remainS just one of a spectrum of techniques that contribute to product quality.

Reflections!

It is not often that burgeoning areas are afforded the luxury of reflecting on both their past and futures. With the contributions contained in this volume the reader has evidence enough to decide the relevance of Gilbert Ryle's warning (*Dilemmas*, The Tarner Lectures, 1953, Cambridge University Press, digital printing 2002, page 14.)

> Karl Marx was sapient enough to deny the impeachment that he was a Marxist. So too Plato was, in my view, a very unreliable Platonist. He was too much of a philosopher to think that anything that he had said was the last word. It was left to his disciples to identify his foot marks with his destination.

Ali E. Abdallah, Cliff B. Jones and Jeff W. Sanders
London, Newcastle and Oxford, January 2005

Sponsors

BCS- Formal Aspect of
Computing Science
specialist group

London South Bank
University, UK

Microsoft Research,
Cambridge, UK

Formal Methods
Europe

Handshake
Solutions, Philips,
Netherlands

Verified Systems
International, GmbH,
Germany

Formal Systems (Europe)
Limited

Table of Contents

Linking Theories

Security

Automated Development and Model Checking

Industrial-Strength CSP

Retracing the Semantics of CSP

Stephen Brookes

Carnegie Mellon University

Abstract. CSP was originally introduced as a parallel programming language in which sequential imperative processes execute concurrently and communicate by synchronized input and output. The influence of CSP and the closely related process algebra TCSP is widespread. Over the years CSP has been equipped with a series of denotational semantic models, involving notions such as communication traces, failure sets, and divergence traces, suitable for compositional reasoning about safety properties and deadlock analysis. We revisit these notions (and review some of the underlying philosophy) with the benefit of hindsight, and we introduce a semantic framework based on action traces that permits a unified account of shared memory parallelism, asynchronous communication, and synchronous communication. The framework also allows a relatively straightforward account of (a weak form of) fairness, so that we obtain models suitable for compositional reasoning about liveness properties as well as about safety properties and deadlock. We show how to incorporate race detection into this semantic framework, leading to models more independent of hardware assumptions about the granularity of atomic actions.

1 Introduction

The parallel programming language CSP was introduced in Tony Hoare's classic paper [15]. As originally formulated, CSP is an imperative language of guarded commands [11], extended with primitives for input and output and a form of parallel composition which permits synchronized communication between named processes. The original language derives its full name from the built-in syntactic constraint that processes belong to the sequential subset of the language. The syntax of programs was also constrained to preclude concurrent attempts by one process to write to a variable being used by another process: this may be expressed succinctly as the requirement that processes have "disjoint local states". These design decisions, influenced by Dijkstra's principle of "loose coupling" [10], lead to an elegant programming language in which processes interact solely by message-passing. Ideas from CSP have passed the test of time, having influenced the design of more recent parallel programming languages such as Ada, occam [18], and Concurrent ML [26].

Most of the subsequent foundational research has focussed on a process algebra known as *Theoretical CSP* (or *TCSP*) in which the imperative aspects of the original language are suppressed [2]. In TCSP (and in occam) processes

A.E. Abdallah, C.B. Jones, and J.W. Sanders (Eds.): CSP**25**, LNCS 3525, pp. 1–14, 2005.

communicate by message-passing along named channels, again using a synchronized handshake for communication. TCSP permits nested parallelism and recursive process definitions, and includes a form of localization for events known as *hiding*. Instead of Dijkstra-style guarded commands TCSP includes two forms of "choice": internal choice, and external choice. The internal form of choice corresponds to a guarded command with purely boolean guards: if more than one guard is true the selection of branch to execute is non-deterministic and made "internally" without consideration of the surrounding context. An external choice corresponds to a guarded command with input guards, for which the "truth" of a guard depends on the availability of matching output in the surrounding context.

Hoare's early paper on CSP [15] presented an informal sketch of a semantics for processes, expressed in intuitive terms with the help of operational intuition. Plotkin later gave a more formal structured operational semantics for a semantically more natural extension of the language [25]. Plotkin employed a more generous syntax allowing nested parallelism, and a more flexible scoping mechanism for process naming. Over the years CSP has become equipped with a series of semantic models of successively greater sophistication, each designed to support compositional reasoning about a specific class of program property.

In 1980 Hoare introduced a mathematical account of communication traces that developed more rigorously from the intuitions outlined in the original CSP paper [16]. In this model a process is taken to denote a set of communication traces, built from events which represent abstract records of communication. A trace here represents a partial history of the communication sequence occurring when a process interacts with its environment; since communication is synchronized an input or output event really stands for a potential for communication. And since traces record a partial behavior it is natural to work with (non-empty) prefix-closed sets of traces. This semantics is suitable for reasoning about simple safety properties of processes, but is too abstract for many purposes since it ignores the potential for deadlock. For example, the processes

$$\textbf{if } (\textbf{true} \to a?x; h!x) \,\square\, (\textbf{true} \to b?x; h!x) \textbf{ fi}$$
$$\textbf{if } (a?x \to h!x) \,\square\, (b?x \to h!x) \textbf{ fi}$$

have the same set of communication traces, but only the first one may deadlock when run in parallel with a process such as $b!0$. Moreover, if **stop** is a process incapable of any communication (so that its only communication trace is the empty trace), the processes

$$\textbf{if } (a?x \to h!x) \textbf{ fi}$$
$$\textbf{if } (a?x \to h!x) \,\square\, (a?x \to \textbf{stop}) \textbf{ fi}$$
$$\textbf{if } (a?x \to h!x) \,\square\, (\textbf{true} \to \textbf{stop}) \textbf{ fi}$$

have the same communication traces (because of prefix-closure) although there are clear operational reasons to distinguish between these processes.

The need to model deadlock led to the *failures* model of Hoare, Brookes and Roscoe [2], in which communication traces were augmented with information about the potential for further communication, represented abstractly (and negatively) as a refusal set. A failure (α, X) consists of a communication trace α and a set X of events, representing the ability to perform the communications in α and then refuse to perform any of the events in X. (Obviously it is equally reasonable to develop a positively formulated notion of acceptance set or ready set rather than refusal [22].) Again operational and observational intuitions suggest that a process should denote a set of failures closed under certain natural rules. The mathematical foundations of the failures model were explored more deeply in the D.Phil. theses of Bill Roscoe and myself [1, 27]. A more readily accessible account, which also discusses a variety of related semantic models, is obtainable in Roscoe's book [28].

The failures model, like the communication traces model from which it evolved, allows compositional reasoning about safety properties; but failures also permit distinctions based on the potential for deadlock. Revisiting the above examples, the processes

$$\textbf{if } (\textbf{true} \rightarrow a?x; h!x) \,\Box\, (\textbf{true} \rightarrow b?x; h!x) \textbf{ fi}$$
$$\textbf{if } (a?x \rightarrow h!x) \,\Box\, (b?x \rightarrow h!x) \textbf{ fi}$$

do *not* denote the same set of failures: only the first process can refuse to input on a (or refuse to input on b). Similarly the processes

$$\textbf{if } (a?x \rightarrow h!x) \textbf{ fi}$$
$$\textbf{if } (a?x \rightarrow h!x) \,\Box\, (a?x \rightarrow \textbf{stop}) \textbf{ fi}$$
$$\textbf{if } (a?x \rightarrow h!x) \,\Box\, (\textbf{true} \rightarrow \textbf{stop}) \textbf{ fi}$$

do not have the same failures. The behavioral distinctions between these examples, expressible in terms of failures, have a natural operational intuition.

The failures model, although offering good support for safety properties and deadlock analysis, still suffers from a deficiency with respect to the phenomenon of *infinite internal chatter*, or *divergence*. We illustrate the problem with an example. The program

$$\textbf{chan } a \textbf{ in}$$
$$(\textbf{while true do } a?x) \parallel (\textbf{while true do } a!0)$$

involves two processes which keep communicating "internally" on the hidden channel a. Externally, no visible communication is apparent, and it is natural to ask what responses, if any, the program should be deemed to provide to its environment if the environment offers a potential for communication. Presumably the environment cannot ever discover in a finite amount of time that the program will never become capable of communication, since the program never reaches a "stable" configuration. There is no way to represent this kind of behavior adequately within the confines of the failures model, since divergence (while doing no external communication) could only be represented by failures containing the empty trace (and all possible refusal sets), but this would be tantamount to equating deadlock with divergence.

In response to this problem, Brookes and Roscoe proposed a further augmentation of failures to incorporate *divergence traces* [3]. A divergence trace represents a sequence of communications leading to a possible divergent behavior. For pragmatic reasons, again based on observability criteria and the view that a well behaved process should respond to its environment in a finite amount of time, divergence is treated as a catastrophe in this model. Thus, a process is taken to denote a failure set F, together with a set D of divergence traces, satisfying the following catastrophic closure rule:

– if $\alpha \in D$ then for all traces β and refusal sets X, $(\alpha\beta, X) \in F$, and for all
   traces β, $\alpha\beta \in D$.

As an example, the simple divergent program listed above has the empty trace as a possible divergence trace, from which it follows from the closure rule that its denotation includes all failures and all divergence traces. In contrast the denotation of a deadlocked process would consist of all failures involving the empty trace, together with the empty set of divergence traces.

The failures/divergences model, despite its rather awkward name, has become the standard semantics for an enormous range of CSP research and implementation [17]. This model underpins the FDR model checker [12], which has been used successfully for the analysis of (and detection of bugs in) parallel systems and protocols [30]. Roscoe and Hoare have also shown how to incorporate state directly into the structure of failure sets, in developing a failure-style semantics for *occam* [29].

2   Reflection

In these early models of CSP the focus is on finite behaviors, with infinite traces either ignored or regarded as being present only by virtue of finite prefixes. Consequently these models did not take fairness into account. Yet fairness assumptions, such as the guarantee that a process waiting for input will eventually be synchronized if another process is simultaneously (and persistently) waiting for a matching output, are vital when trying to reason about liveness properties [24, 23]. As a result it can be argued that these models are, by their very design, less than ideally suited to reasoning about liveness.

Although it is possible to develop straightforward variants of these models that incorporate infinite traces [28], it is not obvious how to augment them in such a way that only *fair* traces get included. Indeed there is a plethora of distinct fairness notions in the literature [13], and it is not clear which (if any) of these notions are simultaneously a reasonable abstraction from network implementation and adaptable to CSP. Susan Older's Ph.D. thesis [21] contains a detailed discussion of the problems that arise as well as a family of models tailored to specific fairness notions. Older's models can be regarded as failures/divergences equipped with infinite traces and book-keeping information about persistently enabled communication [6]. As Older discovered, it can be very difficult to figure out a suitable augmentation regime for extending failures/divergences to match a given notion of fairness, largely because of the fact that enabledness of communication for one process depends on enabledness of matching communication in another process. The difficulties seem less severe when dealing with asynchronous communication [5].

The models described so far were developed specifically with TCSP in mind, and serve this role admirably. However, CSP is not the only paradigmatic parallel programming language and it is natural to compare the semantic framework built for CSP with the models developed over the years for shared memory parallel programs and for networks of asynchronously communicating processes. By the same token, TCSP is not the only process algebra, and the emphasis in CSP on deadlock and divergence is in sharp contrast to the focus on *bisimulation* in calculi based on Milner's CCS [19, 20]. Unfortunately there is frustratingly little similarity in structure between the early semantic models developed for these other paradigms and these CSP models. For instance the *resumptions* of Hennessy and Plotkin [14], and the *transition traces* of Park [24] (later adapted by this author [4]), originally proposed to model shared memory parallel programs, bear no obvious structural relationship with failures.

These semantic disparities make it difficult to apply techniques successful in one setting to similar problems occurring in the other settings. For instance, Older's construction of fair models of CSP does not immediately suggest an analogous construction for a language of asynchronously communicating processes. A further disparity is caused by the emphasis (for obvious reasons) on state in traditional models of shared memory parallelism, in contrast to the prevailing tendency in process algebras such as CSP and CCS to abstract away from state [19, 2].

In a paper presented in tribute to the twentieth anniversary of CSP [7] this author proposed a semantic model based on transition traces, suitable for modelling both shared memory parallel programs and networks of processes communicating asynchronously on named channels. At that time it seemed unlikely that similar techniques would prove suitable for modelling synchronized communication, because of the difficulties encountered by Older in adapting failures to fairness in the synchronous setting. Nevertheless the author discovered later that essentially the same framework can also be made to work for synchronously communicating processes, provided a simple enough notion of fairness is adopted [8]. This is a somewhat surprising turn of events given the prior history of separate development. More recently still, we realized that it is possible to modify this semantic framework in a natural way to handle *race conditions*, leading to an improved semantics in which assumptions about the granularity of atomic actions become less significant [9]. We will now summarize the main technical notions behind this semantics. The key turns out to involve the choice of a suitably general notion of trace, which can be presented in a process algebraic formulation and separately instantiated later in a state-dependent setting.

3 Communicating Parallel Processes

We will work with a language combining shared memory parallelism with communicating processes. Thus processes will be allowed to share state and will be permitted to interact by reading and writing to shared variables as well as by sending and receiving messages. We also include resources and conditional critical regions to allow synchronization and mutually exclusive access to critical data.

Let P range over *processes* and G over *guarded processes*, given by the following abstract grammar, in which e ranges over integer-valued expressions, b over boolean expressions, h over the set **Chan** of channel names, x over the set **Ide** of identifiers, and r over resource names. We omit the syntax of expressions, which is conventional.

$$P ::= \mathbf{skip} \mid x{:=}e \mid P_1; P_2 \mid \mathbf{if}\ b\ \mathbf{then}\ P_1\ \mathbf{else}\ P_2 \mid \mathbf{while}\ b\ \mathbf{do}\ P \mid$$
$$P_1 \| P_2 \mid \mathbf{with}\ r\ \mathbf{when}\ b\ \mathbf{do}\ P \mid \mathbf{resource}\ r\ \mathbf{in}\ P \mid$$
$$h?x \mid h!e \mid \mathbf{if}\ G\ \mathbf{fi} \mid \mathbf{do}\ G\ \mathbf{od} \mid P_1 \sqcap P_2 \mid \mathbf{chan}\ h\ \mathbf{in}\ P$$
$$G ::= (h?x \to P) \mid G_1 \square G_2$$

As in CSP, $P_1 \sqcap P_2$ is "internal" choice, and $G_1 \square G_2$ is "external" choice. We distinguish syntactically between guarded and general processes merely to enforce the constraint that the "external choice" construct is only applicable to input-guarded processes. This allows certain simplifications in the semantic definitions but is not crucial. It is straightforward to extend our semantics to allow mixed boolean and input guards.

The construct **chan** h **in** P introduces a local channel named h with scope P. One can also allow locally scoped variable declarations, but we omit the details. We write $chans(P)$ for the set of channel names occurring free in P. In particular, $chans(\mathbf{chan}\ h\ \mathbf{in}\ P) = chans(P) - \{h\}$.

A process of form **resource** r **in** P introduces a local resource name r, whose scope is P. A process of form **with** r **when** b **do** P is a *conditional critical region* for resource r, with body P. A process attempting to enter such a region must wait until the resource is available, acquire the resource and evaluate b: if b is **true** the process executes P then releases the resource; if b is **false** the process releases the resource and waits to try again. A resource can only be held by one process at a time. We use the abbreviation **with** r **do** P when b is **true**.

4   Actions

The behavior of a process will be explained in terms of the *actions* that it can perform. An action can be regarded as an atomic step which may or may not be enabled in a given state, and if enabled has an effect on the state. Let V_{int} be the set of integers, with typical member v. An *action* has one of the following forms:

- A *read* $x{=}v$, where x is an identifier and v is an integer.
- A *write* $x{:=}v$, where x is an identifier and v is an integer.
- A *communication* $h?v$ or $h!v$, where h is a channel name and v is an integer. Each communication action has a *direction*: $h!$ for output, $h?$ for input, on a specific channel h.
- A *idling action* of form δ_X, where X is a finite set of directions.

- A *resource action* of one of the forms $try(r), acq(r), rel(r)$, where r is a resource name.
- An error action *abort*.

We will not yet provide formal details concerning states and effects, relying instead for now on the following intuitions.

A read $x=v$ is enabled only in a state for which the current value of x is v, and causes no state change. A write $x:=v$ is only enabled in states for which x has a current value, and its effect is to change the value of x to v.

An input action $h?v$ or output action $h!v$ represents the *potential* for a process to perform communication, and can only be completed when another process offers a matching communication on the same channel. We write $match(\lambda_1, \lambda_2)$ when λ_1 and λ_2 are matching actions, i.e. when there is a channel h and an integer v such that $\{\lambda_1, \lambda_2\} = \{h?v, h!v\}$. We let $chan(h?v) = chan(h!v) = h$.

An idling action δ_X represents an unrequited attempt to communicate along the directions in X. When X is a singleton we write $\delta_{h?}$ or $\delta_{h!}$. When X is empty we write δ instead of $\delta_{\{\}}$; the action δ is also used to represent a "silent" local action, such as a synchronized handshake or reading or writing a local variable.

An action of form $try(r)$ represents an unsuccessful attempt to acquire resource r, and $acq(r)$ represents a successful attempt to do so; $rel(r)$ represents the act of releasing the resource. Parallel execution is assumed to be constrained to ensure that at all stages each resource is being held by at most one process. Thus at all stages the sets of resources belonging to each process will be disjoint. Correspondingly, for an action λ and a disjoint pair of resource sets A_1 and A_2 we define a *resource enabling* relation $(A_1, A_2) \xrightarrow{\lambda} (A_1', A_2')$, characterized by the following rules:

$$(A_1, A_2) \xrightarrow{try(r)} (A_1, A_2)$$
$$(A_1, A_2) \xrightarrow{acq(r)} (A_1 \cup \{r\}, A_2) \quad \text{if } r \notin A_1 \cup A_2$$
$$(A_1, A_2) \xrightarrow{rel(r)} (A_1 - \{r\}, A_2) \quad \text{if } r \in A_1$$
$$(A_1, A_2) \xrightarrow{\lambda} (A_1, A_2) \quad \text{otherwise}$$

Since A_1 and A_2 are disjoint, if $(A_1, A_2) \xrightarrow{\lambda} (A_1', A_2')$ it follows that $A_2' = A_2$, and A_1' is disjoint from A_2. Intuitively, when $(A_1, A_2) \xrightarrow{\lambda} (A_1', A_2)$ holds, a process holding resources A_1 can safely perform action λ in a parallel environment that holds resources A_2, and will hold resources A_1' afterwards.

The *abort* action represents a runtime error, is always enabled, and leads to an error state, which we denote **abort**.

5   Action Traces

An action trace is a non-empty finite or infinite sequence of actions. Let **Tr** be the set of action traces; we will use α, β, γ as meta-variables ranging over traces. We write $\alpha\beta$ for the trace obtained by concatenating α and β. We assume that δ behaves as a unit for concatenation, so that $\alpha\delta\beta = \alpha\beta$ for all traces α

and β; this means, effectively, that we ignore finite idling, since $\delta^n = \delta$ for all $n > 0$. However, we still distinguish infinite idling (represented by the trace δ^ω) from δ. We also assume that *abort* behaves as a zero for concatenation, so that $\alpha \, abort \, \beta = \alpha \, abort$, for all traces α and β. This means that we regard an error as fatal, so there is no need to observe what happens "after" *abort*.

We assume given the trace semantics for expressions, so that for an integer expression e we have $[\![e]\!] \subseteq \mathbf{Tr} \times V_{int}$. Similarly for a boolean expression b we have $[\![b]\!] \subseteq \mathbf{Tr} \times \{\mathbf{true}, \mathbf{false}\}$. We let $[\![b]\!]_{\mathbf{true}} = \{\rho \mid (\rho, \mathbf{true}) \in [\![b]\!]\}$ and similarly for $[\![b]\!]_{\mathbf{false}}$. The only actions occurring in expression traces are δ and reads.

A process denotes a set of traces, denoted $[\![P]\!] \subseteq \mathbf{Tr}$. The semantics of processes is defined denotationally, by structural induction. We list here some of the key clauses.

$$[\![h!e]\!] = \delta_{\{h!\}}{}^\infty \{\rho \, h!v \mid (\rho, v) \in [\![e]\!]\}$$
$$[\![h?x]\!] = \delta_{\{h?\}}{}^\infty \{h?v \, x{:=}v \mid v \in V_{int}\}$$
$$[\![P_1; P_2]\!] = [\![P_1]\!] \, [\![P_2]\!]$$
$$[\![P_1 \| P_2]\!] = [\![P_1]\!] \, {}_{\{\}}\|_{\{\}} \, [\![P_2]\!]$$
$$[\![\mathbf{with} \ r \ \mathbf{when} \ b \ \mathbf{do} \ P]\!] = wait^\infty \ enter$$
$$\text{where } wait = \{try(r)\} \cup acq(r) \, [\![b]\!]_{\mathbf{false}} \ rel(r)$$
$$\text{and } \ enter = acq(r) \, [\![b]\!]_{\mathbf{true}} \, [\![P]\!] \ rel(r)$$
$$[\![\mathbf{chan} \ h \ \mathbf{in} \ P]\!] = \{\alpha \backslash h \mid \alpha \in [\![P]\!] \ \& \ h \notin chans(\alpha)\}$$

The semantic clauses for input and output commands include traces that represent infinite waiting for matching output and input, respectively. Sequential composition corresponds to concatenation of traces. The trace set of a conditional critical region reflects the operational behavior discussed earlier: waiting until the resource can be acquired and the test expression evaluates to $\mathbf{true}$. In the special case where b is $\mathbf{true}$ we can derive the following simpler formula:

$$[\![\mathbf{with} \ r \ \mathbf{do} \ P]\!] = try(r)^\infty \ acq(r) \, [\![P]\!] \ rel(r).$$

The clause for a local channel declaration "forces" synchronization to occur on the local channel. We write $\alpha \backslash h$ for the trace obtained from α by deleting $h!$ and $h?$ from all sets of directions occurring in idling actions along α.

The clause for parallel composition involves a form of *mutex fairmerge* for trace sets. When A_1 and A_2 are disjoint sets of resource names and T_1 and T_2 are trace sets, $T_1 \, {}_{A_1}\|_{A_2} \, T_2$ denotes the set of all (synchronizing) interleavings of a trace from T_1 with a trace from T_2, subject to the constraint that the process executing T_1 starts with resources A_1 and the process executing T_2 starts with resources A_2, and at all stages the resources held by the two processes stay disjoint. For each pair of traces α_1 and α_2 we define the set of traces $\alpha_1 \, {}_{A_1}\|_{A_2} \, \alpha_2$, and then we let $T_1 \, {}_{A_1}\|_{A_2} \, T_2 = \bigcup\{\alpha_1 \, {}_{A_1}\|_{A_2} \, \alpha_2 \mid \alpha_1 \in T_1 \ \& \ \alpha_2 \in T_2\}$.

We design this fairmerge operator so that the potential of a *race* (concurrent execution of actions which may interfere in an unpredictable manner) is treated as a catastrophe. We write $\lambda_1 \bowtie \lambda_2$ to indicate a race, given by the following rules:

$$x = v \bowtie x := v'$$
$$x := v \bowtie x = v'$$
$$x := v \bowtie x := v'$$
$$h!v \bowtie h!v'$$
$$h?v \bowtie h?v'$$

In particular, we regard as a race any concurrent attempt to write to a variable being read or written by another process. And we also treat concurrent attempts to input to the same channel, or to output to the same channel, as a race.

For finite traces (including the empty sequence to allow a simpler base case) the set of mutex fairmerges using any given pair of disjoint resource sets can be characterized inductively from the following clauses:

$$\alpha_{A_1} \|_{A_2} \epsilon = \{\alpha \mid (A_1, A_2) \xrightarrow{\alpha} \cdot\}$$
$$\epsilon_{A_1} \|_{A_2} \alpha = \{\alpha \mid (A_2, A_1) \xrightarrow{\alpha} \cdot\}$$
$$(\lambda_1 \alpha_1)_{A_1} \|_{A_2} (\lambda_2 \alpha_2) = \{abort\} \quad \text{if } \lambda_1 \bowtie \lambda_2$$
$$(\lambda_1 \alpha_1)_{A_1} \|_{A_2} (\lambda_2 \alpha_2) =$$
$$\{\lambda_1 \gamma \mid (A_1, A_2) \xrightarrow{\lambda_1} (A_1', A_2) \ \& \ \gamma \in \alpha_{1 \ A_1'} \|_{A_2} (\lambda_2 \alpha_2)\}$$
$$\cup \ \{\lambda_2 \gamma \mid (A_2, A_1) \xrightarrow{\lambda_2} (A_2', A_1) \ \& \ \gamma \in (\lambda_1 \alpha_1)_{A_1} \|_{A_2'} \alpha_2\}$$
$$\cup \ \{\delta \gamma \mid match(\lambda_1, \lambda_2) \ \& \ \gamma \in \alpha_{1 \ A_1} \|_{A_2} \alpha_2\}$$
$$\text{if } \neg(\lambda_1 \bowtie \lambda_2)$$

The above clauses actually suffice for all pairs of traces, one of which is finite. We can extend this mutex fairmerge relation to pairs of infinite traces in a natural manner, imposing a fairness constraint that reflects our assumption that a pair of processes waiting for a matching pair of communications will eventually get scheduled to communicate. This is a variant of weak process fairness adapted to take account of the synchronization mechanism used for CSP-style communication. Although we omit the full definition, note the following special case involving two infinite waiting traces:

$$\delta_X^\omega \ _{A_1} \|_{A_2} \ \delta_Y^\omega = \{\}$$

if $\exists h. \ (h? \in X \ \& \ h! \in Y) \lor (h! \in X \ \& \ h? \in Y)$. This captures formally the fairness assumption from above: there is no fair way to interleave the actions of these two traces because there is a persistent opportunity for synchronization that never gets taken.

6 Examples

We now revisit the examples discussed earlier, previously used to illustrate communication traces, failures, and divergences.

First, we contrast the action traces of an internal choice with those of the corresponding external choice.

$$[\![(a?x \to h!x) \sqcap (b?x \to h!x)]\!] = \delta_{\{a?\}}^\infty \{a?v \, x := v \, h!v \mid v \in V_{int}\}$$
$$\cup \ \delta_{\{b?\}}^\infty \{b?v \, x := v \, h!v \mid v \in V_{int}\}$$

$$[\![\textbf{if } (a?x \to h!x) \,\square\, (b?x \to h!x) \textbf{ fi}]\!] = \delta_{\{a?,b?\}}{}^{\infty}\{a?v\, x:=v\, h!v \mid v \in V_{int}\}$$
$$\cup \, \delta_{\{a?,b?\}}{}^{\infty}\{b?v\, x:=v\, h!v \mid v \in V_{int}\}$$

As with the failures model this semantics distinguishes properly between these processes. There is an obvious sense in which the ability to "refuse" input on a is represented here by the presence of a trace involving infinite waiting for input on b.

Similarly we have

$$[\![a?x \to h!x]\!] = \delta_{\{a?\}}{}^{\infty}\{a?v\, x:=v\, h!v \mid v \in V_{int}\}$$

$$[\![\textbf{if } (a?x \to h!x) \,\square\, (a?x \to \textbf{stop}) \textbf{ fi}]\!] =$$
$$\delta_{\{a?\}}{}^{\infty}\{a?v\, x:=v\, h!v \mid v \in V_{int}\}$$
$$\cup \, \delta_{\{a?\}}{}^{\infty}\{a?v\, x:=v\, \alpha \mid \alpha \in [\![\textbf{stop}]\!] \ \& \ \mid v \in V_{int}\}$$

so that again we distinguish correctly between these processes. (We note in passing here that every process, even **stop**, denotes a non-empty set of traces.)

The divergent program discussed earlier,

> **chan** a **in**
> (**while true do** $a?x$) $\|$ (**while true do** $a!0$),

denotes the action trace set $\{\delta^{\omega}\}$. We see no compelling reason to distinguish this program from a deadlocked process such as **stop** or the process

> **chan** a **in** $(a?x; h!x)$,

which will never be able to engage in external communication on channel h because the local channel a is not in scope for any external process. This process waits forever for input on the local channel, a phenomenon that gives rise to the trace $\delta_{\{\}}{}^{\omega}$. Indeed our semantics gives this program the corresponding trace set $\{\delta^{\omega}\}$. We also choose *not* to interpret divergence as catastrophic, although it would be possible to derive a model along those lines by imposing suitable closure conditions on action trace sets.

The following semantic equivalences illustrate how our model supports reasoning about process behavior.

Theorem 1 (Synchronous Laws)
The following laws hold in the synchronous trace semantics:

1. $[\![\textbf{chan } h \textbf{ in } (h?x; P)\|(h!v; Q)]\!] = [\![\textbf{chan } h \textbf{ in } (x:=v; \ (P\|Q))]\!]$
2. $[\![\textbf{chan } h \textbf{ in } (h?x; P)\|(Q_1; Q_2)]\!] = [\![Q_1; \textbf{chan } h \textbf{ in } (h?x; P)\|Q_2]\!]$
   provided $h \notin \textsf{chans}(Q_1)$
3. $[\![\textbf{chan } h \textbf{ in } (h!v; P)\|(Q_1; Q_2)]\!] = [\![Q_1; \textbf{chan } h \textbf{ in } (h!v; P)\|Q_2]\!]$
   provided $h \notin \textsf{chans}(Q_1)$.

These laws reflect our assumption of fairness, and can be particularly helpful in proving liveness properties. They are not valid in an unfair semantics: if execution is unfair there is no guarantee in the first law that the synchronization will eventually occur, and there is no guarantee in the second or third laws that the right-hand process will ever execute its initial (non-local) code.

7   Granularity

Our semantics involves actions which represent rather high-level operations, such as assignments of an entire integer value to a variable, and communication of an entire integer value along a channel. Rather than assuming that such actions are implemented at the hardware or network level as indivisible atomic operations, we have designed our parallel composition so that any concurrent attempt to perform actions whose combined effect is sensitive to granularity is treated as a catastrophe. As a consequence, our semantics can be shown to be independent of granularity in a precise sense.

Specifically, we can give a "low-level" semantics for processes, based on "low-level" actions that represent fine-grained atomic steps. At low-level we assume that integers are represented as lists of words, with some fixed word size W, and that messages are transmitted as sequences of packets, of some fixed packet size M. A high-level read of the form $x=v$ then corresponds to a sequence of low-level reads of the form $x.0=w_0 \ldots x.k:=w_k$, where $x.0, \ldots, x.k$ represent the various components of x and the sequence of word values $w_0 \ldots w_k$ represents the integer v (for word size W). Similarly a high-level write corresponds to a sequence of low-level writes. A high-level input action $h?v$ corresponds to a sequence of low-level input actions terminated by an end-of-transmission signal, and similarly for an output action. Let us write $v = [w_0, \ldots, w_k]_W$ to indicate that the given word sequence represents v, i.e. that $v = w_0 + 2^W w_1 + \cdots + 2^{kW} w_k$, with a similar notation $v = [m_0, \ldots, m_n]_M$ for messages. In the low-level semantics, which we will denote $\llbracket P \rrbracket_{low}$, we would thus have:

$$\llbracket h!e \rrbracket_{low} = \{\rho \, h!m_0 \ldots h!m_n \, h!\texttt{EOT} \mid (\rho, v) \in \llbracket e \rrbracket \ \& \ [m_0, \ldots, m_n]_M = v\}$$
$$\llbracket h?x \rrbracket_{low} = \{h?m_0 \ldots h?m_n \, h?\texttt{EOT} \, x.0{:=}w_0 \ldots x.k{:=}w_k \mid$$
$$v = [m_0, \ldots, m_n]_M = [w_0, \ldots, w_k]_W\}$$

A high-level state σ describes the values of a finite collection of variables, so that σ is a finite partial function from identifiers to integers. A low-level state can be regarded as a finite partial function τ from identifiers to lists of words. The effect of a high-level action λ can be formalized as a partial function $\overset{\lambda}{\Longrightarrow}$ between high-level states, and similarly for low-level actions and their effect on low-level states. In both cases we use **abort** for an error state. There is an obvious way to define an appropriate notion of correspondence between high- and low-level states: $\sigma \approx \tau$ if $\mathbf{dom}(\sigma) = \mathbf{dom}(\tau)$ and, for each $x \in \mathbf{dom}(\sigma)$, $\sigma(x) = [\tau(x)]_W$. It can then be shown that for all processes P:

- for all high-level traces α of P, if $\sigma \approx \tau$ and $\sigma \overset{\alpha}{\Longrightarrow} \sigma' \neq \mathbf{abort}$ then there is a low-level trace β of P and a low-level state τ' such that $\tau \overset{\beta}{\Longrightarrow} \tau'$ and $\sigma' \approx \tau'$;
- for all low-level traces β of P, if $\sigma \approx \tau$ and $\tau \overset{\beta}{\Longrightarrow} \tau'$ then there is a high-level trace α of P such that either $\sigma \overset{\alpha}{\Longrightarrow} \mathbf{abort}$ or $\sigma \overset{\alpha}{\Longrightarrow} \sigma'$ for some high-level state σ' such that $\sigma' \approx \tau'$.

This formalizes the sense in which our high-level action trace semantics expresses behavioral properties of programs in a manner independent of assumptions about details such as word size or packet size. The role played in this result by the race-detecting clause in our definition of parallel composition is crucial.

8   Asynchrony

To model a language of asynchronously communicating processes, with the same syntax, we need only to make a few modifications in the key semantic definitions concerning communication. Specifically, the clauses for input, sequential composition, and conditional critical regions remain as before but we alter the clauses for output (since waiting is no longer required), parallel composition (since synchronization is no longer needed), and local channel declaration (since an output to a local channel can occur autonomously but we still require the inputs to obey the queueing discipline). The new clauses are:

$$[\![h!e]\!] = \{\rho\, h!v \mid (\rho, v) \in [\![e]\!]\}$$
$$[\![P_1 \| P_2]\!] = [\![P_1]\!]_{\{\}} \|_{\{\}} [\![P_2]\!]$$
$$[\![\textbf{chan } h \textbf{ in } P]\!] = \{\alpha \backslash h \mid \alpha \in [\![P]\!]_h\}$$

We adjust the definition of interleaving, to delete the synchronization case:

$$(\lambda_1 \alpha_1)_{A_1} \|_{A_2} (\lambda_2 \alpha_2) = \{abort\} \quad \text{if } \lambda_1 \bowtie \lambda_2$$
$$(\lambda_1 \alpha_1)_{A_1} \|_{A_2} (\lambda_2 \alpha_2) =$$
$$\{\lambda_1 \gamma \mid (A_1, A_2) \xrightarrow{\lambda_1} (A_1', A_2) \ \& \ \gamma \in \alpha_{1\,A_1'} \|_{A_2} (\lambda_2 \alpha_2)\}$$
$$\cup \{\lambda_2 \gamma \mid (A_2, A_1) \xrightarrow{\lambda_2} (A_2', A_1) \ \& \ \gamma \in (\lambda_1 \alpha_1)_{A_1} \|_{A_2'} \alpha_2\}$$
$$\text{otherwise}$$

We also need to adjust the definition of fairmerge for pairs of infinite traces to fit with the asynchronous interpretation, along the lines of [8] but modified to handle race conditions as above.

   Given a trace set T and channel h, we let T_h be the set of traces α in T along which the actions involving h obey the queue discipline. We write $\alpha \backslash h$ for the trace obtained from α by replacing each action that mentions channel h by δ.

Theorem 2 (Asynchronous Laws)
The following laws hold in the asynchronous trace semantics:

1. $[\![\textbf{chan } h \textbf{ in } (h?x; P)\|(h!v; Q)]\!] = [\![\textbf{chan } h \textbf{ in } (x{:=}v; P)\|Q]\!]$
2. $[\![\textbf{chan } h \textbf{ in } (h?x; P)\|(Q_1; Q_2)]\!] = [\![Q_1; \textbf{chan } h \textbf{ in } (h?x; P)\|Q_2]\!]$
   provided $h \notin \mathtt{chans}(Q_1)$.

Again these laws reflect our assumption of fair execution. There is an obvious similarity with the corresponding pair of laws from the synchronous setting, but note the subtly different positioning of the assignment to x in the first law.

9   Conclusion

We have introduced a semantic framework based on action traces and a form of resource-sensitive, race-detecting, parallel composition. This can be used to provide models for a language combining shared memory parallelism with communicating processes. (We explore the use of such a semantics for shared memory programs, and connections with *separation logic*, in [9].) This language can be viewed as a generalization of CSP that retains and expands on the imperative essence of original CSP yet possesses a semantic model that reflects the elegance of the design principles behind the original language. Action traces allow the expression of concepts such as failures and divergences, familiar from the traditional models of CSP, without the need to commit to a catastrophic treatment of divergence.

The syntactic constraints built into the original version of CSP – disjoint local states, no nested parallelism, and restricted patterns of communication between processes because of the naming discipline – are sufficient to rule out race conditions, so that for programs in the original CSP we could adapt our semantics in the obvious manner, by deleting the race-detection clauses. Our language – and semantics – allow a more generous syntax within which one can reason about program behavior in a manner independent of hardware assumptions.

References

1. Brookes, S., *A model for communicating sequential processes*, D. Phil. thesis, Oxford University (1983).
2. Brookes, S.D. and Hoare, C.A.R., and Roscoe, A.W., *A theory of communicating sequential processes*, JACM 31(3):560–599 (1984).
3. Brookes, S. and Roscoe, A.W., *An improved failures model for CSP*, Proc. Seminar on Concurrency, Springer-Verlag LNCS 197, 1985.
4. Brookes, S., *Full abstraction for a shared-variable parallel language*, Proc. 8th IEEE Symposium on Logic in Computer Science, IEEE Computer Society Press (1993), 98–109.
5. Brookes, S., *Fair communicating processes*, in A.W. Roscoe (ed.), **A Classical Mind: Essays in Honour of C.A.R. Hoare**, Prentice-Hall International (1994), 59–74.
6. Brookes, S., and Older, S., *Full abstraction for strongly fair communicating processes*, Proc. 11th Conference on Mathematical Foundations of Programming Semantics (MFPS'95), ENTCS vol. 1, Elsevier Science B. V. (1995).
7. Brookes, S., *Communicating Parallel Processes*, Symposium in Celebration of the work of C.A.R. Hoare, Oxford University, MacMillan (2000).
8. Brookes, S., *Traces, Pomsets, Fairness and Full Abstraction for Communicating Processes*, Proc. CONCUR'02, Springer-Verlag, 2002.
9. Brookes, S., *A semantics for concurrent separation logic*, to appear in: Proc. CONCUR'04, Springer-Verlag, September 2004.
10. Dijsktra, E. W., *Cooperating sequential processes*, in: **Programming Languages**, in F. Genuys (ed.), Academic Press (1968), 43–112.
11. Dijkstra, E. W., *Guarded Commands, Nondeterminacy, and Formal Derivation of Programs*, Comm. ACM 18(8):453–457 (1975).

12. Formal Systems (Europe) Ltd, *Failures-Divergence Refinement: FDR2 Manual*, 1997.
13. Francez, N., **Fairness**, Springer-Verlag (1986).
14. Hennessy, M. and Plotkin, G.D., *Full abstraction for a simple parallel programming language*, Proc. 8th MFCS, Springer-Verlag LNCS vol. 74, pages 108-120 (1979).
15. Hoare, C. A. R., *Communicating Sequential Processes*, Comm. ACM, 21(8):666–677 (1978).
16. Hoare, C.A.R., *A model for communicating sequential processes*, in: **On the construction of programs**, McKeag and McNaughton (eds.), Cambridge University Press (1980).
17. Hoare, C.A.R., **Communicating Sequential Processes**, Prentice-Hall (1985).
18. Inmos Ltd., occam 2 reference manual, Prentice-Hall (1988).
19. R. Milner, *A Calculus of Communicating Systems*, Springer LNCS 92, 1980.
20. R. Milner, **Communication and Concurrency**, Prentice-Hall, London, 1989.
21. Older, S., *A Denotational Framework for Fair Communicating Processes*, Ph.D. thesis, Carnegie Mellon University, (1997).
22. Olderog, E-R., and Hoare, C.A.R., *Specification-oriented semantics for communicating processes*, Acta Informatica 23, 9-66, 1986.
23. S. Owicki and L. Lamport, *Proving liveness properties of concurrent programs*, ACM TOPLAS, 4(3): 455-495, July 1982.
24. Park, D., *On the semantics of fair parallelism*. In D. Bjørner, editor, **Abstract Software Specifications**, Springer-Verlag LNCS vol. 86 (1979), 504–526.
25. Plotkin, G. D., *An operational semantics for CSP*, In D. Bjørner, editor, **Formal Description of Programming Concepts II**, Proc. IFIP Working Conference, North-Holland (1983), 199-225.
26. Reppy, J., *Concurrent ML: Design, Application and Semantics*, in: **Functional Programming, Concurrency, Simulation and Automated Reasoning**, P. Lauer (ed.), Springer-Verlag LNCS 693, 165–198 (1993).
27. Roscoe, A.W., *A mathematical theory of communicating processes*, D. Phil. thesis, Oxford University (1982).
28. Roscoe, A.W., **The Theory and Practice of Concurrency**, Prentice-Hall (1998).
29. Roscoe, A.W. and Hoare, C.A.R., *The laws of* occam *programming*, Theoretical Computer Science, 60:177–229 (1988).
30. Roscoe, A.W., *Model checking CSP*, in **A Classical Mind: Essays in Honour of C.A.R. Hoare**, Prentice-Hall (1994).

Seeing Beyond Divergence

A.W. Roscoe

Oxford University Computing Laboratory

Abstract. A long-standing complaint about the theory of CSP has been that all theories which encompass divergence are *divergence-strict*, meaning that nothing beyond the first divergence can be seen. In this paper we show that a congruence previously identified as the weakest one to predict divergence over labelled transition systems (LTS's) can be given a non-standard fixed-point theory, which we term *reflected fixed points* and thereby turned into a full CSP model which is congruent to the operational semantics over LTS's.

1 Introduction

The author has long (actually 26 years!) worked on mathematical models for concurrent systems, in particular Hoare's CSP [7]. The models he has used – based on observable behaviours – bear an obvious similarity to the congruences studied, for example, by Valmari and his co-workers [15, 16]. The main difference has been that those in the CSP "school" have sought complete semantic theories in which the semantics of every term – including recursive ones – could be calculated denotationally, whereas Valmari has concentrated on congruences[1] for sets of non-recursive operators. Thus he did not seek to supply a fixed-point theory of recursion over his congruences, being happy to rely on the operational semantics.

The models themselves have been broadly similar, particularly after one factors out the differences (more or less irrelevant to this paper) caused by the different choice operators used: either the CSP $\sqcap$ and $\square$ (the latter not being resolved by a τ) and the CCS + (which is resolved by τ, necessitating knowledge of initial stability). All inhabit the world of finite and infinite traces, divergence traces, and failures/acceptances. The only difference has been that the CSP models have been unable to determine what the non-minimal traces are that a process can diverge on, and what the infinite traces are beyond potential divergence. (The failures/divergences/infinite traces model $\mathcal{U}$ gives all relevant information up to a minimal divergence, and the stable failures/traces model $\mathcal{F}$ gives all information on finite traces and stable failures whether beyond potential divergence or not. See [11] for details of these.)

The main reason for this difficulty is that none of the straightforward ways of finding fixed points give the correct (i.e. operationally correct) answer. We show

---

[1] The semantic value arises here from applying the observations used to determine a congruence to the operational (LTS) semantics of the process under examination.

A.E. Abdallah, C.B. Jones, and J.W. Sanders (Eds.): CSP25, LNCS 3525, pp. 15–35, 2005.

here how this problem can be solved using the model of [9] and a more exotic method of calculating fixed points.

Since divergence is generally considered an error it is possible to argue (and the author has in the past!) that there is little point in being able to see the fine details of what goes on beyond it. In many cases that is true; fortunately so given the complications we will see in this paper. In other circumstances, however, divergence may represent an abstraction of some phenomenon a designer finds acceptable such as a "busy wait", and it is then fair to ask what will happen if the system gets beyond that point by taking a different branch. For example an operating system designer might well require that once a system has accepted a *close down* command then it does so cleanly and finitely, even though it may have passed through many potentially divergent states before this point. The reader should therefore realise that this paper provides a sophisticated option for those who require this extra discernment, rather than a model that should be a natural first choice.

For simplicity in this paper we present a model which predicts only finite and infinite traces and divergences – ignoring failures. The latter can be calculated independently through $\mathcal{F}$, or alternatively an extra component can straightforwardly be added to the model we present.

We adopt the full language of CSP from [11], including the interrupt operator $\triangle$ (which has some interesting properties). We note that since a model without failures identifies $\sqcap$, $\square$ and $+$, this model will also work for languages in the style of CCS. The semantics of CSP over $\mathcal{U}$ and the other standard models can be found in [11], as can the operational semantics of the language. Some of the simpler forms of operational/denotational congruence result are proved in that book, but not the much harder result for $\mathcal{U}$, which is proved in [13]. This paper rests heavily both on this latter result and adaptations of the techniques used in proving it, for example the idea of an approximating sequence of abstraction functions.

The rest of this paper is organised as follows. In the next section we recall two congruences without divergence strictness which would, if a fixed-point theory could be developed, solve our problem. However we see that one of these cannot have a conventional denotational fixed-point theory, which leads us to concentrate on a single model. In the section following that we see why neither the least nor greatest fixed point gives a sensible semantics for recursion over it. In Section 4 we demonstrate a fixed point that does apparently give the correct answer, and we show that it is the operationally correct one.

In appendices we give a summary of notation, models, etc (essentially following [11]), and the new semantics for CSP.

2   Congruences and Fixed Points

The CFFD congruence (see, for example, [14]) records a process's finite and infinite traces, its divergence traces and its stable failures (pairs (s, X) where X is a set of actions that the process can refuse in some stable, namely τ-free, state after trace s, where neither s nor X includes the invisible event τ). Since we are not seeking to model failures in this paper, it makes sense to simplify CFFD to CFFD$_T$, in which the component of stable failures is removed. This remains a congruence since in CSP and similar languages refusal information does not affect traces or divergences through any operator. (For it to do so would correspond to the operational semantics having a form of negation in the antecedents to some transitions.)

Since CFFD and CFFD$_T$ are attractive congruences (seemingly containing just the information we are looking for) it is natural to ask whether we can find a denotational fixed-point theory for them. Unfortunately the answer appears to be no, at least in any conventional sense, if we want that theory to be operationally congruent.

THEOREM 1 . *There are pairs of CSP recursions whose operational semantics yield different values in CFFD and CFFD$_T$, but which generate identical functions from each of these two models to itself. Therefore there can be no operationally congruent definition of recursion derived from the function a recursion represents.*

PROOF.   Let $\Sigma = \{a\}$. Consider the process

$$FA = STOP \sqcap (FA \bigtriangleup a \rightarrow (\mathbf{div} \sqcap STOP))$$

(Here, **div** denotes a process that does nothing but diverge.) This may diverge immediately since the nondeterministic choice may always resolve to the right and interrupt may never occur. However it might perform any finite number of a's thanks to layers of interrupts occurring, and plainly may diverge after any of them. For CFFD, which records failures, it can refuse any set after any trace. However, crucially, it cannot perform an infinite trace of as since whenever it performs its first a the number of subsequent ones has some finite bound. (The bound is the number of recursive unfoldings that have occurred up to the point that the first a occurs.)

Notice that FA has every possible trace, divergence and failure except for the infinite trace a^ω. The same value can be created without interrupt by using, for example, infinite nondeterministic choice.[2]

Now consider these two CSP contexts:

$$F_1(P) = FA \sqcap P$$

$$F_2(P) = FA \sqcap a \rightarrow P$$

The functions F_1 and F_2 that these contexts generate are identical: the nondeterministic choice of FA means that all behaviours other than a^ω belong to

---

[2] The particular version given here in terms of $\bigtriangleup$ is due to Valmari. The author had earlier discovered other examples which made use of infinite nondeterministic choice. Subsequent to the CSP 25 conference he learned that Paul Levy had independently discovered the same result via a similar counterexample to his own.

both $F_i(P)$ independent of the value of P. Furthermore, in each case it is clear that this infinite trace is present if and only if P has it. It follows that F_1 and F_2 are, extensionally, the same function.

However, operationally, the recursions $P_i = F_i(P_i)$ yield different values. P_1 can perform an arbitrarily large finite number of τs and then act like FA, or can simply diverge without reaching FA. The important thing is that it has no way of performing the trace a^ω. On the other hand P_2 can obviously perform this trace by always picking the right-hand of its two nondeterministic options.

It follows that the extensional value of a function over CFFD or CFFD$_T$ does not determine the value of the recursion produced by that function. ∎

The above example works by using the FA process to shroud the difference between what F_1 and F_2 do to P. The example would not work if we removed FA's ability to diverge after any trace since it is clear that P_1 would in any case diverge on $\langle\rangle$, whereas P_2 would not diverge, and if FA could (for example) diverge on the empty trace then P_2 could diverge on all traces.

It turns out that the type of difficulty we have experienced with F_1 and F_2 only occurs in cases like this, where the difference between the two recursions is restricted to infinite traces which belong to $\overline{divergences(P)}$, the closure of the set of divergent traces (namely, the infinite traces that have an infinite chain of divergent prefixes).

The clear lesson to draw from this example is that we either need to add detail to, or remove detail from, our model in order to get a working fixed-point model of recursion. One possibility, which coincides with the abstraction from CFFD made by Puhakka and Valmari for a related reason[3] in [10] (see also [9]), is not to care about whether an infinite trace *which has an infinite chain of divergent prefixes* is present or not: we may choose either to omit all such traces or to include them all. The point of interest here is that the operationally determined values of processes P_1 and P_2 above are identified by this new equivalence: the trace a^ω is put into the don't-care category by the divergences P_1 and P_2 share.

If, as is typically the case in CSP, we want to have a simple theory of refinement, the correct choice is to include, rather than exclude, all traces that are the limits of chains of divergences. For obviously the process $P = a \to P$ refines $P \sqcap FA$, but this would not appear from the usual reverse containment relation if we were forced to exclude a^ω from the representation of the right-hand process.

We therefore use the model $\mathcal{SBD}$ (standing for seeing beyond divergence) in which each process is represented by a triple (T, I, D), where T and D are the finite traces and divergence traces, and I is the union of the infinite traces and the infinite traces in $\overline{D}$. (This model's elements are obviously in 1-1 correspondence with the members of the $Tr - DivTr - Enditr$ congruence from [10].) The healthiness conditions on this model (in the style usually used for CSP models) are

T1 T is nonempty and prefix-closed.

I1 $s \in \Sigma^* \wedge s\hat{\ }u \in I \Rightarrow s \in T$

---

[3] The most abstract congruence capable of detecting all divergence traces.

D1 $D \subseteq T$
D2 $u \in \Sigma^\omega \wedge (\{s \in \Sigma^* \mid s < u\} \cap D)$ is infinite $\implies u \in I$

We term the infinite traces covered by D2 ω-*divergent traces*. Following [10] we term the set of these $DivCl(P)$ for process P.

The above model differs from $Tr - DivTr - Enditr$ in that it specifically includes rather than excludes the members of $DivCl(P)$. That does not affect which processes are considered equivalent, but it gives a smoother definition of refinement, as discussed above.

By extension from the result of [10], this is the weakest congruence which predicts all divergences of a CSP process. We will show in the next section that it is possible to find a working, if complex, fixed-point theory that calculates the values of recursive processes. The reasons why it *is* a congruence for all CSP operators are, in essence

- If we have two processes that differ only in ω-divergent traces, then the result of applying any CSP operator to them could only differ in either a divergence (which can arise because an infinite trace is hidden in one but not the other) or an infinite trace.

- However if the ω-divergent trace u of P generates, in $C[P]$, the divergence trace s, then certainly there is a finite prefix t of u such that all $t \leq t' \leq u$ yield the trace s in $C[P]$. However we know that infinitely many of these t' are divergence traces of P, meaning that $C[P]$ gets the divergence from u's divergent prefixes as well as u itself. (For once $C[P]$ has generated the trace s via t, and has carried on generating internal actions through subsequent actions of u, then as soon as P's trace reaches divergent t' then $C[P]$ can diverge without any more actions of u occurring.) Therefore the divergence would still be in $C[P]$ even if u were removed from P.

- If an ω-divergent trace u of P yields the infinite trace v in $C[P]$ then *either* a finite prefix of u also generates v *or* none do. In the former case the presence of v does not depend on u, so u may be removed without affecting it. In the latter an infinite chain of divergent prefixes of u will yield an infinite chain of divergent prefixes of v: this means that v is ω-divergent in $C[P]$ and so in the category of traces whose presence is immaterial thanks to D2.

In any case removing an ω-divergent trace from P will never affect the presence of any behaviour of $C[P]$ that is recorded in $\mathcal{SBD}$.

3   Greatest and Least Fixed Points

It is clear that $\mathcal{SBD}$ provides a less abstract view of CSP processes than the finite/infinite traces and divergences model $\mathcal{I}$ which is strict after divergence, in the sense that the value of a process in $\mathcal{SBD}$ trivially yields the value in $\mathcal{I}$. (More details of $\mathcal{I}$ and the projection Π which performs the translation are given below.)

This immediately tells us quite a lot about the value of any recursive term in $\mathcal{SBD}$: it must be one that projects to the value calculated in $\mathcal{I}$. The existing theory of CSP models tells us how to compute this as a fixed point. For details on this and why the result is operationally correct, see [13, 11]. In order to understand how we might solve the fixed-point problem for $\mathcal{SBD}$, it is a good idea to review how other CSP models solve this problem.

The first model for CSP [6] was the finite traces model $\mathcal{T}$ in which each process is represented by its (nonempty and prefix-closed) set of finite traces (sequences of visible events). It is straightforward to give a semantics to each non-recursive CSP operator over $\mathcal{T}$ which is operationally correct. The fixed-point theory which has always been quoted as standard for that model is based on least fixed points under subset (corresponding to greatest fixed points under refinement). There is a clear operational intuition for this: if we run the recursive process $\mu\, p.F(p)$ then any actual trace will have occurred after a finite time, so that the recursion can only have been unwound a finite number of times. Since $\mu\, p.F(p)$ can only actually do anything once it has been unwound, it follows that (on the assumption that the operational and semantic representations of F are congruent), every trace comes from $F^n(STOP)$ for some n. The reverse is also true for similar reasons.

Given that every CSP operator is continuous under the subset order (see [11], Chapter 8), this informally justifies the use of this fixed point. For a formal proof that it is correct, see [11], Chapter 9.

The second model for CSP was the failures model of [2] which adopted the opposite fixed-point strategy: it takes the refinement-least. The argument used there[4] was based on a clear rationale: assume the worst and you will not be disappointed. But of course there was a good pragmatic reason too: there is no least element of that model under subset. A consequence of that decision was that ill-defined recursions such as $\mu\, p.p$ were given lots of traces even though there was no operational reason for doing so. This was the origin of the intuition that a divergent process should be identified with the least refined one: however that model did not in fact stand careful examination when it came to divergent terms. This led to the introduction of the divergences component in [3] leading to the now-standard failures/divergences model $\mathcal{N}$.

Brief consideration of how the mathematics of fixed points works reveals that the refinement-least fixed point is necessary in considering divergence. For example the recursion $\mu\, p.p$ plainly is divergent operationally, if it means anything at all, so within $\mathcal{N}$ we *want* it to denote the least refined process, since that is the only one which is immediately divergent. If we were to throw away the refusal components of failures (giving a finite traces/divergences model) so that we regained a $\subseteq$-least element ($STOP$ again), the $\subseteq$-least fixed point would not be operationally correct. The essential point here is that a divergence is not something that can ever arise in a finite number of iterations of $F(\cdot)$ from $STOP$ except where $F(P)$ may diverge even though P does not. So, with this class of exceptions, $\bigcup\{F^n(STOP) \mid n \in \mathbb{N}\}$ cannot diverge either: this is not true of operational fixed points. Rather each particular divergence should be

---

[4] That paper was written before there was a proper operational semantics for CSP.

proved absent in some number of iterations of $F(\cdot)$, which is the essence of the $\sqsubseteq$-least fixed-point calculation.[5] Unless it can be proved absent, it is deemed to be there; and indeed this is accurate since we can again prove congruence with the operational semantics.

An interesting observation that can be made here is that we now know that both $\subseteq$ greatest *and* least fixed points are accurate for computing operationally congruent fixed points for any non-divergent process in (finitely nondeterministic) CSP. It follows that these two are the same, so the fixed point is actually unique. Another way of demonstrating the uniqueness of fixed points for divergence-free processes is via a more rigid divergence-based order as shown in [12]. (The only way $P \le Q$ is if Q's divergences are a subset of P's and P and Q agree precisely on all traces not in $divergences(P)$: this is called the *strong* order, but only makes sense for divergence-strict models.)

Since $\mathcal{T}$ and $\mathcal{N}$, a number of other CSP models on similar lines have been developed. Notable amongst these are the *stable failures model* $\mathcal{F}$ and infinite traces/failures/divergences model $\mathcal{U}$. The former, representing a process as (F, T) (its sets of stable failures – ones generated in a τ-free state – and finite traces) contains only finitely observable behaviours and, like $\mathcal{T}$, uses subset-least fixed points. The latter represents a process as (F, D, I), its sets of failures, divergences and infinite traces, each closed under divergences so as to make the divergent process bottom under refinement. This has a particularly interesting fixed-point theory, since the healthiness conditions relating failures and infinite traces cause the refinement partial order to be incomplete. Nevertheless, as can be shown by various methods [13, 1], refinement-least fixed points do exist for all CSP-definable functions and are operationally congruent. The proof of the congruence between operational and denotational semantics, which is both difficult and crucial to the present paper, may be found in [13]. $\mathcal{U}$ (introduced in that paper) is in essence the minimal extension of $\mathcal{N}$ that can cope accurately with unboundedly nondeterministic operators, and treats divergence in the same way.

As mentioned earlier in relation to CFFD, $\mathcal{U}$ can be simplified to $\mathcal{I}$ in which failures are replaced by finite traces, so a process is represented as (T, D, I). This at least makes the incompleteness problem go away[6], though it does not significantly affect the congruence proof. Once again the model has a refinement top ($STOP$) and since the greatest fixed point of $\mu\,p.a \to p$ has no infinite trace (it can simply perform every finite trace of a's) we see that the use of the $\sqsubseteq$-least fixed point is vital not only for divergences (as discussed above) but also for

---

[5] With respect to $\sqsubseteq$, not all operators are continuous, though they are monotone (see [11] Chapter 8), meaning that fixed-point calculations may need to go to higher ordinals that ω. However this model only turns out to be operationally congruent for finitely nondeterministic CSP, in which operators are continuous. The essence of the proof that that in the finitely nondeterministic case this method predicts the correct divergences is an application of König's Lemma.

[6] Though this is really superficial, since there is still an imperative to demonstrate that the set of infinite traces calculated is consistent with the set of failures calculated via the stable failures model.

infinite traces: operationally, this process obviously does have an infinite trace, which is correctly predicted by the $\sqsubseteq$-least fixed point.

The conclusion to this survey is that the $\sqsubseteq$-least fixed point is necessary to handle infinite behaviours (namely infinite traces and divergences) properly, but that $\subseteq$ is the correct order to use for finitary ones (namely finite traces and stable failures). The latter is emphasised by the fact that $\mathcal{T}$ and $\mathcal{F}$ are accurate for the full language (including unbounded nondeterminism) and predict the correct behaviours even beyond potential divergence (which is just as well since the models don't know when this occurs). We get away with using $\sqsubseteq$-least fixed points for finite traces and failures prior to divergence simply because these parts of a process are uniquely determined so any fixed-point theory would work. And of course in the failures/divergences model we do not have to worry about what happens after divergence because everything is mapped to bottom.

In this section we have switched between component-wise subset ($\subseteq$) and refinement ($\sqsubseteq$) – opposites – in discussing fixed points thanks to historical conventions. However from now on, in discussing the calculation of fixed points over $\mathcal{SBD}$, we will use only $\subseteq$.

4 Reflected Fixed Points

Greatest fixed points do not produce the operationally correct values in $\mathcal{SBD}$: for example the recursion $\mu\, p.p$ is given all finite and infinite traces rather than just the empty trace, which is the right answer. (It is also given all divergences rather than the correct $\{\langle\rangle\}$.) Nor do least fixed points, since the same (divergent) recursion is given the non-divergent value $STOP$, and the process $\mu\, p.a \to p$ is given no infinite trace.

We therefore have to seek a new way of producing a fixed point. In this section we will do this, as part of an overall exercise in demonstrating that the CSP semantics over $\mathcal{SBD}$ including this fixed-point theory is congruent to the operational semantics. These two things go hand in hand since the operational justification of the fixed-point theory only makes sense in the context of congruence proof, which we now develop.

As with any congruence proof, we need to be careful in distinguishing operational terms and semantic values. The proof itself will be by structural induction over all CSP terms in which all free process identifiers are instantiated by nodes of an arbitrary labelled transition system (LTS), perhaps the set of closed CSP terms themselves, *for all such instantiations simultaneously, as opposed to inducting separately for each one*.

Since we need to distinguish between different sorts of semantics, we use the notation $\mathbf{SBD}[\![P]\!]\rho$ to mean the denotational semantics of the term P in $\mathcal{SBD}$ where the *denotational environment* $\rho : PV \to \mathcal{SBD}$ gives the binding of all process variables that might appear free in P. Similarly $\mathbf{I}[\![P]\!]\eta$ is the denotational semantics over $\mathcal{I}$.

Specifically, we will aim for the following result.

THEOREM 2 . *For each CSP term P, and each operational environment σ : $PV \rightarrow \hat{C}$ (C being an arbitrary LTS and $\hat{C}$ its set of nodes), we have*

$$\Psi(P[\sigma]) = \mathbf{SBD}[\![P]\!](\Psi(\sigma))$$

where Ψ is the natural map from the nodes of any LTS to $\mathcal{SBD}$, $P[\sigma]$ is P with the substitution of each variable v by $\sigma[v]$, and $\Psi(\sigma)$ is the function from PV to $\mathcal{SBD}$ (a denotational environment) produced by applying Ψ to $\sigma(v)$ for each variable v[7].

Additionally, the function $\mathbf{SBD}[\![P]\!]$ of denotational environments is monotone. ∎

The second part of this result is necessary to justify some of the constructions and arguments we make below. It is straightforward aside from the case of a recursive term, which requires a more complex inductive argument which we will discuss later. (Note that $\mathbf{SBD}[\![\mu\, p.P]\!]$ is not even defined at present since we don't yet know how to calculate the value of a recursive term.)

To prove this result we need to consider every possible top-level structure for P. These split up into three categories:

- The case where the term P is just a process variable is trivial.
- There are many cases in which P is either a process constant (like $STOP$) or a non-recursive operator. The semantics of all non-recursive operators over $\mathcal{SBD}$ are given in Appendix B. In every case they are identical to the semantics over $\mathcal{I}$ implied[8] in [13] except that the clauses used to enforce divergence strictness are omitted. In each case it is reasonably straightforward to prove that the denotational and operational semantics of the operator are congruent using the same techniques as in [13].

  Of course these results simply parallel the result of [10] that $\mathcal{SBD}$ is a congruence.

- P might be a recursion $\mu\, p.Q$. As in [13], we do not explicitly cover mutual recursion in this proof because of the extra book-keeping, but there is no doubt that the same techniques used below would work for any finite mutual recursion; in infinite mutual recursions similar techniques should work.

  The rest of this section is devoted to developing a fixed-point method which makes the result true for $\mu\, p.Q$ on the assumption that it is true for Q.

Let Φ be the abstraction map (analogous to Ψ) which maps the nodes of any LTS to $\mathcal{I}$ (this is essentially the same as the function of the same name defined in [13]).

Fix an operational environment σ, and let $\Theta = \Psi((\mu\, p.Q)[\sigma])$ be the operationally correct value in $\mathcal{SBD}$ relating to the recursion evaluated over σ.

The recursion (for this fixed σ) yields functions $F_{\mathcal{SBD}} : \mathcal{SBD} \rightarrow \mathcal{SBD}$ and $F_{\mathcal{U}} : \mathcal{I} \rightarrow \mathcal{I}$ defined by

$$F_{\mathcal{I}}(X) = \mathbf{I}[\![Q]\!]\eta[X/p]$$
$$F_{\mathcal{SBD}}(X) = \mathbf{SBD}[\![Q]\!]\rho[X/p]$$

---

[7] This lifting $\Psi(\sigma)$ of Ψ mapping operational to denotational environments actually equals the functional composition $\Psi \circ \sigma$.

[8] The semantics in that paper is given over the more complex model $\mathcal{U}$.

where $\eta = \Phi(\sigma)$ and $\rho = \Psi(\sigma)$ are the denotational environments corresponding to σ over the respective models.

Now let Π be the projection from $\mathcal{SBD}$ to $\mathcal{I}$ obtained by closing up under divergence-strictness . (All extensions of divergences are added to all three components.) By construction we have $\Phi = \Pi \circ \Psi$ and since Q is (by our overall inductive assumption in proving Theorem 2) operationally accurate over $\mathcal{SBD}$ we get, for all members T of an LTS,

$$F_{\mathcal{I}}(\Pi(\Psi(T))) = \Phi(Q[\sigma[T/p]]) = \Pi(\Psi(Q[\sigma[T/p]])) = \Pi(F_{\mathcal{SBD}}(\Psi(T)))$$

Since we can without loss of generality assume that our transition system maps *onto* $\mathcal{SBD}$ under Ψ (analogously to the arguments used in [13]) this tells that for each $x \in \mathcal{SBD}$ we have

$$F_{\mathcal{I}}(\Pi(x)) = \Pi(F_{\mathcal{SBD}}(x))$$

or in other words we have a commuting diagram.

Let Ω be the greatest (i.e. $\sqsubseteq$-least) fixed point of $F_{\mathcal{I}}$. Thanks to the known congruence of that semantics with the operational one, we have

$$\Omega = \Phi((\mu\, p.Q)[\sigma]) = \Pi(\Theta)$$

Furthermore, if K is any member of $\Pi^{-1}(\Omega)$ we get

$$\Pi(F_{\mathcal{SBD}}(K)) = F_{\mathcal{I}}(\Pi(K)) = F_{\mathcal{I}}(\Omega) = \Omega$$

In other words $F_{\mathcal{SBD}}$ maps $\Pi^{-1}(\Omega)$ to itself.

If $\Lambda = (T, D, I)$ is any member of $\mathcal{I}$, then $\Pi^{-1}(\Lambda)$ is the interval (i.e., $\sqsubseteq$-convex subset) in $\mathcal{SBD}$ between its $\sqsubseteq$-greatest element, Λ itself, and its least, which we denote $\tilde{\Lambda}$ and equals (T', D', I') where

$$T' = T \setminus \{t\hat{\ }s \mid t \in D \wedge s \neq \langle\rangle\}$$
$$D' = D \setminus \{t\hat{\ }s \mid t \in D \wedge s \neq \langle\rangle\}$$
$$I' = I \setminus \{t\hat{\ }u \mid t \in D \wedge u \in \Sigma^\omega\}$$

In other words, in all three components, every behaviour following a potential divergence has been removed. So

$$\Pi^{-1}(\Lambda) = \{K \in \mathcal{SBD} \mid \tilde{\Lambda} \subseteq K \subseteq \Lambda\}$$

The preceding two paragraphs show (together with an easy demonstration of the existence of least upper bounds) that $\Pi^{-1}(\Omega)$ is a complete lattice preserved by the function $F_{\mathcal{SBD}}$. The monotonicity of $F_{\mathcal{SBD}}$ then tells us that it has both greatest and least fixed points within $\Pi^{-1}(\Omega)$.

We know that $\Theta \in \Pi^{-1}(\Omega)$. It is also a fixed point of $F_{\mathcal{SBD}}$ since

$$\Theta = \Psi(\mu\, p.Q[\sigma])$$
$$= \Psi(Q[\sigma[\mu\, p.Q[\sigma]/p]]) \qquad (1)$$
$$= \mathbf{SBD}[\![Q]\!](\Psi(\sigma[\mu\, p.Q[\sigma]/p])) \ (2)$$
$$= F_{\mathcal{SBD}}(\Psi(\mu\, p.Q[\sigma])) \qquad (3)$$
$$= F_{\mathcal{SBD}}(\Theta)$$

Here (1) follows by the operational semantics of recursion (which is to execute a τ action and unfold to the term on the right), (2) by our inductive assumption that the denotational and operational semantics of Q are congruent, and (3) by our definition of F_{SBD}.

It follows that Θ lies between the least and greatest fixed points of F_{SBD} within $\Pi^{-1}(\Omega)$. If these are the same, we have no more to do, but unfortunately this is not always the case, as for example in the recursion $\mu\, p.p.$

We will prove, however, that the least fixed point in $\Pi^{-1}(\Omega)$ is always the operationally correct one, and furthermore that it is always given by the standard formula

$$\bigcup_{n=0}^{\infty} F_{SBD}^n(\tilde{\Omega})$$

(bearing in mind that $\tilde{\Omega}$ is the bottom element of the complete lattice we are concentrating on). As is common, the proof that the above term, which we will name Ξ, equals Θ, comes in two parts.

That $\Xi \subseteq \Theta$ is easy, since $\tilde{\Omega} \subseteq \Theta$ and

$$F_{SBD}^n(\tilde{\Omega}) \subseteq \Theta \Rightarrow F_{SBD}^{n+1}(\tilde{\Omega}) \subseteq F_{SBD}(\Theta) = \Theta$$

giving the result for $\Xi = \bigcup_{n=0}^{\infty} F_{SBD}^n(\tilde{\Omega})$ by induction.

The intuition behind the argument up to this point can be explained as follows. We know that Ω is the accurate model of our recursion in $\mathcal{I}$. Therefore all the behaviours recorded in $\tilde{\Omega}$ must actually be present in Θ (for we know that none of them have been inserted by divergence strictness). Since all of these behaviours are present and Θ is a fixed point of F_{SBD} it follows that all the behaviours of every $F_{SBD}^n(\tilde{\Omega})$ are in Θ. Hence $\Xi \subseteq \Theta$.

It is unfortunately more difficult to prove $\Theta \subseteq \Xi$. If this were false, then thanks to the definition of $\mathcal{SBD}$ (especially $D2$), Θ has a behaviour not present in Ξ of one of the following sorts:

- A finite trace.
- A divergence.
- An infinite trace u such that there is some maximal divergence d with $d < u$.
  (Note that any infinite trace without such a maximal divergence would imply the existence of a divergence in $Theta \setminus \Xi$.)

Necessarily the finite trace or divergence s would have to be a *proper* extension of some longest divergence, namely there would have to be a divergence $t < s$ which is maximal subject to this. (Differences cannot appear up to the first divergence since we are operating entirely within $\Pi^{-1}(\Omega)$, a region in which all processes agree up to that point.) We can assume the infinite trace is also the extension of a longest divergence t because if there was no maximal divergence $< u$ then *either* Θ would have a divergence not in Ξ *or* Ξ would have u by axiom $D2$.

This suggests that, in proving $\Theta \subseteq \Xi$, we might try to work by induction based on this maximal divergence. One thought is to count how many divergences there are along a trace, or use the length of trace of the maximal divergence, but these do not work, at least easily, thanks to the complications of hiding. What we actually do is to count how many computation steps (both visible and τ) in the operational semantics of $\mu\, p.F(p)$ are needed to reach this maximal divergence (though not to execute it): clearly this is always a finite number.

We use the technique of an increasing sequence of abstraction functions which approximate Ψ, similar to that used in the main congruence result of [13]. However we only need an ω-sequence of them here rather than the arbitrary ordinals in the Φ_α of that paper. The construction we use is exactly that of the previous paper except for the Φ_0 case, in which we map a process to the subset-least member of $\mathcal{SBD}$ that is consistent with its value in $\mathcal{I}$. (In the previous paper it was mapped to bottom.)

Suppose we are given an LTS C and that $P \in \hat{C}$. Define

$$\Psi_0(P) = \widetilde{\Phi(P)}$$

$$\Psi_{n+1}(P) = ?x : P^0 \to \sqcap\{\Psi_n(Q) \mid P \xrightarrow{x} Q\}$$
$$\text{if } P \text{ is stable}$$

$$\Psi_{n+1}(P) = ?x : P^0 \to \sqcap\{\Psi_n(Q) \mid P \xrightarrow{x} Q\}$$
$$\rhd \sqcap\{\Phi_n(Q) \mid P \xrightarrow{\tau} Q\}$$
$$\text{if } P \text{ is not stable}$$

We can view Ψ_n as $\mathcal{G}^n(\Psi_0)$ where $\mathcal{G} : (\hat{C} \to \mathcal{SBD}) \to (\hat{C} \to \mathcal{SBD})$ is implied by the $n+1$ case above. (Syntactically it is precisely the same as the $\mathcal{G}$ operator in [13], though the model is different.) Since Ψ_0 is the $\subseteq$-minimal abstraction consistent with Φ, and we know that (over $\mathcal{I}$) $\mathcal{G}(\Phi) = \Phi$ it follows that $\Psi_1(P) \supseteq \Psi_0(P)$ and hence inductively that the Ψ_i are a $\subseteq$-increasing sequence.

Let $\Psi^*(P) = \bigcup\{\Psi_n(P) \mid n \in \mathbb{N}\}$, where again $\bigcup$ is component-wise union followed by closure under $D2$.

$\mathcal{G}(\Psi) = \Psi$ by construction, as the natural abstractions of the members of an LTS plainly satisfy the defining equations of $\mathcal{G}$. It therefore follows from induction on the n in Ψ_n that $\Psi^*(P) \subseteq \Psi(P)$ for all P. In fact, $\Psi^* = \Psi$, as demonstrated by the following argument.

If b is any behaviour of $\Psi(P) \setminus \Psi^*(P)$, then (as argued for $\Theta \setminus \Xi$ above) by $D2$ we can assume that b is not an infinite trace with an infinite number of divergent prefixes in $\Psi(P)$. Therefore there is some proper prefix s of the trace of b which is the maximal such trace on which P can diverge. Consider any sequence Q of states in P's operational behaviour which witnesses b. If a is the next event on the trace of b, let b' be the residue of b after $s^\frown\langle a \rangle$ and let Q' be the first state in Q after $s^\frown\langle a \rangle$. No state from Q' to the last of the sequence can be divergent by our assumptions unless it is the last in the sequence and b is a divergence.

By construction b' is in $\Psi_0(Q')$, as no proper prefix of b' is divergent in Q', and inducting backwards along the sequence of states on our path from P to Q' would easily show that $b \in \Psi_n(P)$ (for n the length of the path). This contradicts our assumption that b is not in $\Psi^*(P)$, and we can conclude that indeed $\Psi = \Psi^*$.

The claim that $\Theta \subseteq \Xi$ will be proved if we can show that, for every n,

$$F^n_{\mathcal{SBD}}(\tilde{\Omega})) \supseteq \Psi_n(\mu\, p.Q[\sigma]) \qquad (\mathbf{A})$$

since in the limit this proves $\Xi \supseteq \Theta$, which is what remained to be proved.

This claim is proved by induction: the $n = 0$ case is trivial since both sides equal $\tilde{\Omega}$.

The $n + 1$ case is a corollary to the following result.

LEMMA 1 . *For all terms Q' and operational environments σ,*

$$\Psi_n(Q'[\sigma]) \subseteq \mathbf{SBD}[\![Q']\!](\Psi_n(\sigma))$$

Note that if $Q' = Q$ (Q as in the term $\mu\, p.Q$ we are addressing in main inductive step) and X is an arbitrary member of the underlying transition system, this result implies

$$\Psi_n(Q[\sigma[X/p]]) \subseteq \mathbf{SBD}[\![Q]\!](\Psi_n(\sigma[X/p]))$$

and the right hand side of this inequality is trivially a subset of $F_{\mathcal{SBD}}(\Psi_n(X))$. (It may be a proper subset since Ψ_n is applied to all components of $\sigma[X/p]$, not just the p one.) ∎

That the step case of the proof of $(\mathbf{A})$ above is a corollary follows thanks to the τ which is generated on unfolding $\mu\, p.Q$, which implies:

$$\Psi_{n+1}((\mu\, p.Q)[\sigma]) = \Psi_n(Q[\sigma[((\mu\,.p.Q)[\sigma]/p]]) \subseteq F_{\mathcal{SBD}}(\Psi_n((\mu\, p.Q)[\sigma]))$$

The proof of Lemma 1 is by adding it to the structural induction of the main theorem: they are actually proved together. Note that this is the approach used in [13] for a very similar result involving the functions Φ_α.

Before we look at any technical details of the proof it is helpful to realise that this seemingly very technical result actually has a simple intuition. If we accept that Theorem 2 holds for our given Q, then what this lemma says is that the behaviours of $\Psi(Q[\sigma])$ for which any non-final divergence occurs before the nth state cannot depend on any behaviour of any $\sigma[q]$ which can only happen beyond a non-final divergence later than n. This can be argued at least semi-formally thanks to two properties of the operational semantics:

(1) When any context $C[P]$ runs, the first n steps of its behaviour depend on at most n steps of P. This is because no operational semantic clause ever lets an operand perform an action (visible or invisible) without the overall process doing so as well. (For example, though $P \setminus X$ hides visible actions of P, in the operational semantics these are turned into τ actions, which still count for our purposes.)

Therefore once $Q[\sigma]$ has performed n operational steps, none of the components $\sigma[\![q]\!]$ can have performed more than n.

(2) If the first step of $C[P]$ depends on what actions P has available, and P can immediately diverge, then so can $C[P]$. This is because the operational semantics of every CSP operator ($P \oplus Q$ say) whose immediate actions depend on one of its operands (P say) also has a clause which promotes a τ action of P ($P \xrightarrow{\tau} P'$) to one of $P \oplus Q$, namely $(P \oplus Q) \xrightarrow{\tau} (P' \oplus Q)$.

Let $\underline{Q}$ be any sequence of states that $Q'[\sigma]$ can go through executing a behaviour in which there is no divergent state between step n and any final divergence (namely one reflected in $\Psi_n(Q'[\sigma])$). Necessarily, once a component $\sigma[p]$ has been driven (in $\underline{Q}$) to a point where it diverges beyond its own step n (which because of (1) above is beyond step n overall), then either the overall behaviour does not depend on it at all or is within a divergent tail of its own – so anything the component may do after this point is irrelevant to $\Psi_n(Q'[\sigma])$. For the component of $\underline{Q}$ which contains this state of $\sigma[p]$ is itself divergent by (2).

We can infer that no behaviour in any $\Psi(\sigma[p]) \setminus \Psi_n(\sigma[p])$ is necessary to deduce a behaviour of $\Psi_n(Q'[\sigma])$.

To give a fully formal proof of the Lemma 1 part of our main induction requires separate lemmas for each CSP operator very much in the style of those given in [13] for the corresponding result. For recursion it is necessary to perform inductions which follow the derivation of the fixed point: a transfinite one for the fixed point in $\mathcal{I}$ followed by an ordinary one for the fixed point within $\Pi^{-1}(\Omega)$ we are now justifying. We omit these here for brevity.

The overall fixed-point calculation is summarised in Figure 1. The left-hand side of the picture shows the entire model $\mathcal{SBD}$, and the small diamonds in it are the regions $\Pi^{-1}(X)$ for each value X in the $\subseteq$-greatest or $\sqsubseteq$-least fixed-point iteration within $\mathcal{I}$, whose ultimate fixed point is Ω. Note that since these diamonds are the preimages of the members of $\mathcal{I}$, they are necessarily disjoint; of course the preimage of a divergence-free member of $\mathcal{I}$ is a singleton set. The right-hand side is an expanded view of $\Pi^{-1}(\Omega)$, showing the iteration from its top towards the operationally correct value Θ. The left-hand side is not a very accurate picture of $\mathcal{I}$, since the latter has a top element. Our argument nowhere uses this however, and would work just as well for an expanded model that replaced finite traces by failures. This has no top (and indeed, like the model $\mathcal{U}$ which it extends, is incomplete).

It is mainly because of this potential generalisation that the picture is drawn the way up it is, with refinement from bottom to top (i.e. upside down with respect to $\subseteq$).

The remaining part of Theorem 2 is the monotonicity of $\mathbf{SBD}[\![\mu\, p . Q]\!]\eta$ as a function of the environment η. To prove this we show that each part of the construction illustrated in Figure 1 is monotone in η. If $\eta \subseteq \eta'$ then $\Pi(\eta) \subseteq \Pi(\eta')$, and the monotonicity of the semantics over $\mathcal{I}$ implies $\Omega \subseteq \Omega'$. (We use the obvious convention that primed terms are derived from η' in the same way that unprimed ones are derived from η.) This immediately implies $\tilde{\Omega} \subseteq \tilde{\Omega}'$.

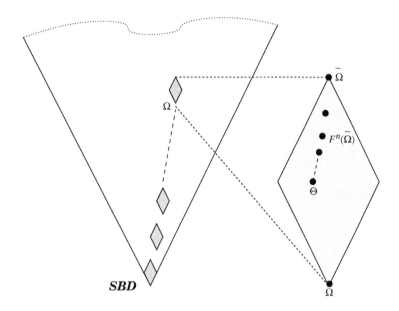

Fig. 1. Illustration of the reflected fixed-point calculation

The fact that $\mathbf{SBD}[\![Q]\!]$ is monotonic by (structural) induction then shows by induction (on n) that

$$F_{\mathcal{SBD}}^n(\tilde{\Omega}) \subseteq (F_{\mathcal{SBD}}')^n(\tilde{\Omega}')$$

for all n.

This concludes our demonstration that Theorem 2 and Lemma 1 hold.

The shape of the process illustrated in Figure 1 leads us to term the new fixed-point method the *reflected fixed point*. We hope it might find use elsewhere, the most obvious possibility being the refinement of other types of programming languages from divergence-strict to not divergence-strict.

Obviously it only produces interesting answers in cases where the value of a recursion is (not necessarily immediately) divergent, since otherwise $\Pi^{-1}(\tilde{\Omega})$ has exactly one point.

The simplest example to check is the recursion $Q_1 = \mu\, p.p$. In this case Ω is the refinement-least element of $\mathcal{I}$ and $\mathcal{SBD}$, and $\tilde{\Omega} = (\{\langle\rangle\}, \{\langle\rangle\}, \emptyset)$, the process which diverges immediately and has no other trace. Since the the function of this recursion is the identity function, it follows that $\tilde{\Omega}$ is the value of the reflected fixed point, which is of course operationally accurate.

As a second example consider

$$Q_2 = ((a \rightarrow Q_2;\ b \rightarrow SKIP) \sqcap SKIP) \setminus \{a\}$$

Like P_1, this can diverge immediately, and so has the same Ω and $\tilde{\Omega}$ as the first example. This time, however, the first iteration from $\tilde{\Omega}$ brings in an extra trace $\langle\checkmark\rangle$, and each subsequent one brings longer and longer ones of the forms $\langle b\rangle^n$ and $\langle b\rangle^{n\frown}\langle\checkmark\rangle$, but no further divergence and no infinite trace. Therefore the reflected fixed point has the single divergence $\langle\rangle$, all these finite traces and no infinite trace. This is operationally correct since the behaviour of Q_2 is rather like that of FA earlier in the sense that once a b is performed there is already a limit on how many more are allowed.

Finally, consider the recursions for the processes P_1 and P_2 defined using FA earlier. Once again we get the same Ω and $\tilde{\Omega}$, but this time every iterate from $\tilde{\Omega}$ in both recursions after the zeroth equals FA, and therefore so do both limits. But of course the model axioms tell us that FA has the infinite trace a^ω thanks to D2, meaning that within the understanding of $\mathcal{SBD}$ this value is operationally accurate for both.

The above method of calculating a fixed point is closely related[9] to the one devised for similar purposes in a language of streams (also using an analogue of our axiom D2) by Manfred Broy in [4], though he uses the Egli-Milner power-domain in place of our divergence-strict model $\mathcal{I}$ to find an approximation.

5   Conclusions

It is fascinating to contemplate the iteration towards a reflected fixed point. The first stage, potentially requiring any ordinal length, manages to characterise accurately all the operational behaviour up to and including the first divergence. Observing what behaviours this proves (under any finite number of iterations) must be present in the fixed point then gives us the correct value in $\mathcal{SBD}$. Nothing can then distinguish the one remaining thing one might want, namely which ω-divergent infinite traces are operationally present.

In a real sense the second stage of our fixed-point process is lifting the calculation done in the first to the post-divergence world, and our (forced) decision to ignore ω-divergent traces means that this can happen relatively simply.

Obviously this fixed-point process is too complex to use regularly to find the semantics of particular processes. Generally speaking this is best done in practice by abstraction from operational semantics. What it does is show how CSP with its $\mathcal{SBD}$ congruence can be viewed as a self-contained theory that can exist without the corresponding operational semantics, and give considerable understanding of the nature of recursions. It will also allow us to derive mathematical properties of fixed points (such as their monotonicity, and forms of recursion induction).

Other two-stage fixed-point techniques have been proposed, such as that of Yifeng Chen in [17] and the one by Broy in [4] already discussed above. Others, such as the *optimal fixed point* [8], have been proposed which yield an answer which is in general between greatest and least.

Similar fixed-point methods (as demonstrated by Broy's work) will apply to other fixed-point calculations based around potentially diverging finite and

---

[9] The author was not aware of the details of Broy's work until his own work was complete.

infinite sequences. They may also apply in other forms of programming languages semantics where one wishes to liberalise a strict interpretation of divergence or undefinedness.

It will, of course, be interesting to compare and reconcile the similar calculations here and in [4].

The infinite-trace component of $\mathcal{SBD}$ is not necessary when the process under consideration is finite-state. It still, of course, has the capability to make finer distinctions than the failures/divergences model $\mathcal{N}$ thanks to the lack of divergence closure. There would be no problem in extending the capabilities of the refinement checker FDR [5] to handle finite-state processes over $\mathcal{SBD}$.

Acknowledgements

This work has benefitted enormously from a number of discussions with Antti Valmari. He, together with others such as Michael Goldsmith, have made helpful suggestions after reading earlier versions of this paper. I have had interesting discussions with Paul Levy in the later stages of writing this paper. I am also grateful for the numerous suggestions of an anonymous referee.

The work reported in this paper was partially supported from EPSRC and the US Office of Naval Research.

References

1. G. Barrett, *The fixed-point theory of unbounded nondeterminism*, Formal Aspects of Computing, **3**, 110–128, 1991.
2. S.D. Brookes, C.A.R. Hoare and A.W. Roscoe, *A theory of communicating sequential processes*, Journal of the ACM **31**, 3, 560–599, 1984.
3. S.D. Brookes and A.W. Roscoe, *An improved failures model for CSP*, Proceedings of the Pittsburgh seminar on concurrency, Springer LNCS 197, 1985.
4. M. Broy, *A theory for nondeterminism, parallelism, communication and concurrency*, Theoretical Computer Science **45**, pp1–61 (1986).
5. Formal Systems (Europe) Ltd., *Failures-Divergence Refinement*, User Manual, obtainable from
   http://www.fsel.com/fdr2_manual.html
6. C.A.R. Hoare, *A model for communicating sequential processes*, in 'On the construction of programs' (McKeag and MacNaughten, *eds*), Cambridge University Press, 1980.
7. C.A.R. Hoare, *Communicating sequential processes*, Prentice Hall, 1985.
8. Zohar Manna and A. Shamir. *The theoretical aspects of the optimal fixed point*, SIAM Journal of Computing, **5**, 14 - 426, 1976.
9. A. Puhakka, *Weakest Congruence Results Concerning "Any-Lock"*, Proc. TACS 2001, Fourth International Symposium on Theoretical Aspects of Computer Software, October 29-31 2001, Sendai, Japan, Lecture Notes in Computer Science 2215, Springer-Verlag 2001, pp. 400-419.

10. A. Puhakka, A and A. Valmari, *Weakest-Congruence Results for Livelock-Preserving Equivalences*, Proceedings of CONCUR '99 (Concurrency Theory), Lecture Notes in Computer Science 1664, Springer-Verlag 1999, pp. 510-524.

11. A.W. Roscoe *The theory and practice of concurrency*, Prentice-Hall International, 1998.

12. A.W. Roscoe, *An alternative order for the failures model*, in "Two papers on CSP", technical monograph PRG-67, Oxford University Computing Laboratory, July 1988. Also Journal of Logic and Computation **2** (5), 557–577, 1992.

13. A.W. Roscoe, *Unbounded nondeterminism in CSP*, in "Two papers on CSP", technical monograph PRG-67, Oxford University Computing Laboratory, July 1988. Also Journal of Logic and Computation, **3** (2), 131–172, 1993.

14. A. Valmari, *A Chaos-Free Failures Divergences Semantics with Applications to Verification*, Millennial Perspectives in Computer Science: Proceedings of the 1999 Oxford–Microsoft Symposium in honour of Sir Tony Hoare, Palgrave "Cornerstones of Computing" series, 2000, pp. 365-382.

15. A. Valmari, *The weakest deadlock-preserving congruence*, Information Processing Letters **53**, 341–346, 1995.

16. A. Valmari and M. Tienari *An improved failures equivalence for finite-state systems with a reduction algorithm*, Protocol Specification, Testing and Verification XI, North-Holland, 1991.

17. Yifeng Chen, *A fixpoint theory for non-monotonic parallelism,* Theoretical Computer Science, Vol. 308 No 1-3, pp.367-392, 2003.

Appendix A: Notation

This paper follows the notation of [11], from which most of the following is taken.

$\mathbb{N}$	natural numbers ($\{0, 1, 2, \ldots\}$)
Σ	(Sigma): alphabet of all communications
τ	(tau): the invisible action
Σ^τ	$\Sigma \cup \{\tau\}$
$\Sigma^\checkmark$	$\Sigma \cup \{\checkmark\}$
$\Sigma^{*\checkmark}$	$\{s, s^\smallfrown\langle\checkmark\rangle \mid s \in \Sigma^*\}$
A^*	set of all finite sequences over A
A^ω	set of all infinite sequences over A
$\langle\rangle$	the empty sequence
$\langle a_1, \ldots, a_n \rangle$	the sequence containing $a_1, \ldots, a_n$ in that order
a^ω	the infinite trace $\langle a, a, a, \ldots \rangle$
$s^\smallfrown t$	concatenation of two sequences
$s \setminus X$	hiding: all members of X deleted from s
$s \underset{X}{\|} t$	the set of traces composed from subsequences s and t which share members of X and are disjoint elsewhere.
$s \leq t$	($\equiv \exists u.s^\smallfrown u = t$) prefix order
$\overline{S}$	closure of S ($= S \cup \{u \in \Sigma^\omega \mid \{s \in S \mid s < u\}$ is infinite$\}$)

Processes:

$\mu\, p.P$	recursion
$a \to P$	prefixing
$?x : A \to P$	prefix choice
$P \,\square\, Q$	external choice
$P \sqcap Q,\quad \sqcap S$	nondeterministic choice
$P \underset{X}{\parallel} Q$	generalised parallel
$P \setminus X$	hiding
$P[\![R]\!]$	renaming (relational)
$P \rhd Q$	"time-out" operator (sliding choice)
$P \,\triangle\, Q$	interrupt
$P[x/y]$	substitution (for a free identifier x)

Transition Systems:

$\hat{C}$	The set of nodes in transition system C.
$P \xrightarrow{a} Q\ (a \in \Sigma \cup \{\tau\})$	single action transition
$P \xRightarrow{s} Q\ (s \in \Sigma^*)$	multiple action transition with τ's removed
$P \xmapsto{t} Q\ (t \in (\Sigma^\tau))^*)$	multiple action transition with τ's retained
$P\ ref\ B$	P refuses B
$P\ div$	P diverges

Models:

$\mathcal{T}$	traces model
$\mathcal{N}$	failures/divergences model (divergence strict)
$\mathcal{F}$	stable failures model
$\mathcal{I}$	finite and infinite traces/divergences model with divergence strictness
$\mathcal{U}$	failures/divergences/infinite traces model with divergence strictness
$CFFD$	failures/divergences/infinite traces congruence/model without divergence strictness
$\mathrm{CFFD}_{\mathcal{T}}$	finite and infinite traces/divergences congruence/model without divergence strictness
$\mathcal{SBD}$	finite and infinite traces/divergences model strict under ω-divergent infinite traces
$\bot_{\mathcal{N}}$ (etc.)	bottom elements of models
$\top_{\mathcal{F}}$ (etc.)	top elements of models
$\sqsubseteq$	refinement over whatever model is clear from the context
$P \le Q$	strong order (over divergence-strict models)
$\mathbf{I}[\![P]\!]\eta$	denotational semantics of P in $\mathcal{I}$
$\mathbf{SBD}[\![P]\!]\rho$	denotational semantics of P in $\mathcal{SBD}$

Appendix B: CSP Semantics Over the New Model

The semantics of recursion has been discussed extensively in the main body of the paper. What remains to be done, therefore, is to provide a recipe for calculating the semantic result of applying any one of the non-recursive operators to the right number of members of $\mathcal{SBD}$. As usual we factor this into recipes for the three components separately.

In general discussions of operators we will refer to a typical binary one $P \oplus Q$. However there is nothing specific to binary operators there and appropriate modifications of the statements hold for all.

In each case the recipe for $traces(P \oplus Q)$ is precisely the same for the traces model $\mathcal{T}$, and depends only on the traces component of the arguments to the relevant operator. This is, of course, not surprising, but it is pleasing since it has not been true of any previous CSP model supporting divergence.

$$traces(STOP) = \{\langle\rangle\}$$
$$traces(SKIP) = \{\langle\rangle, \langle\checkmark\rangle\}$$
$$traces(a \rightarrow P) = \{\langle\rangle\} \cup \{\langle a\rangle\hat{\ }s \mid s \in traces(P)\}$$
$$traces(?x : A \rightarrow P) = \{\langle\rangle\} \cup \{\langle a\rangle\hat{\ }s \mid a \in A \wedge s \in traces(P[a/x])\}$$
$$traces(P \sqcap Q) = traces(P) \cup traces(Q)$$
$$traces(P \parallel_X Q) = \bigcup\{s \parallel_X t \mid s \in traces(P) \wedge t \in traces(Q)\}$$
$$traces(P; Q) = traces(P) \cap \Sigma^* \cup$$
$$\{s\hat{\ }t \mid s\hat{\ }\langle\checkmark\rangle \in traces(P) \wedge t \in traces(Q)\}$$
$$traces(P[\![R]\!]) = \{s' \mid \exists s \in traces(P) \mid s \, R \, s'\}$$
$$traces(P \setminus X) = \{s \setminus X \mid s \in traces(P)\}$$
$$traces(P \triangle Q) = traces(P) \cup$$
$$\{s\hat{\ }t \mid s \in traces(P) \cap \Sigma^* \wedge t \in traces(Q)\}$$

The recipes for divergences involve, in different cases, all three components. They are the same as previous CSP models, but without the closure constructions used to enforce divergence strictness.

$$divergences(STOP) = \emptyset$$
$$divergences(SKIP) = \emptyset$$
$$divergences(a \rightarrow P) = \{\langle a\rangle\hat{\ }s \mid s \in divergences(P)\}$$
$$divergences(?x : A \rightarrow P) = \{\langle a\rangle\hat{\ }s \mid a \in A \wedge s \in divergences(P[a/x])\}$$
$$divergences(P \sqcap Q) = divergences(P) \cup divergences(Q)$$
$$divergences(P \parallel_X Q) = \bigcup\{s \parallel_X t \mid s \in divergences(P) \wedge t \in traces(Q)\}$$
$$\cup \bigcup\{s \parallel_X t \mid s \in traces(P) \wedge t \in divergences(Q)\}$$

$$divergences(P;\ Q) = divergences(P)\ \cup$$
$$\{s\hat{\ }t \mid s\hat{\ }\langle\checkmark\rangle \in traces(P) \wedge t \in divergences(Q)\}$$

$$divergences(P[\![R]\!]) = \{s' \mid \exists\, s \in divergences(P) \mid s\ R\ s'\}$$

$$divergences(P \setminus X) = \{u \setminus X \mid u \in infinites(P) \wedge u \setminus X \text{ is finite}\}$$
$$\cup\, \{s \setminus X \mid s \in divergences(P) \cap \Sigma^* \wedge t \in \Sigma^{*\checkmark}\}$$

$$divergences(P \triangle Q) = divergences(P)\ \cup$$
$$\{s\hat{\ }t \mid s \in traces(P) \wedge t \in divergences(Q)\}$$

In each case the basic recipe for $infinites(P \oplus Q)$ depends only on the sets $Traces(P)$ and $Traces(Q)$ of all finite and infinite traces of the arguments. However in some cases a clause adding the ω-divergent infinite traces is need to make D2 true.

$$infinites(STOP) = \emptyset$$

$$infinites(SKIP) = \emptyset$$

$$infinites(a \rightarrow P) = \{\langle a\rangle\hat{\ }u \mid u \in infinites(P)\}$$

$$infinites(?x : A \rightarrow P) = \{\langle a\rangle\hat{\ }u \mid a \in A \wedge u \in infinites(P[a/x])\}$$

$$infinites(P \,\square\, Q) = infinites(P) \cup infinites(Q)$$

$$infinites(P \,\sqcap\, Q) = infinites(P) \cup infinites(Q)$$

$$infinites(P \,\|_X\, Q) = \{u \in \Sigma^\omega \mid \exists\, s \in Traces(P),$$
$$t \in Traces(Q).u \in s \,\|_X\, t\}$$
$$\cup\, (\Sigma^\omega \cap \overline{divergences(P \,\|_X\, Q)})$$

$$infinites(P;\ Q) = infinites(P)$$
$$\cup\, \{s\hat{\ }u \mid s\hat{\ }\langle\checkmark\rangle \in traces(P) \wedge u \in infinites(Q)\}$$
$$\cup\, (\Sigma^\omega \cap \overline{divergences(P;\ Q)})$$

$$infinites(P[\![R]\!]) = \{u' \mid \exists\, u \in infinites(P).u\ R\ u'\}$$
$$\cup\, (\Sigma^\omega \cap \overline{divergences(P[\![R]\!])})$$

$$infinites(P \setminus X) = \{u' \in \Sigma^\omega \mid \exists\, u \in infinites(P).u \setminus X = u'\}$$
$$\cup\, (\Sigma^\omega \cap \overline{divergences(P \setminus X)})$$

$$infinites(P \triangle Q) = infinites(P) \cup \{s\hat{\ }u \mid s \in traces(P) \wedge u \in infinites(Q)\}$$
$$\cup\, (\Sigma^\omega \cap \overline{divergences(P \triangle Q)})$$

Process Algebra: A Unifying Approach

Tony Hoare

Microsoft Research, 7 J J Thomson Avenue,
Cambridge CB3 0FB, UK

Abstract. Process algebra studies systems that act and react continuously with their environment. It models them by transition graphs, whose nodes represent their states, and whose edges are labelled with the names of events by which they interact with their environment. A trace of the behaviour of a process is recorded as a sequence of observable events in which the process engages. Refinement is defined as the inclusion of all traces of a more refined process in those of the process that it refines. A simulation is a relation that compares states as well as events; by definition, two processes that start in states related by a simulation, and which then engage in the same event, will end in states also related by the same simulation. A bisimulation is defined as a symmetric simulation, and similarity is defined as the weakest of all simulations. In classical automata theory, the transition graphs are deterministic: from a given node, there is at most one edge with a given label; as a result, trace refinement and similarity coincide in meaning.

Research over many years has produced a wide variety of process algebras, distinguished by the manner in which they compare processes, usually by some form of simulation or by some form of refinement. This paper aims to unify the study of process algebras, by maintaining the identity between similarity and trace refinement, even for non-deterministic systems. Obviously, this unifying approach is entirely dependent on prior exploration of the diversity of theories that apply to the unbounded diversity of the real world. The aim of unification is to inspire and co-ordinate the exploration of yet further diversity; in no way does it detract from the value of such exploration.

1 Introduction

Process algebra is the branch of mathematics that has been developed to apply to systems which continuously act and react in response to stimuli from their environment. It is applied to natural systems such as living organisms and societies, and also to artificial systems such as networks of distributed computers. It is applied at many levels of abstraction, granularity and scale, from the entire collection of computers connected to the World Wide Web, through multiple processes time-sharing in a single computer, right down to electronic signals passing between the hardware circuits from which a computer is made. We assume that this is sufficient motivation for the study of process algebra as a branch of Computer Science.

A.E. Abdallah, C.B. Jones, and J.W. Sanders (Eds.): CSP25, LNCS 3525, pp. 36–60, 2005.

With such a range of applications, it is not surprising that there is now a wide variety of process algebras developed to meet differing needs. Fortunately, the axiomatic techniques of modern algebra establish order among the variations, and assist in the selection or development of a theory to meet new needs. The approach taken in this paper emphasises the essential unity of the study of the subject. In particular, it crosses a historical divide between theories that were based on the foundation of Milner's Calculus of Communicating Systems (CCS [4]) and those that owe their origin to the theory of Communicating Sequential Processes (CSP [9]).

In CCS and its variants and successors, the standard method of comparing two processes is by simulation, defined as a relation that is preserved after every action of the pair of processes between which it holds. The relation is often required to be symmetric, and then it is called a bisimulation. Similarity is defined as the existence of a simulation between two given processes [6]; it can be efficiently computed by automatic model checking, or proved manually by an elegant co-inductive technique.

In CSP and its variants, the standard comparison method is refinement, which in its simplest form is defined as inclusion of the traces of the observed behaviour of a more refined process in those of the refining process. This is an intuitive notion of correctness (at least for safety properties), and it has been applied in the stepwise design and development of the implementation of a process, starting from its more abstractly expressed specification. Such reasoning exploits the expressive and deductive power of the mathematics of sets and sequences.

The divergence between CCS and CSP is not accidental, but reflects a slight difference in the primary purposes for which the two calculi were designed. The purpose emphasised by CCS is to model and to analyse the behaviour of existing concurrent systems, including those which occur in nature and which are not implemented on a computer. The purpose emphasised by CSP is to formalise the specification of a concurrent system that is intended to be implemented as a computer program, and to verify that the implementation is correct, in the sense that it satisfies its specification. The only difference is one of emphasis: both CCS and CSP have been successfully used for both purposes. More detailed comparisons of these two calculi may be found in [10, 2].

This paper shows how to combine the particular advantages of similarity with those of refinement, simply by ensuring that they mean the same thing.

The next section introduces the standard theory of deterministic automata by means of an 'after' function, which maps each process and event onto the process that results after occurrence of that event. It defines the basic concepts of simulation and refinement, and proves they are the same. Non-determinism is introduced in Section three by means of a silent transition 'τ', representing an internal choice of an implementation to move from the current state to a different one, without any external cause or externally observable effect. Such internal moves are committed, and cannot be reversed. The reflexive transitive closure of the internal transition is known as reduction, and we postulate that it is a simulation. A weak transition is defined as an observable event preceded and followed by reduction. Weak similarity is defined in terms of weak transitions, in the same way as before. Because reduction is a simulation, weak similarity is proved to be the same as that defined in terms of purely deterministic transitions.

Trace refinement guarantees the safety of an implemented process against what is permitted by the specification that it refines. However, a process should also be adequately responsive to stimuli from its environment, and refinement of simple conventional traces does not guarantee responsiveness. Indeed the most refined process by this definition is the one that does nothing. In Section four, responsiveness is turned into a safety property by introduction of events known as 'barbs' [4, 5, 7], which can be used to record the failure of a process to respond to possibilities of interaction offered by its environment. Barbs are treated as ordinary events, and are recorded at the end of ordinary traces. Barbed simulation is defined as an ordinary simulation that takes these events into account. As a result, barbed simulation is still the same as barbed trace refinement. The problem of divergence can be treated in a similar way.

The paper is illustrated by a series of simple process calculi. The deterministic fragment of the calculus is reminiscent of Milner's lock-step synchronous SCCS, the non-deterministic one is more like CCS, and the barbed calculus is based on a familiar version of CSP. The calculi are defined by recursive definitions of the 'after' function, and by definitions of the tau-successors of each syntactic term; these effectively provide a structured operational semantics [8] for the calculi. Not a single axiom or definition or theorem is lost or changed in moving from one of these calculi to the next.

2   Deterministic Transition Systems

A deterministic transition system is an edge-labelled graph in which all edges leading from the same node have distinct labels. The nodes of the graph stand for the possible states of a process, and the labels stand for observable events in which the process can engage together with its environment.

For a fixed transition system, the existence of an edge labelled e leading from node p to node q is stated by $p \xrightarrow{e} q$; this triple is known as a transition. Its meaning is that a process in state p can move to state q on occurrence of the event denoted by the label e . The corresponding abstract relation on nodes is denoted $\xrightarrow{e}$, defined as the set $\{(p, q) \mid p \xrightarrow{e} q\}$. We will use the relational calculus to simplify the statement and proof of many of the theorems. The semicolon will denote (forward) relational composition

$$S \mathbin{\raisebox{0.2ex}{$\circ$}_{\!\circ}} T =_{\mathsf{def}} \{(p, r) \mid \exists q.\ (p, q) \in S\ \&\ (q, r) \in T\}$$

Our proofs will rely on the fact that composition is associative and has the identity relation as its unit. Also, it distributes through arbitrary unions of relations.

Because of determinism, we can define a function p/e (p after e), which maps a node p to the node at the other end of the edge labelled e. It describes the behaviour of process p after it has engaged in the event e.

Definition of $(\_/e)$

$$p/e =_{\mathsf{def}} q \quad \text{iff} \quad p \xrightarrow{e} q$$

To make this into a total function, it is convenient to introduce a special node $*$, which is not a process, but merely serves as a value for p/e in the case that $p \not\xrightarrow{e}$, where $p \not\xrightarrow{e}$ means that there is no edge from p which is labelled by e. It is also convenient to postulate that $*$ is an isolated node, and has no incoming or outgoing edges. This property effectively defines the purpose of $*$, and is formalised as follows:

$$\forall p, e. \quad * \not\xrightarrow{e} p \ \& \ p \not\xrightarrow{e} *$$

2.1   Traces

The after function can usefully be extended to apply also to sequences of events rather than just single events. If s is such a sequence, p/s is the state that process p reaches after engaging in the whole sequence s of events, one after the other. It can be found in the transition graph by starting with p and following a path along edges labelled by the successive events of s. If there is no such path, the result is $*$. The formal definition is by induction on the length of the trace.

Extended Definition of $(\_/s)$

$$
\begin{aligned}
*/s \quad &=_{\mathsf{def}} \ * \\
p/<> \quad &=_{\mathsf{def}} \ p \\
p/<e>s \ &=_{\mathsf{def}} \ (p/e)/s
\end{aligned}
$$

A trace of a process is defined to be the sequence of labels on the edges of some finite path of consecutive edges starting at p.

Definition of Traces

$$traces(p) =_{\mathsf{def}} \ \{s \mid p/s \neq *\}$$

The non-process $*$ has no traces; the empty sequence is a trace of every process; and the non-empty traces of a process p are all sequences of the form $<e>t'$, where t' is a trace of p/e.

Theorem 2.1.1 Let $labels^\star$ be the set of all finite sequences of labels. The following properties hold.

$$
\begin{aligned}
traces: \ &nodes \ \longrightarrow \ labels^\star \\
traces(p) = \{\} \quad &\text{iff} \quad p = * \\
<> \in traces(p) \quad &\text{iff} \quad p \neq * \\
t \in traces(p/e) \quad &\text{iff} \quad <e>t \in traces(p)
\end{aligned}
$$

Theorem 2.1.2 The function $traces(\_)$ is uniquely defined by the four clauses of Theorem 2.1.1.

Proof: The statement of Theorem 2.1.1 is effectively a definition of the *traces* function by primitive recursion on the length of the trace.

A node q is said to refine p if every trace of q is also a trace of p. The ordering relation $p \geq q$ means that p is refined by q.

Definition of Refinement

$$p \geq q \quad =_{\mathsf{def}} \quad traces(q) \subseteq traces(p)$$

Refinement in a process calculus is used to model program correctness. Let SPEC be a specification, describing the intended behaviour of a process PROG in terms of all the traces that it may give rise to. Being a specification, the description may take advantage of any mathematical concepts that apply to sets of sequences of events. But the actual process PROG must be described in the restricted notations of a process calculus, or an implemented programming language that is based upon it. The semantics of the process calculus (as described in Section 2.3) determines exactly which traces are possible for PROG. Now a proof that PROG refines SPEC shows that no visible behaviour of PROG can ever fall outside the set of behaviours permitted by SPEC. It thereby serves as a proof of the correctness of PROG with respect to SPEC.

Refinement can also be used to justify optimisation of a program. Let OPT be a better version of a program PROG, for example, more efficient in resources of communication or computation, or more responsive to the needs of its users. Then the optimisation is valid just if OPT refines PROG. This is because every specification satisfied by PROG will also be satisfied by OPT, as stated by the following theorem.

Theorem 2.1.3 Refinement is reflexive and transitive, i.e.,

| (reflexive) | $p \geq p$ |
| (transitive) | $p \geq q \ \& \ q \geq r \implies p \geq r$ |

The preceding account of refinement takes safety as an adequate criterion of correctness; it supposes that a process that does less actions is always safer than one that does more. But obviously, failure to respond to the expected stimuli from the environment is also a serious error, one that in practice (all too frequently) manifests itself as deadlock or as livelock of a computer system. A definition of responsiveness states that a process that has more traces is more responsive than one that has less traces. A full specification of correctness should therefore also specify the desired lower bounds on the responsiveness of the system. The introduction of non-determinism in the next section will permit these lower bounds to be specified at the same time as the upper bound, in a single process specification, with the result that a single proof of refinement ensures both safety and responsiveness.

In Section 2.3, we shall define a number of operators, both parallel and sequential, for constructing a complex process, say $F(p, q)$, out of simpler components p and q. These operators can be applied equally well to specifications as to processes written in the calculus or an available programming language that implements it. Suppose we want $F(p, q)$ to satisfy some overall specification F-SPEC, and decide to split the whole task into two sub-tasks: to write a program p and a program q to meet specifications p-SPEC and q-SPEC respectively; the intention is to combine them later by F. Before starting work (may be in parallel) on these two tasks, it would be a good idea to check that we have got their specifications right. This can be done in advance by proving that $F(p$-SPEC, q-SPEC) is a refinement of F-SPEC. Then, when p-SPEC has been correctly implemented by p (i.e., p-SPEC $\geq p$) and similarly q-SPEC has been implemented by q, we can safely plug the implementations p and q into F, in place of their specifications. If such a procedure has been consistently and carefully followed throughout, we can have high confidence that the result $F(p, q)$ is free from design errors (because $F(p, q)$ satisfies $F(p$-SPEC, q-SPEC), which is already known to satisfy F-SPEC). Furthermore, correctness of the assembly has actually been proved before implementation of the components. This method of engineering design is known as step-wise decomposition.

But wait! The validity of the method is dependent on a basic property of the function F: it must respect the ordering relation of refinement between processes. More formally, it must be monotonic in all its arguments.

Definition of Monotonicity. A function F is monotonic wrt $\geq$ iff

$$F(p, q, \dots) \geq F(p', q', \dots) \quad \text{whenever} \quad p \geq p' \ \& \ q \geq q', \text{and} \ \dots$$

An example is provided by the only function on processes that we have defined so far, the after function $\_/e$.

Theorem 2.1.4

$$p \geq q \implies p/e \geq q/e$$

Proof: If q is $*$, $traces(q/e)$ is empty, so the consequent is trivial. Otherwise let t be a trace of q/e. Then by Theorem 2.1.1, $<e>t$ is a trace of q. By the antecedent of this theorem, it is also a trace of p. By Theorem 2.1.1 again, t is a trace of p/e.

The preceding theorem states that every transition respects the ordering $\geq$, in the sense that if two processes are related by $\geq$ before an event, they are still so related after it. An alternative formulation of the same theorem can be given in terms of the relation $\xrightarrow{e}$.

Theorem 2.1.5

$$p \geq q \;\&\; q \xrightarrow{e} r \implies \exists p'. \; p \xrightarrow{e} p' \;\&\; p' \geq r$$

Proof: Let $p \geq q$ and $q \xrightarrow{e} r$. Then $<e>$ is a trace of q, and therefore of p. So $p \xrightarrow{e} p/e$. By Theorem 2.1.4, $p/e \geq q/e$. Because of determinism, $q/e = r$. So $p/e \geq r$, and p/e can play the role of p' in the statement of the theorem.

An even neater formulation of the same theorem can be stated using the relational calculus, as we shall often do from now on. It is weak commutivity principle, which permits interchange of refinement with any e-transition, when they are composed sequentially.

Theorem 2.1.5 (Alternative Formulation)

$$(\geq \,\substack{\circ\\\circ}\, \xrightarrow{e}) \;\subseteq\; (\xrightarrow{e} \,\substack{\circ\\\circ}\, \geq)$$

Here is another example of a relation satisfying the same weak commutivity principle. Let $\equiv$ stand for equality of the trace sets of two processes, formally defined by mutual refinement.

Definition of Trace Equivalence

$$p \equiv q \;\;=_{\text{def}}\; p \geq q \;\&\; q \geq p$$

Theorem 2.1.6

$$(\equiv \,\substack{\circ\\\circ}\, \xrightarrow{e}) \;\subseteq\; (\xrightarrow{e} \,\substack{\circ\\\circ}\, \equiv)$$

In standard automata theory, trace equivalence is taken as a sufficient condition for identity of two processes. We shall not do this, because in the next section we want to make distinctions between processes that have the same traces. In the final section, we will show that trace equivalence is after all an adequate definition of identity of processes.

2.2   Simulation

The principle of weak commutivity introduced in the last two theorems of the previous section suggests that the following definition.

Definition of Simulation. A relation S between processes (i.e., excluding the non-process node $*$) is defined to be a simulation if the relational composition $(S \,\substack{\circ\\\circ}\, \xrightarrow{e})$ is contained in $(\xrightarrow{e} \,\substack{\circ\\\circ}\, S)$, for all labels e. A bisimulation is defined as a simulation that is symmetric.

Examples of bisimulation include the empty relation, the identity relation and $\equiv$, whereas $\geq$ is just a simulation; so is the relation

$$\{(p,q) \mid \text{traces}(q) = \{<>\} \}.$$

Theorem 2.2.1 If S and T are simulations, so is their relational composition.

Proof: The assumptions are:

(A1) $(S \mathbin{⨾} \xrightarrow{e}) \subseteq (\xrightarrow{e} \mathbin{⨾} S)$ and (A2) $(T \mathbin{⨾} \xrightarrow{e}) \subseteq (\xrightarrow{e} \mathbin{⨾} T)$

$$
\begin{aligned}
(S \mathbin{⨾} T) \mathbin{⨾} \xrightarrow{e} \; &= \; S \mathbin{⨾} (T \mathbin{⨾} \xrightarrow{e}) && \text{by associativity of } ⨾ \\
&\subseteq \; S \mathbin{⨾} (\xrightarrow{e} \mathbin{⨾} T) && \text{by A2 and monotonicity of } ⨾ \\
&= \; (S \mathbin{⨾} \xrightarrow{e}) \mathbin{⨾} T && \text{by associativity of } ⨾ \\
&\subseteq \; (\xrightarrow{e} \mathbin{⨾} S) \mathbin{⨾} T && \text{by A1 and monotonicity of } ⨾ \\
&= \; \xrightarrow{e} \mathbin{⨾} (S \mathbin{⨾} T) && \text{by associativity of } ⨾
\end{aligned}
$$

Theorem 2.2.2 The union of any set of simulations is a simulation. The intersection of any non-empty set of simulations is a simulation.

Proof: Relational composition distributes through union; and since $\xrightarrow{e}$ is a partial function, $(\xrightarrow{e} \mathbin{⨾} \_)$ distributes through intersections of non-empty set of relations.

Theorem 2.2.3 If R is a simulation, so is its reflexive transitive closure $R^\star$, defined as the union of the identity relation with R, $(R \mathbin{⨾} R)$, $(R \mathbin{⨾} R \mathbin{⨾} R)$, etc.

Proof: Follows from the previous two theorems.

In CCS and related calculi, bisimulation is the basic relation used to reason about the correctness of programs and their optimisation. Correctness means that there exists a bisimulation between a specification and its program, or between a program and its optimised version. Remarkably, it is not necessary to specify exactly which relation has been used as the bisimulation: any bisimulation will do. It can be chosen to match the needs of each particular proof. Thus what every proof establishes is the bisimilarity of two processes, where bisimilarity (and its asymmetric version similarity) is defined as follows

Definition of Similarity. Similarity is defined as the set union of all simulations. Bisimilarity is the union of all bisimulations.

Theorem 2.2.2 says that similarity is itself a simulation, in fact the largest of all simulations, and the same applies to bisimilarity. In summary, bisimilarity is the correctness relation established by all bisimulation proofs in CCS, and other process calculi which take bisimulation as the basis of reasoning about processes.

Theorem 2.2.4 Similarity is reflexive and transitive.

Proof: Reflexive because identity is a simulation; transitive because similarity composed with itself is a simulation; and every simulation is contained in similarity.

Theorem 2.2.5 Every simulation is relationally contained in refinement.

Proof: By induction on the length of a trace. Let S be a simulation and let $p \, S \, q$. Let t be a trace of q. If t is of length 0, it is the empty sequence, which is a trace of every p. Otherwise, let t be $<e>t'$. Then for some q', $q \xrightarrow{e} q'$ and t' is a trace of q'. Since S is a simulation, there is a p' such that (1) $p \xrightarrow{e} p'$ and $p' \, S \, q'$. Since t' is shorter than t, we can by induction assume that the traces of p' include the traces of q'. Since t' is a trace of q', it is also a trace of p'. Since we proved above at (1) that $p \xrightarrow{e} p'$, $<e>t'$ is a trace of p.

We now state the theorem that is the goal of this whole Section.

Theorem 2.2.6 In a deterministic transition system, similarity and refinement are the same.

Proof: By Theorem 2.1.5, refinement is a simulation, and therefore contained in the largest simulation. Theorem 2.2.5 gives the reverse inclusion.

It is worthy of note that none of the proofs in this section, except that of Theorem 2.2.6 and the second claim of Theorem 2.2.2, relies on the determinacy of the underlying transition system.

2.3   Example: A Synchronous Calculus

The purpose of a process calculus is to define a particular transition system. It first defines the syntax for naming the nodes of the transition system, and then uses induction on the structure of the syntax to define which nodes are connected by transitions, and what the labels on the edges are. The calculus postulates that there is a node in the underlying transition graph that is named by each of the terms of the calculus, as constructed in accordance with its syntax; furthermore, each node of the graph has exactly one name.

In this section we will present a synchronous deterministic calculus based loosely on Milner's SCCS. The primitives of its syntax and their intended meanings are:

STOP   never does anything
RUN   can do anything at any time.

There are two monadic combinators, called prefixing and restriction; they both mean the same as in CCS:

$f.p$ does f first, and then behaves like p
$p \backslash f$ can always do anything that p can do, except f

There are two parallel combinators:

$(p \, |\&| \, q)$ can always do what both p and q can do at the same time
$(p \, |or| \, q)$ can do whatever either p or q can do, as long as possible

These parallel combinators are chosen for their simplicity and elegance. They do not correspond to any of the parallel combinators of either CCS or CSP.

Note that the syntax must not contain in its syntax a notation for $*$, which is not a process. For the same reason, a process calculus cannot include the after operator, because it sometimes gives the result $*$. However, the after operator remains useful in reasoning about the calculus at a more abstract level.

The specification of the labelled edges of the underlying transition system is formalised as an inductive definition of the after operator, where the induction is over the structure of the term that names the parameter. The following table shows a simple way of doing this. For each node p, it tells how to compute (recursively, where necessary) the name of the node at the other end of the edge labelled e. It is easy to check that the formal definition accords with the informal description given above to explain the meaning of each notation.

Definition of $(\_/e)$

$$
\begin{array}{lll}
\text{STOP}/e & = * & \\
\text{RUN}/e & = \text{RUN} & \\[4pt]
f.* & = * & \\[4pt]
(f.p)/e & = p & \text{if } e = f \\
& = * & \text{otherwise} \\[4pt]
(p \,|\&|\, q)/e & = (p/e) \,|\&|\, (q/e) & \text{if } p \xrightarrow{e} \text{ \& } q \xrightarrow{e} \\
& = * & \text{otherwise} \\[4pt]
(p \,|or|\, q)/e & = (p/e) \,|or|\, (q/e) & \text{if } p \xrightarrow{e} \text{ \& } q \xrightarrow{e} \\
& = (p/e) & \text{if } p \xrightarrow{e} \text{ \& } q \not\xrightarrow{e} \\
& = (q/e) & \text{if } p \not\xrightarrow{e} \text{ \& } q \xrightarrow{e} \\
& = * & \text{otherwise} \\[4pt]
(p\backslash f)/e & = (p/e)\backslash f & \text{if } e \neq f \\
& = * & \text{otherwise}
\end{array}
$$

Note the unusual recursion in the first line of the rule for or-parallelism. It reveals that continued parallel computation of both operands is needed if the first event is possible for both of them. Or-parallelism is a deterministic version of a choice operator, as computed by the traditional determinisation procedure of automata theory. That is why the or-parallel operator defined here does not correspond to any of the choice operators in CSP or CCS, which avoid the inefficiency of the parallel computation by resorting to non-determinism. We will return to these more familiar choice operators in Section 3.3.

In the standard deterministic model of CSP, the clauses of the following theorem are presented as a recursive definition of the operators of the calculus; and the clauses of the definition of $(\_/)$ can be proved from them. The equivalence of two different methods of definition is mildly encouraging in a mathematical theory, since it forestalls any controversy over which to choose as definitive.

Theorem 2.3.1

$$traces(\text{STOP}) = \{<>\}$$
$$traces(\text{RUN}) = labels^\star$$
$$traces(f.p) = \{<>\} \cup \{<f>t \mid t \in traces(p)\}$$
$$traces(p \mathbin{|\&|} q) = traces(p) \cap traces(q)$$
$$traces(p \mathbin{|or|} q) = traces(p) \cup traces(q)$$
$$traces(p \backslash f) = \{t \mid t \in traces(p) \,\&\, \mathbf{not}(<f> \mathbf{in}\ t\,)\}$$
$$\text{where } s \mathbf{\ in\ } t =_{\mathsf{def}} \exists u, v.\ u\,s\,v = t$$

Proof (the last clause, for example). By induction on the length of a trace. The hypothesis is that traces with maximum length n on both sides of the assertion are identical.

Base case: $<> \in LHS$ holds because $(p \backslash f) \neq *$. Similarly, $<> \in RHS$ because $<> \in traces(p)$ and (obviously) $<>$ does not contain f.

For the inductive case, we reason as follows.

	$<e>t \in traces(p \backslash f)$	
iff	$t \in traces((p \backslash f)/e)$	by definition of $traces$
iff	$t \in (traces(p/e) \backslash f \ \mathbf{if}\ f \neq e\ \mathbf{else}\ \{\})$	by definition of $((p \backslash f)/e)$
iff	$f \neq e\ \&\ t \in traces(p/e)$	by definition of $\in$
iff	$f \neq e\ \&\ t \in traces(p/e)\ \&\ \mathbf{not}(<f> \mathbf{in}\ t)$	by induction hypothesis
iff	$<e>t \in traces(p)\ \&\ \mathbf{not}(<f> \mathbf{in}\ <e>t)$	by definition of $\mathbf{in}$

The traces of each of the constructions of the calculus can be calculated from the definition of $traces(\_)$ at the beginning of Section 2.1, together with the definition of $\_/e$ given above.

Theorem 2.3.2 All the operators are monotonic with respect to refinement.

Proof: Simple Boolean algebra of sets.

In fact a great many equivalences between processes are immediate consequences of elementary equations between their sets of traces. For example, the following theorems match exactly the properties of the meet operator in a Boolean algebra.

Theorem 2.3.3

$\text{RUN} \mathbin{|\&|} p$	$\equiv p$	RUN is the unit of $\mathbin{|\&|}$
$\text{STOP} \mathbin{|\&|} p$	$\equiv \text{STOP}$	STOP is its zero
$p \mathbin{|\&|} p$	$\equiv p$	$\mathbin{|\&|}$ is idempotent
$p \mathbin{|\&|} q$	$\equiv q \mathbin{|\&|} p$	it commutes
$(p \mathbin{|\&|} q) \mathbin{|\&|} r$	$\equiv p \mathbin{|\&|} (q \mathbin{|\&|} r)$	it associates

Algebraic laws based on trace equivalence help to explain the way in which parallel processes interact with each other by synchronised participation in the same events. Consider the process $((e.p) \ |or| \ (f.q))$, which offers a choice between two initial events, either e or f, which we assume to be distinct. Suppose this is run in and-parallel with an environment $(e.r)$; this process selects e as the next event to occur, rejecting the possibility of f. Then e must be the next event, and the subsequent behaviour of the system will involve p, and q will have no further effect. However, if the environment selects an event, say g, which is not offered by the or-parallel process, the result is deadlock, indicated by the process STOP. These facts are summarised algebraically in the following theorem.

Theorem 2.3.4

$((e.p) \ |or| \ (f.q)) \ |\&| \ (e.r) \equiv e.(p \ |\&| \ r) \quad$ if $e \neq f$

$((e.p) \ |or| \ (f.q)) \ |\&| \ (g.r) \equiv \text{STOP} \qquad$ if $g \neq f \ \& \ g \neq e$

In addition to its collection of operators, a process calculus usually allows definition of the behaviour of a system by means of recursion. For example, a perpetually ticking clock may be defined by the recursive equation

$clock = tick.clock$

The right hand side of such an equation may include any of the operators of the calculus. The fact that all the operators are monotonic guarantees by Tarski's theorem that there exists a trace set that for a process that satisfies the equation. In all reasonable cases, there will only be one such set. When the solution is non-unique, CCS specifies that the least solution is intended. Thus the trivial loop defined by the recursive equation

$loop = loop$

has STOP as its intended solution, rather than RUN. CSP makes the opposite choice. The reason is to make it as difficult as possible to prove correctness of a non-terminating recursion. In the remainder of this paper we will not give further attention to recursion.

In CCS and related calculi, it is usual to present the semantics in a structured operational style. For each nameable node, there are clauses which determine a name for each of its e-derivatives. These essentially determine the structure of the underlying graph.

Theorem 2.3.5

$\text{RUN} \xrightarrow{e} \text{RUN}$

$e.p \xrightarrow{e} p$

$p \ |\&| \ q \xrightarrow{e} p' \ |\&| \ q' \qquad$ if $p \xrightarrow{e} p' \ \& \ q \xrightarrow{e} q'$

$p \ |or| \ q \xrightarrow{e} p' \ |or| \ q' \qquad$ if $p \xrightarrow{e} p' \ \& \ q \xrightarrow{e} q'$

$p \ |or| \ q \xrightarrow{e} p' \qquad$ if $p \xrightarrow{e} p' \ \& \ q \not\xrightarrow{e}$

$p \ |or| \ q \xrightarrow{e} q' \qquad$ if $p \not\xrightarrow{e} \ \& \ q \xrightarrow{e} q'$

$p \backslash f \xrightarrow{e} p' \qquad$ if $e \neq f \quad \& \ p \xrightarrow{e} p'$

There is an implicit understanding that this is the entire set of rules for the transition system, and that if a transition cannot be derived from these rules, it does not exist. Thus the fact the STOP does not appear in any of the rules means that it is the source of no edges. The fact that there is only one transition given for $e.p$ means that if $(e.p) \xrightarrow{f} q$, then $e = f$ and $q = p$. In reasoning about the calculus, the rules must be strengthened to give both necessary and sufficient conditions for each transition. When this has been done, the operational definition of Theorem 2.3.5 can be used to justify the clauses of the definition of $(\_/e)$ given earlier in this section.

3   Non-deterministic Transition Systems

For a deterministic system, all the events that happen are observable, predictable and to some extent controllable (see Theorem 2.3.4) by the environment with which the system interacts. Non-determinism is introduced into the system when there are unobservable internal events that change the internal state of the system without the knowledge or control of the external environment. Let τ be such an internal event. (In fact, there can be many such events, but because they are indistinguishable, we follow convention in letting τ stand for them all). We define a non-deterministic system as a deterministic transition system, plus a set of additional τ-labelled edges between the nodes; these do not have to satisfy the requirement of determinacy: many τ-labelled edges can lead from the same node to many different nodes. Selection between them is non-deterministic, uncontrollable and unobservable by the external environment.

In a program-controlled system, the τ event may model a period of internal computation of the program. In modern process algebras, these internal computations are specified by algebraic reduction rules, which permit the implementation to move the state of a process from one that matches the left hand side of the rule to one that matches the right hand side. In other cases, τ may stand for an internal communication between components of a system, observable only by those components; they are deliberately hidden from its outer environment, in order to present a simpler and more abstract interface.

Non-determinism arises because reduction does not have to satisfy the Church-Rosser property: whenever there is a possibility of two reductions to two different states, there may be no possibility of convergence back to the same state again afterwards. As a result, algebraic reduction involves a commitment that cannot later be withdrawn. That is what makes non-determinism problematic in the design and implementation of computer systems. Another reason is that a program can work perfectly while it is being tested, and still go wrong when put to serious use. Indeed, the solution to these problems is one of the primary motives for the study and application of process algebra to proofs of correctness of computer systems.

In development of an abstract theory of correctness, we are not interested in the exact number of steps involved in a particular computation. In fact, if the theory is to be used for purposes of program optimisation, it is essential to abstract from questions of efficiency, in order that an optimised program can be proved equal to (or a refinement of) its un-optimised version. We are therefore not so much interested in the $\xrightarrow{\tau}$ relation by itself, but rather in its reflexive transitive closure, which we denote by an unlabelled arrow.

Definition of Reduction

$$\longrightarrow \ =_{\mathsf{def}}\ (\xrightarrow{\tau})^{\star}$$

We are also interested in the states for which no further internal computation is possible until after the next externally visible event. In such a stable state, a process is idle, waiting for a response or a new stimulus from the environment. Stable states are defined in the same way as normal forms in algebraic reduction

Definition of Stability

$$p \text{ is stable}\quad =_{\mathsf{def}}\quad p \xcancel{\xrightarrow{\tau}}$$

Occurrence of a τ-transition is intended to be totally unobservable from outside a process. In particular, we cannot tell exactly when the transition took place. In an unstable state, after occurrence of a visible event e we cannot tell whether a τ-transition preceded it or followed it, or maybe never occurred at all. This invisibility is expressed by postulating an algebraic law similar to the definition of a simulation.

Defining Property of τ

$$\xrightarrow{\tau} \ _{9}^{\circ} \xrightarrow{e}\ \subseteq\ \xrightarrow{e}\ _{9}^{\circ} \longrightarrow$$

or equivalently $\longrightarrow$ is a simulation. This condition can also be expressed:

$$p \xrightarrow{\tau} q\ \implies\ p/e \longrightarrow q/e$$

In Section 3.3 we will define the τ transitions of a simple process calculus. Care is needed to show that these definitions are consistent with the axiom. Axioms like this are often called healthiness conditions: the designer of a calculus must ensure that healthiness is preserved by all the operators.

There are three reasons for accepting this as the defining property of a τ transition. First, it represents the invisibility of τ . Secondly, it permits a useful optimisation. If an implementation can detect that an event e will be possible after an internal computation, it may compile code to do e straight away, either avoiding the calculation at run time, or at least postponing it till after: efficiency and responsiveness may thereby be improved. Finally, the postulate achieves our primary goal of reconciliation of similarity with refinement.

Since simulation implies refinement, the defining property of τ means that a non-deterministic choice can only reduce the traces of a process, never change or increase them. Thus the trace set defines the limits of what a process can do, and includes all possible results of any choices it may make internally.

Weak Simulation

In the evolution of a non-deterministic process, internal invisible activity will alternate with externally visible events. Each external event will be preceded and followed by (none or more) internal reductions. We therefore give the usual definition of the concept of a non-deterministic (or weak) transition.

Definition of Weak Transition

$$\stackrel{e}{\Longrightarrow} \;=_{\mathsf{def}}\; (\longrightarrow \mathbin{⨾} \stackrel{e}{\longrightarrow} \mathbin{⨾} \longrightarrow)$$

A weak simulation and weak similarity are defined in the same way as ordinary (strong) simulation and similarity, using the transition $\stackrel{e}{\Longrightarrow}$ in place of $\stackrel{e}{\longrightarrow}$.

The following theorem gives an alternative definition $\stackrel{e}{\Longrightarrow}$, and makes explicit some of its obvious properties.

Theorem 3.1.1

$$\stackrel{e}{\Longrightarrow} \;=\; (\stackrel{e}{\longrightarrow} \mathbin{⨾} \longrightarrow) \;=\; (\longrightarrow \mathbin{⨾} \stackrel{e}{\Longrightarrow}) \;=\; (\stackrel{e}{\Longrightarrow} \mathbin{⨾} \longrightarrow)$$

Proof: $\longrightarrow$ is a reflexive and transitive simulation.

Theorem 3.1.2 If W is a weak simulation, then $(\longrightarrow \mathbin{⨾} W)$ is a simulation.

Proof:

$$
\begin{aligned}
(\longrightarrow \mathbin{⨾} W) \mathbin{⨾} \stackrel{e}{\longrightarrow} \quad
&\subseteq\; \longrightarrow \mathbin{⨾} W \mathbin{⨾} \stackrel{e}{\longrightarrow} \mathbin{⨾} \longrightarrow && \longrightarrow \text{ is reflexive} \\
&=\; \longrightarrow \mathbin{⨾} W \mathbin{⨾} \stackrel{e}{\Longrightarrow} && \text{by Theorem 3.1.1} \\
&\subseteq\; \longrightarrow \mathbin{⨾} \stackrel{e}{\Longrightarrow} \mathbin{⨾} W && W \text{ is a weak simulation} \\
&=\; \longrightarrow \mathbin{⨾} \stackrel{e}{\longrightarrow} \mathbin{⨾} \longrightarrow \mathbin{⨾} W && \text{by Theorem 3.1.1}
\end{aligned}
$$

Theorem 3.1.3 If S is a simulation, then $(S \mathbin{⨾} \longrightarrow)$ is a weak simulation.

Proof: similar to the above.

Theorem 3.1.4 Weak similarity is the same as similarity.

Proof: Let W be the largest weak simulation. Because $\longrightarrow$ is reflexive, W is contained in $(\longrightarrow \mathbin{\text{\textcentoldstyle}} W)$. From Theorem 3.1.2, this is a simulation, and so contained in the largest simulation. The reverse inclusion is proved using Theorem 3.1.3 in place of Theorem 3.1.2. Note that this theorem depends on the defining property for τ.

The introduction of non-determinism has not required any change in the definition of *traces*. So Theorem 3.1.4 achieves our goal of reconciling refinement with weak similarity in a non-deterministic setting.

3.1   Relationship with CCS

A traditional presentation of a non-deterministic transition system is as an edge-labelled graph which allows edges with the same source and label to point to two or more distinct nodes. We can construct such a traditional graph from our definition of a non-deterministic system, simply by using weak transitions $\overset{e}{\Longrightarrow}$ to define its labelled edges, instead of the deterministic transitions $\overset{e}{\longrightarrow}$. The resulting graph will enjoy the following extra properties

(1) $(\overset{\tau}{\longrightarrow} \mathbin{\text{\textcentoldstyle}} \overset{e}{\Longrightarrow}) \;=\; \overset{e}{\Longrightarrow} \;=\; (\overset{e}{\Longrightarrow} \mathbin{\text{\textcentoldstyle}} \overset{\tau}{\longrightarrow})$

(2) $p \overset{e}{\Longrightarrow} q$ iff $p/e \longrightarrow q$

(3) $p \overset{e}{\Longrightarrow} q \;\implies\; p \overset{e}{\Longrightarrow} p/e$

In standard versions of CCS, the property (1) holds by definition of the weak transition; furthermore the after function can be defined in CCS in a way that satisfies the transition rule (2). The only missing property (3) is the one that states that there exists an edge labelled e between p and p/e. For example, consider the graph fragment.

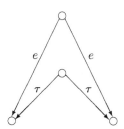

In a transition graph satisfying property (3), there must be an edge labelled e from the top node to the middle node of this diagram. In the underlying transition graph for CCS, such an edge may be missing. Our calculus therefore cannot be applied to a reactive system in which the possible absence of such an edge is a significant feature; for study of such a system, CCS would be a better choice as a model.

In general, our theory can be regarded as a sub-theory of CCS, in that it applies to the subset of CCS processes which happen to satisfy (3).

3.2   Example: An Asynchronous Calculus

The introduction of non-determinism by means of a τ-transition permits distinctions to be made between processes which have the same traces, but which have different reductions. For example the RUN process has all sequences of labels as its traces. So does the CHAOS process of CSP, which is intended to be the most non-deterministic of all processes. Its extreme non-determinism is indicated by the fact that it can unobservably change into any other process whatsoever

$$\forall p. \ \mathrm{CHAOS} \xrightarrow{\ \tau\ } p$$

In this, it is distinguished from RUN, which has no τ-transitions. However, both the processes satisfy similar recursive equations, explaining why RUN and CHAOS have the same traces.

$$\mathrm{RUN}/e \ \ = \mathrm{RUN}$$
$$\mathrm{CHAOS}/e = \mathrm{CHAOS}$$

Before proceeding, we must check that these definitions satisfy the healthiness condition for τ, which is done as follows

$$\mathrm{RUN} \xrightarrow{\ \tau\ } r \quad \Longrightarrow \mathrm{RUN}/e \longrightarrow r/e \quad \text{the antecedent is always false}$$
$$\mathrm{CHAOS} \xrightarrow{\ \tau\ } r \Longrightarrow \mathrm{CHAOS}/e \longrightarrow r/e \ \text{the consequent is always true}$$

In general, a process algebra can define the placing of the τ-labelled edges in a non-deterministic graph by means of a collection of clauses similar to those which defined the meaning of the after operator in Section 2.3. The postulates define a set of τ-transitions which the transition system must include. The definition is completed by saying that these are all the τ-transitions that are included – there must be no more.

Definition of τ-transitions

$$\mathrm{STOP, RUN, \ and} \ f.p \ \text{have no} \ \tau\text{-transitions}$$
$$(p \ |\&| \ q) \xrightarrow{\ \tau\ } (p' \ |\&| \ q) \quad \text{if } p \xrightarrow{\ \tau\ } p'$$
$$(p \ |\&| \ q) \xrightarrow{\ \tau\ } (p \ |\&| \ q') \quad \text{if } q \xrightarrow{\ \tau\ } q'$$
$$(p \ |or| \ q) \xrightarrow{\ \tau\ } (p' \ |or| \ q) \ \text{if } p \xrightarrow{\ \tau\ } p'$$
$$(p \ |or| \ q) \xrightarrow{\ \tau\ } (p \ |or| \ q') \ \text{if } q \xrightarrow{\ \tau\ } q'$$
$$(p \backslash f) \xrightarrow{\ \tau\ } (p' \backslash f) \quad\quad \text{if } p \xrightarrow{\ \tau\ } p'$$

The first line forbids an implementation from making internal transitions in cases where it is not needed or wanted. The next four of these clauses allow reductions to be made independently for both the operands of a parallel combinator. This is what permits an implementation to exploit concurrency in execution of the internal actions of concurrent parallel processes.

Before proceeding further, we must prove that the above definition preserves the healthiness condition for τ. The pattern of the proof is given just for the case $p\backslash f$.

Assume $p\backslash f \xrightarrow{\tau} r$; we need to prove $(p\backslash f)/e \longrightarrow r/e$. Since the traces of $p\backslash f$ include the traces of r , it follows that $p\backslash f \xrightarrow{e}$, and so e cannot be f . The definition given above for τ transitions has only one clause that could justify a τ transition of $p\backslash f$, so the assumption must match that clause; consequently for some p', $r = p'\backslash f$ and $p \xrightarrow{\tau} p'$. The definition of $(\_/e)$ shows that $p'\backslash f \xrightarrow{e}$ only if $p' \xrightarrow{e}$. Now p' is syntactically simpler than $p\backslash f$, so we may assume by induction that it satisfies the healthiness condition. So $p/e \longrightarrow p'/e$, ie, there is a sequence of τ-transitions stretching between them. Applying the definition of $(\_\backslash f)$ to each step of the sequence, we get $(p/e)\backslash f \longrightarrow (p'/e)\backslash f$. From the definition of $(\_/e)$ since $e \neq f$,

$$(p\backslash f)/e \;=\; (p/e)\backslash f \;\longrightarrow\; (p'/e)\backslash f \;=\; (p'\backslash f)/e.$$

As mentioned in Section 2.3, the implementation of or-parallelism has to be prepared to execute both its operands concurrently, for as long as the events that actually happen are possible for both of them. For practical reasons, most process algebras introduce a choice operator that does not require such parallel computation. In fact, CSP introduces two choice operators: internal choice ($\sqcap$), which is made by a process in a manner that cannot be observed or controlled by the environment; and external choice ($\square$), which can be controlled by the environment (as described in Theorem 2.3.4, but only on the first step of their interaction. Although both operators have the same set of traces as $|or|$, they are distinguished by their τ-transitions, as we shall now describe.

For an internal choice, denoted by $(p \sqcap q)$, the choice between the operands can be made internally by a τ-transition; so the following clause should be added to the defining properties of τ-transitions

$$(p \sqcap q) \xrightarrow{\tau} p \;\;\&\;\; (p \sqcap q) \xrightarrow{\tau} q$$

The after function when applied to $(p \sqcap q)$ obeys the same recursion as it does for $(p \,|or|\, q)$

$$
\begin{aligned}
(p \sqcap q)/e &= (p/e) \sqcap (q/e) &&\text{if } p \xrightarrow{e} \,\&\, q \xrightarrow{e}\\
&= (p/e) &&\text{if } p \xrightarrow{e} \,\&\, q \not\xrightarrow{e}\\
&= (q/e) &&\text{if } p \not\xrightarrow{e} \,\&\, q \xrightarrow{e}\\
&= * &&\text{otherwise}
\end{aligned}
$$

For external choice, the two operands can be reduced, even in parallel; but (as in CSP) on this first step it is not permitted to withdraw the external choice between the operands (the CCS + operator does allow such withdrawal). So the τ definition for $\square$ is the same as for $|or|$.

$$(p \,\square\, q) \xrightarrow{\tau} (p' \,\square\, q) \qquad \text{if } p \xrightarrow{\tau} p'$$
$$(p \,\square\, q) \xrightarrow{\tau} (p \,\square\, q') \qquad \text{if } q \xrightarrow{\tau} q'$$

However, after the first visible event, the behaviour is the same for external as for internal choice

$$(p \,\square\, q)/e = (p \,\sqcap\, q)/e$$

The distinction between internal and external non-determinism is sufficient to solve the problem of non-deterministic deadlock. The process $(p \sqcap \text{STOP})$ has the same traces as p; but it is distinguished from p because it can independently and unobservably withdraw its capability to perform the actions of p. The withdrawal is justified by the τ-transition from $(p \sqcap \text{STOP})$ to STOP.

In Section 2.3, the restriction operator $\_ \backslash f$ was defined as in CCS, to conceal the event f by preventing it from happening altogether. CSP introduced a different hiding operator, which we will denote by $\_ \backslash\backslash f$; it allows an f-transition to happen whenever it can, but only as an internally hidden event. This is formally expressed by the postulate

$$(p\backslash\backslash f) \xrightarrow{\tau} (p'\backslash\backslash f) \qquad \text{if } p \xRightarrow{f} p' \vee p \xrightarrow{\tau} p'$$

A process $(p\backslash\backslash f)$ for which all f-transitions are hidden obviously cannot engage in any external occurrence of the event f. But any other event possible for p may occur; or the operand can perform a hidden f-transition first. The choice to perform the f event rather than some other possible event is internally non-deterministic.

$$\begin{aligned}(p\backslash\backslash f)/e &= \ast & \text{if } e = f \\ &= ((p/e)\backslash\backslash f) \,\sqcap\, ((p/f)\backslash\backslash f)/e & \text{otherwise}\end{aligned}$$

4   Barbed Transition Systems

So far we have devoted attention to graphs with labels on their edges; but why shouldn't nodes have labels too? They could be used to denote properties of the internal states of a process, independent of any actions they can perform. Let us introduce a set of node labels B (standing for 'barbs'), disjoint from the set of familiar edge labels, which we will denote by L. All labels e and f mentioned in earlier sections are assumed to be from the set L, which excludes barbs. The barbs cannot be explicitly mentioned in the syntax of our calculus (e.g., $b.p$ is forbidden if b is a barb). Their attachment to the nodes of the graph is governed by specific axioms of the calculus that are known as healthiness conditions.

We use the notation $p \xrightarrow{b} \#$ to state that node p has barb b. To enable us to continue to use the relational calculus, the symbol $\#$ (sharp) will be taken to denote another special node that is not a process; it is distinct from $\ast$ and has no outgoing edges. It will be helpful to draw a barb as an actual barb-labelled edge

of the graph; such edges stick out from the nodes of the graph in the same way
as the barbs stick out from a barbed wire - this is the origin of the name. This
construction ensures that the transition graph satisfies a healthiness condition.

Healthiness Condition for Barbs

$$p \xrightarrow{e} q \implies e \text{ is a barb} \equiv q = \#.$$

A barbed trace of a process p is defined in the same way as before, except that
in addition to normal labels from L, it can also include barbs from B. As
a result of the healthiness condition, a barbed trace can contain only a single
barb, one which labels the node at the end of the trace. This barb represents
the last observation that can be made of a process, and is often used to indicate
the reason for termination. For example, a refusal in CSP can be regarded as a
barb indicating that the process has ended in deadlock; and a divergence barb
indicates the possibility of an infinite sequence of internal actions, often known
as livelock. We will explain these phenomena more fully in Sections 4.2 and 4.3.

A barbed simulation is defined as a simulation in which the range of quantification of the events ranges over B as well as L. In order to apply our theory to
barbs, we require reduction to be a barbed simulation. This has the consequence
that a state inherits all the barbs of its $\longrightarrow$ descendants. Consequently, a barb on
an unstable state describes only the possibility that the state may spontaneously
(and unobservably) change to one that displays the property, – but equally, as
a result of non-determinism, it may not. It is only on a stable state that a barb
denotes a property that can definitely be observed of that state.

These definitions have been carefully formulated to ensure that barbed simulation is the same as barbed trace refinement. In the remaining sections we shall
describe some of the barbs introduced in standard models of CSP.

4.1   Refusals

A refusal '$ref(X)$' in CSP is an observation of the state of a process which
refuses to engage in any of the events in some set X (a subset of L), even
though all of them are possible (and usually even desirable) in the current state
of its environment. The concept of a refusal barb was introduced into CSP in
order to model non-deterministic deadlock as a safety property rather than as
a liveness property of a process, and so ensure that simple refinement reasoning
can prove its absence.

The intended meaning of a meaningful barb is often defined rather abstractly
by means of a healthiness condition imposed on the underlying transition system.
In the case of the refusals of CSP, the healthiness condition states (rather obviously) that a stable process can refuse a set if and only if the set contains none
of the events which it can accept and non-stable processes inherit the refusals of
their descendents.

Healthiness Condition for Refusals

$$p \xrightarrow{ref(X)} \# \text{ iff } \exists q. \ q \text{ is stable } \ \& \ p \longrightarrow q \ \& \ \forall x \in X. \ q \not\xrightarrow{x}$$

As a consequence, every stable state (and all its predecessors under $\longrightarrow$) has an empty refusal set among its barbs. Furthermore, if a state has $ref(X)$ among its barbs, then it also has $ref(Y)$, for all subsets Y of X. However, if a state has no stable successors under reduction, then it has no refusals according to the above definition. We will return to this point in the next section.

The healthiness condition enables us to deduce the refusals of all the processes expressible in the syntax of the calculus. It seems better to deduce the refusals from a general healthiness condition than to make them part of the definition of the operators, which would require a separate proof of the preservation of healthiness.

Theorem 4.1.1

$$\text{STOP} \xrightarrow{ref(X)} \# \quad \text{for all sets } X \text{ that exclude barbs}$$
$$\text{RUN} \xrightarrow{ref(X)} \# \quad \text{iff } X = \{\}$$
$$f.p \xrightarrow{ref(X)} \# \quad \text{iff } f \notin X$$
$$(p \,|or| \, q) \xrightarrow{ref(X)} \# \text{ iff } p \xrightarrow{ref(X)} \# \ \& \ q \xrightarrow{ref(X)} \#$$
$$(p \,|\&| \, q) \xrightarrow{ref(X)} \# \text{ iff } \exists Y, Z. \ X = Y \cup Z \ \& \ p \xrightarrow{ref(Y)} \# \ \& \ q \xrightarrow{ref(Z)} \#$$
$$(p \backslash f) \xrightarrow{ref(X)} \# \quad \text{iff } p \xrightarrow{ref(X-\{f\})} \#$$

The non-deterministic processes introduced in Section 3.3 have their refusals defined in the following theorem

Theorem 4.1.2

$$\text{CHAOS} \xrightarrow{ref(X)} \# \text{ for all sets } X$$
$$(p \sqcap q) \xrightarrow{ref(X)} \# \quad \text{iff } p \xrightarrow{ref(X)} \# \ \vee \ q \xrightarrow{ref(X)} \#$$
$$(p \,\square\, q) \xrightarrow{ref(X)} \# \quad \text{iff } p \xrightarrow{ref(X)} \# \ \& \ q \xrightarrow{ref(X)} \#$$
$$(p \backslash\backslash f) \xrightarrow{ref(X)} \# \quad \text{iff } p \xrightarrow{ref(X \cup \{f\})} \# \ \vee \ (p/f) \xrightarrow{ref(X)} \#$$

4.2   Divergences

In spite of the powerful law of inheritance from descendents, there can be nodes that have no refusal barbs at all. This can happen as a result of concealing an infinite sequence of f-transitions, for example in the process RUN. Because RUN can always do an f, RUN$\backslash\backslash f$ can always make an internal transition

$$\text{RUN} \backslash\backslash f \xrightarrow{\tau} \text{RUN} \backslash\backslash f$$

As a consequence, even after any number of f's, RUN$\backslash\backslash f$ is never stable. Such a process has an empty set of refusals. What is worse, it has an infinite sequence of τ-transitions, and is therefore said to diverge.

Divergence is often considered an undesirable feature of a concurrent system, because there is no way of controlling the amount of system resource that a divergent system may consume. In practice, divergence is a common mechanism of denial-of-service attacks on the World Wide Web, and one would like to prove its impossibility. On the other hand, in some circumstances, maybe the possibility of divergence is of no concern, for example when probabilistic reasoning proves that it is vanishingly unlikely. It is therefore desirable for a process calculus to provide some means of specifying whether a process is allowed to diverge; and that is the purpose of the '*div*' barb; its introduction allows refinement as a means of proving its absence where it is not wanted. A node has a *div* barb if it is the origin of a potentially infinite series of τ-transitions, as stated by the obvious healthiness condition

Healthiness Condition for *div*:

$$p \xrightarrow{div} \# \text{ iff } p \xrightarrow{\tau} p' \xrightarrow{\tau} p'' \xrightarrow{\tau} \ldots \quad \text{forever} .$$

The effect of this new barb on the constants and operators of our process calculus is given by the following theorem

Theorem 4.3.1

$$\text{CHAOS} \xrightarrow{div} \#$$

STOP, RUN and $f.p$ do not have divergence barbs.

$(p \,|\&|\, q), (p \,|or|\, q), (p \sqcap q), (p \,\square\, q)$ and $p\backslash f$ have a divergence barb iff one (or both) of their operands has a divergence barb.

$$(p\backslash\backslash f) \xrightarrow{div} \# \quad \text{iff } \exists\, n.\ p/(f^n) \xrightarrow{div} \# \quad \vee \quad \forall\, i.\ f^i \in traces(P)$$

In the divergence model of CSP, the occurrence of divergence is regarded as so undesirable that it is assumed that no specification will actually allow it, and that any process that allows even just the possibility of divergence is so bad that it is not worth differentiating from any other process that allows it. This very strict view of divergence is taken from Dijkstra's theory of programming, and it is consistent with a simple treatment of recursion as the largest fixed point of its defining equation. The view can be introduced into a process calculus by an additional healthiness condition.

Healthiness Condition for CHAOS (in the divergence model of CSP)

$$p \xrightarrow{div} \# \implies p \xrightarrow{\tau} \text{CHAOS}$$

A consequence of this definition is that even divergent processes will have at least one refusal barb.

In the standard models of CSP, the semantics of a non-deterministic process is given in terms of its traces, its failures, and its divergences. Introduction of barbs enables us to model all of these as just ordinary barbed traces. A failure is just a trace with a refusal barb at the end. A divergence is just a trace with a divergence barb at the end. Thus failures/divergence refinement (FDR) can be considered as simple trace refinement. Theorem 2.2.6 continues to hold. Trace refinement and similarity are the same.

5   Conclusion

In this paper we have started with the classical theory of deterministic automata, and the languages of traces which they generate. In the classical theory, a particular automaton can be completely specified either by its transition graph, with equality implied by mutual similarity, or by equality of the language of traces generated by the labels on all the paths leading from a node. The two methods of defining a process are isomorphic, and so they are mathematically indistinguishable.

Modern process algebras have extended the classical theory of automata, firstly by removing the restriction to finite state automata, and secondly by introduction of non-determinism. The second extension has led to a dichotomy in the study of process algebra, arising from selection of a refinement (as in CSP) or a simulation (as in CCS) as the basis of comparisons between processes. The central goal of this paper has been to re-establish the isomorphism between the two approaches, even in the presence of non-determinism.

CCS provides a fixed collection of primitive processes and operators capable of modelling arbitrary concurrent systems, and it defines them in terms of a fixed set of primitive transitions. All other operators that are needed are expected to be definable in terms of the primitive set. Proofs about the calculus can therefore be made by induction on the structure of the syntax and on the number of operations involved in its execution. The concept of bisimulation gives a way of proving the most essential equations among terms. Bisimulation minimises the risk of obscuring distinctions between processes that may later be required in its potential range of applications.

Bisimilarity has a number of excellent qualities. It is based directly on an operational semantics for the process calculus, which provides an abstract model for its implementation. This kind of semantics appeals to the operational intuition of programmers, which is especially useful when diagnosing errors by testing a program. Bisimulation admits simple and elegant proofs, using co-induction. And for particular programs, proofs can often be replaced by mechanical checking, because bisimulation is a direct description of an algorithm that can be used by an efficient model checker. Subtle variations in the definition of bisimilarity have offered wide scope for research, and new versions can fairly easily be introduced for new purposes. The standard variants are sufficiently powerful to reduce every (finite) process term to a normal form, thereby permitting powerful algebraic techniques to be used in reasoning. For processes containing recursion, a head normal form is available.

CSP is based on the concept of a trace (possibly barbed) as a description of the observable behaviour of a concurrent interactive process. There is an extensible collection of operators defined in terms of the trace sets that they generate. Proofs about the calculus are conducted by standard mathematical theories of sets and sequences. Basic properties of the calculus are postulated by means of healthiness conditions, which must be preserved by each operator that is introduced into the syntax. Further barbs and healthiness conditions can be introduced to model properties of particular systems, but they may require restrictions on the use of any operator that does not preserve the condition. CSP pays particular attention to notions of correctness of implementation. In a specification, the traces may be described in any clear and convenient formalism; whereas implementations are expressed in the notations of the calculus, and intermediate designs can exploit a mixture of notations. Correctness is modelled by trace inclusion, so the calculus supports the standard engineering design strategies of stepwise refinement and stepwise decomposition. The intention is to make refinement and equality as comprehensive as possible, so that programs are easier to prove correct and to optimise. But care has been taken to describe and distinguish undesirable behaviours like deadlock and divergence, which can afflict any real distributed system.

Of course, when bisimulation and refinement are reconciled, all their separate advantages can be combined and exploited whenever the occasion demands. Although in this paper only CCS and CSP have been considered in detail, is hoped that the reconciliation can be extended to more modern process calculi.

The secret of reconciliation of a simulation-based calculus with a trace-based one is to require the reduction relation to be a simulation. This and other healthiness conditions can be expressed as additional transition rules, suitable for inclusion at will in the operational semantics of any calculus that seeks reconciliation. The new transitions may be interpreted by an implementer of the calculus as permission to be kind to the user of the process, in the sense of giving the user more opportunities to avoid deadlock. The new transitions offer additional possibilities for resolving non-determinism at compile time; they validate more algebraic laws, so giving more opportunities for optimisation. But there is no compulsion to be kind – in fact, during system test, it is actually kinder for an implementation to expose all possibilities of error. That too is allowed by the theory.

Acknowledgements

The goal of unification of theories of concurrency was first pursued in the Esprit Basic Research Action CONCUR. This was a Europe-wide research contract aiming at concurrence (in the sense of agreement) between various process algebras current at the time, particularly ACP [1], CCS and CSP.

A renewed attempt to reconcile simulation with refinement was encouraged by the earlier success of power simulation [3]. The inspiration for the particular approach of this paper derives from a Workshop held in Microsoft Research Ltd., at Cambridge on 22-23 July 2002. Those who contributed to the discussion were Ernie Cohen, Cedric Fournet, Paul Gardiner, Andy Gordon, Robin Milner, Sriram Rajamani, Jakob Rehof, and Bill Roscoe. Subsequently, He Jifeng and Jakob Rehof made essential simplifications and clarifications.

The first draft of this paper was published by the Technical University at Munich as lecture notes for the Marktoberdorf Summer School in August 2004. This version was prepared with the kind assistance of Ali Abdallah.

References

1. J.A. Bergstra and J. W. Klop. Algebra of communicating processes with abstraction. *Theoretical Computer Science*, 37(1):77–121, 1985.
2. S. D. Brookes. On the relationship of CCS and CSP. In *Proceedings of the 10th Colloquium on Automata, Languages and Programming*, volume 154 of *Lecture Notes in Computer Science*, pages 83–96. Springer-Verlag, 1983.
3. P.H.B. Gardiner. Power simulation and its relation to Traces and Failures Refinement. *Theoretical Computer Science*, 309(1):157–176, 2003.
4. R. Milner. *Communication and concurrency*. Prentice Hall, 1989.
5. R. Milner and D. Sangiorgi. Barbed bisimulation. In W. Kuich, editor, *Proceeding of the 19th International Colloquium on Automata, Languages and Programming (ICALP '92)*, volume 623 of *Lecture Notes in Computer Science*, pages 685–695. Springer-Verlag, 1992.
6. D.M.R. Park. Concurrency and automata on infinite sequences. In P. Deussen, editor, *Proceedings of 5th GI Conference*, volume 104 of *Lecture Notes in Computer Science*, pages 167–183. Springer-Verlag, 1981.
7. I.C.C. Phillips. Refusal testing. *Theoretical Computer Science*, 50(3):241–284, 1987.
8. G. D. Plotkin. A structural approach to operational semantics. Technical Report DAIMI FN-19, Aarhus University, 1981.
9. A. W. Roscoe. *The theory and practice of concurrency*. Prentice Hall, 1998.
10. R.J. van Glabbeek. Notes on the methodology of CCS and CSP. *Theoretical Computer Science*, 177(2):329–349, 1997.

Linking Theories of Concurrency

He Jifeng[*]

Shanghai East China Normal University

Abstract. Bisimulation is an equivalence relation widely used for comparing processes expressed in CCS and related process calculi [1, 6, 8, 9].
Simulation is its asymmetric variant. The advantages of bisimilarity are
simplicity, efficiency and variety. Proofs based bisimulation for particular programs can often be delegated to a model checker. Refinement is a
weaker asymmetric relation used for the same purpose in CSP [2, 3, 14].
Its advantages are abstraction, expressive power and completeness. Refinement permits proofs of more equations and inequations than bisimilarity. When bisimulation and refinement are reconciled, all their distinctive advantages can be combined and exploited whenever the occasions demands. This paper shows how to link these two approaches by
introducing an observation-preserving mapping, which gives rise a Galois connection between simulation and refinement. The same mapping
is also applicable to coincide barbed simulation with failures/divergence
refinement.

1 Introduction

In the study of process calculi, such as ACP [1], CCS [8], CSP [2, 3, 14], and the
pi-calculus [9], there are two standard approaches to the definition of similarity
or equivalence of processes: bisimulation and refinement.

Bisimulation was firstly introduced in CCS [8] to identify processes of the
same behaviour. It has simulation as an asymmetric version. A bisimulation is
an equivalence relation between the nodes of two directed edge-labelled graphs.
The relation must be preserved by simultaneous passage to a successor node
along any edge which has the same label in both graphs: more precisely, if the
sources of the two transitions are bisimilar, then each transition of one of them
must be matched by some identically labelled transition of the other, and the
targets of the two transitions must be bisimilar. A process calculus is usually
defined by means of a structural operational semantics [13], which ascribes a
node in a graph to each process expressible in the notations of the calculus. This
node represents the initial state of the process. The other nodes of the graph
represent possible subsequent states of the machine executing the process; the
machine can change from the source state of the transition to its target state on

---

[*] On leave from Shanghai East China Normal University. The work is partially supported by the 211 Key project of the Ministry of Education, and the 973 project (no
2002CB312001) of the Ministry of Science and Technology of China.

A.E. Abdallah, C.B. Jones, and J.W. Sanders (Eds.): **CSP25**, LNCS 3525, pp. 61–74, 2005.

occurrence of the event which labels the transition. Two processes are defined as bisimilar if their initial states are bisimilar.

The advantages of bisimulation are simplicity, efficiency and variety. Bisimilarity is based directly on an operational semantics for the process calculus, which provides an abstract model of an implementation; it thereby appeals directly to the operational intuition of programmers, which is especially useful when diagnosing errors in a program. Proofs using bisimulation for particular programs can often be delegated to a model checker.

Refinement is defined in terms of set inclusion. The semantics of the process calculus is presented denotationally. It ascribes to each process the set of all possible observations that could be made of its behaviour in any execution of it. If all possible observations of the implementation are included in those permitted for the specification, the implementation is defined to be correct. The justification of the definition is based on the philosophical principal that no violation of the specification could ever be observed, and requires that the theory must include enough observations to represent all possible ways in which a process can go wrong. In CSP [3], there are four familiar varieties of refinement. The first uses only traces. The second, failures refinement, deals with deadlock by recording the refusals that are allowed at the end of each trace. Either of these can be extended to deal with livelock.

The advantages of refinement are abstraction, expressive power, coarseness and completeness. The observational semantics exploits the familiar abstractions of set theory. This permits a process to be specified by an arbitrary mathematical description of the observations of its behaviour: the specification does not have to be encoded in the syntax of the calculus. New operators can often be defined in the model, without invalidating theorems proved by normal mathematical properties of sets. Refinement permits proofs of more equations and inequations than bisimilarity; and each additional algebraic laws may be useful for program optimisation and for reasoning about program correctness [11].

As described in [5], when bisimulation and refinement are reconciled, all their distinctive advantages can be combined and exploited whenever the occasions demands. This paper shows how to link these two approaches. Section 2 captures the co-algebraic feature of bisimulation by providing it a defining equation. This facilitates algebraic reasonings later in linking bisimulation and refinement theories. Section 3 gives trace refinement a defining equation, and explores its relation with simulation in an algebraic framework. We coincide simulation and traces refinement for transition-deterministic processes in Section 4. Section 5 introduces the notion of *observation-preserving* mapping, and examines its properties. It illustrates how to link traces refinement and simulation by a Galois connection [7]. We discuss barbed simulation in Section 6. It is shown that the link mechanism between traces refinement and simulation can also be applicable to the barbed case. Section 7 characterises communication sequential processes by introducing a simple healthiness condition. It presents a Galois link with the process calculi which distinguish chaotic behaviour from divergent one.

2   Simulation

We use $\mathcal{A}$ to represent the set of all visible actions which appear at the interface of the system, and λ to range over this set. Let τ denote an invisible action that is internal to the system. We will use a to range over the set $\mathcal{A}^\tau =_{df} \mathcal{A} \cup \{\tau\}$.

Definition 2.1 (Labelled Transition System)

A labelled transition system over $\mathcal{A}^\tau$ is a pair $(\mathcal{P}, \mathcal{T})$ consisting of

- a set $\mathcal{P}$ of processes;
- a ternary relation $\mathcal{T} \subseteq \mathcal{P} \times \mathcal{A}^\tau \times \mathcal{P}$

If $(P, a, Q) \in \mathcal{T}$ we write $P \xrightarrow{a} Q$ to indicate that P can move to Q by performing action a.   □

Define $\Rightarrow =_{df} \xrightarrow{\tau}{}^*$ as the reflexive and transitive closure of $\xrightarrow{\tau}$, and define the relation $\xrightarrow{\lambda} =_{df} \Rightarrow; \xrightarrow{\lambda}$, where $';'$ denotes relational composition. Let the predicate $P \xrightarrow{\lambda} =_{df} \exists Q \bullet (P \xrightarrow{\lambda} Q)$.

Definition 2.2 (Weak Simulation)

A binary relation $\mathcal{R}$ over processes is a weak $\mathcal{A}$-simulation if for all $\lambda \in \mathcal{A}$

$$(\mathcal{R}; \xrightarrow{\lambda}) \subseteq (\xrightarrow{\lambda}; \mathcal{R})$$

We use $\leq_\mathcal{A}$ to denote the **greatest** weak simulation, and define $\approx_\mathcal{A}$ to be the greatest symmetric relation satisfying the previous inequation.   □

In the following we are going to prove the existence of $\leq_\mathcal{A}$ and $\approx_\mathcal{A}$ by construction of their defining equations. Let $\mathcal{R}$ be a binary relation over $\mathcal{P}$. For any subsets X and Y of $\mathcal{P}$ we define

$$X \, \mathbf{Pow}(\mathcal{R}) \, Y =_{df} \forall P \in X \bullet \exists Q \in Y \bullet (P \, \mathcal{R} \, Q) \wedge \forall Q \in Y \bullet \exists P \in X \bullet (P \, \mathcal{R} \, Q)$$

and $P \xrightarrow{\lambda} X =_{df} (X = \{S \mid P \xrightarrow{\lambda} S\})$.

We use $\xleftarrow{\lambda}$ to denote the converse of the binary relation $\xrightarrow{\lambda}$.

Theorem 2.1 (Defining equation of weak simulation)

(1) $\mathcal{R}$ is a weak simulation iff $\mathcal{R} \subseteq \bigcap_{\lambda \in \mathcal{A}} (\xrightarrow{\lambda}; \supseteq; \mathbf{Pow}(\mathcal{R}); \xleftarrow{\lambda})$

(2) $\leq_\mathcal{A} = \mu \mathcal{R} \bullet \bigcap_{\lambda \in \mathcal{A}} (\xrightarrow{\lambda}; \supseteq; \mathbf{Pow}(\mathcal{R}); \xleftarrow{\lambda})$

where $\mu X \bullet F(X)$ stands for the greatest fixed point of the equation $X = F(X)$.

Proof. of (1). (only-if-part): Suppose $P \mathcal{R} Q$. Let $P \overset{\lambda}{\hookrightarrow} X$ and $Q \overset{\lambda}{\hookrightarrow} Y$. From Definition 2.2 it follows that

$$\forall T \in Y \bullet \exists S \in X \bullet S \mathcal{R} T$$

Let $X' = \{S \in X \mid \exists T \bullet T \in Y \wedge S \mathcal{R} T\}$. One has

$$P (\overset{\lambda}{\hookrightarrow}; \supseteq) X' \quad \text{and} \quad X' (\mathbf{Pow}(\mathcal{R}); \overset{\lambda}{\hookleftarrow}) Q$$

as required.

(if-part): If $P \mathcal{R} Q$, then from the fact that $\overset{\lambda}{\hookrightarrow}$ is a function we conclude that

$$P \overset{\lambda}{\hookrightarrow} X \wedge Q \overset{\lambda}{\hookrightarrow} Y \Rightarrow \exists X' \bullet (X \supseteq X' \wedge X' \mathbf{Pow}(\mathcal{R}) Y)$$

which is equivalent to

$$P \overset{\lambda}{\hookrightarrow} X \wedge Q \overset{\lambda}{\hookrightarrow} Y \Rightarrow \forall T \in Y \bullet \exists S \in X \bullet S \mathcal{R} T$$

as required by the Definition 2.2.

(2). From (1) and Tarski's fixed-point theory [15], we conclude that $\mu \mathcal{R} \bullet \bigcap_{\lambda \in \mathcal{A}} (\overset{\lambda}{\hookrightarrow}; \supseteq; \mathbf{Pow}(\mathcal{R}); \overset{\lambda}{\hookleftarrow})$ is a weak simulation. The conclusion that it is the greatest weak simulation follows from Tarski's greatest fixed-point theorem and (1). □

$\approx_{\mathcal{A}}$ can also be defined as the greatest fixed point

Theorem 2.2 $\approx_{\mathcal{A}} = \mu \mathcal{R} \bullet \bigcap_{\lambda \in \mathcal{A}} (\overset{\lambda}{\hookrightarrow}; \mathbf{Pow}(\mathcal{R}); \overset{\lambda}{\hookleftarrow})$

Proof. Similar to Theorem 2.1. □

The following properties of weak simulation will be used in the later proof.

Lemma 2.1

(1) $(\overset{\tau}{\rightarrow} \cup id_{\mathcal{P}})$ is a weak simulation, where $id_{\mathcal{P}}$ is the identity relation over $\mathcal{P}$.
(2) $\leq_{\mathcal{A}}$ is transitive.

Proof. (1) From the fact that $(\overset{\tau}{\rightarrow}; \overset{\lambda}{\Rightarrow}) \subseteq \overset{\lambda}{\Rightarrow}$.

(2) First one has $\leq_{\mathcal{A}} = (id_{\mathcal{P}}; \leq_{\mathcal{A}}) \subseteq (\leq_{\mathcal{A}}; \leq_{\mathcal{A}})$. Next we show that $(\leq_{\mathcal{A}}; \leq_{\mathcal{A}})$ is a weak simulation.

$$\leq_{\mathcal{A}}; \leq_{\mathcal{A}}; \overset{\lambda}{\Rightarrow} \qquad\qquad \{(\leq_{\mathcal{A}}; \overset{\lambda}{\Rightarrow}) \subseteq (\overset{\lambda}{\Rightarrow}; \leq_{\mathcal{A}})\}$$

$$\subseteq \quad \leq_{\mathcal{A}}; \overset{\lambda}{\Rightarrow}; \leq_{\mathcal{A}} \qquad\qquad \{(\leq_{\mathcal{A}}; \overset{\lambda}{\Rightarrow}) \subseteq (\overset{\lambda}{\Rightarrow}; \leq_{\mathcal{A}})\}$$

$$\subseteq \quad \overset{\lambda}{\Rightarrow}; \leq_{\mathcal{A}}; \leq_{\mathcal{A}} \qquad\qquad\qquad\qquad\qquad □$$

The following lemma states that the definition of $\leq_{\mathcal{A}}$ is equivalent to the original one given by Robin Milner in [9].

Lemma 2.2

$\leq_{\mathcal{A}}$ is the greatest relation satisfying the inequations

(1) $(\mathcal{R}; \xrightarrow{\tau}) \subseteq (\Rightarrow; \mathcal{R})$

(2) $(\mathcal{R}; \xrightarrow{\lambda}) \subseteq (\xrightarrow{\lambda}; \Rightarrow; \mathcal{R})$.

Proof. Let $\leq$ be the greatest relation satisfying (1) and (2). Similar to Lemma 2.1 we can show

(a) $\xrightarrow{\tau} \subseteq \leq$

(b) $\leq; \leq \, = \, \leq$

First we want to establish $\leq_{\mathcal{A}} \subseteq \leq$ by showing $\leq_{\mathcal{A}}$ satisfies (1) and (2).

$$
\begin{array}{lll}
 & \leq_{\mathcal{A}}; \xrightarrow{\tau} & \{\text{Lemma 2.1(1)}\} \\
\subseteq & \leq_{\mathcal{A}}; \leq_{\mathcal{A}} & \{\text{Lemma 2.1(2)}\} \\
= & \leq_{\mathcal{A}} & \{id_{\mathcal{P}} \subseteq \Rightarrow\} \\
\subseteq & \Rightarrow; \leq_{\mathcal{A}} &
\end{array}
$$

$$
\begin{array}{lll}
 & \leq_{\mathcal{A}}; \xrightarrow{\lambda} & \{\xrightarrow{\lambda} \subseteq \xrightarrow{\lambda}\} \\
\subseteq & \leq_{\mathcal{A}}; \xrightarrow{\lambda} & \{\text{Definition 2.2}\} \\
\subseteq & \xrightarrow{\lambda}; \leq_{\mathcal{A}} & \{id_{\mathcal{P}} \subseteq \Rightarrow\} \\
\subseteq & \xrightarrow{\lambda}; \Rightarrow; \leq_{\mathcal{A}} &
\end{array}
$$

Finally we prove that $\leq$ is also a weak simulation, and so $\leq$ is a subset of $\leq_{\mathcal{A}}$.

$$
\begin{array}{lll}
 & \leq; \xrightarrow{\lambda} & \{\text{Inequation (2)}\} \\
\subseteq & \xrightarrow{\lambda}; \Rightarrow; \leq & \{\text{Fact } (a)\} \\
\subseteq & \xrightarrow{\lambda}; \leq^{*}; \leq & \{\text{Fact } (b)\} \\
\subseteq & \xrightarrow{\lambda}; \leq &
\end{array}
$$

$$
\begin{array}{lll}
 & \leq; \xrightarrow{\tau}^{n}; \xrightarrow{\lambda} & \{\text{Inequation (1)}\} \\
\subseteq & \Rightarrow^{n}; \leq; \xrightarrow{\lambda} & \{\text{Previous proof}\} \\
\subseteq & \Rightarrow^{n}; \xrightarrow{\lambda}; \leq & \{(\Rightarrow^{n}; \xrightarrow{\lambda}) \subseteq \xrightarrow{\lambda}\} \\
\subseteq & \xrightarrow{\lambda}; \leq & \square
\end{array}
$$

3   Traces Refinement

A trace of the behaviour of a process is a finite sequence of names recording the visible events in which the process has engaged up to some moment in time.

$$traces_{\mathcal{A}}(P) =_{df} \{\langle\rangle\} \bigcup \{\langle\lambda\rangle s \mid \lambda \in \mathcal{A} \wedge \exists S \bullet P \overset{\lambda}{\Rightarrow} S \ \wedge \ s \in traces_{\mathcal{A}}(S)\}$$

Definition 3.1 (Traces Refinement)

Q is a traces refinement of P, denoted $P \sqsubseteq_{\mathcal{A}} Q$, if

$$traces_{\mathcal{A}}(Q) \subseteq traces_{\mathcal{A}}(P)$$

We define $P \equiv_{\mathcal{A}} Q =_{df} P \sqsubseteq_{\mathcal{A}} Q \wedge Q \sqsubseteq_{\mathcal{A}} P$ □

Similar to the treatment of $\leq_{\mathcal{A}}$ and $\approx_{\mathcal{A}}$ we are going to form the defining equations for $\sqsubseteq_{\mathcal{A}}$ and $\equiv_{\mathcal{A}}$.

Let X and Y be subsets of $\mathcal{P}$. Define

$$X \supseteq_{tr} Y =_{df} \bigcup\{traces_{\mathcal{A}}(P) \mid P \in X\} \supseteq \bigcup\{traces_{\mathcal{A}}(Q) \mid Q \in Y\}$$

$$X \text{ equal}_{tr} Y =_{df} \bigcup\{traces_{\mathcal{A}}(P) \mid P \in X\} = \bigcup\{traces_{\mathcal{A}}(Q) \mid Q \in Y\}$$

Theorem 3.1 $\sqsubseteq_{\mathcal{A}} = \mu\mathcal{R} \bullet \bigcap_{\lambda \in \mathcal{A}}(\overset{\lambda}{\hookrightarrow}; \supseteq_{tr}; \mathbf{Pow}(\mathcal{R}); \overset{\lambda}{\hookleftarrow})$

Proof. Let $\mathcal{F}_{\lambda}(\mathcal{R}) =_{df} (\overset{\lambda}{\hookrightarrow}; \supseteq_{tr}; \mathbf{Pow}(\mathcal{R}); \overset{\lambda}{\hookleftarrow})$.

First we establish that the inequation $LHS \subseteq RHS$.

$P \sqsubseteq_{\mathcal{A}} Q$ {Definition 3.1}

$\Rightarrow \bigcup\{traces_{\mathcal{A}}(T) \mid Q \overset{\lambda}{\Rightarrow} T\} \subseteq \{traces_{\mathcal{A}}(S) \mid P \overset{\lambda}{\Rightarrow} S\}$ {Definition of $\supseteq_{tr}$}

$\Rightarrow \exists X, Y \bullet P \overset{\lambda}{\hookrightarrow} X \wedge X \supseteq_{tr} Y \wedge Y \overset{\lambda}{\hookleftarrow} Q$ $\{Y \mathbf{Pow}(\sqsubseteq_{\mathcal{A}}) Y\}$

$\Rightarrow P \mathcal{F}_{\lambda}(\sqsubseteq_{\mathcal{A}}) Q$

which together with the greatest fixed point theorem [15] implies that $LHS \subseteq \mu\mathcal{R} \bullet \bigcap_{\lambda \in \mathcal{A}} \mathcal{F}_{\lambda}(\mathcal{R}) = RHS$

The opposite inequation $RHS \subseteq LHS$ can be proved by showing inductively that for any nonempty sequence s of actions of $\mathcal{A}$

$$(P \, RHS \, Q \ \wedge \ Q \overset{s}{\Rightarrow}) \Rightarrow (P \overset{s}{\Rightarrow})$$

where $\overset{\langle\lambda_1,...,\lambda_n\rangle}{\Longrightarrow} =_{df} \overset{\lambda_1}{\Rightarrow}; ...; \overset{\lambda_n}{\Rightarrow}$.   □

Theorem 3.2 (Defining equation of $\equiv_{\mathcal{A}}$)

$\equiv_{\mathcal{A}} = \mu\mathcal{R} \bullet \bigcap_{\lambda \in \mathcal{A}}(\overset{\lambda}{\hookrightarrow}; \mathbf{equal}_{tr}; \mathbf{Pow}(\mathcal{R}); \overset{\lambda}{\hookleftarrow})$

Proof. Similar to Theorem 3.1.   □

Theorem 3.3 Weak simulation implies traces refinement

Proof $\leq_{\mathcal{A}}$ {Theorem 2.1}

$$= \mu \mathcal{R} \bullet \bigcap_{\lambda \in \mathcal{A}}(\stackrel{\lambda}{\hookrightarrow}; \supseteq; \mathbf{Pow}(\mathcal{R}); \hookleftarrow) \qquad \{\supseteq \text{ is a subset of } \supseteq_{tr}\}$$

$$\subseteq \mu \mathcal{R} \bullet \bigcap_{\lambda \in \mathcal{A}}(\stackrel{\lambda}{\hookrightarrow}; \supseteq_{tr}; \mathbf{Pow}(\mathcal{R}); \hookleftarrow) \qquad \{\text{Theorem 3.1}\}$$

$$= \sqsubseteq_{\mathcal{A}} \qquad\qquad\qquad\qquad\qquad\qquad\qquad □$$

4   Transition-Deterministic Processes

Definition 4.1 (Transition-deterministic process)

Define $\mathcal{DP}_{\mathcal{A}} = \{P \mid \forall \lambda \bullet P \stackrel{\lambda}{\hookrightarrow} X \Rightarrow (size(X) \leq 1 \wedge X \subseteq \mathcal{DP}_{\mathcal{A}})\}$
We have for any nonempty sequence s of actions of $\mathcal{A}$

$$P \in \mathcal{DP}_{\mathcal{A}} \wedge P \stackrel{s}{\Rightarrow} S \wedge P \stackrel{s}{\Rightarrow} T \Rightarrow (S = T) \qquad\qquad □$$

Traces refinement implies weak simulation in $\mathcal{DP}$.

Theorem 4.1 If $P \in \mathcal{DP}_{\mathcal{A}}$, then $P \sqsubseteq_{\mathcal{A}} Q$ implies $P \leq_{\mathcal{A}} Q$.

Proof. Let $\mathcal{R} =_{df} \{(P, Q) \mid P \in \mathcal{DP}_{\mathcal{A}} \wedge P \sqsubseteq_{\mathcal{A}} Q\}$

$\quad P \mathcal{R} Q$ {Definition 3.1}

$\Rightarrow \forall \lambda \bullet \forall T \bullet (Q \stackrel{\lambda}{\Rightarrow} T \Rightarrow (\langle \lambda \rangle \cdot traces_{\mathcal{A}}(T) \subseteq traces_{\mathcal{A}}(P))) \qquad \{P \in \mathcal{DP}_{\mathcal{A}}\}$

$\Rightarrow \forall \lambda \bullet \forall T \bullet \exists S \in \mathcal{DP}_{\mathcal{A}} \bullet (Q \stackrel{\lambda}{\Rightarrow} T \Rightarrow (P \stackrel{\lambda}{\hookrightarrow} \{S\} \wedge S \mathcal{R} T)) \quad \{\text{simplification}\}$

$\Rightarrow \forall \lambda \bullet ((Q \stackrel{\lambda}{\Rightarrow}) \Rightarrow$

$\qquad \exists S \bullet (P \stackrel{\lambda}{\hookrightarrow} \{S\} \wedge \{S\} \mathbf{Pow}(\mathcal{R}) \{T \mid Q \stackrel{\lambda}{\Rightarrow} T\}))$

which is equivalent to

$$\mathcal{R} \subseteq \bigcap_{\lambda \in \mathcal{A}}(\stackrel{\lambda}{\hookrightarrow}; \supseteq; \mathbf{Pow}(\mathcal{R}); \stackrel{\lambda}{\hookleftarrow})$$

From Theorem 2.1 we conclude that $\mathcal{R}$ is a weak simulation.   □

Theorem 4.2 If both P and Q lie in $\mathcal{DP}_{\mathcal{A}}$, then $P \equiv_{\mathcal{A}} Q$ implies $P \approx_{\mathcal{A}} Q$.

Proof. Similar to Theorem 4.1.   □

5   Observation-Preserving Mapping

Definition 5.1

$\mathcal{M}$ is an observation-preserving mapping from $\mathcal{P}$ to $\mathcal{DP}_\mathcal{A}$ if

$$\mathcal{M}(P) \equiv_\mathcal{A} P \qquad \qquad \Box$$

Lemma 5.1 If $\mathcal{M}$ is an observation-preserving mapping, then it is a monotonic link [4]:

(1) Monotonic: $P \sqsubseteq_\mathcal{A} Q$ implies $\mathcal{M}(P) \leq_\mathcal{A} \mathcal{M}(Q)$

(2) Weakening: $\mathcal{M}(P) \leq_\mathcal{A} P$

(3) Idempotent: $\mathcal{M}^2(P) \approx_\mathcal{A} \mathcal{M}(P)$

Proof. (1) From the assumption that $\mathcal{M}$ is observation-preserving it follows

$$P \sqsubseteq_\mathcal{A} Q \Rightarrow \mathcal{M}(P) \sqsubseteq_\mathcal{A} \mathcal{M}(Q)$$

which together with Theorem 4.1 implies the conclusion.

(2) From $\mathcal{M}(P) \equiv_\mathcal{A} P$ and Theorem 4.1.

(3) From $\mathcal{M}^2(P) \equiv_\mathcal{A} \mathcal{M}(P)$ and Theorem 4.2. $\qquad \Box$

Theorem 5.1 If $\mathcal{M}$ is observation-preserving, then

(1) $P \sqsubseteq_\mathcal{A} Q$ iff $\mathcal{M}(P) \leq_\mathcal{A} Q$

(2) $P \equiv_\mathcal{A} Q$ iff $\mathcal{M}(P) \approx_\mathcal{A} \mathcal{M}(Q)$

Proof of (1) $P \sqsubseteq_\mathcal{A} Q$ $\qquad\qquad\qquad$ {$\mathcal{M}$ is observation-preserving}

$\qquad\qquad \equiv \mathcal{M}(P) \sqsubseteq_\mathcal{A} Q$ $\qquad\qquad\qquad\qquad$ {Theorem 4.1}

$\qquad\qquad \Rightarrow \mathcal{M}(P) \leq_\mathcal{A} Q$ $\qquad\qquad\qquad\qquad$ {Theorem 3.3}

$\qquad\qquad \Rightarrow \mathcal{M}(P) \sqsubseteq_\mathcal{A} Q$ $\qquad\qquad$ {$\mathcal{M}$ is observation-preserving}

$\qquad\qquad \equiv P \sqsubseteq_\mathcal{A} Q$

(2) can be proved in a similar way. $\qquad \Box$

In the remaining of this section we are going to construct an observation-preserving mapping.

Definition 5.2 (λ-derivative)

Let λ be a visible action, and $P \overset{\lambda}{\Rightarrow}$. The notation P/λ represents a process which behaves like P after the occurrence of λ

$$\frac{P \overset{\lambda}{\Rightarrow} Q}{P/\lambda \overset{\tau}{\to} Q}$$

We call P/λ the λ-derivative of P.   □

$P\backslash\lambda$ can engage in all actions P can perform after the λ-transition.

Lemma 5.2 $P/\lambda \overset{\alpha}{\Rightarrow} Q$ iff $P\,(\overset{\lambda}{\Rightarrow};\overset{\alpha}{\Rightarrow})\,Q$ for all $\alpha \in \mathcal{A}$ □

Corollary $traces(P/\lambda) = \{s \mid \langle\lambda\rangle s \in traces(P)\}$

Proof. From Definition 3.1 and Lemma 5.2.   □

Definition 5.3 (Mapping $\mathcal{H}$)

Let P be a process. The behaviour of the process $\mathcal{H}(P)$ is described by the following transition rules

$$\frac{P \overset{\tau}{\to} Q}{\mathcal{H}(P) \overset{\tau}{\to} \mathcal{K}(Q, P)} \qquad\qquad \frac{Q \overset{\tau}{\to} R}{\mathcal{K}(Q, P) \overset{\tau}{\to} \mathcal{K}(R, P)}$$

$$\frac{P \overset{\lambda}{\to} S}{\mathcal{H}(P) \overset{\lambda}{\to} \mathcal{H}(P/\lambda)} \qquad\qquad \frac{Q \overset{\lambda}{\to} R}{\mathcal{K}(Q, P) \overset{\lambda}{\to} \mathcal{H}(P/\lambda)}$$

$\mathcal{H}(P)$ behaves the same as the process P.

Lemma 5.3

(1) $P \overset{\lambda}{\Rightarrow}$ iff $\mathcal{H}(P) \overset{\lambda}{\Rightarrow}$

(2) $\mathbf{init}(P) = \mathbf{init}(\mathcal{H}(P))$, where $\mathbf{init}(P) =_{df} \{a \mid a \in \mathcal{A}^\tau \wedge \exists Q \bullet (P \overset{a}{\to} Q)$.

(3) If $P \overset{\tau}{\to}^n Q$ for $n \geq 1$, then

(a) $Q \overset{\lambda}{\Rightarrow}$ iff $\mathcal{K}(Q, P) \overset{\lambda}{\Rightarrow}$

(b) $\mathbf{init}(Q) = \mathbf{init}(\mathcal{K}(Q, P))$ □

The following lemma states that $\mathcal{H}(P)$ is a member of $\mathcal{DP}$.

Lemma 5.4

(1) $\mathcal{H}(P) \overset{\lambda}{\Rightarrow} R$ iff $R = \mathcal{H}(P/\lambda)$

(2) $\mathcal{H}(P) \overset{\tau}{\to}^n R$ iff there exists Q such that $P \overset{\tau}{\to}^n Q$ and $R = \mathcal{K}(Q, P)$ □

Now comes the main theorem of this section.

Theorem 5.2 $\mathcal{H}$ is an observation-preserving mapping.

Proof $\langle \lambda \rangle \in traces_{\mathcal{A}}(P)$ {Definition 3.1}

$\equiv \quad P \overset{\lambda}{\Rightarrow}$ {Lemma 5.3(1)}

$\equiv \quad \mathcal{H}(P) \overset{\lambda}{\Rightarrow}$ {Definition 3.1}

$\equiv \quad \langle \lambda \rangle \in traces_{\mathcal{A}}(\mathcal{H}(P))$

$\quad\quad \langle \lambda \rangle s \in traces_{\mathcal{A}}(P)$ {Corollary of Lemma 5.2}

$\equiv \quad P \overset{\lambda}{\Rightarrow} \wedge s \in traces_{\mathcal{A}}(P/\lambda)$ {Lemma 5.3(1) and induction}

$\equiv \quad \mathcal{H}(P) \overset{\lambda}{\Rightarrow} \wedge s \in traces_{\mathcal{A}}(\mathcal{H}(P/\lambda))$ {Lemma 5.4(1)}

$\equiv \quad \langle \lambda \rangle s \in traces_{\mathcal{A}}(\mathcal{H}(P))$ $\square$

$(\mathcal{H}, Id_{\mathcal{P}})$ forms a Galois connection between $(\mathcal{P}, \sqsubseteq_{\mathcal{A}})$ and $(\mathcal{P}, \leq_{\mathcal{A}})$.

Theorem 5.3

(1) $P \sqsubseteq_{\mathcal{A}} Q$ if and only if $\mathcal{H}(P) \leq_{\mathcal{A}} Q$

(2) $P \equiv_{\mathcal{A}} Q$ if and only if $\mathcal{H}(P) \approx_{\mathcal{A}} \mathcal{H}(Q)$

Proof. From Theorems 5.1 and 5.2. $\square$

6   Barbs

A *barb* [10] is used to denote a property of a process, rather than an action which changes the process. For example, the following barbs have suggestive names.

(1) **candiverge** is a property of a process that can engage in an infinite sequence of invisible action τ.

(2) Let X be a subset of $\mathcal{A}$. A process has **canrefuse**(X) if it cannot perform the actions in the set X.

$$P \text{ has } \mathbf{canrefuse}(X) =_{df} \mathbf{init}(P) \cap (X \cup \{\tau\}) = \emptyset$$

(3) **canaccept**(X) indicates a stable process, which can perform all the actions of X.

$$P \text{ has } \mathbf{canaccept}(X) =_{df} \tau \notin \mathbf{init}(P) \wedge X \subseteq \mathbf{init}(P)$$

We are going to adopt a simple coding trick to unify barbed bisimulation and barbed traces with their unbarbed versions. Let $\mathcal{B}$ be the set of barbs of interest, and $\top$ stand for the state which no action or observation may be made, i.e., $traces_{\mathcal{A}}(\top) = \{\langle \rangle\}$, and there is no barb b in $\mathcal{B}$ such that $\top$ has b. It can arise only as described in the following case

$$\text{If } P \text{ has barb } b, \text{ then } P \overset{b}{\rightarrow} \top$$

Lemma 6.1

$$\mathcal{DP}_{\mathcal{A}} = \mathcal{DP}_{\mathcal{A} \cup \mathcal{B}}$$

Proof. From the fact that $\xrightarrow{b}$ is a partial function. □

As in Section 3, we define $P \sqsubseteq_{\mathcal{A} \cup \mathcal{B}} Q =_{df} traces_{\mathcal{A} \cup \mathcal{B}}(Q) \subseteq traces_{\mathcal{A} \cup \mathcal{B}}(P)$

Definition 6.1 (Barbed Simulation [10])

A binary relation $\mathcal{R}$ over processes is a barbed simulation with respect to the barb set $\mathcal{B}$ if it is a weak $(\mathcal{A} \cup \mathcal{B})$-simulation. □

Definition 6.2 (Stable Barbs)

A barb b is stable if P has b only if it is stable, i.e., $\tau \notin \mathbf{init}(P)$, and furthermore,

$$\mathbf{init}(P) = \mathbf{init}(Q) \Rightarrow (P \text{ has } b \text{ iff } Q \text{ has } b) \qquad \square$$

Both **canaccept**(X) and **canrefuse**(X) are stable barbs.

Lemma 6.2 If b is stable, then $P \xRightarrow{b}$ iff $\mathcal{H}(P) \xRightarrow{b}$

Proof. If $\tau \notin P$, the conclusion follows directly from Lemma 5.3(2) and the definition of stable barbs. Now consider the case where $\tau \in \mathbf{init}(P)$. From Lemma 5.3(2) we conclude that $\tau \in \mathcal{H}(P)$.

$$P \xRightarrow{b} \qquad \qquad \{\text{and Def of } \xRightarrow{b}\}$$

$$\equiv \exists n \bullet \exists Q \bullet P(\xrightarrow{\tau}^n) Q \wedge Q \xrightarrow{b} \top \qquad \{\text{Lemma 5.4(2)}\}$$

$$\equiv \exists n \bullet \exists Q \bullet \mathcal{H}(P)(\xrightarrow{\tau}^n)\mathcal{K}(Q, P) \wedge Q \xrightarrow{b} \top \qquad \{\text{Lemma 5.3(3)}\}$$

$$\equiv \exists n \bullet \exists Q \bullet \mathcal{H}(P)(\xrightarrow{\tau}^n)\mathcal{K}(Q, P) \wedge \mathcal{K}(Q, P) \xrightarrow{b} \top \qquad \{\text{ and Def of } \xRightarrow{b}\}$$

$$\equiv \mathcal{H}(P) \xRightarrow{b} \qquad \qquad \square$$

Lemma 6.3

If $b = \mathbf{candiverge}$ then $P \xRightarrow{b}$ iff $\mathcal{H}(P) \xRightarrow{b}$.

Proof. From Lemma 5.4(2). □

In the following we consider the case where $\mathcal{B}$ only consists of stable barbs and **candiverge**.

Theorem 6.1

$\mathcal{H}$ of Section 5 is an observation-preserving mapping from $\mathcal{P}$ to $\mathcal{DP}_{\mathcal{A} \cup \mathcal{B}}$

Proof. From Lemmas 6.2 and 6.3. □

Like in unbarbed case, $(\mathcal{H}, Id_{\mathcal{P}})$ is a Galois connection between barbed traces refinement and barbed simulation.

Theorem 6.2

(1) $P \sqsubseteq_{\mathcal{A} \cup \mathcal{B}} Q$ iff $\mathcal{H}(P) \leq_{\mathcal{A} \cup \mathcal{B}} Q$

(2) $P \equiv_{\mathcal{A} \cup \mathcal{B}} Q$ iff $\mathcal{H}(P) \approx_{\mathcal{A} \cup \mathcal{B}} \mathcal{H}(Q)$

Proof. From Theorems 5.1 and 6.1. □

7 Communicating Sequential Processes

Definition 7.1 (The Chaotic Process)

The behaviour of the chaotic process $\bot$ is totally unpredictable, it can engage in any action, and then move to any process.

$$\bot \xrightarrow{a} P \quad \text{for all } a \in \mathcal{A}^\tau \text{ and } P \in \mathcal{P}.$$

Clearly $\bot \leq_{\mathcal{A}\cup\mathcal{B}} P$ for all $P \in \mathcal{P}$. $\qquad\qquad\Box$

Definition 7.2

For any $P \in \mathcal{P}$, the notation $\mathcal{C}(P)$ represents a process which behaves like P except that it becomes chaotic whenever P enters a divergent state.

$$\frac{P \xrightarrow{a} R}{\mathcal{C}(P) \xrightarrow{a} \mathcal{C}(R)} a \in \mathcal{A}^\tau \qquad \frac{P \xrightarrow{b} \top}{\mathcal{C}(P) \xrightarrow{b} \top} \qquad \frac{P \xrightarrow{candiverge} \top}{\mathcal{C}(P) \xrightarrow{\tau} \bot}$$

Like the observation-preserving mappings, $\mathcal{C}$ is a monotonic link.

Lemma 7.1

(1) $P \sqsubseteq_{\mathcal{A}\cup\mathcal{B}} Q$ implies $\mathcal{C}(P) \sqsubseteq_{\mathcal{A}\cup\mathcal{B}} \mathcal{C}(Q)$

(2) $\mathcal{C}(P) \leq_{\mathcal{A}\cup\mathcal{B}} P$

(3) $\mathcal{C}^2(P) \approx_{\mathcal{A}\cup\mathcal{B}} \mathcal{C}(P)$ $\qquad\qquad\Box$

Definition 7.3 (**Communicating Sequential Processes**)

P is a communicating sequential process if $P \equiv_{\mathcal{A}\cup\mathcal{B}} \mathcal{C}(P)$.

We use $\mathcal{CSP}$ to stand for the set of all communicating sequential processes. $\quad\Box$

From Lemma 7.1(3) it follows that $\mathcal{C}$ is a mapping from $\mathcal{P}$ to $\mathcal{CSP}$. Moreover, $(\mathcal{C}, \mathcal{H})$ forms a Galois connection between $(\mathcal{P}, \leq_{\mathcal{A}\cup\mathcal{B}})$ and $(\mathcal{CSP}, \sqsubseteq_{\mathcal{A}\cup\mathcal{B}})$.

Theorem 7.1 $P \sqsubseteq_{\mathcal{A}\cup\mathcal{B}} \mathcal{C}(Q)$ **iff** $\mathcal{H}(P) \leq_{\mathcal{A}\cup\mathcal{B}} Q$ for all $P \in \mathcal{CSP}$ and $Q \in \mathcal{P}$.

Proof $\mathcal{H}(P) \leq_{\mathcal{A}\cup\mathcal{B}} Q$ $\qquad\qquad$ {Theorem 6.2}

$\equiv \quad P \sqsubseteq_{\mathcal{A}\cup\mathcal{B}} Q$ $\qquad\qquad$ {Lemma 7.1(1)}

$\Rightarrow \quad \mathcal{C}(P) \sqsubseteq_{\mathcal{A}\cup\mathcal{B}} \mathcal{C}(Q)$ $\qquad\qquad$ {$P \in \mathcal{CSP}$}

$\equiv \quad P \sqsubseteq_{\mathcal{A}\cup\mathcal{B}} \mathcal{C}(Q)$ $\qquad\qquad$ {Theorem 6.2}

$\equiv \quad \mathcal{H}(P) \leq_{\mathcal{A}\cup\mathcal{B}} \mathcal{C}(Q)$ $\qquad\qquad$ {Lemma 7.1(2)}

$\Rightarrow \quad \mathcal{H}(P) \leq_{\mathcal{A}\cup\mathcal{B}} Q$ $\qquad\qquad\qquad\Box$

8   Conclusion

Process algebras and calculi serve two complementary purposes. The first is to model and to analyse the behaviour of concurrent systems at various levels of abstraction. The second is to formalise the specification of a concurrent system, as well as its implementation as a program, and to verify that the implementation is correct, in the sense that it satisfies its specification. CCS and CSP have been used for both purposes, but CCS gives more emphasis on modelling and CSP to correctness. In modelling concurrent behaviour, CCS and related calculi define the behaviour of a process by the operational semantics, which provides an abstract model of an implementation. To compare processes, CCS introduces an equivalence relation known as bisimilarity, defined co-inductively on the structure of the behavioural graph of the two processes. The arrows of the graph are the transitions in which the process may engage. Bisimilarity appeals directly to the operational intuition of programmers. In addressing the question of correctness, CSP expresses both specification and implementation in the same algebraic notations, and correctness is identified with an ordering relation known as refinement. This relation holds between an implementation and a specification when all possible observations of any execution of the implementation are included in those described and therefore allowed by the specification. The observational semantics exploits the familiar abstraction of set theory. This permits a process to be specified by an arbitrary mathematical description of the observations of its behaviour. After reconciliation of simulation with refinement, their advantages can be combined and exploited. This was the primary motivation for the research reported in this paper.

The basic technique for reconciling refinement with simulation we have adopted here was to construct an observation-preserving mapping, which gives rise a Galois link between refinement and simulation. The mapping defined in this paper is actually a monotonic link which converts processes to healthy ones. It was built by introducing a number of additional non-standard transitions into the operational semantics of the process algebra. The additional transitions that are needed have a justifiable intuitive contents, and they turn out to be useful in dealing with a variety of simulations.

Acknowledgement

The inspiration for this paper derives from a Workshop held in Microsoft Research Ltd., at Cambridge on 22-23 July 2002. Those who contributed to the discussions were Ernie Cohen, Cedric Fournet, Paul Gardiner, Andy Gordon, Tony Hoare, Robin Milner, Sriram Rajamani, Jacob Rehof and Bill Roscoe.

References

1. J.A. Bergstra and J.W. Klop. *Algebra of communicating processes with abstraction.* Theoretical Computer Sciences, Vol 37(1): 77–121, 1985.

2. S.D. Brookes, C.A.R. Hoare and A.W. Roscoe. *A theory of communicating sequential processes.* Journal of the ACM, Vol 31, 1984.
3. C.A.R. Hoare. *Communicating sequential processes.* Prentice Hall, 1985.
4. C.A.R. Hoare and He Jifeng. *Unifying theories of programming.* Prentice Hall, 1998.
5. C.A.R. Hoare. *Process Algebra: a Unifying Approach.* In A.E. Abdallah, C.B. Jones and J.W. Sanders, editor, *Twenty-five Years of Communicating Sequential Processes*, Lecture Notes in Computer Science, Springer-Verlag, 2005.
6. K.G. Larsen and A. Skou. *Bisimulation through probabilistic testing.* Information and control 94(1), 1991.
7. S. Mac Lane. *Categories for the Working Mathematicians.* Springer-Verlag, 1971.
8. R. Milner. *Communication and concurrency.* Prentice Hall, 1989.
9. R. Milner. *Communicating and mobile systems: the π -calculus.* Cambridge University Press, 1999.
10. R. Milner and D. Sangiorgi. *Barbed bisimulation.* In W. Kuich, editor, *Proceedings of the 19th International Colloquium on Automata, Languages and Programming (ICALP'92)*, Lecture Notes in Computer Science, Vol 623, 685–695, Springer-Verlag, 1992.
11. R. De Nicola and M. Hennessy. *Testing equivalence for processes.* Theoretical Computer Science 34, 1983.
12. D.M.R. Park. *Concurrency and automata on infinite sequences.* Lecture Notes in Computer Science, Vol 14, 167–183, Springer-Verlag, 1981.
13. G.D. Plotkin. *A structural approach to operational semantics.* Report DAIMI-FN-19, Computer Science Department, Aarhus University, Denmark, 1981.
14. A.W. Roscoe. *The theory and practice of concurrency.* Prentice Hall, 1998.
15. A. Tarski. *A lattice-theoretical fixed-point theorem and its applications.* Pacific Journal of Mathematics, Vol 5: 285–309, 1955.

CSP, occam and Transputers

David May

Bristol University

The following is based on an after-dinner speech at the conference to celebrate the 25th anniversary of CSP. It's an informal - and personal - account of the development of CSP and the related work on the occam language and the Inmos transputer. This involved many exceptional people, and I've only been able to mention a few of them - but before I start - I'd like to thank them all.

1   The 25th Anniversary of CSP

It's over 25 years since the publication of Tony's CSP paper [4] and over 30 years since I first became interested in concurrent systems. In 1973 I was at Warwick University working on autonomous mobile robots, and had started to think about how to build control systems to handle a lot of sensors and actuators. I decided to spend a few months sorting out these problems ... !

At that time microprocessors had only just appeared, but it was already clear to me that they would open up the potential for low cost, compact, systems with multiple processors. And, on a larger scale, experimental computer networks and distributed systems were under construction. In fact, we set up a research project on programming languages for distributed computing and I tried to persuade our UK research council to let me build a system with ten processors - but they inisisted that *three* processors would be enough! Anyway, we built single-board microcomputers directly connected with communications links and programmed in a language I'd designed called EPL which had processes and messages - and a very efficient implementation.

Over the 1970s there was a lively debate in the UK about architectures and languages for these systems. I met Tony around 1977 and I think we both realised that we were working with very similar ideas. Tony had been working on the CSP language ideas for a while by then, and I'd spend a lot of time on architecture, compilers and implementation techniques.

The CSP paper was a significant step in that it described a simple language with considerable expressive power; beyond that it was clear to me that I knew how to implement most of it efficiently. I think it's true to say that the CSP paper provided the first accessible and widely read paper about the principles of concurrent programming languages and concurrent programs - a point of reference for a lot of people already working in the field and an invitation to many more to join it.

A.E. Abdallah, C.B. Jones, and J.W. Sanders (Eds.): CSP 2004, LNCS 3525, pp. 75–84, 2005.

2   The 25th Anniversary of Inmos

The publication of CSP in 1978 coincided with the foundation of the microelectronics company Inmos, with an investment of £50m of venture capital from the UK government. Iann Barron, one of the founders of Inmos, planned on establishing UK design and manufacture of microprocessors. Viewing a microcomputer as a component for the construction of complex electronic systems just as the transistor is a component for logic gates, he coined the word 'transputer' (transistor + computer) to describe such a device.

It was always planned that Inmos would introduce a new language for the design and programming of concurrent systems. This language was designed between 1979 and 1983 and was eventually called occam [10]; the development continued and produced occam2 in 1985 [9]. Looking over the many drafts I still have, it's possible to trace the development of occam and to see the influence of the original CSP paper. There are differences, for example at some point we added channels; we introduced *protocols* to describe the messages sent through channels; we never adopted automatic termination of repetitive guards. All the time we were concerned about delivering a practical language which could be efficiently implemented. I wrote the first experimental compiler and designed the first transputer instruction set around 1981.

And at the same time, Tony and his group in Oxford were working on the formal models for CSP. I remember the first algebraic definition of occam which arrived unexpectedly in 1982; this subsequently had a significant influence on various aspects of the language and the way it was described - and led into Bill Roscoe's work on the 'laws of occam programming' [6] and the project to build an automated program transformation system.

Inmos in Bristol turned out to be a highly innovative environment, not least because an attempt to recruit a small number of graduating students actually resulted in twenty being recruited - more than the complement of 'experienced' staff - most of whom weren't very experienced! I've come to realise that most creative computer scientists at the time wanted to design their own architecture, programming language and development tools - just like I did - but fortunately most of them didn't get the opportunity! Anyway, we rapidly found ourselves innovating in almost every area - architecture, programming language, development environment, computer aided design system - even the style of the documentation and the packaging of the evaluation boards!

And we took an innovative approach to marketing too - first introducing occam and then the transputer to the Japanese market. A group of us - including Tony - went to Japan to present occam to research organisations including the Institute for new-generation Computing Technology (ICOT). In assembling the presentations for this trip we struggled to find a suitable simple example of the use of occam. Eventually we came up with an example of an embedded control program - the occam *tea-maker* - for the kind of bedside alarm and tea-maker which was common in the UK at the time. I've never been sure what the Japanese made of this program as their way of preparing tea is quite different from ours - but it appeared all over the Japanese technical press anyway!

We went to Japan again - this time with Bill Roscoe - to give two presentations at the second 5th generation conference. Here I presented the transputer as the implementation of occam [14] whilst Bill tried to persuade his audience that occam was a logic programming language [5]! But I'm not sure they were ever convinced by this - or by my remark during the final panel session that occam was a way of doing *logical* programming without *logic* programming!

3   The 20th Anniversary of Transputer (Announcement)

So we can today also celebrate the 20th anniversary of the transputer - or at least, the 20th anniversary of its *announcement*! The transputer's architecture was a hardware embodiment of occam. Its instruction set had specific instructions to support concurrent processes, synchronised communication and guarded commands. To construct systems with multiple processors, the transputer had serial communication links through which the interprocessor messages were passed.

The implementation of these functions in terms of microcode took around a year - significant complexity arose from the fact that the transputer process scheduler provided timer-based scheduling and two priority levels. The end result was to embed a microkernel in around 300 micro-instructions - about 4kbytes of read-only-memory in total.

To my knowledge, the transputer design remains the best integration of processing and communication yet achieved - at a time when processor clock speeds were less than 10Mhz, it took a few microseconds to transfer a short message between two processes on different transputers. It's notable that this has been one of the neglected areas of computer design over the last 20 years, so that despite a hundredfold increase in processor clock speeds and communications rates, the time taken to pass a short message between processes in two different computers is typically between 100 microseconds and 1 millisecond.

It was inevitable that releasing a microcomputer which could be used to build multiprocessors easily would lead to research groups and companies building concurrent 'supercomputers'. Soon there was a spin-out from Inmos - Meiko - selling concurrent supercomputers; they were followed by several others. And many students who passed through computing courses in the 1980s learnt about occam and programmed small collections of transputers.

In 1985 we started the design of an enhanced transputer with a floating point unit, resulting in the launch in 1987 of the world's fastest single-chip floating-point microcomputer [7]. Although we had expected this to be of interest in embedded applications, it had much more impact as a component for concurrent supercomputers.

In fact, many concurrent computing systems were built using transputers and occam - whenever I watch animated films I'm reminded of the concurrent implementation of the the Renderman system now used for rendering movies such as Jurassic Park. This took us into the area of general purpose architectures which could support programmable and dynamically changing communication patterns.

So we started to investigate ways of implementing communications. There was a lot of debate at the time arising from work on VLSI interconnection networks which claimed that low-dimensional networks were the most efficient. We soon realised that this was based on the inappropriate assumptions - optimising a network for minimum delay under low-load conditions is not the same as optimising a network for bounded delay under high-load conditions - which is what concurrent computation is all about!

Fortunately, at this time Les Valiant was in Oxford and Tony re-introduced him to me - I had lost contact with him since he left Warwick in the 1970s. A series of meetings and letters resulted in us designing the first VLSI message-routing switch; unfortunately this design was never understood in the company and it was not used in any commercial products - although we did demonstrate them and I still have one on my shelves. This switch was designed as a component for interconnection networks and included hardware mechanisms to avoid hot-spots in parallel communication [15]. At the same time, the network protocols were designed to support synchronised message communication between processes [12].

The legacy of this work remains today - similar ideas were adopted by the Inmos spin-out Meiko, and the Meiko technology was subsequently acquired by Quadrics. They are still based in the UK, and have developed it further into the interconnection system used in many of the world's largest supercomputers.

4   Formal Methods

The development of the floating point transputer - and indeed the floating point software package which preceded it - highlighted the need for better design verification techniques. Inmos had already pioneered a number of techniques including automatic circuit connectivity checking and design rule checking. Thanks to an invitation from Tony, I was fortunate to hear Don Good talking about formal program verification at the Royal Society [3]. This led to my suggesting the formal verification of a software package to implement the proposed IEEE754 standard for floating point arithmetic - a suggestion which was taken up by Geoff Barrett, at that time a PhD student at Oxford.

Geoff succeeded in this work - within three months we had the specification - and proof - of the package [1]. Subsequently we employed the outcome of our project to develop an interactive transformation system based on the 'laws of occam programming' in order to check - by transformation - that the floating point microprograms could be transformed into the programs in Geoff's package. I think this was the earliest use of formal methods in microprogramming [11].

Geoff went on to construct a verification of the transputer process scheduler as his PhD thesis, and then joined Inmos where he continued to develop novel verification tools; the inspiration for the FDR refinement checker was a checker initially written by Geoff to verify the design of the communications processing system of our next-generation transputer - the T9000 [2].

It had always been our intention to move into applications-specific products and to this end occam was intended to be usable as a hardware design and synthesis language. There is a great advantage of being able to use the same language for both hardware design and software design - the implementation of a specific operation can be easily moved between hardware and software. In fact, in 1987 we completed an experimental synthesiser which used the optimised library of modules designed for the transputer as a target - potentially exploiting a significant investment [13]. We couldn't pursue this work because of the market conditions in 1988 although it did give rise to the developments at Oxford of Handel - now Handel-C. I've never understood why our approach to hardware synthesis has not been taken forward more generally but I'm still optimistic!

5   Market Resistance

It had always been the Inmos strategy to introduce a new concurrent programming language and then to introduce the transputer as the best implementation of it. The problems with this strategy soon became apparent - selling a language is much harder than selling a chip!

In fact, it's very difficult to persuade engineers and programmers to adopt new tools - especially as replacements for the tools they are familiar with - and if you imply that their existing tools are out-of-date it appears that you are saying that their skills are out-of-date! And of course, we didn't have the resources to supply occam implementations for lots of other processors and operating systems prior to the introduction of the transputer.

And another problem emerged as we started to launch the transputer - the Motorola 68000 had taken over most of the teaching laboratories in the US and to some extent in Europe, and the transputer's stack architecture with only a few registers - chosen to minimise code-size and context-switch overheads - was just *too* different. We often encountered the comment: 'It's not like a 68000, it can't be a microprocessor ...'!

And we were very naive about the market. We introduced a development system with the price of a typical PC software product - within weeks we were contacted by an engineer telling us that his management wouldn't take our product seriously because it was too cheap! On checking, we discovered that our competitors were charging almost 10 times as much as we were for a development system. So we released the 'professional development system' - just the same but much more expensive - and the problem went away!

Another problem was that the potential market for 32-bit embedded processors was much too low to sustain the development of new products; few embedded systems required the performance of more than one processor. At the time, most embedded systems used a single 8-bit microprocessor programmed in assembler, and so we had taken on the task of trying to educate most of our customers in the use of concurrency and high-level languages!

I think that those of us used to CSP or occam don't realise how much there is to learn. These languages are small because they don't provide many different syntactic representations for the same idea - but you actually have to learn more ideas and the ways they interact. So even when a programmer has mastered the concurrent processes and communications, there's still a long way to go to grasp guarded commands.

However, in the end I think programmers will have to learn how to use tools like CSP and occam. I watched the growth of this expertise within Inmos and saw the chaos resulting from experienced programmers trying to write concurrent programs without the right tools - in fact when we released the first version of the occam compiler which checked for aliases and disjointness - we found numerous mistakes in existing programs!

But I think few programmers realise that such techniques are the key to fast and reliable programming. And they are also the key to simple, efficient, optimisng compilers. Unfortunately there is still a widespread view - fostered by historic features in our programming languages - that efficient programs will be full of source-level 'optimisations'. But even if programmers can understand the impact of their detailed work at source-level on execution efficiency, they only have the time to work in this way on tiny programs.

6   Principles

CSP and occam were designed around a number of principles. These included the close integration of communications and processing within a programming language. This principle was followed in the transputer, which provided instructions directly corresponding to the input and output statements [8].

But one of the most important CSP principles was 'scheduling invariance', or the absence of 'race conditions'. This was achieved by the combination of synchronised communication and disjointness; checking this at compile-time also required the prevention of aliases. Twenty years ago I came to the view that it's not possible to construct concurrent programs of any complexity quickly and easily without this principle - and having watched people struggling with libraries supporting concurrency - and the concurrency support in languages such as Java - has simply reinforced my view.

I still find myself explaining these principles today! Its a strange phenomenon that the computing world seems to forget fundamental ideas: as a student I was taught about the idea of *the quit-key which always restores a computer to a known state* - this doesn't exist on the computer I'm using to write this! In the 1970's UNIX introduced the idea that *anything that can be done from the command line can also be done from a program* - but today most of the world uses software which doesn't follow this principle. I could give many more examples. Nevertheless, I believe that we can only advance computer design - and software design - by identifying such principles, applying them - and *remembering* them!

And finally - simplicity. In a rationale for an early version of occam, we were able to write:

"Consequently, the major part of this rationale concentrates on justifying the omission of features from the language. These include syntax, jumps, case con-

struction, functions, recursion, types, process names, output guards, automatic termination/abortion, monitors, signals, semaphores, pointers, delays and exceptions".

In the end a few of these crept back into the design, but only after we had tried to manage without them!

7 Computer Architecture

At this celebration of 25 years of CSP, it seems important to contemplate what has been achieved in computer architecture and languages, where there are headed, and what CSP might have to contribute.

First, a disappointment. It is widely accepted that hardware efficiency doubles ever 18 months, following Moore's law. Let me now introduce you to May's law - software efficiency halves every 18 months, compensating Moore's law! It's not clear what has caused this, but the tendency to add features, programming using copy-paste techniques, and programming by 'debugging the null-program' - starting with a debugger and an empty screen and debugging interactively until the desired program emerges - have probably all contributed.

In general purpose processors, it seems we are finally reaching the limits to 'sequential' processing - or at least the advances will be more difficult and expensive. In the last few years we have seen rapidly escalating costs of design, as geometries have shrunk and the number of transistors on a chip has increased. Further difficulties have arisen in the manufacturing process technology, especially as regards power consumption; it has become increasingly important to switch off any part of a system which is not in use.

I think we will see the emergence of single-chip symmetric multiprocessors, an attempt to hide the costs of shared variables with coherency protocols, and a re-iteration of the claims that these machines are easy to program - just like it was with multi-processors 20 years ago! My belief is that with this approach, performance improvements by use of concurrency will remain around a factor of two - as it does with super-scalar techniques - regardless of the number of processors. A good way to avoid this problem would be to follow the CSP principles - and in this case the hardware coherency mechanisms aren't needed!

With hardware enhancements becoming more difficult, I believe that the pressure to improve software will increase. I don't believe that this is about complex optimisation tools or tools for managing the development and maintenance of massive programs - it's about using the right ideas and tools and using them with care. And it's about creating the right abstractions in both hardware and software. We are already seeing some of this with the increased use of standard hardware platforms such as Field Programmable Gate Arrays in place of Applications Specific designs. There is now the potential to fill chips with arrays of processors which are customised entirely by writing programs and configurations. An important part of the next generation of semiconductor companies may well be specialists purely in writing high quality software for specific applications - they'll own no hardware designs and no manufacturing capability!

And in computing, there is always a new opportunity ...

8   The Future of CSP

We are now at the early stages of the ubiquitous computing era - with computer-based wireless devices distributed around the environment or used in wearable - or even implantable - systems. Over the next few years, we will see the integration of sensors, processors and actuators in a vast range of mobile devices.

These devices will effectively consume no power; they will scavenge power from their environment or will be driven by small batteries which last years. Many of them will be high performance - but only in very short bursts. They must be engineered for power-efficiency at all levels from process technology to applications software.

And the mobile devices will communicate with fixed devices - which will be based on single-chip supercomputers - multiple processors combined on a single chip. Key issues will be power-efficiency, responsiveness and programmability; processors will need to switch between idling with no power and delivering results according to the demands from the environment. We will also have to reverse the trend of using ever-increasing amounts of memory, which uses both space and power.

So these systems need small programs and event-driven processing. And their compilers need to be able to do a lot of static analysis so that they can optimise for power minimisation. And of course, this is what alias and disjointness checking do - as well as helping to get the programs right in the first place.

I can't think of a better way to do all this than to use CSP, which provides a natural way of describing event-driven systems and also brings the benefit of building concurrent systems using libraries instead of kernels and operating systems. And, by embedding the concurrency mechanisms in the language it enables concurrency optimisations in the compilers and tools.

It's worth pointing out that these systems pose some new challenges for research. Two examples come to mind. The first is *mobility* - we'd like to be able to move processes and channels around securely. The second is *wireless connectivity* - what are the appropriate abstractions in an environment where connections are being made and broken frequently?

9   How Can CSP Have an Impact?

I don't think I should finish without considering how the CSP community here in the UK can make a bigger impact than it has. The experience of trying to develop innovative ideas here and promote them overseas made me observe two problems. 'Not-invented-here' is something most cultures are guilty of - but the British also have the complementary version - 'invented here'. We also have a tendency identified by Charles Babbage who wrote:

"Propose to an Englishman any principle, or any instrument, however admirable, and you will observe that the whole effort of the English mind is directed to find a difficulty, a defect, or an impossibility in it. If you speak to him of a machine for peeling a potato, he will pronounce it impossible: if you peel a

potato with it before his eyes, he will declare it useless, because it will not slice a pineapple".

We must get much better at valuing the things we are good at - and we do excel in minimal, efficient designs - whether processors, languages or theories. The ARM processor, the transputer processor now known as the ST20, the BCPL programming language (as Tony might have said - a significant advance on its successors) and of course CSP are all obvious examples.

I'd suggest to the industrial community - and the investors here - that in the immediate future using powerful tools like CSP to tackle applications directly may provide rich rewards - enabling rapid design of efficient and reliable electronic products. It just doesn't make sense to try to sell powerful tools - especially to an unreceptive market - *you have to use them.*

I'd suggest to the research community - and to those who fund it - that turning ideas like CSP into fully supported platforms for future research - with compilers, tools and libraries - is an important part of the research agenda - especially in computer science. We have to be able base new research on previous achievements - which can only happen if the achievements are consolidated in this way.

And I'd suggest to the educational community - both in universities and schools - that teaching programming is vital - and it should be *concurrent* programming. As I've come to realise over the years, in addition to their usefulness in dealing with computers, concurrent programs can be used to explore - and design - the techniques used by human organisations to tackle large and complex tasks. So I find it very odd that business process management experts promote flow-charts - I'm sure that these help to formalise parts of a process, but they can't possibly capture how business processes actually work. We all carry out tasks concurrently, and we all selectively wait for sets of events! And I'm sure that the renewed interest in understanding biological systems will draw on - and cause us to extend - our research on concurrency.

10   Summary

CSP combines three things: concurrency, minimalism and logical structure. And these principles were also followed in the occam and transputer designs. And both of these strengths in language design and architecture are still here - CSP is still very much alive in our research community and the most significant concentration of microprocessor systems designers in Europe has grown from the original Inmos team - an extraordinarily successful example of government intervention to try to establish a new industry.

Recent programming languages have made a virtue of features - aliases, exceptions, dynamic resource management - adding complexity both in design and implementation. And the same has happened in hardware design - most new processor designs add complexity in both architecture and implementation. None of this is a good basis for the next generation of computers - or programmers!

So, 25 years on, I believe CSP is still a sound and relevant basis for microcomputer architecture, design and programming. It has immediate relevance to single-chip multiprocessors, and provides a starting point for ubiquitous computing components.

In 1978 Tony Hoare wrote in his abstract for the CSP paper:

"This paper suggests that input and output are basic primitives of programming and that parallel composition of communicating sequential processes is a fundamental program structuring method. When combined with a development of Dijkstra's guarded command, these concepts are surprisingly versatile".

This proposal seems to me every bit as relevant - and innovative - today as it was when it was written. And I suggest to you that despite it's age - *CSP is the most recent major innovation in programming language design!*

References

1. G. Barrett. Formal methods applied to a floating point number system. *IEEE transactions on software engineering*, 15(5):611–621, May 1989.
2. G. Barrett. Model checking in practice: the t9000 virtual channel processor. *IEEE transactions on software engineering*, 21(2):69–78, February 1995.
3. D. I. Good. Mechanical proofs about computer programs. In C. A. R. Hoare and J. C. Shepherdson, editors, *Mathematical Logic and Programming Languages*, pages 55–74. Prentice Hall, 1985.
4. C. A. R. Hoare. Communicating sequential processes. *Communications of the ACM*, 21(8):666–677, August 1978.
5. C. A. R. Hoare and A. W. Roscoe. Programs as executable predicates. In *Second International Conference on Fifth Generation Computer Systems*, pages 220–228, Tokyo, November 1984.
6. C. A. R. Hoare and A. W. Roscoe. The laws of occam programming. *Theoretical Computer Science*, 60(2):177–229, September 1988.
7. M. Homewood, D. May, and R Shepherd. The ims t800 transputer. *IEEE Micro*, 7(5):10–26, October 1987.
8. Inmos. *The Transputer Instruction set: a compiler writer's guide*. Prentice hall, 1988.
9. Inmos Ltd. occam-*2 Reference Manual*. Prentice Hall, 1988.
10. D. May. occam. *Sigplan Notices*, 18(4):69–79, 1983.
11. D. May. Use of formal methods by a silicon manufacturer. In C. A. R. Hoare, editor, *Developments in Concurrency and Communication*, pages 107–129. Addison-Wesley, 1990.
12. David May. Transputers and routers: components for concurrent machines. In *Proceedings of the 3rd Transputer/occam International Conference, Japan*, pages 3–20, Tokyo, May 1990. IOS Press.
13. David May and Catherine Keane. Compiling occam into silicon. In *Twentieth Hawaii International Conference on System Sciences*, Hawaii, May 1987. IEEE.
14. David May and Roger Shepherd. The transputer implementation of occam. In *Second International Conference on Fifth Generation Computer Systems*, pages 533–541, Tokyo, november 1984.
15. L. G. Valiant. A scheme for fast parallel communication. *SIAM Journal on Computing*, 11(2):350–361, May 1982.

Models for Data-Flow Sequential Processes

Mark B. Josephs

Centre for Concurrent Systems and Very-Large-Scale Integration,
Faculty of BCIM, London South Bank University,
103 Borough Road, London SE1 0AA, UK
josephmb@lsbu.ac.uk

Abstract. A family of mathematical models of nondeterministic data flow is introduced. These models are constructed out of sets of traces, successes, failures and divergences, cf. Hoare's traces model, Roscoe's stable-failures model and Brookes and Roscoe's failures/divergences model of Communicating Sequential Processes. As in CSP, operators are defined that are convenient for constructing processes in the various models.

1 Introduction

Consider sequential processes that communicate via input streams and output streams (FIFO buffers of unlimited storage capacity), as in Kahn-MacQueen data-flow networks [17, 18]. They are capable of the following actions:

- selectively reading data from their input streams,
- unreading (pushing back) data to their input streams,
- writing data to their output streams, and
- termination.

Processes can be composed in parallel. In particular, an output stream of one process may be connected to an input stream of a second process. Any datum written to the output stream by the first process should be transferred (eventually and automatically) to the input stream, where it becomes available for reading by the second process.

Processes can also be composed in sequence. When one process terminates its successor starts to execute. An important point here (implicit in [10]) is that *termination does not destroy the contents of input streams and output streams.*

Some years ago, the author, Hoare and He [16, 9] devised a process algebra for (nondeterministic) data flow, as a variant of Communicating Sequential Processes (CSP) [12]. (Part of this work was reproduced in [13].) We showed how to simplify the failures/divergences model [4] of CSP so that refusal sets were no longer required; failures could instead be identified with (finite) 'quiescent traces' [7, 14] or 'traces of completed computation sequences' [23].

At the time we did not consider a binary angelic choice operator, nor sequential composition. One purpose of this article is to rectify those omissions. Note that termination is modelled in CSP by a special symbol $\sqrt{}$ (success) [11],

A.E. Abdallah, C.B. Jones, and J.W. Sanders (Eds.): CSP25, LNCS 3525, pp. 85–97, 2005.

but that would not work for what we shall call Data-Flow Sequential Processes (DFSP). The solution is to create a 'stub' (a sequence of unread inputs) when termination occurs and there are no pending outputs, cf. [10, 6].

Another purpose of this article is to show how the more recent stable-failures model [27] of CSP can be adapted for DFSP. Indeed, a series of increasingly sophisticated models for DFSP will be introduced in a step-by-step manner, cf. [22]. Note that fairness issues, the focus of [23, 2, 3], are not addressed in these models.

The rest of this article is organised as follows. In Section 2, we recall the reordering relation [16, 9] between traces of directed events, a relation that captures the essence of data-flow communication. Subsequently, we define partial-correctness models (in Sections 3–5) and a total-correctness model (in Section 6) for DFSP, guided by what Roscoe [27] has done for CSP. In each case we consider the semantics of operators appropriate to the model. Conclusions are drawn in Section 7.

2   Directed Events, Traces and Reordering

A process is associated with an alphabet A, a (possibly infinite) set of symbols[1], partitioned into an input alphabet I and an output alphabet O. A symbol in I designates the transfer of a particular datum to a particular input stream; a symbol in O designates the transfer of a particular datum from a particular output stream. Such *directed events* are considered to be atomic, i.e., instantaneous.

Following Hoare [11], we define a *trace* to be a finite sequence (string) of symbols in A that expresses the occurrence of events over time as a linear order. In respect of a process that communicates through streams of unbounded capacity, however, two facts are noteworthy:

1. Events are independent if they are in the same direction but act upon different streams.
2. The occurrence of an input event does not depend upon the prior occurrence of an output event.

The first fact would justify taking a more abstract approach, namely, to follow Mazurkiewicz [21] by defining a trace to be an equivalence class on A^*. The two facts taken together would justify being more abstract still, namely, to follow Pratt [24] by defining a trace to be a partially-ordered multiset (pomset) on A. For example, if a and b are independent input events and c and d are independent output events, then the strings $cabd$ and $cbad$ are equivalent, but the only ordering between events is given by $a < d$ and $b < d$.

---

[1] To be more concrete, we have in mind compound symbols with $s.d$ referring to stream s and datum d. We would then require that $s_0.d_0 \in I$ and $s_1.d_1 \in O$ implies that $s_0 \neq s_1$. Moreover, if D is a data type associated with stream s, then $s.d \in A$ for all $d \in D$.

Anyway, the possibility of *reordering* a trace without affecting the behaviour of a process was recognized in [7, 28] and was formalised as a relation $t \ltimes u$ (t reorders u) between strings t and u in [16]. Reordering allows

- input symbols to be moved in front of other symbols
- output symbols to be moved behind other symbols

provided the symbols being swapped are associated with different streams. In other words, it is the strongest reflexive transitive relation (i.e. preorder) such that $tabu \ltimes tbau$ if $a \in I$ or $b \in O$, a and b designating transfers on different streams. For example, if a and b are independent input events and c and d are independent output events, then $badc \ltimes cabd$. Various properties of the reordering relation have been proved in [19, 20].

More abstractly, t and u are equivalent ($t \bowtie u$) if and only if $t \ltimes u$ and $u \ltimes t$. Note that, if two traces are equivalent, then reordering one into the other involves only the swapping of input symbols and the swapping of output symbols, not the swapping of input symbols with output symbols.

Not only does $\ltimes$ give us Mazurkiewicz's equivalence classes, but it also becomes a partial order on them. Note that a trace t is minimal (up to equivalence) if and only if $t \in I^*O^*$. Kahn [17] modelled a class of data-flow networks by means of continuous functions from the histories of input streams to the histories of output streams. For that class, the minimal traces are all that are needed. Moreover, reordering of a trace corresponds to 'augmentation' [25] or 'subsumption' [8], a partial order on pomsets.

3   Traces Model

A process with alphabet A (partitioned into I and O) can be modelled by a set T of traces, i.e., $T \subseteq A^*$. (Pratt [24] similarly models a process by a set of pomsets, and Gischer [8] investigates closure under subsumption.) This model avoids the Brock-Ackerman anomaly [1]. It embodies the following assumptions:

1. Divergence is always possible, i.e., a process may remain unstable indefinitely.
2. Quiescence (also referred to as stable failure) is always possible, i.e., a process that has become stable may refuse to output.

3.1   Healthiness Conditions

Four conditions must be satisfied by such a set T:
It contains the empty sequence.

$$\varepsilon \in T \tag{1}$$

It is prefix-closed.[2]

$$\{t, u : tu \in T : t\} \subseteq T \tag{2}$$

---

[2] The set comprehension $\{l : D : E\}$ denotes the set of all values E obtained by substituting values that satisfy domain predicate D for the variables in the list l.

It is receptive.

$$TI^* \subseteq T \tag{3}$$

It is closed under reordering.

$$\{t, u : t \in T \wedge u \ltimes t : u\} \subseteq T \tag{4}$$

Observe that the space of healthy sets of traces is a complete lattice, with least (greatest) member A^* and greatest (least) member I^*, under the superset (subset) order. Also, for any non-empty subset S of healthy sets of traces, $\bigcap S$ is the least upper (greatest lower) bound and $\bigcup S$ is the greatest lower (least upper) bound.

3.2   Operators

It is convenient to construct a process P out of CSP-like operators. traces(P) is then the set of traces denoted by P. For a given I and O, P is refined by Q if traces(P) $\supseteq$ traces(Q). It is essential that the operators preserve the healthiness conditions and are monotonic with respect to the refinement order. It turns out that the operators are also continuous in the reverse (subset) order [27].

Quiescence. The process **stop** does nothing, though data can always be transferred to its input streams. Thus

traces(**stop**) = I^*

and we can see that **stop** refines every other process in the traces model.

Recursion. The meaning of a recursively-defined process $\mu X. F(X)$ is given by $\bigcup_{0 \leq i} F^i(\textbf{stop})$, the least fixed point of continuous function F with respect to the subset order.

Nondeterministic Choice. The process $P_0 \sqcap P_1$ behaves like P_0 or like P_1. (Broy [5] calls this 'erratic' choice because it is outside the control of the environment.)

traces($P_0 \sqcap P_1$) = traces(P_0) $\cup$ traces(P_1),

the greatest lower bound $\sqcap$ with respect to the superset order.

Conditional Choice. Given a Boolean expression B, the process $P_0 \triangleleft B \triangleright P_1$ behaves like P_0 or like P_1, depending upon whether or not B is true.

Prefixing. Given a minimal trace t (i.e. $t \in I^*O^*$), the process $t \rightarrow P$ reads data from its input streams and writes data to its output streams in the order given by t, and then behaves like P. The representation of such a sequence of internal data transfers as a single step is a convenient abstraction.

traces($t \rightarrow P$) = $I^* \cup \{u, v, w : u \in \text{traces}(P) \wedge vw \ltimes tu : v\}$.[3]

---

[3] When the input streams referenced in t are each associated with a data type of cardinality one, the union with I^* is redundant.

stop is a fixed-point of input-prefixing:

$$t \to \mathbf{stop} = \mathbf{stop}, \text{ if } t \in I^*.$$

Guarded Choice. Quiescence and prefixing generalise to guarded choice: the process $|_{0 \leq i < n} t_i \to P_i$ is constructed from an indexed set t of minimal traces (guards) and an indexed set P of processes.

$\text{traces}(|_{0 \leq i < n} t_i \to P_i)$
$= I^* \cup \{i, u, v, w : 0 \leq i < n \wedge u \in \text{traces}(P_i) \wedge vw \Join t_i u : v\}.$

Observe that *in the traces model* guarded choice is simply a nondeterministic choice between prefixed processes.

After. The behaviour of P after the occurrence of t is given by the process P/t, for any trace $t \in \text{traces}(P)$. In particular, P/t is always meaningful for $t \in I^*$ and behaves like P with the contents of its input streams determined by t.

$$\text{traces}(P/t) = \{u : tu \in \text{traces}(P) : u\}.$$

We have the following cancellation law:

$$(t \to P)/u = P, \text{ if } t \Join u.$$

Observe also that

$$P/t \text{ is refined by } P/u, \text{ if } t \Join u,$$

which follows from the definitions of refinement and $/$, and the property of $\Join$ that $t_0 \Join t_1$ implies $t_0 u \Join t_1 u$.

Parallel Composition. Parallel composition corresponds to blending [28] (in which internal communication is concealed). Let input alphabet I_i and output alphabet O_i of P_i partition A_i, for $i = 0, 1$, with $I_0 \cap I_1 = \emptyset$ and $O_0 \cap O_1 = \emptyset$. Then the process $P_0 \parallel P_1$ has input alphabet $(I_0 \cup I_1) \setminus C$ and output alphabet $(O_0 \cup O_1) \setminus C$, where $C = A_0 \cap A_1$, and

$\text{traces}(P_0 \parallel P_1)$
$= \{t : t \in (A_0 \cup A_1)^* \wedge t \upharpoonright A_0 \in \text{traces}(P_0) \wedge t \upharpoonright A_1 \in \text{traces}(P_1) : t \setminus C\}.$

(Closure under reordering is proved in [19].) Pratt proposes a similar operator on sets of pomsets in [24].

Output-prefixing distributes through parallel composition, as follows:

$$t \to (P_0 \parallel P_1) = (t_0 \to P_0) \parallel (t_1 \to P_1),$$
$$\text{where } t \Join t_0 t_1, \text{ if } t_0 \in (O_0 \setminus I_1)^* \text{ and } t_1 \in (O_1 \setminus I_0)^*.$$

Trading is also allowed between output-prefixing and after-input:

$$(t \to P_0) \parallel P_1 = P_0 \parallel (P_1/t), \text{ if } t \in (O_0 \cap I_1)^*.$$

4   Traces/Successes Model

A problem with the traces model is that it says nothing about successful termination and so one cannot define sequential composition. This is remedied by modelling the set S of successes, where $S \subseteq A^* \times I^*$. Often we are only interested in the first component of each pair in S, the set of such traces being $\mathrm{dom}(S)$.

The structure of S (viz. a set of pairs of traces) is new[4] and can be understood as follows. For any $t \in A^*$, $u \in O^*$ and $v \in I^*$, $(tu, v) \in S$ records the ability of the process, after engaging in t, to terminate with u determining the contents of its output streams (i.e. pending outputs) and v determining the contents of its input streams (i.e. unread inputs). Of course, this implies that if $u = u_0 u_1$, then the process is also able to terminate after tu_0, leaving u_1 pending and v unread. The second component of a member of S might be referred to as a 'stub', being what is left over upon termination of a process.

Broy and Lengauer [6] provide another way to model terminating processes. They generalise from deterministic processes represented by functions from states to states, to nondeterministic processes represented by sets of such functions.

4.1   Healthiness Conditions

Three conditions must be satisfied by a pair (T, S) in addition to the four stated above for T:

The first component of every success is a trace.

$$\mathrm{dom}(S) \subseteq T \tag{5}$$

S is receptive.

$$\{t, u, v : (t, u) \in S \wedge v \in I^* : (tv, uv)\} \subseteq S \tag{6}$$

S is closed under reordering of both components.

$$\{t, u, v, w : (t, u) \in S \wedge v \bowtie t \wedge w \bowtie u : (v, w)\} \subseteq S \tag{7}$$

Note that, in spite of Condition (6), symbols in the stub v of a success (u, v) are not necessarily present in u. Such successes can arise from the application of the after operator and from unreading, as we are about to see.

The space of healthy pairs (T, S) is a complete lattice under the pair-wise superset (subset) order.

---

[4] Roscoe discusses at length in [27] how termination is modelled in CSP with $\sqrt{}$. He does mention as an alternative, however, that 'the termination traces (at least) would have to be included as a separate component'.

4.2   Operators

The refinement order remains superset (now in each component). The operators previously introduced for the traces model can be lifted to the traces/successes model by defining their successes, and several more operators are now meaningful.

$\text{successes}(\textbf{stop}) = \emptyset$.

$\text{successes}(P_0 \sqcap P_1) = \text{successes}(P_0) \cup \text{successes}(P_1)$.

$\text{successes}(t \to P) = \{u, v, w : (u, v) \in \text{successes}(P) \wedge w \ltimes tu : (w, v)\}$.

$\text{successes}(|_{0 \leq i < n} t_i \to P_i)$
$= \{i, u, v, w : 0 \leq i < n \wedge (u, v) \in \text{successes}(P_i) \wedge w \ltimes t_i u : (w, v)\}$.

$\text{successes}(P/t) = \{u, v : (tu, v) \in \text{successes}(P) : (u, v)\}$.

Parallel composition requires distributed termination [27] (in which both components must terminate before the composite process can).

$\text{successes}(P_0 \parallel P_1) = \{t, u : t \in (A_0 \cup A_1)^* \wedge u \in (I_0 \cup I_1)^*$
$\wedge (t \upharpoonright A_0, u \upharpoonright I_0) \in \text{successes}(P_0)$
$\wedge (t \upharpoonright A_1, u \upharpoonright I_1) \in \text{successes}(P_1) : (t \setminus C, u \setminus C)\}$.

Termination. The process **skip** differs from **stop** in that it terminates successfully.

$\text{traces}(\textbf{skip}) = I^*$

$\text{successes}(\textbf{skip}) = \{u, v : u \in I^* \wedge u \bowtie v : (u, v)\}$.

Reaction. The process t, where t is a minimal trace, reads data from its input streams and writes data to its output streams in the order given by t, and then terminates successfully. (So ε is the same as **skip**.)

$\text{traces}(t) = I^* \cup \{u, v, w : u \in I^* \wedge vw \ltimes tu : v\}$

$\text{successes}(t) = \{u, v : u \in I^* \wedge v \ltimes tu : (v, u)\}$.

It is a special case of prefixing:

$$\boxed{t = t \to \textbf{skip}, \text{ if } t \in I^* O^*.}$$

Unreading. The process t^{-1}, $t \in I^*$, unreads (pushes back) data on its input streams before terminating successfully. (So ε^{-1} is also the same as **skip**.)

$\text{traces}(t^{-1}) = I^*$

$\text{successes}(t^{-1}) = \{u, v : u \in I^* \wedge tu \bowtie v : (u, v)\}$.

Sequential Composition. The process $P_0; P_1$ behaves like P_0 until that terminates successfully, allowing P_1 to take over.

traces$(P_0; P_1)$
= traces(P_0)
$\quad \cup \{t_0, t_1, t, u, v : (t_0, v) \in \text{successes}(P_0) \wedge vt_1 \in \text{traces}(P_1) \wedge tu \bowtie t_0 t_1 : t\}$

successes$(P_0; P_1)$
= $\{t_0, t_1, t, v, w : (t_0, v) \in \text{successes}(P_0)$
$\qquad\qquad \wedge (vt_1, w) \in \text{successes}(P_1) \wedge t \bowtie t_0 t_1 : (t, w)\}$.

Compare the following law to how division by a non-zero number relates to multiplication by the reciprocal of that number:

$$\boxed{P/t = t^{-1}; P \,, \text{ if } t \in I^* \,.}$$

Iteration $^*P$ is a special case of recursion [12]: $\mu X. P; X$.

5   Traces/Successes/Failures Model

A problem with the above models is that quiescence is always a possibility. This is remedied by modelling the set F of (stable) failures, where $F \subseteq A^*$.

The structure of F (viz. a set of traces) is the same as in the author's earlier work [16, 15]. For any $t \in A^*$, $t \in F$ records the ability of the process, after engaging in t, to refuse to output after becoming stable, cf. Roscoe's stable-failures model[5] [27].

5.1   Healthiness Conditions

Two conditions must be satisfied by a triple (T, S, F) in addition to the seven stated above for a pair (T, S):

F is a subset of T.
$$F \subseteq T \tag{8}$$

F is closed under reordering.
$$\{t, u : t \in F \wedge u \bowtie t : u\} \subseteq F \tag{9}$$

Note that whether or not a process, after engaging in $t \in T$, is able to terminate is independent of whether or not it is able to become quiescent. That is, $t \notin \text{dom}(S) \cup F$, $t \in \text{dom}(S) \setminus F$, $t \in F \setminus \text{dom}(S)$ and $t \in \text{dom}(S) \cap F$ are all possible.

The space of healthy triples (T, S, F) is a complete lattice under the componentwise superset (subset) order.

---

[5] Consider a trace t that can be extended by $u \in O^*$ to $tu \in F$ and, for simplicity, define a refusal set to be a set of streams. Then we may associate with t any refusal set consisting of output streams that are not involved in the events recorded in u [9].

5.2   Operators

The refinement order remains superset. The operators previously introduced .
can be lifted to the traces/successes/failures model by defining their failures, and
several more operators are now meaningful. In particular, the first approximation
to a recursion is now **div** rather than **stop**.

$\text{failures}(\textbf{stop}) = I^*$.

$\text{failures}(P_0 \sqcap P_1) = \text{failures}(P_0) \cup \text{failures}(P_1)$.

$\text{failures}(t \rightarrow P)$
$= (I^* \setminus \{u, v, w \ : \ \{u, v\} \subseteq I^* \wedge w \in O^* \wedge vw \ltimes tu \ : \ v\})$
$\quad \cup \{u, v \ : \ u \in \text{failures}(P) \wedge v \ltimes tu \ : \ v\}$.

A guarded choice is between those prefixed-processes for which all the inputs
required by their guards are available.

$\text{failures}((|_{0 \leq i < n} t_i \rightarrow P_i)$
$= (I^* \setminus \{i, u, v, w \ : \ 0 \leq i < n \wedge \{u, v\} \subseteq I^* \wedge w \in O^* \wedge vw \ltimes t_i u \ : \ v\}$
$\quad \cup \{i, u, v \ : \ 0 \leq i < n \wedge u \in \text{failures}(P_i) \wedge v \ltimes t_i u \ : \ v\}$.

$\text{failures}(\textbf{skip}) = \text{failures}(t^{-1}) = \emptyset$.

$\text{failures}(t) = I^* \setminus \{u, v, w \ : \ \{u, v\} \subseteq I^* \wedge w \in O^* \wedge vw \ltimes tu \ : \ v\}$.

$\text{failures}(P/t) = \{u : tu \in \text{failures}(P) : u\}$.

$\text{failures}(P_0; P_1)$
$= \text{failures}(P_0)$
$\quad \cup \{t_0, t_1, t, v : (t_0, v) \in \text{successes}(P_0) \wedge vt_1 \in \text{failures}(P_1) \wedge t \ltimes t_0 t_1 : t\}$.

$\text{failures}(P_0 \parallel P_1)$
$= \{t : t \in (A_0 \cup A_1)^* \wedge (\ (t \restriction A_0 \in \text{dom}(\text{successes}(P_0)) \wedge t \restriction A_1 \in \text{failures}(P_1))$
$\qquad\qquad\qquad \vee (t \restriction A_0 \in \text{failures}(P_0)) \wedge t \restriction A_1 \in \text{dom}(\text{successes}(P_1))$
$\qquad\qquad\qquad \vee (t \restriction A_0 \in \text{failures}(P_0) \wedge t \restriction A_1 \in \text{failures}(P_1))\ ) : t \setminus C\}$.

Divergence. The process **div** never becomes stable.

$\text{traces}(\textbf{div}) = I^*$

$\text{successes}(\textbf{div}) = \text{failures}(\textbf{div}) = \emptyset$.

Angelic Choice. The process $P_0 \square P_1$ [6] behaves like P_0 or like P_1, except that
it can only refuse to produce its *first* output if both P_0 and P_1 can so refuse.
(In CSP, a similar operator can only refuse to engage in its first event if both
arguments can so refuse.)

$\text{traces}(P_0 \square P_1) = \text{traces}(P_0) \cup \text{traces}(P_1)$

$\text{successes}(P_0 \square P_1) = \text{successes}(P_0) \cup \text{successes}(P_1)$

$\text{failures}(P_0 \square P_1) = ((\text{failures}(P_0) \cup \text{failures}(P_1)) \setminus I^*) \cup (\text{failures}(P_0) \cap \text{failures}(P_1))$.

---

[6] Unfortunately, Broy [5] uses the symbol ∇ for angelic choice and $\square$ for erratic choice.

The following 'step' law [27] relates angelic choice to guarded choice.

Let $Q = |_{0 \leq i < m} t_i \rightarrow P_i$ and $R = |_{m \leq i < n} t_i \rightarrow P_i$. Then
$Q \square R = |_{0 \leq i < n} t_i \rightarrow ((P_i \square ((R \triangleleft i < m \triangleright Q)/t_i)) \triangleleft t_i \in I^* \triangleright P_i)$.

---

6   Successes/Failures/Divergences Model

One may object to the above models on the grounds that they imply that divergence is the best thing that can happen. An alternative approach goes to the opposite extreme, as in Brookes and Roscoe's failures/divergences model [4]. Divergence is modelled as chaos, being the worst thing that can happen. The set D of divergences is a subset of A^*.

In the traces/successes/failures model, T had to be given explicitly because after certain traces no stable state might be reachable. Now, however, we shall consider every divergence to be a failure too, enabling us to extract T from F and S, by means of the following definition:

$$T = \{t, u : u \in O^* \wedge tu \in F \cup \mathrm{dom}(S) : t\} .$$

All nine conditions of the previous sections must still be satisfied. There is some redundancy, however, since Conditions (4), (5) and (8) follow from the definition of T and Conditions (7) and (9).

6.1   Healthiness Conditions

There are five more healthiness conditions:

Every divergence is a failure.
$$D \subseteq F \tag{10}$$

Every divergence paired with any sequence of input events is a success.
$$D \times I^* \subseteq S \tag{11}$$

D is extension-closed.
$$DA^* \subseteq D \tag{12}$$

D is closed under reordering.
$$\{t, u : t \in D \wedge u \ltimes t : u\} \subseteq D \tag{13}$$

Every trace that gives rise to unbounded nondeterminism is a divergence.
$$\{t : |\{u : u \in O^* \wedge tu \in F : u\}| \tag{14}$$
$$+ |\{u, v : u \in O^* \wedge (tu, v) \in S : (u, v)\}| = \infty : t\} \subseteq D$$

Note that Conditions (10), (12) and (14) together imply that $\{t, u : u \in O^* \wedge tu \in D : t\} \subseteq D$. Note also that, if $O \neq \emptyset$, then D can be defined to be

$\{t : |\{u : u \in O^* \wedge tu \in F : u\}| + |\{u, v : u \in O^* \wedge (tu, v) \in S : (u, v)\}| = \infty : t\}$,

Condition (13) becoming redundant because it follows from the definition of D and Conditions (7) and (9).

This time the conditions that we impose mean that our space of healthy tuples is not a complete lattice, but only a complete partial order (cpo) under the component-wise superset order.

6.2   Operators

The refinement order remains component-wise superset. Recursion is now the least fixed point with respect to this order.

As T, F and S have to be augmented to reflect the chaos that arises after divergence, we need new semantic functions $\text{traces}_\perp(P), \text{successes}_\perp(P), \text{failures}_\perp(P)$ and $\text{divergences}(P)$.

The semantic clauses for each operator will be omitted here, but it is worth making the following point. In the successes/failures/divergences model, if $t \in O^*$, then $(t \rightarrow \mathbf{div}) = \mathbf{div}$ and so $\mu X. (t \rightarrow X) = \mathbf{div}$. Thus the model is unsuitable for analysis of networks relying upon processes that output forever without waiting for input. The traces/successes/failures model should be used instead.

7   Conclusion

A mathematical framework has been developed for Data-Flow Sequential Processes, a CSP-like language that assumes buffered communication between processes. DFSP operators include **stop**, **skip**, **div**, recursion, reaction, unreading, after, nondeterministic choice, angelic choice, conditional choice, prefixing, guarded choice, sequential composition, iteration and parallel composition. Each term in DFSP denotes a process in an abstract model. The traces/successes/ failures model is an adaptation of the stable-failures model of CSP; the successes/ failures/divergences model is an adaptation of the failures/divergences model of CSP.

Upon termination of a process, the contents of its input streams and output streams remain available to its successor. It suffices to know how that successor behaves for the single case in which all of the streams are empty, in order to determine the effect of this sequential composition! This contrasts with the semantics of occam [26], for example. Stubs allow state information to be passed through a sequence of processes. Alternatively, Broy and Lengauer's approach [6] is adequate for nondeterministic choice, but does not handle angelic choice (as found in 'nonstrict merge', for example) [5]. Failures-based models are more expressive in this respect.

Note that program variables can be accommodated within DFSP: each variable is represented by an input stream on which read and unread actions are performed; their states are passed through stubs.

This paper has highlighted just a few of the algebraic laws of DFSP, focusing instead on its denotational semantics. As future work one might follow the same research agenda for DFSP as for CSP [27], namely, algebraic semantics, operational semantics, relationships between the various semantics, a full-abstraction result for the denotational models, a characterization of deterministic processes, application of the theory and provision of tool support.

Acknowledgment

The author is grateful to the anonymous reviewer for his insightful comments.

References

1. J.D. Brock, W.B. Ackerman. Scenarios: A Model of Non-Determinate Computation. In J. Dia, I. Ramos (editors) *Formalization of Programming Concepts*, Lect. Notes in Comp. Sci. **107**, pp. 252–259, Springer-Verlag, 1981.
2. S.D. Brookes. On the Kahn Principle and Fair Networks. Technical Report CMU-CS-98-156, School of Computer Science, Carnegie Mellon University, Pittsburg, USA, 1998.
3. S.D. Brookes. Traces, Pomsets, Fairness and Full Abstraction for Communicating Processes. In L. Brim, P. Janar, M. Ketinsky, A. Kuera (editors) *CONCUR 2002 — Concurrency Theory*, Lect. Notes in Comp. Sci. **2421**, pp. 466–482, Springer-Verlag, 2002.
4. S.D. Brookes, A.W. Roscoe. An improved failures model for CSP. In S.D. Brookes (editor) *seminar on Semantics of Concurrency*, Lect. Notes in Comp. Sci. **197**, pp. 281–305, Springer-Verlag, 1985.
5. M. Broy. A Theory for Nondeterminism, Parallelism, Communication, and Concurrency. *Theoretical Computer Science* **45**, pp. 1–61, 1986.
6. M. Broy, C. Lengauer. On Denotational versus Predicative Semantics. *Journal of Computer and System Sciences* **42**(1), pp. 1–29, 1991.
7. K.M. Chandy, J. Misra. Reasoning about networks of communicating processes. *Unpublished.* Presented at INRIA Advanced NATO Study Institute on Logics and Models for Verification and Specification of Concurrent Systems, La Colle-sur-Loupe, France, 1984.
8. J.L. Gischer. The Equational Theory of Pomsets. *Theoretical Computer Science* **62**, pp. 299–224, 1988.
9. He Jifeng, M.B. Josephs, C.A.R. Hoare. A Theory of Synchrony and Asynchrony. In M. Broy, C.B. Jones (editors) *Programming Concepts and Methods*, pp. 459–478, Elsevier Science Publishers (North-Holland), 1990.
10. E.C.R. Hehner. Predicative Programming Part II. *Communications of the ACM* **27**(2), pp. 144–151, 1984.
11. C.A.R. Hoare. A model for communicating sequential processes. In R.M. McKeag, A.M. MacNaughten (editors) *On the construction of programs*, pp. 229–254, Cambridge University Press, 1980.
12. C.A.R. Hoare. *Communicating Sequential Processes.* Prentice Hall, 1985.
13. C.A.R. Hoare, He Jifeng. *Unifying Theories of Programming.* Prentice Hall, 1998.
14. B. Jonsson. A model and proof system for asynchronous networks. Proc. 4th Annual ACM Symp. on Principles of Distributed Computing, pp. 49–58, 1985.
15. M.B. Josephs, Receptive process theory. *Acta Informatica* **29**, pp. 17–31, 1992.

16. M.B. Josephs, C.A.R. Hoare, He Jifeng. A theory of asynchronous processes. Technical Report PRG-TR-6-89, Oxford University Computing Laboratory, Oxford, England, 1989.

17. G. Kahn. The semantics of a simple language for parallel programming. In J.L. Rosenfeld (editor) *Information Processing '74*, pp. 471–475, North-Holland, 1974.

18. G. Kahn, D.B. MacQueen. Coroutines and networks of parallel processes. In B. Gilchrist (editor) *Information Processing '77*, pp. 993–998, North-Holland, 1977.

19. P.G. Lucassen. A Denotational Model and Composition Theorems for a Calculus of Delay-Insensitive Specifications. PhD Thesis, University of Groningen, Groningen, The Netherlands, 1994.

20. W.C. Mallon. Theories and Tools for the Design of Delay-Insensitive Communicating Processes. PhD Thesis, University of Groningen, Groningen, The Netherlands, 2000.

21. A. Mazurkiewicz. Concurrent Program Schemes and their Interpretation. Technical Report DAIMI PB-78, Århus University, Denmark, 1977.

22. E.-R. Olderog, C.A.R. Hoare. Specification-Oriented Semantics for Communicating Processes. *Acta Informatica* **23**, pp. 9–66, 1986.

23. P. Panangaden, V. Shanbhogue. The Expressive Power of Indeterminate Dataflow Primitives. *Information and Computation* **98**, pp. 99–131, 1992.

24. V.R. Pratt. On the composition of processes. Proc. 9th Annual ACM Symp. on Principles of Programming Languages, pp. 213–223, 1982.

25. V.R. Pratt. Modeling Concurrency with Partial Orders. *International Journal of Parallel Programming* **15**(1), pp. 33–71, 1986.

26. A.W. Roscoe. Denotational semantics for occam. In S.D. Brookes, A.W. Roscoe, G. Winskel (editors) *Seminar on Concurrency, Lecture Notes in Computer Science* **197**, pp. 306–321, Springer-Verlag, 1984.

27. A.W. Roscoe. *The Theory and Practice of Concurrency.* Prentice Hall, 1998.

28. J.T. Udding. Classification and Composition of Delay-Insensitive Circuits. PhD Thesis, Eindhoven University of Technology, Eindhoven, The Netherlands, 1984.

Implementation of Handshake Components

Ad Peeters

Handshake Solutions, Philips Electronics, Eindhoven, The Netherlands
Ad.Peeters@philips.com
http://www.handshakesolutions.com

Abstract. Handshake Technology is a clockless design style for digital circuits, targeted at applications where low energy consumption and ease of integration are essential. Communicating Sequential Processes play a role at various levels of representation. The design-entry language has parallel composition operators, communication channels for broadcast and narrowcast, and input and output actions on these channels. The intermediate architecture is based on Handshake Circuits, which is a network of components connected by handshake channels. In the implementation of these components in VLSI, models of communication again play a role.

This paper presents how in Handshake Technology the specification and implementation of handshake components is addressed. It is based on a formal definition of handshake protocols, and outlines the obligation for an implementor to establish a relation between handshake events in the implementation and the specification. Examples of two phase, four phase, and spurious-acknowledge implementations of handshake control circuits are discussed.

1 Introduction

Communicating Sequential Processes [1, 2] play a role in all approaches towards the design of asynchronous VLSI circuits — for good reasons. First of all, today's VLSI circuits present a medium with an abundant amount of parallelism, for which CSP has native operators, both in the language and its formalisms. Secondly, asynchronous circuits in particular require an explicit handling of communication between parallel processes, since one cannot rely on the magic presence of a clock for synchronization. In addition, the abstraction level of channel communication in CSP is just right, whether that has been intentionally or not. On the one hand, the use of atomic input and output actions abstracts from the way this is to be implemented, which makes it an extremely useful primitive for design and modeling languages. On the other hand, the input/output mechanism is buffer free, which makes it well-suited for hardware implementation, where unbuffered implementation is thus left open as an option. This combination allows for simple and cheap implementation, such in contrast to e.g. the unbounded buffering primitives in Kahn process networks [3].

CSP is omnipresent in Handshake Technology, which is an extremely disciplined asynchronous circuit style developed at Philips Research between 1986

A.E. Abdallah, C.B. Jones, and J.W. Sanders (Eds.): CSP25, LNCS 3525, pp. 98–132, 2005.

and 2001. This technology has been applied in dozens of products in domains such as wireless communication (pagers, cordless telephones, game controllers), identification (e-passports and smartcards for access control, public transport, credit cards, e-purses, and combinations of such functions), and automotive (various in-vehicle control networks).

In this paper we discuss the implementation of Handshake Technology, in which we focus on the implementation of handshake protocols in handshake components. Many different implementations are possible. To properly address their correctness, a formalization of handshake protocols is required, and the relation between implementation and specification must be covered. This has been established by introducing a formal notion of handshake channels, and one for handshake implementations. It is the obligation of an implementor to present a so-called *handshake reduction*, which specifies which events in an implementation are to be interpreted as which handshake events in the specification. Such a reduction also introduces the inverse challenge, namely given a specification to find implementations that *modulo* the reduction will satisfy the specification.

1.1   Handshake Technology

We use the term *Handshake Technology* to refer to the rigorous asynchronous circuit style and associated tool set that has been developed since 1986 at Philips Research, and which today is commercialized by Handshake Solutions. The idea behind this technology is to make the potential benefits of asynchronous circuits available to designers that are specialists in application domains rather than in the domain of gate-level asynchronous circuit design. To that end a design flow has been developed in which the circuit level details are hidden for the designer. This design flow is shown in Fig. 1, and is described briefly here. For a more detailed introduction we refer to [4, 5, 6, 7, 8]. A handshake technology tool set has also been developed by Manchester University, under the name Balsa [9, 10].

Handshake circuits [6] form the central representation in the Handshake Technology design flow. A handshake circuit is a network of handshake components, which use handshake protocols to communicate with each other and the environment. At the handshake circuit level, the specific handshake protocols and data encoding for implementation in e.g. VLSI are not determined yet.

The asynchronous knowledge is hidden in the *Handshake Compiler*, which is based on a library that specifies the implementation of each handshake component for a given handshake protocol and a given standard-cell library. The library consists of some fifty different components, most of them parameterized in e.g., the type of data (signed, unsigned), the number of bits for data, and the number of handshake ports.

If a designer would have access only to the library of components and the handshake compiler, then productivity would still be low. That is why a design language has been added on top of this. The design language, called *Haste* (formerly known as Tangram) [11], can be considered as a parallel programming language, and has constructs for parallelism and synchronized channel communication that are borrowed directly from CSP. Naturally it also supports sequential

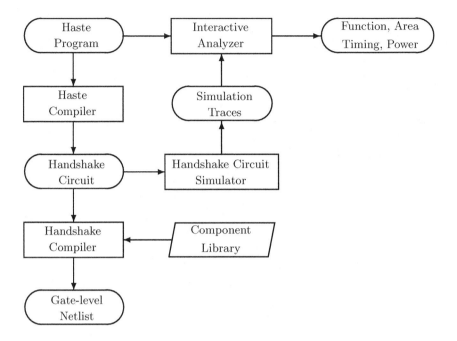

Fig. 1. The Handshake Technology design flow: boxes denote design tools, ovals denote design representations

composition, data-dependent guarded command constructs, datapath operators, procedures, functions, and modular compilation. The compilation from Haste to handshake circuits by the Haste compiler is syntax-directed and transparent [4,5], which means that a designer can make design decisions at the Haste level, and have predictable results.

The design flow offers a simulator at the handshake circuit level, and an interactive analysis tool that enables the inspection of simulation results directly at the Haste level. The compilation to gate-level implementations also includes support for logic optimization, timing characterization, test-pattern generation, and placement and routing, all based on standard third-party EDA tools.

1.2   Outline

In this paper we focus on the step from a handshake circuit to a gate-level netlist, and then particularly on the handshake protocols that can be used for the control part of such a circuit. We start with the formalization of handshake protocols by introducing handshake channels and handshake descriptions. Several implementations of handshake channels then pass in review, such as two-phase, four-phase, and spurious-acknowledge handshake protocols. Subsequently, handshake components are introduced, and several implementations are presented to illustrate the lifting of protocol implementation from channels to components.

2   Handshake Protocols

This section introduces a formal framework in which handshake protocols and implementations thereof can be discussed. The central notion is that of a handshake channel, which is used to describe handshake protocols. Implementations can be related to this by means of so-called handshake reduction. This is illustrated by several examples, such as two- and four-phase handshake implementations.

2.1   Handshake Channels

Handshake signaling is a communication protocol that establishes point-to-point synchronization. A handshake involves two partners which play a different role, called *active* and *passive*. The partners exchange so-called *request* and *acknowledge* signals. The passive partner waits for a request to arrive and after receipt of such a request responds with sending an acknowledge. The active partner starts with issuing a request and then waits for the corresponding acknowledge to arrive. Such a combination of a request and an acknowledge is called a handshake.

In this paper we assume the active and passive roles to be fixed, which means that one partner will always be active, and the other will always be passive. The communication medium between the partners is called a *handshake channel*. Throughout this paper we conform to the convention to denote an active handshake partner with a fat dot (●), and a passive partner with an open circle (○), see Fig. 2.

One may think of handshake communication as the exchange of tokens. Initially the active partner has the token. Sending a request is then interpreted as passing the token from the active to the passive partner. An acknowledge is represented by sending the token from the passive to the active partner. The fat dot and open circle can then be thought of as indicating the initial distribution of the tokens.

A handshake essentially synchronizes the active and the passive partner. In addition to pure synchronization, handshakes can also establish communication between the partners by encoding data in the request, in the acknowledge, or in both.

Handshake channels with no data encoded are called *nonput* channels. A handshake on a nonput channel establishes a synchronization only; no data is communicated.

The second type of handshake channels are those with data encoded in the request. These channels connect an active sender and a passive receiver. So,

Fig. 2. A handshake channel represents the communication medium between an active and a passive handshake partner

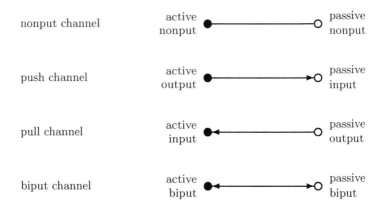

Fig. 3. Symbols for the four types of handshake channels

the sender takes the initiative for a communication action. One might say that the sender *pushes* the data through the channel, therefore these channels are referred to as *push* channels. From a data-flow point of view, push channels are *data driven.*

On a *pull* handshake channel data is encoded in the acknowledge. Such a channel connects a passive sender and an active receiver. The sender issues data after receiving a request from the receiver, so one could say that the receiver *pulls* the data through the channel. From a data-flow perspective, pull channels are *demand driven.*

The fourth type of handshake channels are *biput* channels, on which data is encoded in both the request and the acknowledge. One handshake then establishes the exchange of values between the two partners. The active partner now initiates the handshake by sending data to the passive partner. The passive partner then responds by sending data back. The handshake partners alternatingly act as sender and receiver.

The four types of handshake channels are depicted in Fig. 3. On data channels, arrows indicate the direction(s) of data-flow.

A formalization of the relation between handshake protocols and implementations thereof requires a formal specification of handshake protocols. This is captured in the definition of handshake channels given below.

A handshake protocol is the sequence of events that can be observed on a handshake channel. In a handshake, two types of events can be distinguished, namely *request* and *acknowledge* events. It is therefore relevant to distinguish these two types in the formalization. The behavior that can be observed by recording the sequence of events at handshake channels are characterized by handshake traces, which are sequences of events that satisfy the *semaphore* property [12, 13]. In these traces, request and acknowledge symbols alternate, and the first symbol (if any) is a request symbol.

Definition 1 (Handshake Channel, $\mathcal{H}$).
A handshake channel h is a triple $\langle \text{req}(h), \text{ack}(h), \text{trc}(h) \rangle$. The sets $\text{req}(h)$ and $\text{ack}(h)$ are disjoint, non-empty sets of request and acknowledge symbols. The set of handshake symbols, $\text{req}(h) \cup \text{ack}(h)$, is denoted by $\text{sym}(h)$.

The *handshake traces* of h, denoted by $\text{trc}(h)$, is the set of traces defined by $\text{sem}(\text{req}(h), \text{ack}(h))$, where, for disjoint non-empty sets R and A, set $\text{sem}(R, A)$ is defined by:

$$\text{sem}(R, A) = \{t : t \in (R \cup A)^* \wedge (\forall s : s \le t : 0 \le len(s \lceil R) - len(s \lceil A) \le 1) : t\}$$

A handshake channel is uniquely defined by its request and acknowledge set, which is also called its *signature*. The handshake channel with request set R and acknowledge set A (signature $\langle R, A \rangle$) is denoted by $\mathcal{H}(R, A)$. The set of all handshake channels is denoted by $\mathcal{H}$.   □

A *nonput* channel is a handshake channel for which both the request and the acknowledge set consist of only one symbol. The request set of a *push* handshake channel contains at least two symbols, representing the different data that can be communicated; its acknowledge set exactly one symbol. A *pull* handshake channel is characterized by a singleton request set and an acknowledge set containing at least two (data) symbols. For push and pull channels the set of data items is also called the *type* of that channel.

For a handshake channel p with a singleton request set we generally use p_r to represent that request. In the case where the acknowledge set of p contains only one element we use p_a. When representing sequences of events (traces) we use $p_a(x)$ to denote the communication of x in the acknowledge of p (for $x \in \text{ack}(p)$). Similarly, we use $p_r(x)$ to denote request x on handshake channel p (for $x \in \text{req}(p)$). If it is clear from the context with which handshake channel an event is associated we sometimes omit the $p_r()$ and $p_a()$.

A push handshake channel a used to communicate booleans can be modeled by $\mathcal{H}(\{true, false\}, \{a_a\})$. A trace that may be observed on channel a is

$$a_r(true)\ a_a\ a_r(false)\ a_a\ a_r(false).$$

This may also be described by

$$true\ a_a\ false\ a_a\ false.$$

This trace describes the communication of the value *true*, which is acknowledged by a_a. After this the value *false* is communicated and acknowledged, and *false* is communicated again. The receipt of this last value has not yet been acknowledged by the receiver.

Similarly, $\mathcal{H}(\{a_r\}, \{-1, 0, 1\})$ can be used to model a pull channel for three-valued symbols (trits), on which in each handshake the receiver first requests new data, which is then acknowledged by sending a value from the set of symbols. A sequence that may be observed on this channel is $a_r\ 0\ a_r\ -1\ a_r\ 1$, or alternatively $a_r\ a_a(0)\ a_r\ a_a(-1)\ a_r\ a_a(1)$.

In the rest of the paper we typically use regular expressions to define trace sets. The traces for a push boolean channel would be specified by expression $*((true \mid false); a_a)$, these for the pull trits channels by $*(a_r; (-1 \mid 0 \mid 1))$.

3 Handshake Implementation

Handshake communication can be implemented many different ways. The goal of this section is to formalize the relation between handshake specifications and these implementations. This relation is established in two steps, called *abstraction* and *reduction*. The inverse operations corresponding to these two are realization and refinement, respectively. The relation between the various terms introduced in this section is illustrated in Fig. 4.

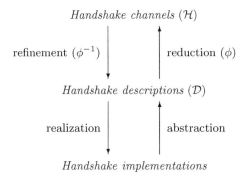

Fig. 4. Location of terms; up arrows refer to functions, down arrows refer to relations

3.1 Handshake Descriptions

We presume that any implementation of a handshake protocol can be described by three characteristics, namely, the request and acknowledge events that can be distinguished and the sequences of such events that can be observed. To capture this we introduce handshake descriptions.

Definition 2 (Handshake Description).
A handshake description D is a triple $\langle \mathrm{req}(D), \mathrm{ack}(D), \mathrm{trc}(D) \rangle$, where $\mathrm{req}(D)$ and $\mathrm{ack}(D)$ are non-empty, disjoint sets of symbols, and $\mathrm{trc}(D)$ is a prefix-closed non-empty set of traces over $\mathrm{sym}(D) = \mathrm{req}(D) \cup \mathrm{ack}(D)$.
The set of all handshake descriptions is denoted by $\mathcal{D}$.   □

One may observe that in the definition of handshake descriptions, request and acknowledge events are distinguished, but alternation of these events in the trace set is not required. This allows for redundant events that do not obey the semaphore (alternation) property. This redundancy is filtered out by a so-called handshake reduction, which will be presented shortly.

3.2 Handshake Abstraction

The relation between a 'physical' implementation and its (handshake) description is usually straightforward. In CMOS implementations, typically wires are used to implement handshake channels. The events that can be observed at these wires are *transitions*, that is, changes between low and high voltages.

We distinguish up (from low to high) and down (from high to low) transitions in the abstractions. Transitions on wires are denoted by pairs, identifying the wire and the direction of the transition. For a wire w an up transition is denoted by $\langle w, \uparrow \rangle$ and a down transition by $\langle w, \downarrow \rangle$. As shorthands $w\uparrow$ and $w\downarrow$ are used.

We do not formalize abstractions further. Some work has been done by others to formalize transitions with dynamical systems theory [14]. There appears to be a relation between restrictions on the phase diagram and proper complete monotonic transitions. These restrictions are also practical in the sense that they are required to guarantee proper sequential behavior of an asynchronous circuit [15, 16].

3.3   Handshake Reduction

Handshake reduction formalizes the relation between a description of an implementation of a handshake protocol and its specification as a handshake channel. A reduction defines which events have to be interpreted as the actual requests and which as the actual acknowledges.

In general a handshake reduction is a function from handshake descriptions ($\mathcal{D}$) to handshake channels ($\mathcal{H}$) that satisfies certain restrictions.

The basis of a reduction is formed by a (partial) function that maps symbols (events) from $\mathcal{D}$ onto symbols from $\mathcal{H}$. This function is referred to as the *kernel* of the reduction.

Definition 3 (Handshake Reduction).
A (handshake) reduction ϕ is a function $\mathcal{D} \mapsto \mathcal{H}$, derived from the partial function (kernel) ϕ that maps symbols from $\mathcal{D}$ onto symbols from $\mathcal{H}$.

Let $D \in \mathcal{D}$, then the request, acknowledge, and trace set of $\phi(D)$ are defined by

- $\mathrm{req}(\phi(D)) = \phi(\mathrm{req}(D)) = \{x : x \in \mathrm{req}(D) \wedge \phi(x) \text{ is defined} : \phi(x)\}$;
- $\mathrm{ack}(\phi(D)) = \phi(\mathrm{ack}(D)) = \{x : x \in \mathrm{ack}(D) \wedge \phi(x) \text{ is defined} : \phi(x)\}$;
- $\mathrm{trc}(\phi(D)) = \phi(\mathrm{trc}(D)) = \{t : t \in \mathrm{trc}(D) : \phi(t)\}$.

The trace set of $\phi(D)$ is based on function ϕ which is obtained by lifting kernel ϕ to traces. This lifting is the constructive part of the reduction and should satisfy the following rules.

1. $\phi(\varepsilon) = \varepsilon$,
2. For all $s \in \mathrm{trc}(D), x \in \mathrm{sym}(D)$ such that $s\,x \in \mathrm{trc}(D)$:
   if $\phi(x)$ is defined,
     then $\phi(s\,x) \in \{\phi(s), \phi(s)\,\phi(x)\}$,
     else $\phi(s\,x) = \phi(s)$.   □

The rationale behind the above definition is simple. The kernel defines with which handshake event an event from $\mathcal{D}$ has to be associated. This is a partial function, which implies that some events in the descriptions may be redundant to the handshake protocol.

From the kernel, reductions can be constructed. This construction is based on lifting the kernel from symbols to traces. In this lifting, there is a choice in defining the reduction of traces $s\,x$ for which the kernel of x ($\phi(x)$) is defined. This choice allows for redundant occurrences of handshake events, that is, events that are identified by the kernel as being handshake events may sometimes be ignored.

Most reductions that pass in review in throughout this paper do not allow for redundant handshake events. These reductions are called *direct* handshake reductions. Reductions that do allow for redundant occurrences of handshake events are called *spurious event* reductions.

Throughout this paper, handshake reductions are typically defined as direct reductions based on a kernel that maps transition events ($\langle w, \uparrow \rangle$ or $\langle w, \downarrow \rangle$) onto handshake events (w).

The reduction of a description need not necessarily result in a proper handshake channel, since alternation of requests and acknowledges is not guaranteed by the lifted version of the kernel reduction.

Definition 4 (Reduction Modulo ϕ).
Let ϕ be a handshake reduction, D a handshake description and H a handshake channel. Then H is the reduction modulo ϕ of D if and only if $\phi(D) = H$. $\square$

3.4   Handshake Refinement

Given a reduction it is interesting to know what behaviors in its domain of descriptions would result in proper handshakes. This is covered by *refinement*. A handshake description is called a refinement of a handshake channel if its reduction results in that handshake.

Definition 5 (Handshake Refinement).
Let ϕ be a handshake reduction, $D \in \mathcal{D}$, and $H \in \mathcal{H}$, then D is a refinement of H modulo ϕ if and only if $\phi(D) = H$. $\square$

An essential difference between reduction and refinement is that reduction is a function, whereas refinement is a relation. This means that given a handshake reduction ϕ and a handshake channel H, there may be more than one handshake description that is a refinement of H modulo ϕ.

3.5   Handshake Realization

Handshake realization is the inverse of handshake abstraction, similar to the relation between refinement and reduction. Realization is based on the abstraction function and defines how handshake descriptions can be implemented. In later sections handshake realization is applied to obtain implementations of handshake components.

3.6   Transition Descriptions

All handshake implementations addressed in this paper are targeted at VLSI implementation, which is why we will use a special class of handshake descriptions based on transition symbols and transition traces. Request and acknowledge events will thus consist of pairs of a wire name and a transition direction, and will be of the form $w \times \{\uparrow, \downarrow\}$. A restriction on the trace set of such descriptions is that for all wires the up and down transitions in any trace should alternate. In this paper we restrict ourselves to such descriptions where the initial state has all wires low, and hence the first transition is a rising one.

Definition 6 (Transition Descriptions, $\mathcal{D}_{\mathcal{T}}$).
A transition description d is a handshake description with $\text{sym}(d) = \text{req}(d) \cup \text{ack}(d) = \text{wires}(d) \times \{\uparrow, \downarrow\}$, in which $\text{wires}(d)$ is a non-empty set of symbols, and where the trace set $\text{trc}(d)$ is a prefix-closed trace set that satisfies the following alternation property:

$$(\forall s, x : s \in \text{trc}(d) \land x \in \text{wires}(d) : 0 \leq len(s\lceil x\uparrow) - len(s\lceil x\downarrow) \leq 1)$$

The set of all transition descriptions is denoted by $\mathcal{D}_{\mathcal{T}}$.   □

One may observe that both up and down transitions on a certain wire should be in the symbol set, but should not necessarily be both requests or both acknowledges.

4   Handshake Protocols for Control

In this section several implementations for control (nonput) handshake channels are reviewed. For each protocol the corresponding description and reduction are given.

4.1   Two Phase

In two-phase handshake protocols *each* transition in an implementation has a meaning, so there is no redundancy, neither in the symbol set, nor in the trace set of the corresponding handshake description. The two-phase handshake reduction is therefore rather straightforward, as it simply abstracts from the direction of the transitions. Two-phase handshaking is also known as transition or two-stroke signaling.

Definition 7 (Transition Handshake Channel, $\mathcal{T}$).
A transition handshake channel h with request r and acknowledge a, denoted by $\mathcal{T}(\{r\}, \{a\})$, is a handshake structure

$$\langle \{r\uparrow, r\downarrow\}, \{a\uparrow, a\downarrow\}, \text{trc}(*(r\uparrow\,; a\uparrow\,; r\downarrow\,; a\downarrow))\rangle$$

The set of all such channels is denoted by $\mathcal{T}$ (clearly $\mathcal{T} \subset \mathcal{D}_{\mathcal{T}}$).   □

The two-phase handshake reduction is a direct reduction of $\mathcal{T}$ in which no event is redundant. The kernel of this reduction is therefore simple; it strips the direction of the transition from the symbols.

Definition 8 (Two-phase Reduction, ϕ_2).
For a transition handshake channel h, its two-phase reduction $\phi_2(h)$ is the direct handshake reduction based on the following kernel function. For all $x \in \text{wires}(h)$: $\phi_2(x\uparrow) = x$, and $\phi_2(x\downarrow) = x$. □

The absence of redundancy implies that the inverse of ϕ_2 is also a function. This two-phase refinement alternatingly extends occurrences of symbols with up and down transitions.

Two-phase control handshaking is commonly explained using the timing diagram of Fig. 5. It is based on two wires, *req*, and *ack*, both assumed to be initially low. Two kinds of handshakes can then be distinguished, namely *Up* (*req*↑ *ack*↑) and *Down* (*req*↓ *ack*↓). Up and Down handshakes alternate, and after an Up handshake all wires are high. After each Down handshake all wires are low.

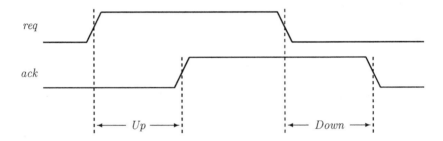

Fig. 5. Two-phase handshaking

The behavior on such channels can easily be described by recording the events in nonput transition handshakes. The timing diagram in Fig. 5 then depicts two consecutive handshakes of $\mathcal{T}(\{req\}, \{ack\})$. The reduction that defines the relation with plain handshakes channels is $\phi_2 : \mathcal{T} \mapsto \mathcal{H}$.

4.2 Four Phase

A communication in a four-phase handshake protocol consists of four phases. In the first two phases up-going request and acknowledge events take place. In the last two phases the equivalent down-going events take place. This means that in comparison to two-phase protocols, messages are sent twice, such that after each complete communication the channel is back in its initial state. Four-phase handshake protocols are also known as return-to-zero (RTZ), four-stroke, four-cycle, and level signaling.

For nonput channels we can re-use the transition handshake descriptions that were introduced for the two-phase protocol earlier. In a four-phase handshake protocol half of the events are redundant, since the handshake protocol requires only one request and one acknowledge event. Three kernel reductions can be identified that result in proper handshakes, namely, early, broad, and late. These reductions differ in the partition between redundant and functional handshake events.

Definition 9 (Four-phase Reduction, ϕ_4).
Three different four-phase reductions $\mathcal{T} \mapsto \mathcal{H}$ are defined, namely ϕ_{4b}, ϕ_{4e}, and ϕ_{4l}. For a transition handshake channel $\mathcal{T}(\{r\}, \{a\})$, these reductions are based on the following three kernel reductions:

- broad: $\phi_{4b}(r\uparrow) = r$, and $\phi_{4b}(a\downarrow) = a$.
- early: $\phi_{4e}(r\uparrow) = r$, and $\phi_{4e}(a\uparrow) = a$.
- late: $\phi_{4l}(r\downarrow) = r$, and $\phi_{4l}(a\downarrow) = a$.   □

Property 1. For symbols r and a, and reduction $\phi \in \{\phi_2, \phi_{4b}, \phi_{4e}, \phi_{4l}\}$, transition handshake channel $\mathcal{T}(\{r\}, \{a\})$ is a refinement modulo ϕ of $\mathcal{H}(\{r\}, \{a\})$ (and $\mathcal{H}(\{r\}, \{a\})$ is a reduction modulo ϕ of $\mathcal{T}(\{r\}, \{a\})$).   □

The three four-phase reductions that are defined for this protocol are depicted (for $\mathcal{T}(\{req\}, \{ack\})$) in the timing diagram in Fig. 6.

The *broad* reduction (sometimes referred to as *complete* four-phase [6]), defines the up-going request signal as its actual request, and the down-going acknowledge signal as its actual acknowledge.

The *early* reduction (sometimes referred to as *quick* four-phase [6]) filters out down-going requests and acknowledges. In this interpretation the down-going (return-to-zero) phase of the protocol is functionally redundant.

The counterpart of early is the *late* reduction, obtained by projection on down-going requests and acknowledges. When this reduction is applied the up-going phase of the handshake protocol is basically redundant.

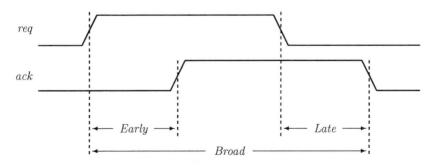

Fig. 6. Four-phase nonput handshake reductions

4.3   Spurious Events

The handshake reductions that have been introduced so far are all direct reductions, that is, no redundant occurrences of handshake events are allowed. This is reflected in the definition of transition handshake traces, which dictates a strict alternation of request and acknowledge symbols.

Spurious event protocols are a way of introducing more freedom in this behavior, which allows for more implementation freedom. Naturally, a restriction remains that one should still be able to reconstruct proper handshakes from the sequences of events (traces) that can be observed, which implies that a proper reduction must be defined for such protocols.

An interesting protocol turns out to be a four-phase *spurious acknowledge* protocol that allows for redundant acknowledge pulses to occur between true handshakes. The active partner of a handshake can ignore pulses on the acknowledge wire (pairs of up and down transitions) when the handshake protocol on that channel is in-active, that is, when its request wire is low. An example of such a scenario is sketched in Fig. 7. This protocol gives rise to some interesting non-trivial optimizations in control handshake circuits [7, 17]. The corresponding reduction is based on the kernel of the broad four-phase reduction.

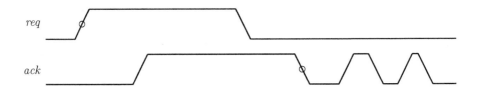

Fig. 7. A four-phase handshake followed by two spurious acknowledge pulses. The actual request and acknowledge events, which remain after reduction and constitute the reconstructed handshake, are marked by a circle

First the descriptions that characterize the (four-phase) spurious acknowledge protocol are introduced. A generalization towards spurious requests or the combination of the two is straightforward and omitted here.

Definition 10 (Spurious Acknowledge Descriptions, $\mathcal{S}_\mathcal{A}$).
For disjoint symbols r and a, spurious acknowledge description $\mathcal{S}_\mathcal{A}(\{r\}, \{a\})$ is a handshake structure

$$\langle \{r{\uparrow}, r{\downarrow}\}, \{a{\uparrow}, a{\downarrow}\}, \mathrm{trc}(*(\ (a{\uparrow} \,; a{\downarrow}) \mid (r{\uparrow} \,; a{\uparrow} \,; r{\downarrow} \,; a{\downarrow}) \ ))\rangle$$

The set of all spurious event descriptions is denoted by $\mathcal{S}_\mathcal{A}$.   □

The associated reduction, ϕ_{4s}, is based on the same kernel as the broad four-phase reduction. A direct lifting of this kernel to traces would result in a reduction that is equivalent to ϕ_{4b}. However, the lifting of ϕ_{4s} should filter out redundant events to arrive at proper handshakes. For the step to the trace set we introduce an auxiliary function φ_{4s} that has an additional parameter from $\{req, ack\}$, which encodes the expected handshake event.

Definition 11 (Spurious-event Reduction, ϕ_{4s}).
Let $d = \mathcal{S}_\mathcal{A}(\{r\}, \{a\})$ be a spurious-event description. The kernel of the reduction is characterized by $\phi_{4s}(r\!\uparrow) = r$ and $\phi_{4s}(a\!\downarrow) = a$.

For trace $t \in \text{trc}(d)$, $\phi_{4s}(t) = \varphi_{4s}(t, req)$, where φ_{4s} is defined as follows. For $x \in \text{sym}(d)$ and $s \in \text{sym}(d)^*$:

- $\varphi_{4s}(\varepsilon, req) = \varphi_{4s}(\varepsilon, ack) = \varepsilon$
- if $x \in \text{req}(d)$ and $\phi_{4s}(x)$ is defined
   then $\varphi_{4s}(x\,s, req) = \phi_{4s}(x)\,\varphi_{4s}(s, ack)$
   else $\varphi_{4s}(x\,s, req) = \varphi_{4s}(s, req)$
- if $x \in \text{ack}(d)$ and $\phi_{4s}(x)$ is defined
   then $\varphi_{4s}(x\,s, ack) = \phi_{4s}(x)\,\varphi_{4s}(s, req)$
   else $\varphi_{4s}(x\,s, ack) = \varphi_{4s}(s, ack)$

The lifting of the reduction from traces to descriptions is now standard:

$$\phi_{4s}(d) = \langle\{r\}, \{a\}, \phi_{4s}(\text{trc}(d))\rangle. \qquad\qquad \Box$$

Property 2. For symbols r and a, $\mathcal{H}(\{r\}, \{a\})$ is the reduction modulo ϕ_{4s} of $\mathcal{S}_\mathcal{A}(\{r\}, \{a\})$, and thus $\mathcal{S}_\mathcal{A}(\{r\}, \{a\})$ is a refinement modulo ϕ_{4s} of $\mathcal{H}(\{r\}, \{a\})$. Furthermore, $\mathcal{T}(\{r\}, \{a\})$ modulo $\phi_{4s} = \mathcal{H}(\{r\}, \{a\})$. $\qquad\qquad \Box$

5   Handshake Components

Handshake channels form the basis on which handshake components are built. The most important characteristic of a handshake component is its handshake interface, that is, the handshake channels via which it interacts with its environment. This interface restricts the behavior of the component, since it must adhere to the handshake protocol on all channels. The specification of a handshake component may furthermore impose additional restrictions on its behavior, such as mutual inclusion or exclusion of handshakes on certain channels.

The implementation of handshake components is also founded on handshake channels. An implementation comprises a choice of a handshake refinement *per* channel. This results in the notions reduction and refinement, but also abstraction and realization, built on these notions for handshake channels.

The way handshake components are treated in this paper differs notably from the way they are introduced in [6], in which handshake reduction is defined on the level of handshake circuits, that is, networks of handshake components. For all channels the same handshake reduction is then chosen. The approach taken here allows for a more general strategy when striving for efficient implementations of handshake circuits.

In this section we first formally introduce handshake components and the formal definitions of reduction and refinement. This is then applied to several

handshake components. An important class of components are protocol converters, which are refinements of so-called connectors, and which are used to convert
between different handshake reductions. These converters can be applied in the
implementation of other handshake components.

5.1   Handshake Component Descriptions

A handshake component interacts with its environment via handshakes. The
interface with its environment consists of so-called handshake ports, which come
in two flavors, namely *active* and *passive*.

The description of handshake components has to cover its relevant characteristics. First of all, the active and passive handshake ports have to be part
of the description. The distinction between active and passive is important for
components, because it dictates how to interact with the other partner in the
handshake on that port. The active handshake ports define on which handshake channels the component is supposed to initiate handshakes; the passive
handshake ports define the handshake channels on which the component should
acknowledge handshakes.

A second characteristic is the behavior, or the allowed sequences of events,
at the interface of the component. An essential restriction on the behavior is
that on each handshake channel the handshake protocol should be obeyed. If all
components would only follow this restriction, then it would not be possible to
build anything interesting from handshake components, so there is more to it.
In general a handshake component restricts its external behavior, for example,
to establish mutual exclusion in access to a resource, or to establish mutual
inclusion to synchronize two otherwise independent parties.

Most of these protocols can be described as a composition of a number of
handshake channels, where the behavior of the composite satisfies the conjunction of the constituent handshake protocols.

Definition 12 (Composition).
Let H be a set of handshake channels. The composition of H, denoted by
$\text{weave}(H)$, is the triple $\langle \text{req}(H), \text{ack}(H), \text{trc}(H) \rangle$ defined by:

- $\text{req}(H) = (\cup h : h \in H : \text{req}(h))$
- $\text{ack}(H) = (\cup h : h \in H : \text{ack}(h))$
- $\text{sym}(H) = (\cup h : h \in H : \text{sym}(h)) = \text{req}(H) \cup \text{ack}(H)$
- $\text{trc}(H) = \{t : t \in \text{sym}(H)^* \wedge (\forall h : h \in H : t\lceil \text{sym}(h) \in \text{trc}(h)) : t\}$ □

The request and acknowledge sets of the handshake channels in H may have
symbols in common. This is the interesting case, for this means that in the
definition of the trace set of H, the projection requirement is a restriction.

Definition 13 (Handshake Component).
A handshake component P is a triple $\langle \text{pas}(P), \text{act}(P), \text{trc}(P) \rangle$, in which $\text{pas}(P)$
and $\text{act}(P)$ are lists of handshake channels, and $\text{trc}(P)$ is the trace set of P.
Trace set $\text{trc}(P)$ should at least obey the handshake protocols at the individual
handshake channels. This is formalized in the following restrictions.

1. $\text{port}(P) = \text{pas}(P) \cup \text{act}(P) \subset \mathcal{H}$
2. $(\forall p, q : p, q \in \text{port}(P) \wedge p \neq q : \text{sym}(p) \cap \text{sym}(q) = \emptyset)$
3. $\text{trc}(P) \subseteq \text{trc}(\text{weave}(\text{port}(P)))$
4. $\text{trc}(P)$ is non-empty and prefix-closed

The pair $\langle \text{pas}(P), \text{act}(P) \rangle$ is called the *handshake signature* of P.   □

Two things can be noticed in this definition. First, the handshake channels involved should have disjoint symbol sets. This implies that two handshake channels should not share a signal. The motivation behind this requirement will become clear when refinements of handshake components are discussed in Sect. 6.2. The second observation is an implication of this, namely that, because the symbol sets of the handshake channels are disjoint, the composition (weave) of their traces does not introduce any additional restrictions.

The handshake components discussed in this paper generally impose additional restrictions on the trace set, and thereby enforce interaction between the different handshakes involved.

Now that we have handshake ports, we can also distinguish inputs and outputs. Inputs are events that are initiated by the environment of the component, and that are not under direct control of the component itself. Outputs, on the other hand, are initiated by the component and can be observed by the environment.

Definition 14 (Input, Output).
For handshake component P, its inputs and outputs are defined by

$$\text{in}(P) = (\cup p : p \in \text{pas}(P) : \text{req}(p)) \cup (\cup p : p \in \text{act}(P) : \text{ack}(p));$$
$$\text{out}(P) = (\cup p : p \in \text{pas}(P) : \text{ack}(p)) \cup (\cup p : p \in \text{act}(P) : \text{req}(p)).$$ □

6   Handshake Component Implementation

The definition of handshake components is based on handshake channels. It seems therefore a natural choice to introduce implementations of handshake components on basis of implementations of the handshake channels. The basic idea is that we can for each channel choose an implementation. The associated handshake reduction then identifies which events are relevant to the handshake protocol.

For handshake channels, handshake reduction was introduced as the essential function that relates specifications and implementations. For handshake components a derivative thereof is used. First of all the domain and codomain of such a function should be identified. Therefore we introduce handshake component descriptions, which are based on handshake channel descriptions. Basically, all concept that are introduced for handshake channels can be applied to handshake components as well, see Fig. 8.

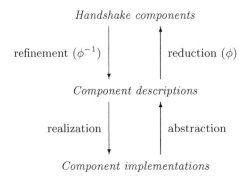

Fig. 8. Location of terms

6.1   Descriptions

Handshake channels are covered by $\mathcal{H}$, and for their implementation we can garner from $\mathcal{T}$ and $\mathcal{S}_\mathcal{A}$, and in general from $\mathcal{D}$. Since handshake components are composed from elements of $\mathcal{H}$ we can compose elements of $\mathcal{D}$ to obtain implementations of handshake components.

Definition 15 (Component Descriptions).
A handshake component description D is a triple $\langle \mathrm{pas}(D), \mathrm{act}(D), \mathrm{trc}(D)\rangle$, in which $\mathrm{pas}(D)$ and $\mathrm{act}(D)$ are lists of handshake channel descriptions, and $\mathrm{trc}(D)$ is the trace set of D.

1. The active and passive ports of D range over $\mathcal{D}$.
   $\mathrm{port}(D) = \mathrm{pas}(D) \cup \mathrm{act}(D) \subset \mathcal{D}$
2. Handshake ports have no symbols in common.
   $(\forall p, q : p, q \in \mathrm{port}(D) \wedge p \neq q : \mathrm{sym}(p) \cap \mathrm{sym}(q) = \emptyset)$
3. The trace set of D satisfies the handshake protocols of all constituent channels: $\mathrm{trc}(D) \subseteq \mathrm{trc}(\mathrm{weave}(\mathrm{port}(D)))$
   Alternatively: $(\forall d : d \in \mathrm{port}(D) : \mathrm{trc}(D)\lceil\mathrm{sym}(d) \subseteq \mathrm{trc}(d))$
4. $\mathrm{trc}(D)$ is non-empty and prefix-closed

The pair $\langle \mathrm{pas}(D), \mathrm{act}(D)\rangle$ is called the *handshake signature* of D.   □

Special handshake component descriptions can be identified for which the handshake channels involved range over a particular subset of handshake descriptions only. For control components, for example, the handshake channels are generally taken from $\mathcal{T}$ (and occasionally from $\mathcal{S}_\mathcal{A}$).

6.2   Reduction

Several handshake reductions for handshake channels have been introduced, which define, for an implementation of a handshake channel, which events are redundant and which events contribute to the handshake protocol. These reductions can be lifted to handshake components. With each handshake channel that is used to implement a handshake component a handshake reduction can be associated. The handshake reduction of the component description is then obtained by taking the handshake reductions on a per channel basis.

Definition 16 (Reduction).
Let P be a handshake component with $n \geq 0$ passive ports $\langle i : 0 \leq i < n : h_i \rangle$, and $m \geq 0$ active ports $\langle i : n \leq i < n + m : h_i \rangle$.
Furthermore, let D be a handshake component description with $n \geq 0$ passive ports $\langle i : 0 \leq i < n : d_i \rangle$, and $m \geq 0$ active ports $\langle i : n \leq i < n + m : d_i \rangle$.
Finally, let $L = \langle i : 0 \leq i < n + m : \phi_i \rangle$ be a list of handshake reductions from $\mathcal{D}$ to $\mathcal{H}$.

Component P is a reduction of D (and D a refinement of P) *modulo* L if the following conditions are satisfied.

1. $(\forall i : 0 \leq i < n + m : \phi_i(d_i) = h_i)$
2. $\phi_L(\mathrm{trc}(D)) = \mathrm{trc}(P)$

Reduction ϕ_L is defined inductively as follows.

1. $\phi_L(\varepsilon) = \varepsilon$
2. For trace $t \in \mathrm{trc}(D)$, $0 \leq i < n + m$, and $a \in \mathrm{sym}(d_i)$ such that $t\, a \in \mathrm{trc}(D)$:
   $\phi_L(t\, a) = \phi_L(t)\, \phi_i(a)$
3. $\phi_L(\mathrm{trc}(D)) = \{t : t \in \mathrm{trc}(D) : \phi_L(t)\}$ $\hfill\square$

6.3   Refinement

Now that we have lifted handshake reduction from handshake channels to handshake components, we have also defined the challenge of handshake refinement. One needs to choose a handshake protocol for each channel and then to come up with an appropriate component description that can be reduced to the specification using the reduction that was selected.

For the two-phase implementation of a handshake component, the refinement is trivial because it is a deterministic function. A four-phase implementation of a components is more challenging, as one can garner from the early, broad, late, and spurious protocol. This freedom of choosing different protocols, and the freedom that the redundant events offer in this choice, is sometimes referred to as *handshake reshuffling* [18].

Throughout this paper, refinements of nonput handshake channels are denoted by a, b, c, etcetera, and will be taken from transition handshake descriptions $\mathcal{T}$ and spurious-acknowledge descriptions $\mathcal{S_A}$.

6.4   Realization

Circuit realizations of handshake components can be arrived at by decomposing the behavior specified for the refinements of component specifications with the compilation method of Martin [18] for example. Other methods, such as automated STG-based tools such as Petrify [19] could also be applied. The way from transition components to CMOS circuits is not the main subject of this paper, so circuit implementations (when given) are postulated rather then derived. In the circuit diagrams, standard symbols are used for standard gates such as AND and OR gates [20]. The notation for typical asynchronous elements such as (generalized) C-elements and mutual-exclusion elements are adopted from [21].

In all handshake descriptions that have been introduced it is assumed that in the initial state all handshake wires are low. A circuit realization requires a procedure to force all handshake channels in their initial state. The property of *self-initialization* has been introduced [6] to avoid a global reset, and two forms of initialization play a role. A circuit realization of a handshake component is *weakly* initializable if all its outputs are forced low when all its inputs are low. The circuit is furthermore *strongly* initializable if in addition all outputs of all active ports can be forced low by making all inputs of all passive ports low.

Sometimes one can determine from the handshake refinement that any circuit realization thereof is not initializable. This is, for instance, the case for the late refinement of the connector component, cf. the D-element in Sect. 7.3. Self-initialization is generally hardly a constraint in the realization of early and broad refinements. Late refinements, however, are generally not initializable.

7   Protocol Converters

The *connector* handshake component is used for propagating handshakes. It has two nonput ports, one active and one passive. Such a component awaits a request on its passive port, propagates this on its active port, waits for the corresponding acknowledge, and propagates this via its passive port. A connector with passive port a and active port b thus satisfies not only handshake protocols $\mathcal{H}(\{a_r\}, \{a_a\})$ and $\mathcal{H}(\{b_r\}, \{b_a\})$ on its ports a and b, respectively, but in addition also adheres to $\mathcal{H}(\{a_r\}, \{b_r\})$ and $\mathcal{H}(\{b_a\}, \{a_a\})$. The specification and symbol for the connector are shown in Fig. 9.

The specification of the connector is not too interesting as it does not really perform a function. In a silicon compiler such as the Haste compiler system, it proves useful mostly as a renaming operator. Later in this section we discuss its use as protocol converter, where different handshake protocols are applied to the two handshake interfaces.

7.1   Connector

The most straightforward four-phase implementation of the connector is based on the two-phase refinement of the connector protocol, as specified in (1). This is

$$\text{CON}(a^\circ, b^\bullet) =$$
$$\langle\langle a\rangle, \langle b\rangle, \text{trc}(*(p_r \,;\, q_r \,;\, q_a \,;\, p_a))\rangle$$

Fig. 9. Specification and symbol for connector component

indeed a refinement modulo $\langle \phi_2, \phi_2 \rangle$ of the connector protocol, but a lot of other refinements can be applied as well. First of all, for all four-phase refinements ϕ_4 the specified behavior is also a refinement modulo $\langle \phi_4, \phi_4 \rangle$. Two mixtures can also be applied however, namely $\langle \phi_{4b}, \phi_{4e} \rangle$ and $\langle \phi_{4b}, \phi_{4l} \rangle$.

$$* (a_r\uparrow \, ; b_r\uparrow \, ; b_a\uparrow \, ; a_a\uparrow \, ; a_r\downarrow \, ; b_r\downarrow \, ; b_a\downarrow \, ; a_a\downarrow) \tag{1}$$

The implementation of this connector refinement is trivial; two wires are needed to do the renaming at the wire level, as shown in Fig. 10.

Fig. 10. Connector implementation

When different handshake reductions are used in a four-phase handshake circuit, protocol converters may be required. A *protocol converter* is a refinement of a connector with possibly different reductions for the active and the passive channel. An element is said to be a converter from protocol A to protocol B if it has the same port signature as the connector and its behavior according to reduction A on its passive channel a and reduction B on its active channel b satisfies the connector protocol.

7.2 S-Element

The *S-element* is a converter from early to broad. The four-phase refinement of the connector with early for the passive channel and broad for the active one is unique, that is, there is only one specification that satisfies these requirements, which is the fully sequential specification given in (2).

$$* (a_r\uparrow \, ; b_r\uparrow \, ; b_a\uparrow \, ; b_r\downarrow \, ; b_a\downarrow \, ; a_a\uparrow \, ; a_r\downarrow \, ; a_a\downarrow) \tag{2}$$

It is readily verified that the appropriate reduction (modulo $\langle \phi_{4e}, \phi_{4b} \rangle$) indeed results in the connector protocol. Five more reductions of (2) exist that result in the connector protocol, namely, all reductions $\langle \phi_{4e}, \phi_4 \rangle$ and $\langle \phi_{4b}, \phi_4 \rangle$ for all $\phi_4 \in \{\phi_{4e}, \phi_{4b}, \phi_{4l}\}$.

A speed-independent implementation of the S-element is depicted in Fig. 11. This circuit is also known as Q-element [18].

The S-element implementation shown here is strong initializable. When input a_r is forced low, output b_r immediately follows via the AND-gate, and the C-element's output goes high. This then forces a_a low. So, forcing the input of the passive channel low forces all outputs low and the state-holding element in a known state.

The asymmetric C-element may also be replaced by other asymmetric C-elements and even by a fully symmetric C-element. This does not change the initialization argument for b_r, but for a_a the cases where input b_a is low and high have to be distinguished. These both lead to a_a low.

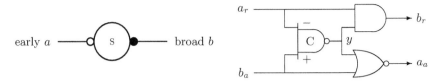

Fig. 11. S-element: symbol and implementation

7.3   D-Element

The *D-element* [18] converts from late to broad. Like the S-element, its behavior, given in (3) is fully sequential and unique.

$$* (a_r\uparrow ; a_a\uparrow ; a_r\downarrow ; b_r\uparrow ; b_a\uparrow ; b_r\downarrow ; b_a\downarrow ; a_a\downarrow) \tag{3}$$

Again, it can be readily verified that the behavior of the D-element modulo $\langle \phi_{4l}, \phi_4 \rangle$, for any $\phi_4 \in \{\phi_{4e}, \phi_{4b}, \phi_{4l}\}$ reduces to the connector protocol.

From the specified behavior in (3) one can already deduce that the D-element cannot be self initializable. After $a_r\downarrow$ the handshake on b still has to start, so b_r has to go high. This implies that making a_r low can never force b_r low. In Fig. 12 a speed-independent implementation of the D-element is given with an active-high reset (*res*).

7.4   T-Element

The *T-element* is a four-phase refinement of the connector that only sequences the up-going phase of the handshake protocol and then synchronizes again at the end. It thus decouples the return-to-zero phase of b from that of a.

The protocol for the T-element is given by

$$* (a_r\uparrow ; b_r\uparrow ; b_a\uparrow ; (a_a\uparrow ; a_r\downarrow \parallel b_r\downarrow ; b_a\downarrow) ; a_a\downarrow). \tag{4}$$

In terms of Martin's handshake notation this protocol is specified as follows:

$$*([a_r] ; b_r\uparrow ; [b_a] ; (a_a\uparrow \parallel b_r\downarrow) ; [\neg a_r \wedge \neg b_a] ; a_a\downarrow).$$

Three reductions of the T-element behavior result in the connector protocol, namely, modulo $\langle \phi_{4b}, \phi_{4b} \rangle$, modulo $\langle \phi_{4e}, \phi_{4e} \rangle$, and modulo $\langle \phi_{4b}, \phi_{4e} \rangle$. The T-element can thus be used as a broad or as an early connector, and as a converter

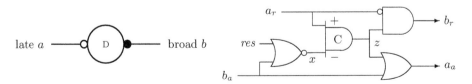

Fig. 12. D-element: symbol and implementation

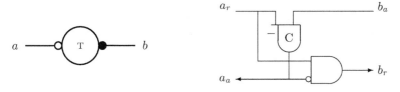

Fig. 13. T-element: symbol and implementation

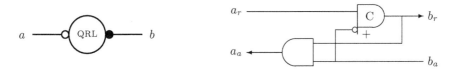

Fig. 14. Quick Return Linkage: symbol and implementation

from broad to early. On the other hand, the reduction according to the late protocol, for instance, violates the connector specification.

A speed-independent implementation of the T-element is given in Fig. 13. The T-element is also known as 'autosweeping module' (ASM in [22]), and is used in the implementation of the parallel in [23]. In this paper it is used in the implementation of an early sequencer (Sect. 8) and the parallel (Sect. 9).

7.5   Quick Return Linkage

The *Quick Return Linkage* (QRL) [24, 25], which is generally contributed to Seitz, is a protocol converter that is specified by:

$$a_r\uparrow\,; *(b_r\uparrow\,; b_a\uparrow\,; a_a\uparrow\,; a_r\downarrow\,; (a_a\downarrow\,; a_r\uparrow \parallel b_r\downarrow\,; b_a\downarrow)) \tag{5}$$

The QRL acts as a connector in the up-going phase and after this decouples the return-to-zero phase on the active port from that of the passive port. Essentially it thereby gives an early acknowledge. It can therefore be used as an 'early' connector and as a converter from 'broad' to 'early.' So, the QRL is a refinement modulo $\langle\phi_{4e}, \phi_{4e}\rangle$, and modulo $\langle\phi_{4b}, \phi_{4e}\rangle$, of the connector protocol.

The QRL is insensitive to spurious acknowledgements on its active port. It is applied in interfaces, for example to handshake with a clock-signal, which is then connected to b_a. A possible speed-independent implementation is given in Fig. 14. The implementation of the QRL sequences the two outputs $b_r\downarrow$ and $a_a\downarrow$, thereby exploiting the implementation freedom of the specification, which allows for parallelism between these events.

The specification in terms of traces does not give too much insight in the operation of the QRL. A more operational specification can be given in terms of Martin's handshake notation, because inputs and outputs are then explicit. The operation of QRL is then specified by:

$$*([a_r \wedge \neg b_a]\,; b_r\uparrow\,; [b_a]\,; a_a\uparrow\,; [\neg a_r]\,; (a_a\downarrow \parallel b_r\downarrow)).$$

Filtering out the actions of the a-protocol gives $*([\neg b_a] ; b_r\uparrow ; [b_a] ; b_r\downarrow)$, a protocol that is also known as the *lazy active* protocol [18].

7.6   Spurious-Ack Filter

A *spurious acknowledgement filter* is a protocol converter from early, broad, or late to the spurious acknowledge protocol. It allows for redundant events on its active port (as long as it has not been activated along its passive port) and it prevents propagation of these redundant acknowledges to the passive side, cf. (6). One may observe that this restricts the behavior of the environment as well, as redundant events are not allowed while a handshake on a is in progress.

$$* ((a_r\uparrow ; b_r\uparrow ; b_a\uparrow ; a_a\uparrow ; a_r\downarrow ; b_r\downarrow ; b_a\downarrow ; a_a\downarrow) \mid (b_a\uparrow ; b_a\downarrow)) \qquad (6)$$

The symbol and implementation for this filter are given in Fig. 15. The asymmetric C-elements will filter out pulses on b_a while a_r is low, and propagate them when a_r is high.

Fig. 15. Symbol and implementation of spurious ack filter

8   Sequencer

A *sequencer* is a handshake component with one passive ports and several active ports. When activated along its passive port, it will sequentially perform a handshake on each active port in order, and then complete the handshake on its passive 'activation' port. A sequencer with passive port a and n ($n \geq 1$) active ports $b(i)$ ($0 \leq i < n$) is specified (in addition to the handshake protocols on the individual ports) by handshake protocols $\mathcal{H}(\{a_r\}, \{b(0)_r\})$, $\mathcal{H}(\{b(i)_a\}, \{b(i+1)_r\})$ (for all i, $0 \leq i < n-1$), and $\mathcal{H}(\{b(n-1)_a\}, \{a_a\})$.

One may observe that for $n = 1$ the sequencer is equivalent to a connector. The first interesting case is the binary sequencer given in Fig. 16. We first address this component further and then briefly discuss the implementation of the multi-channel sequencer.

The two-phase refinement of the sequencer is unique, and given in (7).

$$* (a_r\uparrow ; b_r\uparrow ; b_a\uparrow ; c_r\uparrow ; c_a\uparrow ; a_a\uparrow ; a_r\downarrow ; b_r\downarrow ; b_a\downarrow ; c_r\downarrow ; c_a\downarrow ; a_a\downarrow) \qquad (7)$$

Reduction modulo ϕ_2 for all ports indeed results in the sequencer specification. This refinement of the sequencer can be implemented with wires only, as depicted in Fig. 17.

$$\text{SEQ}(a^\circ, b^\bullet, c^\bullet) =$$
$$\langle\langle a\rangle, \langle b, c\rangle, \text{trc}(*(a_r\,;b_r\,;b_a\,;c_r\,;c_a\,;a_a)))\rangle$$

Fig. 16. Specification and symbol of binary sequencer

The two-phase refinement also satisfies some four-phase reductions. The most straightforward reductions that apply are those that select the up or down cycles of the two-phase refinement, that is, the reduction modulo ϕ_{4e} for all ports, and the reduction modulo ϕ_{4l} for all ports. The four-phase reductions of (7) that result in the sequencer protocol are listed in Fig. 17. In the rest of this section, the two-phase wire-only sequencer implementation will be denoted by the same symbol as the sequencer in the specification in Fig. 16.

With respect to progress the wire-only sequencer has to be applied with care because the return-to-zero phase on b can only complete after the first (up) phase on c has been acknowledged. This might cause deadlock when the completion of the first phase on c depends on the completion of the return-to-zero phase on b.

The T-element can be used to decouple return-to-zero phases. If a T-element is connected to channel b, as depicted in Fig. 18, the sequencer still satisfies the early reduction and will not give rise to deadlock. The return-to-zero phase on c can furthermore be decoupled from the acknowledge on a by also adding a T-element to channel c.

The refinement that corresponds to the implementation in Fig. 18 is given in (8). It is clear that this refinement indeed allows for parallelism between the down-phase on b and the up-phase on c. This allows the handshake on b to complete before the first acknowledge on c is given.

$$* (a_r\uparrow\,;b_r\uparrow\,;b_a\uparrow\,;(b_r\downarrow\,;b_a\downarrow \,\|\, c_r\uparrow\,;c_a\uparrow\,;a_a\uparrow\,;a_r\uparrow)\,;c_r\downarrow\,;c_a\downarrow\,;a_a\downarrow) \qquad (8)$$

Several reductions of this refinement result in the sequencer protocol. First of all, the all-early reduction applies, and this is the only reduction with early on a. There is no reduction to the sequencer protocol with late on a. Four reductions with broad on a can be applied, three of which have early on b, as listed in Fig. 18.

Broad refinements of the sequencer can be obtained by applying protocol conversion to the two-phase refinement. Two possible refinements are give below.

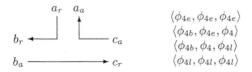

$$\langle\phi_{4e}, \phi_{4e}, \phi_{4e}\rangle$$
$$\langle\phi_{4b}, \phi_{4e}, \phi_4\rangle$$
$$\langle\phi_{4b}, \phi_4, \phi_{4l}\rangle$$
$$\langle\phi_{4l}, \phi_{4l}, \phi_{4l}\rangle$$

Fig. 17. Sequencer implementation and four-phase reductions of (7)

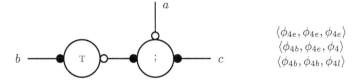

$\langle\phi_{4e},\phi_{4e},\phi_{4e}\rangle$
$\langle\phi_{4b},\phi_{4e},\phi_4\rangle$
$\langle\phi_{4b},\phi_{4b},\phi_{4l}\rangle$

Fig. 18. Early sequencer that avoids deadlock

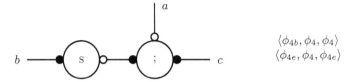

$\langle\phi_{4b},\phi_4,\phi_4\rangle$
$\langle\phi_{4e},\phi_4,\phi_{4e}\rangle$

Fig. 19. Broad sequencer based on S-element

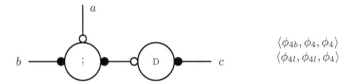

$\langle\phi_{4b},\phi_4,\phi_4\rangle$
$\langle\phi_{4l},\phi_{4l},\phi_4\rangle$

Fig. 20. Broad sequencer based on D-element

In the first one the protocol on b is converted from early to broad by adding an S-element. In the second one conversion from late to broad is applied to c by adding a D-element.

The implementation depicted in Fig. 19 is based on the refinement in (9), the implementation based on the D-element in Fig. 20 on (10). These refinements have in common that they are fully sequential, and that the behavior restricted to b and c is $*(b_r\uparrow;b_a\uparrow;b_r\downarrow;b_a\downarrow;c_r\uparrow;c_a\uparrow;c_r\downarrow;c_a\downarrow)$. Therefore we can apply any reduction to b and c, provided that we choose the broad reduction on a. Especially, the all-broad reduction applies, therefore these implementations are also called broad implementations.

$$* (a_r\uparrow;b_r\uparrow;b_a\uparrow;b_r\downarrow;b_a\downarrow;c_r\uparrow;c_a\uparrow;a_a\uparrow;a_r\downarrow;c_r\downarrow;c_a\downarrow;a_a\downarrow) \tag{9}$$

$$*(a_r\uparrow;b_r\uparrow;b_a\uparrow;a_a\uparrow;a_r\downarrow;b_r\downarrow;b_a\downarrow;c_r\uparrow;c_a\uparrow;c_r\downarrow;c_a\downarrow;a_a\downarrow) \tag{10}$$

For the implementation of multi-channel sequencers we can follow the same approach as for the binary sequencer, which was presented above. One can start with a wire-only backbone, e.g. consisting of a tree-structure, and then add converters to the leafs of this tree. In the Haste system this is exactly the approach that is followed. In general, a broad refinement may be preferred, especially when the sequencer has the task to guarantee mutual-exclusive access to a shared resource, e.g. through a mixer, cf. Sect. 10. However, several cases exist where wire-only or T-element branches can be exploited, for instance when interfacing to a non-handshake environment via QRL elements. Several efficient multi-channel sequencer implementations based on broad-only refinements are presented in [26].

9   Parallel

The *parallel* component has the same handshake signature as the sequencer. When activated along its passive port, it sends a request on each active port, then waits until each handshake has completed, and subsequently signals this by sending an acknowledge on its passive channel. A parallel component with passive port a and n $(n \geq 1)$ active ports $b(i)$ $(0 \leq i < n)$ is thus specified (in addition to the handshake protocols on the individual ports) by handshake protocols $\mathcal{H}(\{a_r\}, \{b(i)_r\})$ and $\mathcal{H}(\{b(i)_a\}, \{a_a\})$ (for all i, $0 \leq i < n$).

For $n = 1$ the parallel is equivalent to a connector. The simplest interesting case is the binary parallel, which is introduced in Fig. 21.

The traces corresponding to the two-phase refinement of this binary parallel are specified in (11).

$$* \, (a_r\uparrow \, ; (b_r\uparrow \, ; b_a\uparrow \, \| \, c_r\uparrow \, ; c_a\uparrow) \, ; a_a\uparrow \, ; a_r\downarrow \, ; (b_r\downarrow \, ; b_a\downarrow \, \| \, c_r\downarrow \, ; c_a\downarrow) \, ; a_a\downarrow) \qquad (11)$$

This behavior can be realized with a wire-fork to distribute the incoming request and a C-element to combine the corresponding acknowledgements, as shown in Fig. 22.

Both the all-early and the all-late reduction of this implementation result in the behavior specified for the parallel. However, the all-broad reduction (modulo $\langle \phi_{4b}, \phi_{4b}, \phi_{4b} \rangle$) results in the more limited protocol, namely that of the *fork* component, whose symbol and specification are given in Fig. 23. Fork satisfies the parallel specification but in addition synchronizes the handshakes on its active port. In a two-phase refinement this can only be taken care of by the environment, but in a four-phase refinement of the parallel this can occur because of an excess of synchronization in the component itself, as is the case in the all-broad reduction of Fig. 22. In a four-phase circuit, this additional synchronization may give rise to deadlock.

The fork-implementation can be taken as a starting point to arrive at broad four-phase implementations. One may for instance connect S, T, or D-elements to the active ports of the fork component, as shown in Fig. 24. (In the reductions given in the figure, ϕ_4 is used to freely refer to early, broad, and late four-phase

$\text{PAR}(a^\circ, b^\bullet, c^\bullet) =$
$\quad \langle\langle a \rangle, \langle b, c \rangle, \text{trc}(*(a_r \, ; (b_r \, ; b_a \, \| \, c_r \, ; c_a) \, ; a_a))\rangle\rangle$

Fig. 21. Specification and symbol of binary parallel component

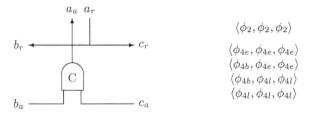

$$\langle \phi_2, \phi_2, \phi_2 \rangle$$

$$\langle \phi_{4e}, \phi_{4e}, \phi_{4e} \rangle$$
$$\langle \phi_{4b}, \phi_{4e}, \phi_{4e} \rangle$$
$$\langle \phi_{4b}, \phi_{4l}, \phi_{4l} \rangle$$
$$\langle \phi_{4l}, \phi_{4l}, \phi_{4l} \rangle$$

Fig. 22. Two-phase refinement of parallel component and applicable reductions

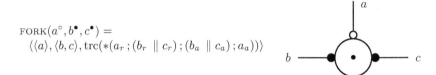

FORK$(a^\circ, b^\bullet, c^\bullet) =$
$$\langle \langle a \rangle, \langle b, c \rangle, \mathrm{trc}(*(a_r\,;(b_r \parallel c_r)\,;(b_a \parallel c_a)\,;a_a))) \rangle$$

Fig. 23. Specification and symbol of fork component

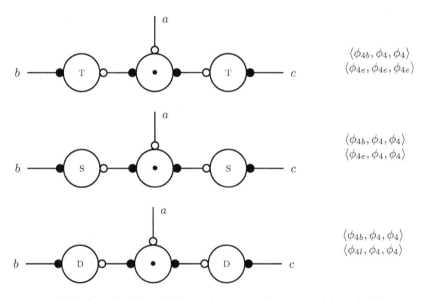

$$\langle \phi_{4b}, \phi_4, \phi_4 \rangle$$
$$\langle \phi_{4e}, \phi_{4e}, \phi_{4e} \rangle$$

$$\langle \phi_{4b}, \phi_4, \phi_4 \rangle$$
$$\langle \phi_{4e}, \phi_4, \phi_4 \rangle$$

$$\langle \phi_{4b}, \phi_4, \phi_4 \rangle$$
$$\langle \phi_{4l}, \phi_4, \phi_4 \rangle$$

Fig. 24. Three implementations of parallel with applicable reductions

reductions.) In the T-element variant, the excess of synchronization offered by the fork is removed by decoupling the return-to-zero phases of b and c.

Multi-channel implementations of the parallel component can be based on a back-bone of fork components. T-elements can be added to convert to the broad four-phase reduction and avoid the risk of deadlock on the branches where needed.

10   Mixer

The *mixer* component has several passive ports and one active handshake port. When activated via a passive port it will perform a handshake on its active port and then complete the handshake on the initiating passive port.

A mixer component with n ($n \geq 1$) passive ports $a(i)$ ($0 \leq i < n$) and active port b is specified by handshake protocols $\mathcal{H}(\{i : 0 \leq i < n : a(i)_r\}, \{b_r\})$ and $\mathcal{H}(\{b_a\}, \{i : 0 \leq i < n : a(i)_a\})$, plus, naturally, the protocols on the individual ports.

The handshake requirements imply that the handshakes on the different passive ports should be non-overlapping, that is, pair-wise mutually exclusive. Since this restricts the requests on the passive ports to not arrive while a handshake on a different passive port has not yet completed, this clearly is a restriction that should be implemented by the environment of the component, and can be exploited in the implementation of the mixer component itself.

Again, the unary mixer is equivalent to a connector, and the first interesting case is the binary mixer, which is shown in Fig. 25.

For the mixer component, the two-phase refinement is not a viable starting point when looking at implementations, due to the mutual-exclusion constraint at the passive ports. As an alternative, we start from the sequential broad four-phase refinement of (12).

$$*(\ a_r{\uparrow}\ ;c_r{\uparrow}\ ;c_a{\uparrow}\ ;a_a{\uparrow}\ \ ;a_r{\downarrow}\ ;c_r{\downarrow}\ ;c_a{\downarrow}\ ;a_a{\downarrow}$$
$$|\ b_r{\uparrow}\ ;c_r{\uparrow}\ ;c_a{\uparrow}\ ;b_a{\uparrow}\ \ ;b_r{\downarrow}\ ;c_r{\downarrow}\ ;c_a{\downarrow}\ ;b_a{\downarrow} \tag{12}$$
$$)$$

From this refinement, the implementation of the request circuit is simple, as the incoming requests can be implemented with an OR-gate. If we decide to broadcast the acknowledge from the active port to all passive ports we obtain the circuit shown in Fig. 26.

Interestingly, this circuit is a correct implementation of the mixer if the spurious-acknowledge protocol is applied to channel a and b. In that case the behavior of the circuit is specified by (13), and reduction modulo $\langle \phi_{4s}, \phi_{4s}, \phi_4 \rangle$ results in the mixer specification.

$$*(\ a_r{\uparrow}\ ;c_r{\uparrow}\ ;c_a{\uparrow}\ ;(a_a{\uparrow}\ \|\ b_a{\uparrow})\ ;a_r{\downarrow}\ ;c_r{\downarrow}\ ;c_a{\downarrow}\ ;(a_a{\downarrow}\ \|\ b_a{\downarrow})$$
$$|\ b_r{\uparrow}\ ;c_r{\uparrow}\ ;c_a{\uparrow}\ ;(b_a{\uparrow}\ \|\ a_a{\uparrow})\ ;b_r{\downarrow}\ ;c_r{\downarrow}\ ;c_a{\downarrow}\ ;(b_a{\downarrow}\ \|\ a_a{\downarrow}) \tag{13}$$
$$)$$

MIX$(a^\circ, b^\circ, c^\bullet) =$
   $\langle\langle a, b \rangle, \langle c \rangle, \mathrm{trc}(*(a_r\ ;c_r\ ;c_a\ ;a_a\ |\ a_r\ ;c_r\ ;c_a\ ;b_a)))\rangle$

Fig. 25. Specification and symbol for mixer component

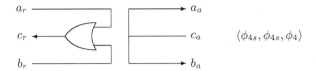

Fig. 26. Mixer implementation and its applicable reductions

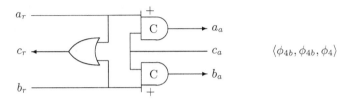

Fig. 27. Four-phase implementation of two-party mixer and applicable reductions

To arrive at a clean four-phase implementation, we can add a protocol converter that implements a spurious acknowledge filter to each passive port. Adding the circuit from Fig. 15 to Fig. 26 results in the implementation presented in Fig. 27. Clearly, the function of the filters is make sure that acknowledges are sent in the right direction, and to protect the side that did *not* issue the request from receiving a spurious acknowledge pulse.

This implementation of the mixer uses *two* state-holding elements to remember where to forward the incoming acknowledge to. Implementations that use only a single sequential element are also possible. However, an important advantage of the implementation shown here is that it generalizes to a multi-channel implementation straightforwardly. Furthermore, in a multi-channel implementation, the C-element on a passive port can be omitted if the corresponding active partner is robust against the spurious acknowledges thus introduced [7, 17].

11   Mutual Exclusion

Two handshakes are *mutually exclusive* if they do not overlap, that is, the request of the one does not occur between the request and the acknowledge of the other. For the mixer, it was a requirement to the environment to guarantee this for the passive ports. In this section we look into how to guarantee mutual exclusion, and how to covert between different four-phase refinements of mutual exclusion.

A set of n $(n > 1)$ handshake channels $a(i)$ $(0 \le i < n)$ is mutual exclusive if the channels can essentially be considered as one single handshake channel, that is, if their behavior is restricted to that of handshake channel

$$\mathcal{H}(\{i : 0 \le i < n : a(i)_r\}, \{i : 0 \le i < n : a(i)_a\}).$$

Naturally, in addition each individual protocol $\mathcal{H}(\{a(i)_r\}, \{a(i)_a\})$ (for all i, $0 \le i < n$) should also apply. For instance, three channels a, b, and c are mutually exclusive if their interaction is restricted to

$$*(a_r\,;a_a \mid b_r\,;b_a \mid c_r\,;c_a).$$

11.1   Arbiter

Mutual exclusion between independent handshakes can be assured by an arbiter. The arbiter, which is depicted below, acts as a connector from a to p, and as a connector from b to q, so handshakes on a and b are simply propagated. However, the arbiter guarantees the handshakes on p and q to be mutual exclusive. Therefore it stalls an incoming request when the other handshake is still active, and arbitrates and sequences such simultaneous requests, thereby eliminating overlap.

$$\text{ARB}(a^\circ, b^\circ, p^\bullet, q^\bullet) =$$
$$\langle\langle a, b\rangle, \langle p, q\rangle, \text{trc}(AP\|BQ\|PQ)\rangle$$

Fig. 28. Specification and symbol for handshake arbiter

The specification of the trace set of the arbiter is given as the composition of three behaviors. Expression AP specifies that the arbiter acts as a connector between a and p. Similarly BQ specifies that handshakes along b are propagated through q. The third expression, PQ, specifies that handshakes on p and q are mutually exclusive.

$$AP = *(a_r\,;p_r\,;p_a\,;a_a)$$
$$BQ = *(b_r\,;q_r\,;q_a\,;b_a)$$
$$PQ = *(p_r\,;p_a \mid q_r\,;q_a)$$

An early four-phase implementation of the arbiter is shown in Fig. 29. It is based on a so-called *mutual-exclusion element*, which is also known as interlock element or basic arbiter [27, 18]. This element adheres to the handshake protocols on $\mathcal{H}(\{a_r\}, \{p_r\})$ and $\mathcal{H}(\{b_r\}, \{q_r\})$, and in addition guarantees that p_r and q_r are not high simultaneously.

Modulo the early four-phase reduction on p and q the implementation of Fig. 29 satisfies exactly the arbiter protocol specified in Fig. 28. For a broad four-phase implementation, however, we have to delay the rising of e.g. p_r not only until b_r and q_r are low, but further until q_a is low as well. This can be achieved by adding a mutex converter, which is introduced next.

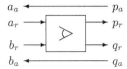

Fig. 29. Implementation of arbiter based on mutual-exclusion element

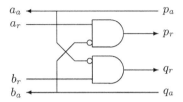

Fig. 30. Implementation of early-to-broad mutex converter

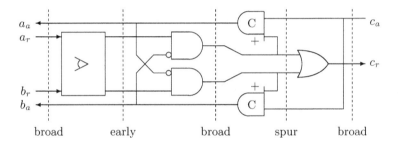

broad   early   broad   spur   broad

Fig. 31. Different protocols in an implementation of the arbitrated mixer

11.2   Mutex Converter

Conversion between early and broad mutual exclusion can be implemented efficiently, for instance as shown in Fig. 30. The early reductions of the handshakes on a and b are assumed to be mutually exclusive. Given this, this component guarantees that the broad reductions of the handshakes on p and q are mutually exclusive. This is implemented by stalling an incoming handshake until the other has fully completed.

11.3   Arbitrated Mixer

The mixer presented in Sect. 10 has as a restriction for the environment that the handshakes on the passive ports should be mutual exclusive. In the context of a silicon compiler, such mutual exclusion can be guaranteed by having strict sequential access, for instance, by a sequencer. An alternative is to make the mixer *receptive*, which means that it should be able to receive request on the different passive ports independently.

A receptive mixer can be obtained by connecting an arbiter component to the mixer implementation of Fig. 27. As the mixer requires broad mutual exclusion, a mutex converter is required at the interface of the arbiter and the mixer. In such an implementation, several handshake protocols play a role, as illustrated in Fig. 31.

12   Conclusion

We presented a systematic approach to the specification and implementation of handshake protocols. Handshake protocols are specified by handshake channels, which characterize the request and acknowledge events and the allowed sequences thereof. For an implementation of such a handshake channel two notions are important, namely description and reduction. Handshake descriptions are used to specify the behavior of the implementation, again in terms of its request and acknowledge events and the sequences that can be observed. Handshake reduction then defines which events should be interpreted as handshake events, and thus contribute to the handshake protocol, and which events should be considered redundant.

Handshake reduction also introduces a design challenge, which is covered by its inverse, refinement. Handshake refinements can be used to explore the handshake descriptions for implementations of a handshake protocol. Especially for the four-phase implementation of handshake components a rich domain is available, and early, broad, late, and spurious protocols can be combined freely.

This approach has turned out to work well in the context of the Haste silicon compiler. Multi-channel components (e.g., for sequencer, parallel, mixer) have been taken into account from the start, rather than building them from binary components only. The latter would have required the introduction of extensive (peephole) optimization steps in the design flow [28].

In this paper we have focused on four-phase implementations of handshake components for control functions. The approach sketched in this paper can be (and has been) applied to other components and to other handshake protocols as well. In cases where the implementations have clean transitions on the signals involved, one can typically record the events in a specialized handshake description. This for instance applies to the following cases.

Single track [29] control circuits, in which a single wire can carry both the request event (in the form of an up transition) and the acknowledge event (as a down transition). Such single-track handshakes can be recorded in handshake descriptions of the form $\langle \{w\uparrow\}, \{w\downarrow\}, \mathrm{trc}(*(w\uparrow \,;\, w\downarrow))\rangle$. The associated handshake reduction maps $w\uparrow$ onto a request event and $w\downarrow$ onto an acknowledge event.

Pulse mode [30, 31, 32] circuits, where request and acknowledge events are not encoded as transitions on wires, but rather as pulses on these wires. Often, non-overlapping pulses are used, which can be modeled through handshake description $\langle\{r\uparrow,r\downarrow\},\{a\uparrow,a\downarrow\},\mathrm{trc}(*(r\uparrow;r\downarrow;a\uparrow;a\downarrow))\rangle$, and where a reduction that maps the $r\uparrow$ onto a request and $a\downarrow$ onto an acknowledge can be applied.

One hot datapath circuits use one wire for each symbol, which can be modeled directly as a transition refinement of a handshake channel, and which can be used both in two-phase and in four-phase form.

Double rail [27] datapath circuits, which can be modeled as the composition of one-hot channels, where (for a push channel) the different requests share a single acknowledge wire. The handshake reductions can be based on the two- and four-phase reductions for control circuits.

Handshake descriptions are not suited to record events on signals where glitches (transitions that are not complete or clean) are allowed. This applies for instance to single-rail datapath circuits or sample-based control circuits. In these cases, it may be preferred to record the state on such signals only when 'valid' or 'sample' signals indicate that such a recording is safe, that is, results in a well-defined value.

Single rail [27, 33, 7] datapath circuits use a single wire per bit, and rely on a data-valid signal and a data-release signal, of which one is encoded in the request and the other in the acknowledge signal of the handshake protocol. Data-valid protocols can be expressed directly in the handshake reductions that apply to these control signals, such as four-phase, two-phase, single-track, and pulse mode. In four-phase implementations, one may for instance distinguish early, broad, and late data-valid schemes [7, 21].

Synchronous [34, 35] implementations of handshake protocols go even one step further, as these (in addition to datapath signals) also allow for glitches on handshake control signals. A separate *sample* or *clock* signal defines the moments at which the handshake wires may be observed. This additional signal may well be the only signal in such an implementation on which clean transitions are guaranteed, and on which the interpretation of all other signals depends. Naturally, such implementations are less suited for handshake descriptions, and a different approach is needed, although the formal specifications of handshake channels and components themselves can be maintained.

Handshake circuits allow for a wide variety of implementations, which can be based on many different handshake protocols, both asynchronous and synchronous. This makes these circuits an interesting target for compilation from high-level languages, such as CSP-based parallel programming languages. The combination of such powerful design languages and the handshake circuit intermediate architecture facilitates the exploration of the rich domain offered by todays VLSI circuits.

References

1. Hoare, C.A.R.: Communicating sequential processes. Communications of the ACM **21** (1978) 666–677
2. Hoare, C.A.R.: Communicating Sequential Processes. Prentice-Hall (1985)
3. Kahn, G.: The semantics of a simple language for parallel programming. Information Processing **74** (1974) 471–475
4. Berkel, C.H.K.v., Niessen, C., Rem, M., Saeijs, R.W.J.J.: VLSI programming and silicon compilation. In: Proc. International Conf. Computer Design (ICCD), Rye Brook, New York, IEEE Computer Society Press (1988) 150–166
5. Berkel, K.v., Kessels, J., Roncken, M., Saeijs, R., Schalij, F.:   The VLSI-programming language Tangram and its translation into handshake circuits. In: Proc. European Conference on Design Automation (EDAC). (1991) 384–389
6. Berkel, K.v.: Handshake Circuits: an Asynchronous Architecture for VLSI Programming. Volume 5 of International Series on Parallel Computation. Cambridge University Press (1993)
7. Peeters, A.M.G.: Single-Rail Handshake Circuits. PhD thesis, Eindhoven University of Technology (1996)
8. Kessels, J., Peeters, A.: The Tangram framework: Asynchronous circuits for low power. In: Proc. of Asia and South Pacific Design Automation Conference. (2001) 255–260
9. Bardsley, A., Edwards, D.: Compiling the language Balsa to delay-insensitive hardware. In Kloos, C.D., Cerny, E., eds.: Hardware Description Languages and their Applications (CHDL). (1997) 89–91
10. Bardsley, A.: Implementing Balsa Handshake Circuits. PhD thesis, Department of Computer Science, University of Manchester (2000)
11. Peeters, A., de Wit, M.: Haste manual. Technical report, Handshake Solutions (2004)
12. Dijkstra, E.W.: Cooperating sequential processes. Programming Languages (1968) 43–112
13. Snepscheut, J.L.A.v.d.: Trace Theory and VLSI Design. Volume 200 of Lecture Notes in Computer Science. Springer-Verlag (1985)
14. Brockett, R.W.: Smooth dynamical systems which realize arithmetical and logical operations. In Nijmeijer, H., Schumacher, J.M., eds.: Three Decades of Mathematical Systems Theory: A Collection of Surveys at the Occasion of the 50th Birthday of J. C. Willems. Volume 135 of Lecture Notes in Control and Information Sciences. Springer-Verlag (1989) 19–30
15. Berkel, K.v.: Beware the isochronic fork. Integration, the VLSI journal **13** (1992) 103–128
16. Mohammadi, S., Furber, S., Garside, J.: Designing robust asynchronous circuit components. IEE Proceedings, Circuits, Devices and Systems **150** (2003) 161–166
17. Negulescu, R., Peeters, A.: Verification of speed-dependences in single-rail handshake circuits. In: Proc. International Symposium on Advanced Research in Asynchronous Circuits and Systems. (1998) 159–170
18. Martin, A.J.: Programming in VLSI: From communicating processes to delay-insensitive circuits. In Hoare, C.A.R., ed.: Developments in Concurrency and Communication. UT Year of Programming Series, Addison-Wesley (1990) 1–64
19. Cortadella, J., Kishinevsky, M., Kondratyev, A., Lavagno, L., Yakovlev, A.: Logic Synthesis of Asynchronous Controllers and Interfaces. Springer-Verlag (2002)
20. Weste, N.H.E., Eshraghian, K.: Principles of CMOS VLSI Design: a Systems Perspective. Addison-Wesley (1993) Second Edition.

21. Sparsø, J., Furber, S., eds.: Principles of Asynchronous Circuit Design: A Systems Perspective. Kluwer Academic Publishers (2001)
22. Nanya, T., Ueno, Y., Kagotani, H., Kuwako, M., Takamura, A.: TITAC: Design of a quasi-delay-insensitive microprocessor. IEEE Design & Test of Computers **11** (1994) 50–63
23. Bisseling, H., Eemers, H., Kamps, M., Peeters, A.: Designing delay-insensitive circuits. Technical report, IVO, Eindhoven University of Technology (1990)
24. Rem, M.: Partially ordered computations with applications to VLSI design. In de Bakker, J.W., van Leeuwen, J., eds.: Distributed Systems, part 2: Semantics and Logic. Number IV in Foundations of Computer Science. (1983)
25. Udding, J.T.: Classification and Composition of Delay-Insensitive Circuits. PhD thesis, Dept. of Math. and C.S., Eindhoven Univ. of Technology (1984)
26. Bailey, A., Josephs, M.: Sequencer circuits for VLSI programming. In: Asynchronous Design Methodologies, IEEE Computer Society Press (1995) 82–90
27. Seitz, C.L.: System timing. In Mead, C.A., Conway, L.A., eds.: Introduction to VLSI Systems. Addison-Wesley (1980)
28. Chelcea, T., Nowick, S.M.: Resynthesis and peephole transformations for the optimization of large-scale asynchronous systems. In: Proc. ACM/IEEE Design Automation Conference. (2002)
29. Berkel, K.v., Bink, A.: Single-track handshaking signaling with application to micropipelines and handshake circuits. In: Proc. International Symposium on Advanced Research in Asynchronous Circuits and Systems, IEEE Computer Society Press (1996) 122–133
30. Keller, R.M.: Towards a theory of universal speed-independent modules. IEEE Transactions on Computers **C-23** (1974) 21–33
31. Plana, L.A., Unger, S.H.: Pulse-mode macromodular systems. In: Proc. International Conf. Computer Design (ICCD). (1998) 348–353
32. Nyström, M., Martin, A.: Asynchronous Pulse Logic. Kluwer Academic Publishers (2002)
33. Sutherland, I.E.: Micropipelines. Communications of the ACM **32** (1989) 720–738
34. Peeters, A., van Berkel, K.: Synchronous handshake circuits. In: Proc. International Symposium on Advanced Research in Asynchronous Circuits and Systems, IEEE Computer Society Press (2001) 86–95
35. Page, I., Luk, W.: Compiling **occam** into FPGAs. In Moore, W., Luk, W., eds.: FPGAs. (1991) 271–283

A Trace Semantics for Long-Running Transactions

Michael Butler[1], Tony Hoare[2], and Carla Ferreira[3]

[1] School of Electronics and Computer Science, University of Southampton, UK
mjb@ecs.soton.ac.uk
[2] Microsoft Research Cambridge, UK
[3] Department of Computer Science,
Technical University of Lisbon

Abstract. A long-running transaction is an interactive component of a distributed system which must be executed as if it were a single atomic action. In principle, it should not be interrupted or fail in the middle, and it must not be interleaved with other atomic actions of other concurrently executing components of the system. In practice, the illusion of atomicity for a long-running transaction is achieved with the aid of compensation actions supplied by the original programmer: because the transaction is interactive, familiar automatic techniques of check-pointing and rollback are no longer adequate. This paper constructs a model of long-running transactions within the framework of the CSP process algebra, showing how the compensations are orchestrated to achieve the illusion of atomicity. It introduces a method for declaring that a process is a transaction, and for declaring a compensation for it in case it needs to be rolled back after it has committed. The familiar operator of sequential composition is redefined to ensure that all necessary compensations will be called in the right order if a later failure makes this necessary. The techniques are designed to work well in a highly concurrent and distributed setting. In addition we define an angelic choice operation, implemented by speculative execution of alternatives; its judicious use can improve responsiveness of a system in the face of the unpredictable latencies of remote communication. Many of the familiar properties of process algebra are preserved by these new definitions, on reasonable assumptions of the correctness and independence of the programmer-declared compensations.

1 Introduction

Business transactions involve hierarchies of activities whose execution needs to be orchestrated. Business transactions typically involve interactions and coordination between multiple partners. Business transactions need to deal with faults that arise at any stage of execution. In standard atomic transactions, such as database transactions, rollback mechanisms are used to protect against faults by providing all or nothing atomicity for transactions [7]. In long-running business transactions, rollback is not always possible because parts of a transaction will

A.E. Abdallah, C.B. Jones, and J.W. Sanders (Eds.): **CSP25**, LNCS 3525, pp. 133–150, 2005.

have been committed or because parts of a transaction (e.g., communications with external agents) are inherently impossible to undo using any automatic technique. The only solution in principle is to ask the system designer to provide ways of compensating actions that cannot be undone automatically. A language for long-running transactions can provide constructs through which the application developer declares compensations for actions. The language will then orchestrate the compensations in the appropriate way to achieve the desired effect.

In the context of business transactions, Gray and Reuter [7] define a compensation as the action taken to recover from error or cope with a change of plan. Consider the following example: a client buys some books in an on-line bookstore and the bookstore debits the client's account as the payment for the book order. The bookstore later realises that one of the books in the client's order is out of print. To compensate the client for this problem, the bookstore can credit the account with the amount wrongfully debited and send a letter apologising for their mistake. This example shows that compensation is more general than traditional rollback in database transactions. Compensation is important when a system cannot control everything, such as when interaction with other agents (including humans) is involved. Garcia-Molina and Salem [6] use compensation to define the concept of *sagas*. A saga partitions a long-running transaction into a sequence of several smaller subtransactions, where each of the subtransactions has an associated compensation. If one of the subtransactions in the sequence aborts, the compensation associated with those committed subtransactions is executed in reverse order.

This paper constructs a model of long-running transactions within the framework of the CSP process algebra [8], showing how the compensations are orchestrated to achieve the illusion of atomicity. Section 2 of this paper gives an introduction to the Compensating CSP language. Section 3 provides a description of the standard trace semantics of the sequential and the concurrent operators of CSP, slightly adapted to the needs of our model. The three following sections put together ideas from the standard semantics to construct the transaction processing model, and prove the relevant theorems.

Our compensation constructs are not intended to replace atomic transactions. Instead they extend transaction mechanisms to a higher level of granularity. The goal of our design is that shorter-running transactions should be nested inside longer-running transactions, so as to deal with many levels of granularity, from milliseconds to (say) months. Backtracking will be minimised, by use of compensations at the appropriate level of granularity, so as to preserve as much progress-to-date as possible. Where possible, basic activities of a long-running transaction could be implemented as atomic transactions with automatic rollback rather than explicit compensation.

The inspiration of this paper derives from the transaction processing features of Microsoft Biztalk [11], IBMs WSFL [10], IBM's Business Process Beans [4], Structured Activity Compensation [3] and the OASIS draft standard for BPEL4WS [5]. However no attempt has been made to model the particular semantics of any of these languages.

2   Compensating CSP

The behaviour of an interactive process (typically denoted $P, Q, \ldots$) can be recorded as a sequential trace (typically denoted $p, q, \ldots$) of all its environmentally observable actions (typically denoted $A, B, \ldots$), and of certain special internal actions (like $\checkmark$, indicating successful termination of a process). For example, the trace $\langle A, B, \checkmark \rangle$ is a behaviour of the process $A;B$ that executes action A, then action B and then terminates successfully. In the CSP process algebra, processes are modelled using such traces [8]. The traces of composite processes, such as a sequential composition $(P;Q)$ or a parallel composition $(P \parallel Q)$, are defined in terms of the traces of their constituent processes. The trace model means that each action that occurs cannot be anything but atomic in the two usual senses: (1) it either occurs as a whole, or it does not occur at all; (2) it occurs either wholly before or wholly after every other action.

If a long-running transaction actually fails before successfully completing, the effect must be as if it had not occurred at all. In a conventional (short running) transaction system, the effect of the transaction can be undone at any time by restoring a checkpoint of local state that has been taken before its start. But a long-running transaction may have interacted with the real world before failing, and the real world cannot be check-pointed. To solve this problem, the programmer of the original transaction is asked to provide for each fine-grained action A a compensation action (often called A°); its occurrence after the action A will restore the world to a state which is an acceptable approximation to the state that it had before the start of the transaction. Thus the primitive component of a long-running transaction can be written $A \div A^\circ$, where A is a fine-grained atomic action, and A° is its compensation, which will be invoked if a failure later in the transaction makes it necessary. Since a complete transaction P is an atomic action at a coarser level of granularity, it too may be declared to have its own compensation, for example $P \div Q$. The coarse-grained compensation Q over-rides the fine-grained compensations declared inside P.

An implementation of a transaction processing system must ensure that on failure of a transaction, all the necessary atomic compensations are performed in an appropriate order to compensate for the effect of everything that has actually happened so far. For example, if a failure occurs after sequential execution of the two fine-grained actions $\langle A, B \rangle$, the compensations should occur in the reverse order $\langle B^\circ, A^\circ \rangle$. To model this strategy, we distinguish between standard processes $P, Q, \ldots$), and compensable processes $(PP, QQ, \ldots)$. We represent a behaviour $(pp, qq, \ldots)$ of a compensable process using a pair of sequential traces with a forward part and a compensation part. For example, the trace pair $(\langle A, B, \checkmark \rangle, \langle B^\circ, A^\circ, \checkmark \rangle)$ is a behaviour of the process $(A \div A^\circ); (B \div B^\circ)$. Sequential composition of compensable processes is redefined in a non-standard way to ensure that the compensations for all actions performed will be accumulated in the reverse order to their original performance. Parallel composition of compensable processes is defined so that compensations for performed actions will be accumulated in parallel.

Failure of a transaction is signified by another special symbol $!$, which appears like $\checkmark$ at the end of a trace. The intended effect of the $!$ event is to throw an interrupt. For example, the primitive process $THROW$ which fails immediately contains the trace $\langle ! \rangle$. In a purely sequential process, the exception causes an immediate disruption to the flow of control. An interrupt handler may be used to catch interrupts: in $P \rhd Q$, an interrupt raised by P triggers execution of the handler Q. In parallel processes, the whole group of parallel processes may fail when one of the processes throws an exception and all the other processes are willing to disrupt their flow of control and yield to the exception. A process that is ready to terminate (indicated by $\checkmark$) is also willing to yield to an interrupt. A process may also yield at mid points in its execution, indicated by the special symbol $?$ which again appears at the end of a trace. Parallel composition is defined so that $!$ in one process synchronises with $!$, $\checkmark$ or $?$ in another process and the combined event is $!$. A compensation pair $P \div Q$ is always willing to yield to an interrupt either before starting P or immediately after completing P. For example, $A \div A^\circ$ will contain the compensable behaviours $(\langle ? \rangle, \langle \checkmark \rangle)$ and $(\langle A, \checkmark \rangle, \langle A^\circ, \checkmark \rangle)$.

A complete transaction is formed from a compensable process PP by enclosing PP in a transaction block $[PP]$. This converts PP back into a standard process. The standard behaviours of a transaction block $[PP]$ are defined in terms of the compensable behaviours of PP. Successful forward traces of PP represent successful completion of the whole transaction. The compensations are no longer needed, and they are discarded. The failed traces of PP need to involve actual execution of the compensations. The intention in forming a complete transaction from a compensable process is that, in the case of failure, the compensations will cancel all the forward actions, leaving only a trace containing no observable actions as a result. We introduce a framework for proving that a transaction either does nothing, because its forward actions will have been cancelled, or completes successfully. This is the fundamental principle for a process algebra that models long-running transactions. In these proofs, we will assume that any trace is equivalent to one in which any action and its following compensation have been cancelled. The unrealism of this abstraction should be mitigated in engineering practice, by ensuring that failures with less desirable compensations are adequately rare.

External choice $(P \,\square\, Q)$ is defined in our model as the union of the traces of the alternatives P and Q, just as in CSP. In implementation, the choice is made between P and Q according to whichever of them is the first to be able to start. This choice operation is often used to mitigate the unpredictable variations in latency that are characteristic of remote interactions on the world wide web. In a transaction processing system, further improvement is possible, by delaying the choice until the first of P and Q have not only started but completed; the actions of the other are then just compensated. This strategy is a kind of speculative execution; it has been called optimistic scheduling in distributed system simulation. Its definition is the final achievement of this paper.

Standard processes:

$$P, Q ::= A \qquad \text{(atomic action)}$$

$$\begin{aligned}
&|\ P\ ;\ Q &&\text{(sequential composition)}\\
&|\ P \ \square\ Q &&\text{(choice)}\\
&|\ P \parallel Q &&\text{(parallel composition)}\\
&|\ SKIP &&\text{(normal termination)}\\
&|\ THROW &&\text{(throw an interrupt)}\\
&|\ YIELD &&\text{(yield to an interrupt)}\\
&|\ P \rhd Q &&\text{(interrupt handler)}\\
&|\ [PP] &&\text{(transaction block)}
\end{aligned}$$

Compensable processes:

$$PP, QQ ::= P \div Q \qquad \text{(compensation pair)}$$

$$\begin{aligned}
&|\ PP\ ;\ QQ\\
&|\ PP\ \square\ QQ\\
&|\ PP \parallel QQ\\
&|\ SKIPP\\
&|\ THROWW\\
&|\ YIELDD
\end{aligned}$$

Fig. 1. Syntax of Compensating CSP

$$\begin{aligned}
OrderTransaction &= [\ ProcessOrder\ ]\\
ProcessOrder &= (AcceptOrder \div RestockOrder)\ ;\ FulfillOrder\\
FulfillOrder &= BookCourier \div CancelCourier\ \parallel\\
&\quad\ PackOrder\ \parallel\\
&\quad\ CreditCheck\ ;\ (\ \ Ok;\ SKIPP\\
&\qquad\qquad\qquad\quad \square\ NotOk;\ THROWW\ )\\
PackOrder &= \parallel i \in Items\ \bullet\ (PackItem(i) \div UnpackItem(i))
\end{aligned}$$

Fig. 2. Order transaction example

To keep the semantic definitions simple in this paper, we have avoided supporting synchronised communication between parallel processes. Synchronisation in parallel process blocks is limited to joint execution of compensations, joint termination and joint interruption. Dealing with synchronised communication is a desirable longer term aim.

The syntax of compensating CSP is summarised in Figure 1. Figure 2 presents a transaction for processing of customer orders in the compensating CSP language. The first step in the transaction is a compensation pair. The primary action of this pair is to accept the order and deduct the order quantity from the inventory database. The compensation action simply adds the order quantity back to the total in the inventory database. After an order is received from a customer, the order is packed for shipment, and a courier is booked to deliver the goods to the customer. The *PackOrder* process packs each of the items in the order in parallel. Each *PackItem* activity can be compensated by a corresponding *UnpackItem*. Simultaneously with the packing of the order, a credit check is performed on the customer. The credit check is performed in parallel because it normally succeeds, and in this normal case the company does not wish to delay the order unnecessarily. In the case that a credit check fails, an interrupt is thrown causing the transaction to stop its execution, with the courier possibly having been booked and possibly some of the items having being packed. In case of failure, the semantics of the transaction block will ensure that the appropriate compensation activities will be invoked for those activities that did take place.

3   Trace Semantics for Standard Processes

We assume a process has an alphabet of actions Σ which does not include any of the special events in $\Omega = \{\checkmark, !, ?\}$. For traces s and t, we write st for their concatenation. Standard processes are defined as non-empty sets of traces each of the form $s\langle\omega\rangle$ where $s \in \Sigma^*$ and $\omega \in \Omega$. Thus all traces of standard processes are of one of the following forms:

- $s\langle\checkmark\rangle$ trace leading to normal termination
- $s\langle!\rangle$ trace leading to interrupt throw
- $s\langle?\rangle$ trace leading to interrupt yield

Unlike the traces model for CSP in [8], we include only completed traces in our traces model, not prefixes of traces. This simplifies many definitions since the nature of a trace is indicated by its final symbol.

3.1   Sequential Operators

The process that performs a single atomic event and terminates successfully consists of a single complete trace:

Definition 1 (Atomic Action). *For $A \in \Sigma$,* $A = \{\langle A, \checkmark\rangle\}$

As in CSP the choice between two process is defined as the union of their traces:

Definition 2 (Choice). $P \square Q = P \cup Q$

With sequential composition $P;Q$, execution of Q commences when P has completed successfully; thus successful traces of P are extended with traces of Q, while other traces of P remain unchanged. We define a sequential operator on traces and then lift it to processes in the following way:

Definition 3 (Sequential Composition).

$$p\langle\checkmark\rangle \; ; \; q = pq$$
$$p\langle\omega\rangle \; ; \; q = p\langle\omega\rangle, \textbf{ where } \omega \neq \checkmark$$
$$P \, ; Q = \{p\,;q \mid p \in P \wedge q \in Q\}$$

The process *SKIP* immediately terminates successfully:

Definition 4 (Skip). $SKIP = \{ \langle \checkmark \rangle \}$

THROW is the process that immediately raises an interrupt. *YIELD* is the process that yields or terminates. These processes are defined as follows:

Definition 5 (Throw and Yield).

$$THROW = \{ \langle ! \rangle \} \qquad YIELD = \{ \langle ? \rangle, \langle \checkmark \rangle \}$$

The process $P; YIELD; Q$ may yield to an interrupt from the environment after executing P and before executing Q.

Sequential processes satisfy the following laws:

$$P;(Q \,\Box\, R) = (P;Q) \,\Box\, (P;R)$$
$$(P \,\Box\, Q);R = (P;R) \,\Box\, (Q;R)$$
$$P;(Q;R) = (P;Q);R$$
$$P;SKIP = P$$
$$SKIP;P = P$$
$$THROW;P = THROW$$
$$YIELD;YIELD = YIELD$$

We look now at defining an operator for handling interrupts. For processes P and Q, $P \rhd Q$ represents a process that behaves as P until an interrupt is raised by P, at which point it behaves as Q. The interrupt handling operator is defined as follows:

Definition 6 (Interrupt Handler).

$$p\langle ! \rangle \rhd q = pq$$
$$p\langle \omega \rangle \rhd q = p\langle \omega \rangle, \textbf{ where } \omega \neq !$$

$$P \rhd Q = \{ p \rhd q \mid p \in P \wedge q \in Q \}$$

Laws for interrupt handling:

$$(P \rhd Q) \rhd R = P \rhd (Q \rhd R)$$
$$SKIP \rhd P = SKIP$$
$$YIELD \rhd P = YIELD$$
$$THROW \rhd P = P$$

3.2   Concurrency

In this paper we do not support synchronous execution of observable actions. A parallel block of processes will synchronise only on joint termination or joint interruption. We represent this by defining a synchronisation operator on the special terminal events from the set Ω. If ω and ω' are terminal events of distinct concurrent processes, we denote by $\omega\&\omega'$ the joint terminal event of their concurrent execution. Evaluations of this operator are enumerated in Table 1. The first three rows of the table show that the synchronisation of an interrupt throw with any other terminal event results in an interrupt throw. The next two rows show that the synchronisation of a yield with either a yield or a successful termination result in a yield. The first five rows are motivated by our decision that if a process is willing to terminate (in any of the three ways), then it is willing to yield to an interrupt from its environment. The last row of Table 1 shows that a pair of parallel processes may terminate successfully when both processes are willing to terminate successfully. We also define the synchronisation operator to be commutative; from this and from Table 1 it can be seen that the operator is well-defined for all operands in the set Ω. Case analysis shows the synchronisation operator to be associative.

As usual in process algebra, we model asynchronous execution of actions in separate processes as occurring in an interleaved fashion. Asynchronous actions can lead to different interleavings; for example, $A \parallel B$ can execute A followed by B or B followed by A. For traces p and q, we write $p \parallel\!\parallel\!\parallel q$ to denote the set of all interleaving of p and q:

$$p \parallel\!\parallel\!\parallel \langle\rangle \;=\; \{p\}$$
$$\langle\rangle \parallel\!\parallel\!\parallel q \;=\; \{q\}$$
$$\langle x\rangle p \parallel\!\parallel\!\parallel \langle y\rangle q \;=\; \{\,\langle x\rangle r \mid r \in (p \parallel\!\parallel\!\parallel \langle y\rangle q)\,\} \;\cup\; \{\,\langle y\rangle r \mid r \in (\langle x\rangle p \parallel\!\parallel\!\parallel q)\,\}$$

We define parallel composition of traces to be the set of interleavings of their observable part followed by the synchronisation of their terminal events. This is then lifted to sets of traces to define parallel composition of processes:

Definition 7 (Parallel Composition).

$$p\langle\omega\rangle \parallel q\langle\omega'\rangle \;=\; \{\,r\langle\omega\&\omega'\rangle \mid r \in (p \parallel\!\parallel\!\parallel q)\,\}$$
$$P \parallel Q \;=\; \{\,r \mid r \in (p \parallel q) \wedge p \in P \wedge q \in Q\,\}$$

Table 1. Synchronisation of terminal events

ω	ω'	$\omega\&\omega'$
!	!	!
!	?	!
!	✓	!
?	?	?
?	✓	?
✓	✓	✓

Parallel composition is commutative and associative:

$$P \parallel Q = Q \parallel P$$
$$(P \parallel Q) \parallel R = P \parallel (Q \parallel R)$$

If P does not contain any yields, then $YIELD; P$ is only willing to yield to an interrupt either before P commences or when P terminates. This is shown in the following law (for P not containing any yields):

$$THROW \parallel (YIELD; P) = THROW \ \Box \ P; THROW$$

This law shows that interrupt does *not* have priority over other events. This is what we would expect in a distributed setting where we cannot expect an entire distributed system to respond immediately to an attempt by one party to raise an exception.

4   Compensable Processes

A compensable process contains forward behaviour and compensation behaviour. The intention is that the compensation can be executed to compensate for the forward action, if necessary (e.g., when an error or interrupt occurs later). Compensable behaviour is modelled by pairs of traces of the form $(p\langle \omega \rangle, p'\langle \omega' \rangle)$, where $p\langle \omega \rangle$ represents a forward trace and $p'\langle \omega' \rangle$ represents the corresponding compensation trace. A compensable process is modelled by a non-empty set of such pairs.

The choice of compensable processes is as for standard processes:

Definition 8 (Compensable Choice).

$$PP \ \Box \ QQ \ = \ PP \cup QQ$$

Parallel composition of compensable processes is similar to the standard case:

Definition 9 (Compensable Parallel Composition).

$$(p, p') \parallel (q, q') \ = \ \{ \ (r, r') \mid r \in (p \parallel q) \ \wedge \ r' \in (p' \parallel q') \ \}$$

$$PP \parallel QQ \ = \ \{ \ rr \mid rr \in (pp \parallel qq) \ \wedge \ pp \in PP \ \wedge \ qq \in QQ \ \}$$

We redefine the sequential composition operator so that the compensation behaviour of the first process is made to happen after that of the second process. Behaviours of PP where the forward trace is unsuccessful remain unchanged.

Definition 10 (Compensable Sequential Composition).

$$(p\langle \checkmark \rangle, p') \ ; \ (q, q') \ = \ (pq, \ q'; p')$$
$$(p\langle \omega \rangle, p') \ ; \ (q, q') \ = \ (p\langle \omega \rangle, p'), \ \textbf{where} \ \omega \neq \checkmark$$

$$PP \ ; \ QQ \ = \ \{ \ pp \ ; \ qq \mid pp \in PP \ \wedge \ qq \in QQ \ \}$$

A compensation pair is a compensable process constructed from two standard processes. In the pair $P \div Q$, successfully terminating forward behaviour of P is augmented by compensation behaviour from Q resulting in a compensable process. If P throws or yields, the compensation is empty. The rationale for our definition is that a compensation is intended to be used to compensate, at a later stage, for a successfully completed forward unit of work and not for an interrupted unit of work. As before we define the pairing operator on compensable behaviours and then lift it to processes. When lifting to processes, we include an extra behaviour which allows the compensation pair to yield immediately with the empty compensation. The operator is defined as follows:

Definition 11 (Compensation Pair).

$$p\langle\checkmark\rangle \div q \;=\; (p\langle\checkmark\rangle, q)$$
$$p\langle\omega\rangle \div q \;=\; (p\langle\omega\rangle, \langle\checkmark\rangle), \quad \textbf{where } \omega \neq \checkmark$$

$$P \div Q \;=\; \{\,((\langle?\rangle, \langle\checkmark\rangle))\,\} \;\cup$$
$$\{\, p \div q \mid p \in P \wedge q \in Q \,\}$$

The operators on compensable processes are designed to ensure the correct compensation is accummulated even when an interrupt is yielded to. For example, consider the traces of the following process:

$$A \div A'; \; B \div B' \;=\; \{\, ((\langle?\rangle, \langle\checkmark\rangle),$$
$$(\langle A, ?\rangle, \langle A', \checkmark\rangle),$$
$$(\langle A, B, \checkmark\rangle, \langle B', A', \checkmark\rangle) \,\}$$

If this process yields immediately, the compensation is empty. If it yields after executing A, the compensation is A'. If it completes successfully, the compensation is B' followed by A'.

Definition 12 (Compensable Basic Processes).

$$SKIPP = SKIP \div SKIP$$
$$THROWW = THROW \div SKIP$$
$$YIELDD = YIELD \div SKIP$$

Laws:

$$PP \parallel QQ = QQ \parallel PP$$
$$(PP \parallel QQ) \parallel RR = PP \parallel (QQ \parallel RR)$$
$$(PP; QQ); RR = PP; (QQ; RR)$$
$$PP; SKIPP = PP$$
$$SKIPP; PP = PP$$
$$THROWW; PP = THROWW$$
$$YIELDD; (P \div Q) = P \div Q$$

A transaction block involves running the compensation part of interrupted forward traces, discarding the compensation parts of terminating forward traces and completely removing traces whose forward parts are yielding. A transaction block converts a compensable process into a standard process:

Definition 13 (Transaction Block).

$$[PP] \; = \; \{\, pp' \mid (p\langle ! \rangle, p') \in PP \,\} \; \cup$$
$$\{\, p\langle \checkmark \rangle \mid (p\langle \checkmark \rangle, p') \in PP \,\}$$

Note that non-emptiness of PP is not sufficient to ensure non-emptiness of $[PP]$. If PP only contained yielding behaviours, then $[PP]$ would be empty. The following healthiness conditions, declaring that all processes P and PP consist of some terminating or interrupting behaviour, will ensure that $[PP]$ is non-empty:

- $p\langle \checkmark \rangle \in P$ or $p\langle ! \rangle \in P$, for some p
- $(p\langle \checkmark \rangle, p') \in PP$ or $(p\langle ! \rangle, p') \in PP$, for some p, p'

These conditions are true of the basic processes and are preserved by all the operators.

The transaction block masks interrupts and yields in forward behaviour:

$$[THROWW] \; = \; SKIP$$
$$[YIELDD] \; = \; SKIP$$

Assume P is non-yielding. The following laws show that installed compensation is run in the case of an interrupt and discarded in the case of successful termination:

$$[\, P \div P' ; \; THROWW \,] \; = \; P; P'$$
$$[\, P \div P' \,] \; = \; P$$

Assume P, P', Q, Q' terminate successfully, neither raising nor yielding to interrupts. The following laws show the effect of the parallel and sequential composition operators on the order of compensations:

$$[\, P \div P' ; \; Q \div Q' ; \; THROWW \,] \; = \; P; Q; Q'; P'$$
$$[\, (P \div P' \parallel Q \div Q'); \; THROWW \,] \; = \; (P \parallel Q) \, ; \, (P' \parallel Q')$$
$$[\, (P \div P' ; \; Q \div Q') \parallel THROWW \,] \; = \; SKIP \; \square \; (P; P') \; \square \; (P; Q; Q'; P')$$

$$[\, P \div P' \parallel Q \div Q' \parallel THROWW \,] \; =$$
$$SKIP \; \square \; (P; P') \; \square \; (Q; Q') \; \square \; (P \parallel Q); (P' \parallel Q')$$

5   Cancellation Semantics for Transactions

So far we have said very little about the relationship between forward actions and their compensations other than the relative order in which they may occur.

In this section we develop a theory of cancellation for compensable processes in which the effect of forward actions is cancelled by compensation actions. We take a very abstract view of cancellation in which we can declare that an atomic action, say A, is compensated by A° and that the behaviour exhibited by A followed by A° is the same as *SKIP*. We will introduce a cancellation function that removes cancelling forward and compensation actions from process traces. We will introduce a correctness criteria on compensable processes which says they should be *self-cancelling*. We will introduce a rule which says that when the cancellation function is applied to a self-cancelling transaction, then the overall effect is either to perform the normal forward behaviour of the transaction or to do nothing (*SKIP*). We will show under what conditions the self-cancellation property is preserved by the operators of our language.

Assume F is a set of forward actions and C is a set of compensation actions with F and C being disjoint. We assume that *cancel* is a relation between F and C so that $cancel(A, A^\circ)$ means that A° cancels the effect of A. We can also declare that certain actions are independent so that they can occur in either order. This would typically be the case for compensations of parallel processes. We write $independent(A, B)$ to indicate that A and B may be transposed in a trace as they do not interfere with each other. We assume that *independent* is symmetric (unlike *cancel*).

We now define our cancellation function ($\mathcal{C}$) on traces. If a trace t is of the form $p\langle A\rangle q\langle A^\circ\rangle r$ and if $cancel(A, A^\circ)$ and $\forall B \in q \cdot independent(A^\circ, B)$, then:

$$\mathcal{C}(\, p\langle A\rangle q\langle A^\circ\rangle r\,) \;=\; \mathcal{C}(\, pqr\,)$$

If trace t does not satisfy the above conditions then no further cancellation can be applied:

$$\mathcal{C}(t) \;=\; t, \;\textbf{otherwise}$$

For example, assuming A°, B° and C° cancel A, B and C respectively and A° and B° are independent:

$$
\begin{aligned}
\mathcal{C}(\,\langle A, B, C, C^\circ, A^\circ, B^\circ\rangle\,) &= \mathcal{C}(\,\langle A, B, A^\circ, B^\circ\rangle\,) \\
&= \mathcal{C}(\,\langle A, A^\circ\rangle\,), \;\; \text{since } independent(A^\circ, B^\circ) \\
&= \mathcal{C}(\,\langle\rangle\,) \\
&= \langle\rangle
\end{aligned}
$$

Cancellation is lifted to processes by mapping the cancellation function to each trace. We refer to a transaction block to which cancellation has being applied, $\mathcal{C}[PP]$, as being *closed*.

A compensation behaviour $(p\langle\omega\rangle, p'\langle\omega'\rangle)$ is self-cancelling if the forward and compensation parts together are equivalent to the empty trace and the compensation terminates sucessfully:

$$self\_cancelling(p\langle\omega\rangle, p'\langle\omega'\rangle) \;=\; \mathcal{C}(pp') = \langle\rangle \;\wedge\; \omega' = \checkmark$$

A compensable process PP is self-cancelling, $self\_cancelling(PP)$, when all its behaviours are self cancelling. Self-cancelling transactions enjoy some important properties. If we force an interrupt, then the closed transaction behaves simply as $SKIP$:

$$\frac{self\_cancelling(PP)}{C[\,PP;THROWW\,]\;=\;SKIP} \tag{1}$$

The closure of a self-cancelling transaction either completes a forward trace successfully or, if an exception occurs, terminates immediately with no observable effect:

$$\frac{self\_cancelling(PP)}{C[PP]\;\subseteq\;PP_{\checkmark}\;\square\;SKIP} \tag{2}$$

Here, $PP_{\checkmark}$ represents successfully completing executions of PP:

$$PP_{\checkmark}\;=\;\{\,t\langle\checkmark\rangle\;|\;(t\langle\checkmark\rangle,t')\in PP\,\}$$

Inequality arises in rule (2) because PP might not have any successful behaviours or might not have interrupted behaviours. This rule is quite powerful as it allows us to reason separately about the normal behaviour and the compensation behaviour of a closed transaction block. The abstract specification of a transaction block might be to achieve a certain goal or to do nothing. We verify this by verifying that $PP_{\checkmark}$ achieves that goal and by verifying that PP is self-cancelling.

The following rules allow $PP_{\checkmark}$ to be derived through simple structural calculation:

$$(A \div A^{\circ})_{\checkmark} = A$$
$$(PP \;\square\; QQ)_{\checkmark} = PP_{\checkmark} \;\square\; QQ_{\checkmark}$$
$$(PP \parallel QQ)_{\checkmark} = PP_{\checkmark} \parallel QQ_{\checkmark}$$
$$(PP\,;\;QQ)_{\checkmark} = PP_{\checkmark}\;;\;QQ_{\checkmark}$$
$$THROWW_{\checkmark} = NULL$$

Here $NULL$ stands for the empty set of traces. $NULL$ does not correspond to a valid process but is a useful calculational artefact. $NULL$ satisfies the following laws:

$$NULL\,;\;PP = NULL$$
$$PP\,;\;NULL = NULL$$
$$NULL \parallel PP = NULL$$
$$NULL \;\square\; PP = PP$$

The final law above shows that $NULL$ is absorbed by choice. This means that the result of applying cancellation to a self-cancelling transaction block (rule (2) above) is a well defined process even if $PP_{\checkmark} = NULL$. Figure 3 shows the result of calculating the forward behaviour of the order process example of Figure 2.

$$ProcessOrder_\checkmark \; = \; AcceptOrder \; ; \; FulfillOrder_\checkmark$$

$$\begin{aligned} FulfillOrder_\checkmark \; = \; & BookCourier \; \parallel \\ & PackOrder_\checkmark \; \parallel \\ & CreditCheck \; ; \; Ok \end{aligned}$$

$$PackOrder_\checkmark \; = \; \parallel i \in Items \; \bullet \; PackItem(i)$$

Fig. 3. Forward behaviour for order transaction example

We look now at how self cancellation relates to the operators of our language.

$$cancel(A, A^\circ) \; \Rightarrow \; self\_cancelling(\, A \div A^\circ \,)$$

SKIPP, *THROWW* and *YIELDD* are all self-cancelling. Self-cancellation is preserved by sequential composition and choice:

$$\frac{self\_cancelling(PP) \quad self\_cancelling(QQ)}{self\_cancelling(PP; QQ)} \qquad \frac{self\_cancelling(PP) \quad self\_cancelling(QQ)}{self\_cancelling(PP \; \Box \; QQ)}$$

Parallel composition preserves self-cancellation provided the compensations from parallel processes are independent:

$$\frac{\begin{array}{c} self\_cancelling(PP) \\ self\_cancelling(QQ) \\ \forall \, A \in comp(PP), \; B \in comp(QQ) \cdot independent(A, B) \end{array}}{self\_cancelling(PP \parallel QQ)}$$

Here, $comp(PP)$ represents the set of compensation actions of PP.

From the above rules, we see the result that, if the programmer of a transaction ensures

– an action A is directly paired with its compensation A° and
– every compensation is independent of compensations in parallel processes,

then the transaction will be self-cancelling under our theory.

6   Speculative Choice

When the goal of a transaction can be achieved in different ways, responsiveness may be improved by attempting these different means in parallel. When one attempt succeeds, the other attempts may be abandoned. Compensation can be used to cancel the effect so far of the abandoned attempts. In this section, we define a form of speculative choice which can be shown to be equivalent to standard choice under the right conditions.

We write $PP \boxtimes QQ$ for the speculative choice of PP and QQ. The effect of $PP \boxtimes QQ$ is to run the forward behaviour of PP and QQ in parallel until one of them terminates successfully. If PP terminates successfully, then the compensation accumulated for QQ is run while the compensation for PP is preserved:

$$(p\langle\checkmark\rangle, p') \boxtimes (q\langle\omega\rangle, q') \;=\; \{\,(rq', p') \mid r \in (p \;|||\; q)\,\}$$

Here and below we assume $\omega, \omega' \neq \checkmark$. Trace r above represents any interleaving of the forward trace p with the forward trace q. The compensation q' is run immediately, i.e., appended to r, while the compensation trace p' is preserved. The case where QQ terminates successfully is similar:

$$(p\langle\omega\rangle, p') \boxtimes (q\langle\checkmark\rangle, q') \;=\; \{\,(rp', q') \mid r \in (p \;|||\; q)\,\}$$

Behaviours in which both processes terminate successfully result in a choice between one or the other succeeding:

$$(p\langle\checkmark\rangle, p') \boxtimes (q\langle\checkmark\rangle, q') \;=\; \{\,(rq', p') \mid r \in (p \;|||\; q)\,\} \,\cup$$
$$\{\,(rp', q') \mid r \in (p \;|||\; q)\,\}$$

Behaviours in which neither terminate successfully are also, in which case the compensations are run in parallel:

$$(p\langle\omega\rangle, p') \boxtimes (q\langle\omega'\rangle, q') \;=\; \{\,(rr', \langle\checkmark\rangle) \mid r \in (p \;|||\; q) \wedge r' \in (p' \;\|\; q')\,\}$$

The operator on compensable behaviours is lifted to compensable processes:

Definition 14 (Speculative Choice).

$$PP \boxtimes QQ \;=\; \{\, pp \boxtimes qq \mid pp \in PP \wedge qq \in QQ \,\}$$

To illustrate the effect of the operator, consider the following example transaction block containing speculative choice:

$$[A \div A' \boxtimes B \div B'] \;=\; A \;\square\; B \;\square\; ((A \;\|\; B)\,;\,(A' \;\square\; B'))$$

Here, either A succeeds (because $B \div B'$ yields immediately) or B succeeds or both succeed with one of A or B being compensated.

If PP and QQ are self-cancelling and their compensations are independent, then their speculative choice is self-cancelling:

$$\frac{\begin{array}{c} self\_cancelling(PP) \\ self\_cancelling(QQ) \\ \forall A \in comp(PP),\, B \in comp(QQ) \cdot independent(A, B) \end{array}}{self\_cancelling(PP \boxtimes QQ)}$$

Under the same conditions, a transaction block consisting of $PP \boxtimes QQ$ is the same as one consisting of $PP \Box QQ$:

$$\frac{\begin{array}{c} self\_cancelling(PP) \\ self\_cancelling(QQ) \\ \forall\, A \in comp(PP),\ B \in comp(QQ) \cdot independent(A, B) \end{array}}{\mathcal{C}[\![\, PP \boxtimes QQ\,]\!] \ = \ \mathcal{C}[\![\, PP \Box QQ\,]\!]}$$

Unlike our other operators, speculative choice is not associative. For example consider the process $(A \div A' \boxtimes B \div B') \boxtimes C \div C'$ and the case where B succeeds overall. This case results in the compensations for the non-succeeding branches being run in the order A' then C'. On the other hand, if B succeeds overall in the process $A \div A' \boxtimes (B \div B' \boxtimes C \div C')$, then the compensations for the non-succeeding branches will be run in the order C' then A'. We could get around this problem by defining an n-ary version of the operator which would select one succeeding branch, if possible, and run the compensations for the other branches in parallel.

7   Related Work

Korth *et al.* [9] define compensating transactions as a way to overcome the limitations of atomicity when dealing with long-running transactions. The authors propose the use of compensating transactions to allow access to uncommitted data and to undo committed transactions. In their work compensation is formalized in terms of the properties it has to guarantee. Consider a transaction T, its compensating transaction CT, and a set of dependent transactions on T (dependent transactions of T are those transactions that read data values written by T). The authors say that a compensation is sound when "compensation does not disturb the outcome of dependent transactions", i.e., the compensation has to:

- reverse the effects of execution of T, and
- assure the outcome of the dependent transactions after the execution of the CT must be the same as if the transaction T did not occur.

As the definition of compensation soundness can be too restrictive the authors present a definition for weaker forms of soundness. Clearly, there are similarities between [9] and our cancellation semantics. One main difference is that [9] does not provide a rich language as the work presented here does. Transaction's operations are limited to reading or writing a set of data, as the focus is on transactional databases.

Two of the authors (Butler and Ferreira) developed the StAC (Structured Activity Compensation) language [2,3] for modelling long-running business transactions which includes compensation constructs. An important difference between StAC and the work presented here is that instead of the execution of compensations being part of the definition of a transaction block, StAC has explicit primitives for running or discarding installed compensations (*reverse* and *accept* respectively). StAC gives a precise interpretation to the mechanics of compensation, including the combination of compensation with parallel execution, hierarchy and exceptions. However, the design of the language does not lend itself to reasoning about the intended effect of a transaction in a compositional way. In particular the separation of the *accept* and *reverse* operators from compensation scoping prevents the definition of a compositional semantics: the semantics of the reverse operator cannot be defined on its own as its behaviour depends on the context in which it is called. These shortcomings were addressed in the work presented here.

Recently Bruni et al [1] have developed an operational semantics for a language with similar operators to ours, including compensation pairs and transaction blocks (or sagas as they call them). Like our work, and unlike StAC, the execution of compensation is part of the definition of a saga which leads to a neater operational semantics. They provide a richer form of exception than us whereby whether or not compensations were run in a saga is visible outside the saga. They also define a form of speculative choice similar to ours.

8   Conclusions

The operators of our language are quite powerful in the way they take care of orchestration of compensation and interrupt handling in a nested way. By working with a trace semantics we have developed a language that supports compensation in the desired way and has a compositional semantics supporting modular reasoning about long-running transactions. Our cancellation semantics is somewhat purist but we believe it points towards what should be achievable with a language for long-running transactions that is designed with correctness in mind. In particular, the way in which the cancellation semantics allows reasoning about normal behaviour and compensation behaviour to be separated is very powerful. The design of our proposed structures has been through many iterations, in which we have sought simpler and simpler formal definitions. We have also tried to make definitions of each feature logically independent of every other feature, so as to reduce the risk of complex interaction effects.

Compensating CSP can be regarded as a design pattern for a tightly-disciplined form of error handling for transactions. The advantage of a special orchestration language is that the implementation is responsible for avoiding the deadlocks and race conditions that almost universally accompany a programmer's attempt to implement the necessary error recovery protocols.

For this paper we have chosen to use a simple trace semantics making strong use of the special terminal events. This trace semantics allowed us to develop simple elegant definitions of the operators which facilitated the proof of the various laws. However we have avoided modelling several important and well understood features of process algebras for concurrent and distributed systems. In particular we have avoided synchronous communication, event hiding and the distinction between internal and external choice. These will require a richer semantic model and now that we have achieved a better grasp of compensation through the trace model, we are in a better position to tackle these other features in combination with compensation. In our self-cancellation rule for compensation pairs, we have only allowed for pairs of atomic actions. To deal with the more general case, our current belief is that we need a semantic model that admits a notion of event refinement where an atomic event at a course level of granularity is replaced by a whole process at a finer-grained level.

Acknowledgements

Thanks to Peter Welch, Marc Shapiro, Roberto Bruni, Hernan Melgratti, Peter Henderson, Mandy Chessell, David Vines and Catherine Griffin for valuable discussion on compensation and exceptions. Thanks to the anonymous referee for suggesting improvements in the presentation and thanks to Bertrand Meyer for pointing out that 'compensable' was preferable to 'compensatable'.

References

1. R. Bruni, H. Melgratti, and U. Montanari. Theoretical foundations for compensations in flow composition languages. In *POPL 2005*, 2005.
2. M. Butler and C. Ferreira. A process compensation language. In *Integrated Formal Methods(IFM'2000)*, volume 1945 of *LNCS*, pages 61 – 76. Springer-Verlag, 2000.
3. M. Butler and C. Ferreira. An operational semantics for StAC, a language for modelling long-running business transactions. In *Coordination 2004*, volume 2949 of *LNCS*. Springer-Verlag, 2004.
4. M. Chessell, D. Vines, C. Griffin, V. Green, and K. Warr. Business process beans: System design and architecture document. Technical report, Transaction Processing Design and New Technology Development Group, IBM UK Laboratories, January 2001.
5. F. Curbera, Y. Goland, J. Klein, F. Leymann, D. Roller, S. Thatte, and S. Weerawarana. Business process execution language for web services, version 1.1. http://www-106.ibm.com/developerworks/library/ws-bpel/, 2003.
6. H. Garcia-Molina and K. Salem. Sagas. In *Proceedings of ACM SIGMOD*, pages 249–259, 1987.
7. J. Gray and A. Reuter. *Transaction Processing: Concepts and Techniques*. Morgan Kaufmann Publishers, 1993.
8. C.A.R Hoare. *Communicating Sequential Processes*. Prentice-Hall, 1985.
9. H. Korth, E. Levy, and A. Silberschatz. A formal approach to recovery by compensating transactions. In *16th VLDB Conference*, Brisbane, Australia, 1990.
10. F. Leymann. Web services flow language, version 1.0. http://www-3.ibm.com/software/solutions/webservices/pdf/WSFL.pdf, 2001. IBM.
11. B. Metha, M. Levy, G. Meredith, T. Andrews, B. Beckman, J. Klein, and A. Mital. BizTalk Server 2000 Business Process Orchestration. *IEEE Data Engineering Bulletin*, 24(1):35–39, 2001.

Practical Application of CSP and FDR
to Software Design

Jonathan Lawrence

IBM United Kingdom Ltd.,
MP 154, IBM Hursley Park,
Winchester, SO21 2JN, UK
jlawrence@uk.ibm.com

Abstract. Most published material on CSP and the FDR tool is theoretical and mathematically rigorous, which can be daunting to the less mathematical software engineer. It is also often difficult to relate the elegant but abstract examples in the literature to the problems of the software engineer who must eventually produce an executable program expressed in a procedural programming language This paper outlines a number of techniques which may be used to model procedural designs in CSP and to structure the refinements so as to render them tractable to verification by the FDR model-checking tool. A simple example, taken from a recent IBM Software Services engagement, is used to illustrate some of the ideas presented in the paper.

1 Introduction

This paper describes some of the author's experiences applying CSP in conjunction with the FDR model-checking tool to a range of small design problems which have arisen in the course of recent IBM Software Services consultancy projects.

1.1 Indebtedness to CSP

 The author has been using the CSP notation and FDR tool intermittently for about ten years; initially for the formalization of a concurrent design for the logging component of a transaction processing system, and subsequently for a few other minor pieces of design work and an MSc project.

More recently, and perhaps surprisingly, considerable scope for the application of CSP and FDR has been found in a number of services engagements involving the delivery of bespoke software components or system designs. In all such cases to date, the client has not required and has not been aware that CSP has been used for some aspect of the project; so use of the notation and tools could not be permitted to adversely affect other factors such as performance, function and cost.

That the application of CSP is viable in a commercial environment where cost and delivery schedules are of almost equal importance to quality and reliability, and where neither safety nor security are critical concerns, is a good indication that the combined CSP and FDR approach is sufficiently mature for wider use in software engineering.

A.E. Abdallah, C.B. Jones, and J.W. Sanders (Eds.): CSP25, LNCS 3525, pp. 151 – 174, 2005.

Even in cases where CSP has not been formally used for a design, the conceptual principles behind the notation, and a slightly extended form of CSP communication diagram, have been found helpful in formulating and recording designs.

1.2 Suitability

The CSP approach is most suitable for tackling problems where communication or concurrency is a key concern. In this context, communication includes not only the domain of transport protocols, but also for example a pattern of communication between tightly-coupled components of a software system; while concurrency would include interactions with independent entities such as users and external devices as well as the obvious application to multi-threaded operating environments. It is less well suited to dealing with systems with large and complex state, for which state-based notations such as Z, B or VDM are more appropriate.

An important factor in the successful application of CSP and FDR has been a high degree of selectivity in the choice of problem to tackle. The scope must be sufficiently well-defined to be able to isolate a portion of the system to treat, while being sufficiently complex that there is benefit to be gained from the investment of effort involved. For this reason, the approach has not been applied to every project, and then, typically, only to one aspect of the design.

The remainder of this paper is devoted to an example exemplifying the type of problem to which the approach has been applied, concluding with a summary of the benefits which have been achieved through the use of CSP in software design.

2 Example: A Multi-threaded Connection Pool

The example presented in this paper was developed as part of a recent IBM Software Services engagement. It illustrates some techniques for the use of CSP and FDR to model and verify software designs; in this case, applied to a multi-threaded connection pooling mechanism forming part of a communications adapter between a Web Server and a transaction processing system.

2.1 Overview

A transport layer to be used for communication provides the notion of a *connection* which may be thought of as an established link between the two systems. Once created, a connection may be used to transmit requests and receive responses on behalf of any client thread; however only one thread at a time may use a connection (this restriction is not policed, but if violated leads to unpredictable results). The creation and destruction of connections is expensive, and the overhead of creating a fresh connection for each client request would be prohibitive. It is therefore necessary to maintain a pool of persistent connections and allocate them to client threads as required, while ensuring that no two threads are ever allocated the same connection concurrently.

Connections are also a limited resource and costly to maintain, so the number of open connections must be carefully controlled, and will usually be less than the number of potential client threads which wish to use them. The design envisaged allows for a fixed maximum number, `poolsize`, of connections to be permanently allocated; but in order to cater for short-term peaks in demand the system may allocate further connections up to an additional maximum, `extpoolsize`. These extra connections are closed when no longer required. In the event that more concurrent requests are received than can be accommodated within the total, (`maxconn=poolsize+extpoolsize`), the system may suspend up to `queuesize` threads to wait for a connection to become free; but requests exceeding this limit are rejected. This queueing scheme allows some requests to succeed rather than be rejected, at the cost of some delay, but prevents the system from becoming clogged with suspended threads.

poolsize	extpoolsize	queuesize	reject

0   Number of concurrent requests

───▶

2.2 Specification

Although there is some value in modelling just the design of a software component and then perhaps using a model-checking tool to verify certain desirable properties such as deadlock-freedom; much greater benefit is derived if a specification of the required behaviour is constructed, and the design verified against it. Typically such a specification will be much simpler than the design, such that it can be shown to meet the requirements by inspection or informal arguments, possibly supplemented by additional formal checks using a tool. The level of abstraction to be used in a design is also usually established at the specification stage.

Definitions

Before the specification can be constructed it is necessary to define some datatypes and constants used to label entities and determine system parameters. The datatype `ConnId` introduces a set of tokens used to identify connection instances.

```
datatype ConnId = nil | c1 | c2 | c3
```

`nil` is a special 'null' connection ID which does not refer to a real connection, and is excluded from the set of actual connection IDs.

```
ConnSet = diff(ConnId,{nil})
```

The maximum number of connections which may exist at any time is equal to the number of valid connection IDs, and there must be at least one connection available otherwise all requests will deadlock or be rejected.

```
maxconn = card(ConnSet)
assert maxconn > 0
```

In a multi-threaded design such as this, it is almost always necessary to be able to identify the thread taking part in a particular action, and so the datatype `ThreadId` is defined to provide labels for threads.

```
datatype ThreadId = t1 | t2 | t3 | t4
```

Some constants determining system parameters:

```
poolsize = 2   -- no. of connections to keep open
extpoolsize = maxconn - poolsize   -- extras
queuesize = 2   -- no. of threads allowed to queue
```

All the above size parameters must be non-negative.

```
assert poolsize     >= 0
assert extpoolsize >= 0
assert queuesize    >= 0
```

Possible responses from a call to the pool are defined by the datatype `Response`.

```
datatype Response = ok | error | full
```

`ok` and `error` both indicate that a link request to the target system was made, and it succeeded or failed respectively. `full` indicates that the request was rejected because all available connections were in use, and the queue was full at the time of the request. The level of abstraction to be used in the design is thus already beginning to become apparent from the definition of the possible responses.

Threads

The structure we will use for the specification is a set of independent threads, represented by interleaved processes, handling requests to the system. `call` is the channel on which requests are received at the external interface. `enter` and `exit` are internal channels representing a thread being accepted into, and later leaving the connection pool. All of these carry a label identifying the thread taking part in the event, in order to keep track of which threads are in which state and to tie target links back to the originating thread.

```
channel call,enter,exit:ThreadId
```

Note that no actual request data is represented here, even on the `call` channel. This is a deliberate abstraction from the real system, simply because we do not care about the data for the purposes of this specification – we are solely concerned with the management of the connections, and believe that the transmission of data is a detail which can safely be added at the implementation stage.

The event `reject` is used when a request cannot be processed because the system is full. There is no need to identify a thread on this channel.

```
channel reject
```

The channel link represents an invocation of the target system. The thread must be identified on this channel since otherwise an implementation would be free to return a response (and probably any associated data) to any thread, rather than the one which made the request.

```
channel link:ThreadId.{ok,error} -- no 'full' on link
channel return:ThreadId.Response -- any poss. Response
```

The process Thread(t) models the behaviour of the single thread with label t, at the specification level. What we are actually modelling is the behaviour of a thread within the connection pool, which initially only accepts a call for that thread, then offers an external choice of reject or enter. This choice is later resolved by a supervisor process which is monitoring the state of the connection pool.

```
Thread(t) = call.t -> (reject -> return.t.full -> SKIP
                  []   enter.t -> link.t?r ->
                       exit.t -> return.t!r -> SKIP);
                  Thread(t)
```

Depending on the branch chosen, the thread either returns immediately with a full response, or issues a link to the target system before registering its completion via the exit channel and returning control to the caller via return. Since the channels enter, exit and reject will be hidden when the specification is assembled, the external view of a thread may be represented by the following diagram:

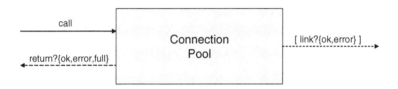

The diagram represents the connection pool as a black box which accepts call requests, may optionally issue a link, and then returns to the caller. The response on return depends on whether the link is issued and if so, what the result was. Threads do not communicate directly with each other, only indirectly through their interactions with shared data or synchronization components; so the combined behaviour of all threads is simply the interleaving of the individual threads.

```
Threads = ||| t : ThreadId @ Thread(t)
```

If the internal events were to be hidden at this stage, the external choice on each iteration of a Thread would become nondeterministic, and the system would be anarchic, choosing arbitrarily whether to process or reject each request.

Supervisor

To impose order on the system corresponding to our informal requirements for the connection pool, we introduce a supervisor process which maintains a global view of the state of the system, monitoring and controlling the possible actions of the threads according to that view.

The following diagram represents the Supervisor process for the connection pool. Its state comprises two variables: active, the set of threads which have been allocated a connection and are in the process of linking to the target system; and queue, a sequence of threads which have been accepted but are awaiting the allocation of a connection. Potential example values are given for each variable.

Supervisor

| active : Set(ThreadId) : {t3,t2} |
| queue : Seq(ThreadId) : <t1,t4> |

```
empty(inter(active,set(queue)))
card(active) <= maxconn
#queue <= queuesize
card(active) == maxconn or
                     null(queue)
```

reject

enter

link

exit

The lower portion of the diagram gives an invariant for the state, which is not necessarily complete, i.e. a partial invariant.

- No thread may be simultaneously active and in the queue.
- The number of active threads is limited to the number of available connections.
- The size of the queue is limited to queuesize.
- All available connections must be in use for a thread to be queued.

The full CSP definition of the Supervisor process is given below. Note that if the stated invariant becomes false after any event, the process deadlocks immediately,

```
Supervisor(active,queue)=
empty(inter(active,set(queue))) and
card(active) <= maxconn and
#queue <= queuesize and
(card(active) == maxconn or null(queue)) &
```

The choice between enter and reject is based on the state, which is then updated to reflect that choice.

```
(if card(active) < maxconn
  then enter?t -> Supervisor(union(active,{t}),queue)
  else if #queue == queuesize  -- full
       then reject -> Supervisor(active,queue)
       else enter?t -> Supervisor(active,queue^<t>))
[]
```

Threads which are active (i.e. have an allocated connection) are permitted to engage in link or exit. In the latter case the state is updated as the connection is no longer required by that thread.

```
([]t : active @  -- active threads only
     link.t?_ -> Supervisor(active,queue)
  [] exit.t ->
     let left = diff(active,{t}) within
     if null(queue)
     then Supervisor(left,queue)
     else Supervisor(union(left,{head(queue)}),
                     tail(queue)))
```

The style of expressing a CSP process in the form:

```
P(s) = Inv(s) & [] e : E(s) -> P(s')
```

is useful as it allows us to formalize an invariant in a way which will be flagged by FDR if ever violated since it will quickly result in a total deadlock of the whole system. Alternatively divergence could be used in a similar pattern.

Assembly

The complete specification for the connection pool is given by the parallel combination of the threads with the supervisor process in its initial state, synchronizing on the channels shared by the threads and the supervisor, and hiding the internal events.

```
PoolSpec =
     (Threads                               -- all threads
      [|{|enter,exit,reject,link|}|]       -- shared channels
      Supervisor({},<>))                    -- initial state
      \ {|enter,exit,reject|}               -- hide internals
```

The structure of the specification is illustrated in the following diagram.

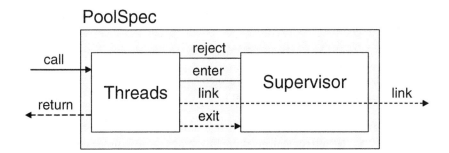

Validation

At this point, it is appropriate to ask whether what we have specified is actually what we intended, since clearly if it is not, then even a perfect implementation of it will not meet the requirements. There are several techniques which can help to validate the specification:

1. Careful inspection or peer review, paying attention to synchronization and hiding, which are common sources of error.
2. Use of a tool such as ProBe to explore possible behaviour of the specification.
3. Formulation of expected properties of the specification as CSP processes, and then using FDR to check those properties.

A couple of quick checks which require little effort to formulate and are sometimes valid are deadlock and divergence freedom, which both happen to apply in this case. The deadlock freedom check also implicitly checks that the stated invariant for the Supervisor state is not violated.

```
assert PoolSpec :[ deadlock free[FD] ]
assert PoolSpec :[ divergence free ]
```

An example of a stronger check of the validity of the specification can be formulated if we consider how we would expect the specification to behave if its `link` channel is hidden. In this case, and abstracting the internal state of the supervisor so that the choice between `reject` and `enter` becomes nondeterministic, each thread may perform an infinite sequence of `call-return` pairs with a nondeterministic choice of response on each `return` event.

```
ThreadInterface(t) = |~| r : Response @
    call.t -> return.t!r -> ThreadInterface(t)
```

The multi-threaded version of the interface should be the interleaving of each thread separately, with no interference between threads. This independence of the threads only holds with `link` hidden since otherwise the refusal of the environment to engage in `link` for one thread may block another waiting in the queue for a connection.

```
PoolInterface = ||| t : ThreadId @ ThreadInterface(t)
```

The FDR refinement check can now be expressed, that our abstract nondeterministic interface specification is refined by `PoolSpec` with the `link` channel hidden. The validity of this assertion in fact includes the deadlock and divergence freedom properties by inspection.

```
assert PoolInterface [FD= PoolSpec \ {|link|}
```

Frequently, the failure of an eventual refinement check of the design will indicate errors or inaccuracies in the specification which need to be corrected. In other words, a 'correct' design can be found not to meet the specification originally formulated because the latter is too prescriptive, or some unforeseen subtlety of the operational semantics renders the refinement invalid. In such cases it is the specification rather than the design which needs to be revised and revalidated.

2.3 Design

Design remains the responsibility of the software engineer. CSP and FDR can only help to model, record and verify a design; they cannot help to conceive it. Often, the engineer will have an outline design in mind at the specification stage and this will inform the construction of the specification.

The design for the connection pooling mechanism has four components:

1. The connections provided by the transport layer.
2. A control component which maintains a record of the state of the pool and queue. This is a single shared data component which is used by all threads and which does not provide any synchronization except to protect itself.
3. A dispatcher component which has two functions: synchronization (suspend/ resume) of threads in the queue, and connection passing.

4. The threads. Each client thread is a separate process, identical apart from the label used to identify it. These represent independent copies of the same algorithm executing on separate threads, while accessing the same shared components, and as such are similar to the `Thread` processes of the specification.

It would probably be possible to conceive a design (especially in Java) in which the control and dispatcher functions are combined, but separation of these concerns results in a cleaner, more understandable, maintainable and portable structure.

Connections

Although we will not need to implement connections, as they are provided by the transport layer, we need to model them in order to include them in the design. The technique used here is one way to model resources which can be obtained and released, such as memory, objects or in this case, connections. The channels `create` and `close` respectively represent the actions of obtaining and releasing a particular connection, and hence are labelled with a valid connection ID.

```
channel create,close : ConnSet
```

The channel `start_link` is used to represent the use of a particular connection, by a specified thread, to access the target system. The thread ID is necessary for the same reason that it appears on the `link` channel used in the specification; indeed, `end_link` will later be renamed to `link` when the design is fully assembled.

```
channel start_link    : ConnSet.ThreadId
channel end_link      : ConnSet.ThreadId.{ok,error}
```

The link channel of the specification has been split into two separate channels for the design. This allows the model to include the possibility of interleaving of link requests which we wish to guard against, so that its occurrence can be detected by FDR. The complete interface of the transport layer is given by the following set definition and will be useful later.

```
ConnInterface = {|create,close,start_link,end_link|}
```

It is useful to define a divergent process which can be used to represent a broken component – often one which has been used in some invalid way. If this state is reached in an FDR check of the design it will cause the check to fail. A simple divergent process is:

```
DIV = STOP |~| DIV
```

Before a connection has been created, or while a `link` request is being processed by a connection on behalf of a thread, it should be invalid for any `close` or `start_link` event to occur for a connection. `ConnError` is a process which may always accept any such event and then immediately diverge, causing FDR to flag its occurrence during a refinement check.

```
ConnError(c) = [] e : {|close.c,start_link.c|} @
                  e -> DIV
```

Initially, a connection may be considered to be in a latent, unobtained state in which it can only validly engage in the action of being created.

```
Connection(c) = create.c -> Active(c)
                [] ConnError(c)
```

Any attempt to close or use a connection before it has been created will result in divergence, so if our design does this it will be detected by FDR. After creation, a connection may be closed, or used by any thread to initiate a link to the target system. In the latter case it moves to a distinct Linking state.

```
Active(c) = close.c -> Connection(c)
            [] start_link.c?t -> Linking(c,t)
```

In the Linking state a connection may complete the link request and return to the Active state ready for other requests, but we also allow the possibility of an invalid event (close or start_link), leading to divergence. If this scenario can arise in the assembled design it will be detected by FDR, allowing us to police the requirement that link requests are not interleaved on a connection. This could not be done if a link remained as a single atomic event in the design.

```
Linking(c,t) = end_link.c.t?_ -> Active(c)
               [] ConnError(c)
```

In fact, although a connection is modelled as remaining active after end_link we will regard an error response as indicating a possible problem with that connection, and close it without further reuse. Connections are independent of each other, so the complete transport layer is represented by the interleaving of all possible valid connections.

```
Connections = ||| c : ConnSet @ Connection(c)
```

The following diagram illustrates the structure of Connections, showing how it is composed of the interleaving of several independent Connection processes labelled by unique connection IDs. The meaning of the arrows, dashed and dotted lines for the channels is as explained earlier for the high-level description of the Connection Pool.

The diagram also anticipates the eventual renaming of end_link to link in the final system, to conform to the external interface of the specification. This is explained further when the complete system is assembled later.

This simple model of the transport layer relies for its validity on the way it is used by the threads: when creating a connection a thread must use an external choice over all valid connection IDs (... -> create?c -> ...) – it may not attempt to create a particular connection although this is not prohibited by the model.

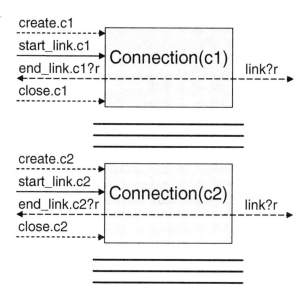

Control

The `Control` component keeps track of the state of the pool. It provides two functions: 1) obtain a connection from the pool; and 2) return a connection to the pool after use. Often when modelling a shared data component such as this, each function will be represented by a single channel, but in this case a more complicated pattern is used where each function can result in a choice over several channels, this choice being determined by the values of the state variables.

The following channels (plus `reject` which has already been defined) are used to request a connection from the `Control` component. The client thread must offer an external choice of these channels when requesting a connection from `Control`, and subsequently act according to the channel actually chosen.

```
channel allocate,reject  -- create a new connection
channel reuse : ConnSet  -- reuse a pooled connection
channel wait : ThreadId   -- suspend thread
```

In a similar way, the following channels are used to return a connection to the pool:

```
channel repool:ConnId -- this may be nil indicating
that the connection is closed
channel release -- release the connection if not
already closed
channel pass:ThreadId -- pass the connection to this
thread
```

It is convenient, and reduces the likelihood of errors when assembling the complete system, to define the set of all events in the client interface of `Control`:

```
ControlInterface = {|reject,allocate,reuse,wait,
                     repool,release,pass|}
```

The channel `close` is not included in this definition as it is a demonic event of the component and is not synchronized with the client threads.

`Control` may be represented by the following diagram, following a similar pattern to that for the `Supervisor` process of the specification:

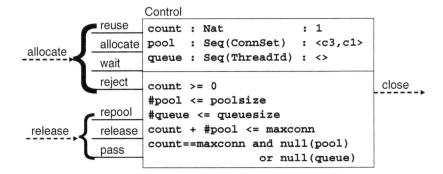

As for `Supervisor`, potential example values are given for each state variable, and an invariant is specified in the lower portion of the diagram, which as before, may be only partially complete.

The complete CSP definition for the Control component follows.

```
Control(count,pool,queue) =
count >= 0                 and
#pool <= poolsize          and
#queue <= queuesize        and
count + #pool <= maxconn   and
((count == maxconn and null(pool)) or null(queue)) &
((not null(pool) & let front^<last> = pool within
  STOP |~| close!last -> Control(count,front,queue))
[]          -- cases when requesting a connection
( if count==maxconn
  then if #queue < queuesize
       then wait?t -> Control(count,pool,queue^<t>)
       else reject -> Control(count,pool,queue)
  else if null(pool)
       then allocate -> Control(count+1,pool,queue)
       else reuse!head(pool) ->
            Control(count+1,tail(pool),queue) )
[]          -- cases when returning a connection
( if null(queue)
  then if #pool == poolsize
       then release -> Control(count-1,pool,queue)
       else repool?c ->
            if c == nil
            then Control(count-1,pool,queue)
            else Control(count-1,<c>^pool,queue)
  else pass!head(queue) ->
       Control(count,pool,tail(queue))))
```

Dispatcher

The dispatcher component combines two functions: explicit thread synchronization (suspend / resume) and connection passing. The suspend channel identifies the thread which is to be suspended:

```
channel suspend : ThreadId
```

The channels `resume` and `dispatch` each identify the thread being resumed, but also transmit a connection to be used by that thread. This is an input on the resume channel, and an output on dispatch.

```
channel resume,dispatch : ThreadId.ConnId
Ready(t,c) = dispatch.t.c -> Ready(t,c)
              [] suspend.t -> Suspended(t)
              [] resume.t?c -> Resumed(t,c)
Suspended(t) = resume.t?c -> Ready(t,c)
              [] suspend.t -> DIV
Resumed(t,c) = suspend.t -> Ready(t,c)
              [] resume.t?_ -> DIV
```

A state transition diagram illustrating the Ready process for a thread is given below.

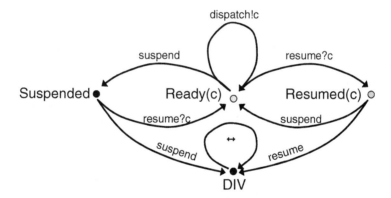

The complete Dispatcher function for all threads is simply the interleaving of each individual thread's dispatcher, initialized with a null connection.

```
Dispatcher = ||| t : ThreadId @ Ready(t,nil)
```

As with Control it is convenient to define the set of all events in the interface of Dispatcher.

```
DispatchInterface = {|suspend,resume,dispatch|}
```

Threads

We now model the actions of a client thread interacting with `Control`, `Dispatcher` and `Connections`. We call this `Client(t)`, labelled by `ThreadId`. Essentially this is a CSP model of the algorithm to be followed by a thread invoking the call function of the connection pool. There are 3 stages to the processing:

1. Obtain a connection from the pool if possible, or wait for one to become available (if neither of these is possible then the request is rejected).
2. Use the connection obtained in stage 1 to link to the target system.
3. Release the connection to the pool and return to the caller.

As in the specification, each thread is modelled as a separate copy of identical processes with events labelled with a `ThreadId`.

```
Client(t) = call.t ->           -- caller initiates process
(   reject -> return.t!full -> Client(t)
[] wait.t -> suspend.t -> dispatch.t?c ->    -- suspend
                (if c != nil then Execute(t,c)   -- valid
                 else create?d -> Execute(t,d)) -- need new
[] allocate -> create?d -> Execute(t,d)        -- need new
[] reuse?c -> Execute(t,c) )    -- connection from pool
```

The process `Execute(t,c)` represents thread `t` once it has obtained a valid connection `c`. It initiates a link to the target system via `start_link` using the connection, and then waits to engage in the corresponding `end_link` event.

```
Execute(t,c) =   -- thread has valid connection c to use
start_link.c.t -> end_link.c.t?r -> -- link to target
if r == ok then Release(t,c,r)      -- retain connection
else close.c -> Release(t,nil,r)    -- close due to error
```

Finally the thread must release the connection back to `Control` and return to its caller. As when obtaining a connection, the thread must offer an external choice over the `Control` channels used for release, and take appropriate action depending on the channel chosen by `Control`. In all cases, the last event is to return the response from the link, before reverting to the initial state to await the next call on that thread.

```
Release(t,c,r) =
( repool!c -> SKIP -- c is back in pool, no more to do
[] release -> (if c==nil then SKIP    -- already closed
                else close.c -> SKIP) -- must close c
[] pass?u -> resume.u!c -> SKIP); -- pass c to thread u
    return.t!r -> Client(t) -- return response to caller
```

Threads do not communicate except indirectly through their interactions with the shared components, so the combined behaviour of all the client threads is simply the interleaving of the individual threads.

```
Clients = ||| t : ThreadId @ Client(t)
```

Assembly

The following diagram illustrates how the complete CSP model of the implementation is assembled from its component parts.

Starting with `Clients`, we add the other components one at a time, synchronizing on the shared interface events and then hiding them at each stage. `DispatchClients` is the combination of `Clients` with `Dispatcher`.

```
DispatchClients = ( Clients
                       [|DispatchInterface|]
                       Dispatcher ) \
                       DispatchInterface
```

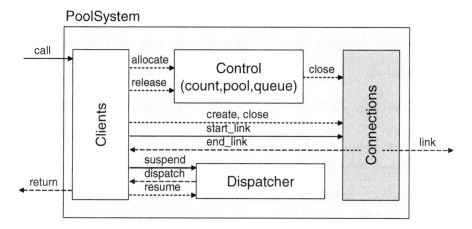

Next, we add the `Control` component. Note that because `close` is not in `ControlInterface`, `close` events from `Clients` and from `Control` are interleaved rather than synchronized and so may occur independently.

```
ControlClients = ( DispatchClients
                       [|ControlInterface|]
                       Control(0,<>,<>) ) \
                       ControlInterface
```

Next, the `Connections` are added in a similar way. The `end_link` channel remains exposed at this stage as it will become the `link` channel from the specification.

```
ConnClients = ( ControlClients
                   [|ConnInterface|]
                   Connections ) \
                   {|create,close,start_link|}
```

Finally, all `end_link` events are renamed to `link` for compatibility with the specification. This involves removing the `ConnId` labels from the events as they are no longer relevant.

```
PoolSystem = ConnClients [[end_link.c <- link |
                                       c <- ConnSet]]
```

Verification

The required refinement relationship between the specification and design is expressed as an FDR assertion using the most general semantic model.

```
assert PoolSpec [FD= PoolSystem
```

We are now ready to perform the verification using FDR. The structure of the system means that any check of the above assertion implicitly subsumes the corresponding checks for any subset of ThreadId; however it is still useful to start with one thread and work up as this will detect errors which become apparent only when a certain number of threads access the system concurrently, as well as ensuring that we begin well within the capacity of the tool.

For all combinations of system parameters which have been tried and for which the check completed, the assertion holds. Typical output from the end of a check is given below, in this case for four threads, three available connections, a poolsize of 2 and a queuesize of 1.

```
. . .
+.41,850,000 *
+.*
+.*
+.... 41,855,808
Refine checked 41,855,808 states
With 198584320 transitions
Took 7166(6791+57) seconds
```

The following table gives the corresponding number of states and transitions for a few different checks, which are of interest if only to show how the size of the check depends on the number of threads and other parameters.

#t	#c	pool size	queue size	States	transitions
3	1	0	0	1,847	5,916
3	1	1	1	48,392	146,032
3	2	0	1	87,708	278,538
3	2	1	1	110,712	376,926
4	2	2	1	54,781,182	241,887,276
4	3	2	1	41,855,808	198,584,320

2.4 Implementation

This section illustrates how a CSP design such as our connection pool can be recast into an executable procedural program, in this case in the Java language. The translation process is manual, and involves not only a change of language, but also the removal of abstractions present in the design and some minor enhancements not reflected in the CSP model.

The Java code presented here is a simplified version of the actual implementation from the project, intended to make the relationship to the CSP design clearer.

Dispatcher

The Dispatcher class implements the Ready process for a thread, so there will be a separate instance of this class for each thread in the queue. The methods of this class, suspend() and resume(), are both synchronized (in the Java sense), so that their actions are effectively atomic as in the CSP model, as well as being necessary in order to use the Java wait()/notify() mechanism.

constants

Three constants are defined corresponding to the possible states of the dispatcher as follows.

```
private static final int ready    = 1;  -- Ready(c)
private static final int suspended = 2; -- Suspended
private static final int resumed   = 3;  -- Resumed(c)
```

variables

Each Dispatcher instance has two variables; state, which takes one of the three constant values defined above, and conn, which is the Connection passed to the thread by resume(). The initial values of the variables correspond to the process Ready(t,nil) as in the CSP definition of the Dispatcher component.

```
private int         state = ready;
private Connection conn   = null;
```

suspend()

The action of suspend() depends on the state at the time it is invoked. If ready, it is moved to the suspended state and caused to wait for the corresponding call to resume(). If already resumed, there is no need to wait and the thread can proceed immediately. The connection stored on resume() is returned to the caller.

```
synchronized Connection suspend() { // suspend.t ->
  switch (state) {
    case ready :
      state = suspended;
      try { wait(); }
      catch (InterruptedException e) {}
      break;
    case suspended :
      exception("Already suspended");
    case resumed :
      state = ready;
      break;
  } // switch()
  return conn;  // -> dispatch.t!conn
} // suspend()   // -> Ready(conn)
```

resume()

The `resume()` method stores the connection being passed to the target thread in the instance and then modifies the state depending on its initial value in accordance with the CSP. If a thread is already suspended, then it is notified to allow its `wait()` to complete.

```
synchronized void resume(Connection c) {
  conn = c;
  switch (state) {
    case ready :
      state = resumed;
      break;
    case suspended :
      state = ready;
      notify();
      break;
    case resumed :
      exception("Already resumed");
  } // switch()
} // resume()
```

Pool

The Java class `Pool` combines the implementations of two components of the design: `Control` and `Client(t)`. Roughly speaking, the instance variables together with the `synchronized()` blocks within the `allocate()` and `release()` methods correspond to `Control`; whilst `call()` and the remaining code from the other methods together implement `Client(t)`. The melding of the two CSP processes is an implementation convenience partly due to the fact that Java allows only a single return parameter on a method call. Note that the thread executing this code is never identified explicitly as it is in the CSP but is always present by implication.

constants

Three constants are defined corresponding to the CSP datatype `Response`.

```
public static final int ok    = 1;
public static final int error = 2;
public static final int full  = 3;
```

variables

The instance variables of `Pool` have an obvious correspondence with the state variables of the CSP `Control` process in the design. `count` is a simple integer, whilst the two sequences `pool` and `queue` are each implemented by a Java `Vector` object. The initial values of these variables correspond to the initial state of `Control` in the assembled `PoolSystem`, i.e. `Control(0,<>,<>)`.

```
private int    count = 0;
private Vector pool  = new Vector();
private Vector queue = new Vector();
```

allocate()

The `synchronized()` block in this method implements the CSP choice between the possible connection allocation events of `Control`. The choice which is made is communicated to the subsequent code (part of `Client(t)`) by different combinations of local variables.

```
private Connection allocate() {
  Dispatcher thread = null;
  Connection conn = null;  // allocate
  boolean queue = false;
  synchronized (this) {
    if (count >= maxconn) {
      if (queue.size() < queuesize) {
        thread = new Dispatcher();
        queue.add(thread);
        queue = true; // wait
      }
      else return null; // reject
    }
    else {
      if (!pool.isEmpty()) // reuse
        conn = pool.remove(pool.size()-1);
      count++;
    }
  } // synchronized()
  if (queue) conn = thread.suspend();
  if (conn == null) conn = create();
  return conn;
} // allocate()
```

release()

As with allocate(), the synchronized() block here implements the CSP choice between the possible connection release events of Control. The choice is communicated to the subsequent code by different combinations of the local variables waiter and conn, which then behaves according to the corresponding path of the Client(t) CSP process.

```
private void release(Connection conn) {
  Dispatcher waiter = null;
  synchronized (this) {
    if (queue.isEmpty()) {
      count--;
      if (conn != null) pool.add(conn); // repool
      if (pool.size() > poolsize)
        conn = pool.remove(0); // release
      else conn = null;
    }
```

```
      else waiter = queue.remove(0); // pass
    } // synchronized()
    if (waiter != null) waiter.resume(conn);
    else if (conn != null) conn.close();
  } // release()
```

call()

This is the only public method of `Pool`, and implements those sections of the `Client(t)` process not included within the `allocate()` or `release()` methods, including the top-level `call` and `return` events. Note the introduction here of data to be exchanged with the target system on `link()`. The omission of this data from the CSP model is one of the abstractions employed in the design.

```
  public int call(byte[] data) {
    Connection conn = allocate();
    if (conn==null) return full; // return.t!full -> ...
    else { // Execute(t,conn)
      boolean success = conn.link(data);   // ok | error
      if (!success) { // r != ok
        conn.close;     // close.conn ->
        conn = null;   // Release(t,nil,r)
      }
      release(conn);   // Release(t,conn,r)
      if (success) return ok;   // return.t!r -> Client(t)
      else return error;
    } // else()
  } // call()
```

3 Summary

The original design and implementation of the connection pooling component described in this paper was completed in three days, from the preliminary CSP specification to initial testing of the Java code, including verification of the design using FDR. This time was split approximately equally between developing and verifying the CSP design, and recasting it as executable Java. Following delivery of the system containing the connection pooling mechanism to the client shortly thereafter, no errors have been detected in the implementation in spite of thorough testing and heavy usage of the system by the client.

The implementation was subsequently enhanced with some functions not included in the CSP model, notably the ability to cause threads which have been queueing for more than a certain interval to time out. These modifications were not added to the CSP model (although it would have been perfectly feasible to do so), because it was thought that the effort involved would not be justified by the likely benefit in verifying the enhancements. Rather it was considered that the clear structure and design intent engendered by the original use of CSP meant that the necessary modifications could be made without risk to the integrity of the core design; and this appears to have been borne out in practice.

Other Techniques
The example in this paper has illustrated some techniques for modelling procedural, and in particular multi-threaded, designs in CSP such that they may be checked by the FDR tool. For example:

- Abstraction.
- Specification; and validation of specification properties.
- Modelling multiple threads including non-interleaving properties.
- Design – decomposition into data / synchronization / processing elements.
- Resource allocation and deallocation.
- Specifying and checking state invariants of processes.
- Design verification with FDR refinement assertions.
- Implementation by translation of CSP to procedural code.

A single example, however, can only exemplify a small cross-section of the techniques which might need to be applied to model and verify a wider range of problems. In particular the example used in the paper is sufficiently simple that one stage of refinement is sufficient to reach an (almost) directly implementable level of design. This is by no means always the case and several techniques may need to be applied to deal with larger problems. Some of these are summarized below.

- Stepwise refinement. A crucial property of CSP semantics is that all CSP operators are monotonic with respect to refinement. This allows an abstract or not directly implementable process to appear at one level of a design, and for it to be refined and checked separately. An unmanageably large design may thereby be broken down into several more manageable design steps, each independently verifiable by FDR.
- Interface wrapping. Often, where stepwise refinement is used, the intermediate abstract component may not be directly refineable because its interface refers directly to events which will not exist or will not be exposed in the design. In such cases an additional call-return interface layer may be inserted to encapsulate the component and the wrapped version then refined. The validity of the introduction of this additional interface layer may itself be checked, often at a single thread level.
- Interface protocols and rely-guarantee contracts. A 'correct' design may not be a true CSP refinement of the specification because of some reliance on the way the system will be used. It is usually possible to deal with such cases by formalizing the permissible usage scenarios as a CSP process and including this in parallel with the specification to be refined.
- Avoidance of unbounded state. The FDR tool is not able to check systems with unbounded or even very large state spaces and there are several ways of reducing or avoiding such problems; for example:

      o Factor out unbounded state components from the system.

      o Use modulo arithmetic to reduce state space of numeric types.

      o Place bounds on counts by introducing artificial deadlock or divergence in a specification.

- Data independence. This idea has already been mentioned elsewhere and involves replacing a large datatype with a much smaller one for the purpose of the model.

Even for the example in the paper, the step from the CSP `Control` component of the design to the implementation of the `allocate()` and `release()` methods of the Java `Pool` class is not entirely obvious, and an additional stage employing interface wrapping and stepwise refinement might have been added.

A couple of other techniques which can be useful for certain special classes of problem are:

- Discrete time modelling. FDR does not include support for the semantics of Timed CSP, however some timing aspects can be modelled and checked by FDR using a technique of 'untimed time', in which the 'tocks' of a clock are represented as CSP events in the untimed language.
- Fairness modelling. CSP does not have any built-in notion of fairness, in other words there is nothing in the language to prevent infinite overtaking from occurring. However, it is perfectly feasible to construct an explicit representation of a concept of fairness for any given system. The form of this representation is typically system dependent but can be similar to the way that lossy channels are sometimes represented in communication protocols.

4 Conclusion

This paper has presented one example of the application of an approach to software development involving the CSP notation for modelling combined with the use of the FDR model-checking tool for validation and verification of the specification and design respectively.

Benefits
Apart from the obvious benefit of the capability for automated verification of designs from their specifications, the use of CSP in software engineering has other advantages.

- Discipline for structuring designs. The use of CSP naturally encourages the decomposition of a design into clearly defined logical units, resulting in a more understandable and maintainable implementation structure.
- Elegance and efficiency. In the author's opinion, the use of CSP tends to result in designs which are more elegant and economical, both in terms of the amount of code required and its runtime efficiency.
- Design documentation. In common with other design methodologies, the CSP approach inevitably results in the production of design documentation at a higher level of abstraction than the eventual code. Where connection diagrams

are used, the diagrams record the overall structure, whereas the details of the behaviour of individual components are in the CSP.

- Hierarchical decomposition. In larger systems, a natural consequence of stepwise refinement is that the design is split up into manageable chunks which can be understood and implemented largely independently of each other.

Limitations

Probably the main limitation of the approach discussed in the paper is the restriction on the size of system which can be checked by the tool. For example, the example in this paper can be checked with up to four threads and any given combination of the other parameters in the space of a few hours on a modern workstation. However, the state space which needs to be explored increases approximately exponentially with the number of threads and when an additional thread is defined the check can only be completed for a small subset of combinations of the other parameters.

Consequently, verification of such a design by FDR for certain specific cases can provide a considerable level of confidence in the correctness of a design, but cannot prove it to be correct as the system is scaled up. An exception is where data-independence is exploited, as this is known to scale up without affecting the validity of checks performed with small datatypes. For certain very restricted classes of problem the scalability limitation can be overcome by an inductive technique but this is not applicable to designs such as that presented in this paper.

Other Examples

Some other recent examples of the use of the combined CSP and FDR approach from the author's consultancy work include:

- A design for a concurrent twin-buffering logger.
- A transport protocol for transmitting 'unbounded' data in finite segments.
- A design for the Web-enablement of a CICS 3270 application.
- A mechanism to ensure once-only initialization under race conditions.
- A model of a bimodal locking algorithm for Java objects.

These have mostly been of a similar size and complexity to the example in this paper and the results, in terms of the benefit from the application of the approach have also been comparable. A few other examples where adapted connection diagrams only have been applied to formulate and document a design are:

- A CICS TCP/IP socket listener-server.
- A framework to demonstrate tightly-coupled transactional interoperation between independent Java and C applications.
- Control flow in an XML reformatting tool.

In these and other cases not mentioned, the diagrams have proved beneficial in imposing a discipline of decomposing a system into logically organized components, defining the possible interactions between them, and subsequently providing a record of the design to aid in the construction of the system.

It is also worth mentioning that the part-time MSc in software engineering run by Oxford University Computing Laboratory has proved extremely popular with Hursley employees, several of whom have chosen to undertake projects using CSP and FDR for the dissertation element of their studies. These projects are normally based on an aspect of the student's work responsibilities.

Future Outlook
The software engineering community would undoubtedly benefit from a wider knowledge and application of CSP and CSP-based model-checking tools, such as FDR, even in areas where safety and reliability are not overriding priorities. Developments which might help to facilitate this would be:

1. Free availability of FDR, preferably as an open-source project.
2. Availability of a *practical* manual on the use of CSP and associated tools for software modelling, design and verification.
3. Inclusion of CSP connection diagrams in UML, perhaps with some extensions such as those employed in this paper.

CSP is an extremely powerful language for specification and modelling the design of software, especially system components in which communication or concurrency are central issues. Used in conjunction with a model-checking tool such as FDR, the notation provides unparalleled capability for the automated checking of designs which would otherwise be extremely difficult to verify.

Bibliography

- *Communicating Sequential Processes*, C.A.R. Hoare, Prentice-Hall International, 1985.
- *The Theory and Practice of Concurrency*, A.W. Roscoe, Prentice Hall, 1998.
- *Failures-Divergences Refinement*, FDR2 User Manual, Formal Systems (Europe) Ltd., 1998. (www.fsel.com).

Trademarks

- The following terms are trademarks of International Business Machines Corporation in the United States, or other countries, or both: IBM, CICS.
- Java and all Java-based trademarks and logos are trademarks or registered trademarks of Sun Microsystems, Inc. in the United States and other countries.

Communicating Mobile Processes

Introducing occam-pi

Peter H. Welch and Frederick R.M. Barnes

Computing Laboratory, University of Kent,
Canterbury, Kent, CT2 7NF, England
{P.H.Welch, F.R.M.Barnes}@kent.ac.uk

Abstract. This paper introduces occam-π, an efficient and safe binding of key elements from Hoare's CSP and Milner's π-calculus into a programming language of industrial strength. A brief overview of classical occam is presented, before focussing on the extensions providing data, channel and process mobility. Some implementation details are given, along with current benchmark results. Application techniques exploiting mobile processes for the direct modelling of large-scale natural systems are outlined, including the modelling of locality (so that free-ranging processes can locate each other). Run-time overheads are sufficiently low so that systems comprising millions of dynamically assembling and communicating processes are practical on modest processor resources. The ideas and technology will scale further to address larger systems of arbitrary complexity, distributed over multiple processors with no semantic discontinuity. Semantic design, comprehension and analysis are made possible through a natural structuring of systems into multiple levels of network and the compositionality of the underlying algebra.

1 Introduction

1.1 Mobile Processes in occam-π

A process, embedded anywhere in a dynamically evolving network, may suspend itself mid-execution, be safely disconnected from its local environment, moved (by communication along a channel), reconnected to a new environment and reactivated. Upon reactivation, the process resumes execution from the same state (i.e. data values and code positions) it held when it suspended. Its view of its environment is unchanged, since that is abstracted by its synchronisation (e.g. channel and barrier) interface and that remains constant. The actual environment bound to that interface will usually be different at each activation. The mobile process itself may contain any number of levels of dynamically evolving sub-network.

1.2 Structure of this Paper

The rest of this section describes the background to this work, along with some of the forces motivating it. Section 2 provides an overview of process and network construction in the occam-π language, with specific details on mobile data,

A.E. Abdallah, C.B. Jones, and J.W. Sanders (Eds.): CSP25, LNCS 3525, pp. 175–210, 2005.

mobile channels and dynamic process creation. The main work presented in this paper concerns mobile processes, covered in section 3. Performance benchmarks and figures for the various occam-π mechanisms are given in section 4. A notion of *duality* between mobile channel and mobile process mechanisms, arising from two of the benchmarks, is considered in section 4.6. Some application areas are explored in section 5. Finally, section 6 draws some conclusions and discusses the scope for future work.

1.3   Background

Twenty years ago, improved understanding and architecture independence were the goals of the design by Inmos of the occam [1, 2] multiprocessing language and the Transputer. The goals were achieved by implementation of the abstract ideas of process algebra (primarily CSP) and with an efficiency that is today almost unimaginable and certainly unmatchable.

We have been extending the classical occam language with ideas of mobility and dynamic network reconfiguration [3, 4, 5, 6, 7] which are taken from the π-calculus [8]. We have found ways of implementing these extensions that involve significantly less resource overhead than that imposed by the rather less structured concurrency primitives of existing languages (such as Java) or libraries (such as Posix threads). As a result, we can run applications with the order of millions of processes on modestly powered PCs. We have plans to extend the system, without sacrifice of too much efficiency and none of logic, to simple clusters of workstations, wider networks such as the Grid and small embedded devices.

We are calling this new language, for the time being at least, occam-π. Classical occam built CSP primitives and operators into the language as first-class entities with a semantics that directly reflected those of CSP. occam-π extends this by judicious inclusion of the mobility features of the π-calculus. In the interests of provability, we have been careful to preserve the distinction between the original static point-to-point synchronised communication of occam and the dynamic asynchronous multiplexed communication of the π-calculus; in this, we have been prepared to sacrifice the elegant sparsity of the π-calculus. We conjecture that the extra complexity and discipline introduced will make the task of developing and proving concurrent and distributed programs easier.

A further, minor, difference between occam-π and the underlying process algebra is its focussing on *channel-ends* in some places, rather than *channels*; this is to constrain the direction of data-flow over any particular channel to *one-way* only. More significant differences are apparent because of the direct language support for state information and transformation (such as variables, block structure and assignment). These are orthogonal to concurrency considerations — thanks largely to the strict control of aliasing inherited from the classical occam— and greatly simplify its application to industrial scale problems.

We view occam-π as an *experiment* in language design and implementation. It is sufficiently small to allow modification and extension, whilst being sufficiently powerful to build significant applications. The abstractions and semantics captured are not settled and may change in the light of future experience and theory (for example, into its formal semantics). However, it is sufficiently stable and efficient to invite others to play. The semantics will be denotational, retaining properties of compositionality derived from CSP and a calculus of refinement. This mathematics is built into the language design, its compiler, run-time system and tools, so that users benefit automatically from that foundation — without themselves needing to be experts in the theory. The new dynamics broadens its area of direct application to a wide field of industrial, commercial and scientific practice. The key safety properties of classical occam are retained by occam-π, giving strong guarantees against a range of common programming errors (such as aliasing accidents and race hazards). The language also provides high visibility of other classic problems of concurrency (such as deadlock, livelock and process starvation) and is supported by a range of formally verified design guidelines for combating them. Its close relationship with the process algebra allows, of course, these problems to be eliminated formally before implementation coding.

1.4   Natural Process Metaphors for Computing

The natural world exhibits concurrency at all levels of scale — from atomic, through human, to astronomic. This concurrency is endemic: a central point of control never remains stable for long, ultimately working against the logic and efficiency of whatever is supposed to be under that control. Natural systems are very resilient, efficient, long-lived and evolving.

Natural mechanisms should map on to simple engineering principles that offer high benefits with low costs, but the mapping has first to be accurate. In this case, the underlying mechanisms seem to be processes, communication and networks — precisely those addressed by our process algebra. Our belief, therefore, is that the basis for a good mapping exists, so that concurrency can and should be viewed as a *core design mechanism* for computer systems — not as something that is advanced and difficult, and only to be used as a last resort to boost performance. Concurrency should *simplify* the design, construction, commissioning and maintenance of systems.

This is not the current state of practice. Standard concurrency technologies are based on multiple threads of execution plus various kinds of locks to control the sharing of resources. Too little locking and systems mysteriously corrupt themselves — too much and they deadlock. Received wisdom from decades of practice is that concurrency is very hard, that we are faced with a barrage of new hazards, that our intuition derived from experience in serial computing is not valid in this context and that our solutions will be fragile. We are advised to steer well clear if at all possible [9].

On top of these logical problems, there are also problems for performance. Standard thread management imposes significant overheads in the form of additional memory demands (to maintain thread state) and run time (to allocate and garbage-collect thread state, switch processor context between states, recover from cache misses resulting from switched contexts and execute the protocols necessary for the correct and safe operation of locks). Even when using *'lightweight'* threads, applications need to limit implementations to only a few hundred threads per processor — beyond which performance catastrophically collapses (usually because of memory thrashing).

Threads are an engineering artifact derived from our successes in serial computing. Threads do not correspond well with nature. They support only a transient concept of ownership (as they lock resources for temporary use), an indirect form of communication (through their side-effects on shared data) and no notion of structure (to reflect natural layering of process networks).

Processes, however, have strong ownership of their internal resources (other processes cannot see or change them), communication (synchronous or asynchronous) as fundamental primitives and structure (a network of processes is itself a process, available for use as a component of a higher-level network).

We do claim performance wins from this *process-oriented* model of computing, but they are not the primary concern. The primary concern is a model of concurrency that is mathematically clean, yields no engineering surprises and scales well with complexity. We must be careful not to damage any of this as we extend the classical occam/CSP model with the dynamics of mobility from the π-calculus (and learn to exploit a few more tricks from nature).

2   An Overview of occam-π

The occam-π language is an extension of classical occam, incorporating: mobile data, channels and processes; dynamic process creation; recursion; extended rendezvous; process priority; protocol inheritance; and numerous other less language-centric enhancements. For instance, a (generally) faster ALT implementation, a fix to a long-standing bug with tagged-protocol communication, and greatly enhanced support for interacting with the system environment outside of occam-π. A more concise list of new features can be found on the KRoC web-page [3].

An example of an 'integrator' component is used throughout this and the following section. This particular component is a well-used teaching example, due to its simplicity and range of implementations. The basic interface to the process is two channels, one input and one output. Given the input sequence x, y, z, the integrator will output running sums: $x, (x + y), (x + y + z)$ and so on.

2.1   Defining Processes

Figure 1 shows the design and implementation of a *serial* integrator. The code is largely classical occam, with the exceptions of the removal of the 'OF' keyword in channel declarations, the introduction of *channel direction specifiers* ('?', '!') on channel variables, and the use of an 'INITIAL' declaration [10, 11] (with the obvious behaviour).

Channel direction specifiers declare channels as either being for input or output, as shown by the arrows in the diagrams. In fact, the classical occam compiler always deduced this information. This extension just makes that information explicit, bringing design and representation closer and enabling more accurate compiler error messages if the programmer contradicts herself.

```
PROC integrate (CHAN INT in?, out!)
   INITIAL INT total IS 0:
   WHILE TRUE
     INT x:
     SEQ
       in ? x
       total := total + x
       out ! total
 :
```

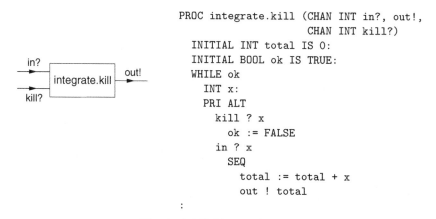

Fig. 1. Serial integrate design and implementation

Note that this process never terminates — evident from its 'WHILE' loop condition. Neither occam nor occam-π provide mechanisms for forcefully, and externally, terminating a process — this is dangerous. If we wish the process to be 'killable', that behaviour must be engineered into it. Adding such support to this serial integrator is trivial, as shown in figure 2.

```
PROC integrate.kill (CHAN INT in?, out!,
                                CHAN INT kill?)
   INITIAL INT total IS 0:
   INITIAL BOOL ok IS TRUE:
   WHILE ok
     INT x:
     PRI ALT
       kill ? x
         ok := FALSE
       in ? x
         SEQ
           total := total + x
           out ! total
 :
```

Fig. 2. A killable serial integrator

The process alternates between its two input channels, giving priority to the 'kill?' channel. Ordinary input data values are added to the running total and output as before. A communication on the 'kill?' channel causes the process to stop looping and terminate normally.

It should be noted that certain behaviours by the environment can cause deadlock with these processes. It would help to declare a "contract" [12] that formally specifies how a process is prepared to interact with its environment. For integrate.kill, the contract might specify that each communication on 'in?' will only be followed by a communication on 'out!', before any other communication (either on 'in?' or 'kill?') is accepted. Further, that a communication on the 'kill?' channel will only be followed by termination. Such a contract guides both the implementation of the process and its safe positioning in an environment. This becomes even more of an issue for mobile processes, whose position with respect to its environment may change! Contracts are discussed further in section 3.5.

2.2   Process Networks

Static process networks in occam-π are no different from occam. Figure 3 shows a parallel version of the integrator process. It is a network of *stateless* components: an adder (that waits, in parallel, for a number on each input channel and then outputs their sum), a stream splitter (that outputs each input number, in parallel, on each output channel) and a prefixer (that initially generates a zero and, then copies input to output). State (the running-sum) emerges from the feedback loop in the network.

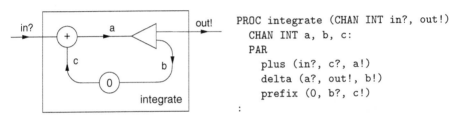

```
PROC integrate (CHAN INT in?, out!)
    CHAN INT a, b, c:
    PAR
        plus (in?, c?, a!)
        delta (a?, out!, b!)
        prefix (0, b?, c!)
    :
```

Fig. 3. Parallel integrator design and implementation

Figure 3 implements a slightly relaxed version of the contract honoured by the process in figure 1. Internal buffering allows two 'in?' events to occur before there must be an 'out!'. Formally, figure 1 is a *refinement* of figure 3.

A killable parallel version requires some careful engineering to avoid internal deadlock. The *"graceful termination"* protocol described in [13] can be used to this effect. Figure 4 shows the modified process network.

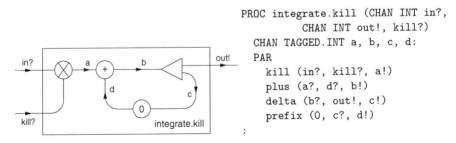

```
PROC integrate.kill (CHAN INT in?,
                     CHAN INT out!, kill?)
    CHAN TAGGED.INT a, b, c, d:
    PAR
        kill (in?, kill?, a!)
        plus (a?, d?, b!)
        delta (b?, out!, c!)
        prefix (0, c?, d!)
    :
```

Fig. 4. A killable parallel integrator

In order for the 'integrate.kill' process to terminate, all its parallel sub-components must terminate. This requires some changes to those components. The internal channels now carry a 'TAGGED.INT' protocol consisting of a boolean and an integer, where the boolean indicates whether the integer data is 'good' or this is a 'kill' signal. The implementation of each component must forward a 'kill' and then terminate. Care must be taken to do this in the right order or deadlock (not termination) will result! Further discussion of this protocol is postponed to section 3.4, where it is considered in the context of (mobile) process *suspension* (which is a little more delicate than termination, since network state must also be preserved).

2.3   Mobile Data

occam-π adds the concept of *mobility* to classical occam, incorporating mobile data, mobile channels and mobile processes. Mobile processes are discussed in section 3.

Communication and assignment in classical occam have a *copying* semantics. That is, the 'source' in output or assignment remains safely usable after the operation — the 'target' has received a copy. Clearly this precludes the creation of aliases, but has implications for performance if the data size is large (on shared-memory systems).

Mobile data types on the other hand have a *movement* semantics. That is, the 'source' in output or assignment is not available after the operation — it has moved to the target. This also precludes the creation of aliases. On shared-memory systems, this is a constant-time operation (effectively a pointer copy). If the communication is between memory spaces, copying has to happen — but the semantics remain that of movement (i.e. the 'source' always loses the data).

Mobile data types are declared simply by adding the 'MOBILE' keyword. For example:

```
DATA TYPE FOO
  RECORD
    ...  data fields
:
```

declares a classical occam data type; whereas:

```
DATA TYPE FOO
  MOBILE RECORD
    ...  data fields
:
```

declares the mobile version. No changes are required to process codes operating on the type, but the semantics of communication and assignment on its variables become those of movement.

Figure 5 illustrates the difference between copying and movement semantics. Picture (a) shows the state of the system just before its communication — with the 'x' variable in process 'A' initialised and the 'y' variable in 'B' undefined.

If 'FOO' were a classical (non-mobile) type, picture (b) shows system state just after communication — where 'x' still has its data and 'y' has a copy. If 'FOO' were a mobile type, picture (c) shows a different state following communication — where the data has moved to 'y' and 'x' has no data (i.e. is undefined).

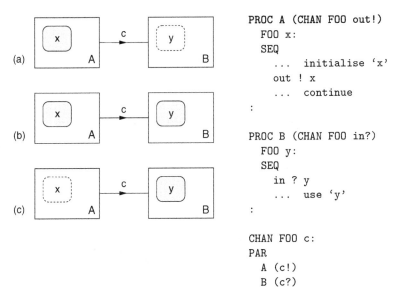

```
PROC A (CHAN FOO out!)
  FOO x:
  SEQ
    ...  initialise 'x'
    out ! x
    ...  continue
  :

PROC B (CHAN FOO in?)
  FOO y:
  SEQ
    in ? y
    ...  use 'y'
  :

CHAN FOO c:
PAR
  A (c!)
  B (c?)
```

Fig. 5. Copying and movement semantics

The movement semantics leaves the 'x' variable undefined after the output — picture (c). Any subsequent attempt by process 'A' to use the value of 'x', before 'x' is reset, will result in a compile-time 'undefined' error. This *undefinedness-check* is an addition to the occam-π compiler, that now (pessimistically) tracks the *defined* status for all variables and channels — not just the mobile ones. There is also a 'DEFINED' prefix operator, applicable to any mobile variable, that may be used to resolve ambiguity in the defined status at run-time. It is impossible to write code that causes a *null-pointer* to be followed.

A copying semantics can be enforced on mobile data by use of the 'CLONE' operator. This creates a temporary mobile containing a copy of the data and it is this copy that is moved. For example:

```
PROC A.copy (CHAN FOO out!)
  FOO x:
  SEQ
    ...  initialise 'x'
    out ! CLONE x
    ...  'x' still defined
  :
```

Dynamic Mobile Arrays. The mobile data described above has fixed-size memory requirements, allowing the compiler to pre-allocate space statically — despite their dynamic semantics.

occam-π has run-time sized arrays, whose allocation and deallocation must be performed dynamically. Such arrays are always mobile. Non-mobile dynamic arrays are currently not permitted — they are not strictly necessary, since 'CLONE' can be used to enforce copying semantics where necessary.

Dynamic mobile arrays are declared in a similar way to fixed-size mobile arrays. For example:

```
MOBILE []REAL64 data:
SEQ
  ... process using 'data'
```

Unlike a fixed-size array, this 'data' initially has no elements. Any attempt to assign one of its elements would result in a run-time (array-bound) error. Before the elements can be accessed, the array must be sized and allocated. This is done using a special form of assignment:

```
data := MOBILE [n]REAL64
```

where 'n' is an integer expression, computable at run-time. Once allocated, the elements may be accessed, but they must be written (defined) before they can be read. The current occam-π compiler does not fully track this nested 'definedness' state, treating all elements as a single block — they are either all defined or all undefined.

The semantics for assignment and communication of these dynamic mobiles arrays are the same as for the static sized mobiles. Note that, because of the *single-reference* rule maintained by the semantics of mobility, no garbage-collection is needed to manage these dynamic types. The compiler always knows when that single reference is lost and automatically generates deallocation code.

The memory-allocation mechanism for these dynamic mobile arrays is based on Brinch-Hansen's allocator for parallel recursion [14], which is also used to provide memory for the other occam-π dynamic mechanisms that require it.

2.4 Mobile Channel Types

Mobile channels types in occam-π provide a mechanism for moving *channel-ends* — either by assignment or communication. This behaviour is not described in standard CSP, where processes (or parallel operators) are bound to *fixed* event alphabets. Moving channel-ends around means those alphabets are changing as the system evolves. The π-calculus [8] however is centered on this concept of channel mobility, allowing only channels to be communicated over channels in its purest form. We have an operational semantics for mobile channel-end communication, but do not yet have a denotational semantics.[1]

---

[1] It is important for this to be addressed in the future — see section 6.

The mobile channels of occam-π are defined by means of a structured channel-type (an idea partly taken from occam3 [10]). These define a group of one or more channels, accessed individually using a record subscript syntax. For example:

```
CHAN TYPE IO.KILL
  MOBILE RECORD
    CHAN INT in?:
    CHAN INT out!:
    CHAN INT kill?:
  :
```

Variables of the channel-type hold its *ends* and must indicate which end explicitly. The terms 'server' and 'client' are used informally to refer to the two ends, with '?' and '!' as respective formal symbols. The *server-end* uses the component channels in the directions indicated by the channel-type declaration; the *client-end* uses them in the opposite directions. The usage pattern need not be 'client-server', however. For the above example, the channel-end types are written 'IO.KILL?' and 'IO.KILL!', for 'server' and 'client' ends respectively.

Mobile channels are created dynamically, by means of an assignment similar to that for mobile data, but where the right-hand side of the assignment produces the two ends of newly created channel 'bundle'. For example:

```
IO.KILL? io.svr:
IO.KILL! io.cli:
SEQ
  io.svr, io.cli := MOBILE IO.KILL
  ... continue
```

Once allocated, the channel-ends 'io.svr' and 'io.cli' may be used for communication or be themselves communicated (or assigned) to other processes (or variables). The semantics of the latter operations are the same as those for mobile data — the channel-end *moves* and the source variable becomes undefined.

Figure 6 shows a simple network consisting of three processes 'P', 'Q' and 'R', that communicate an 'IO.KILL' client channel-end (which is, of course, a bundle of three scaler channel-ends). The server-end of the mobile channel-bundle is marked with an arrow pointing from the client-end — even though communication over the bundle will probably be in both directions.

Initially, processes 'P' and 'R' have no direct means of communication. 'P' creates a channel-bundle and passes its client-end, via 'Q', to 'R'. 'P' and 'R' may now communicate directly over the channel bundle, observing some agreed usage pattern. For example:

```
INT x:                    INT v:
SEQ                       SEQ
  svr[in] ? x               cli[in] ! 42
  svr[out] ! f(x)           cli[out] ? v
```

where the code on the left is in process 'P' and the right is in 'R'.

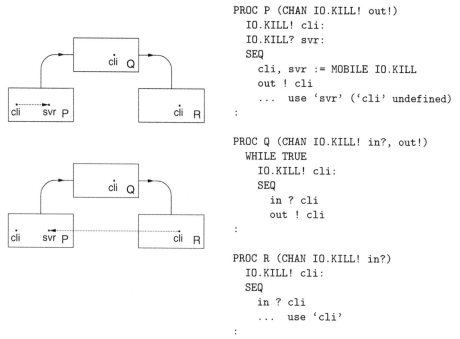

```
PROC P (CHAN IO.KILL! out!)
  IO.KILL! cli:
  IO.KILL? svr:
  SEQ
    cli, svr := MOBILE IO.KILL
    out ! cli
    ... use 'svr' ('cli' undefined)
:

PROC Q (CHAN IO.KILL! in?, out!)
  WHILE TRUE
    IO.KILL! cli:
    SEQ
      in ? cli
      out ! cli
:

PROC R (CHAN IO.KILL! in?)
  IO.KILL! cli:
  SEQ
    in ? cli
    ... use 'cli'
:
```

Fig. 6. Mobile channel-end communication

Currently, there are no restrictions on the communication of mobile channel-ends, enabling process networks to re-wire themselves arbitrarily. Some discipline will need to be enforced to render deadlock analysis, for example, manageable.

They also break another principle of occam that we hold dear, which is that that there should be no hidden ties between processes — all the plumbing should be visible (*WYSIWYG*) or their reusability as system components is compromised. We have plans to restore this principle through the explicit declaration of (typed) 'HOLE's in process interfaces, through which dynamically acquired channel-ends must be wired before they can be used for communication [15]. This will assist the behavioural specification of processes using mobile channels and maintain the compositionality of their semantics.

2.5   Shared Mobile Channel Types

In addition to the *point-to-point* mobile channels described above, occam-π supports 'shared' channel-ends. These allow channel-ends (server or client) to be connected to *any* number of processes, although only one may be conducting business over it at a time.

A shared channel-end is communicated and assigned in the same way as a non-shared one, except that output and assignment automatically 'CLONE' that end — leaving it defined locally. Before a process may use any of the component channels within a shared end, it must 'CLAIM' exclusive access. Whilst so

'CLAIM'ed, the channel-end loses its mobility, preventing its communication or assignment.

Figure 7 shows a network of client and server processes connected using a shared channel-bundle.

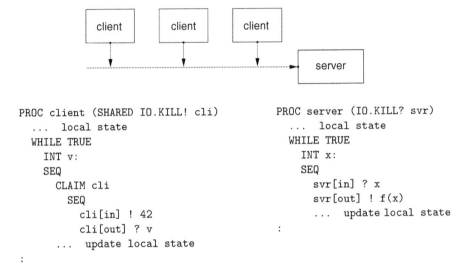

```
PROC client (SHARED IO.KILL! cli)        PROC server (IO.KILL? svr)
  ... local state                          ... local state
  WHILE TRUE                               WHILE TRUE
    INT v:                                   INT x:
    SEQ                                      SEQ
      CLAIM cli                                svr[in] ? x
        SEQ                                    svr[out] ! f(x)
          cli[in] ! 42                         ... update local state
          cli[out] ? v                     :
      ... update local state
:
```

Fig. 7. Shared mobile channel bundles

The code to create this network is:

```
SHARED IO.KILL! cli:
IO.KILL? svr:
SEQ
  cli, svr := MOBILE IO.KILL
  PAR
    server (svr)
    PAR i = 0 FOR n.clients
      client (cli)
```

In this example the mobile channel-ends are "hard-wired" into the processes as they are created, but they could be communicated dynamically, if desired. An earlier paper describing mobile channels [4] shows this in detail.

Simple *request-answer* patterns of use across a channel-bundle correspond to simple CSP *interleaving* of the clients with respect to the shared channel-end. Richer patterns require semaphore processes to manage the locking. Locking of a resource, of course, opens new opportunities for deadlock. To reduce this risk, the occam-π compiler disallows any 'CLAIM' inside the 'CLAIM' of a client-end, but allows 'CLAIM's inside the 'CLAIM' of a server-end. This prevents the deadlock of "partially acquired resource", if multiple clients try to acquire the same set of channel-ends.

2.6   Dynamic Process Creation

Shared channel-ends are useful in their own right, but particularly so when combined with dynamic process creation.

In classical occam, networks are statically organised, with all potential configurations of all processes known in advance. occam-π enables dynamic network creation, in response to run-time decisions. Four mechanisms are provided for this: mobile processes (covered in section 3); (self-)recursive processes; run-time specified replicated 'PAR' counts (as in the network code from the previous section); and the run-time "forking" of a parallel process. The last of these is examined here.

Forking a process is expressed in a similar way to an ordinary procedure call, but with an additional 'FORK' keyword. Classical occam (and occam-π) use a *renaming* semantics for normal parameter-passing. Forked processes use a communication semantics for their parameters, since the forked process may out-live its given arguments — and that would break renaming. The use of communication semantics places restrictions on the parameter types that may be used: specifically, the parameters must be communicable — e.g. no reference parameters. Mobile parameters (data, channel-ends and processes) are allowed, since they have a well-defined communication semantics.

A common use of dynamic process creation is for setting up process 'farms'[4]. The network creation code for figure 7, for example, could also be written as:

```
SHARED IO.KILL! cli:
IO.KILL? svr:
SEQ
  cli, svr := MOBILE IO.KILL
  FORK server (svr)
  SEQ i = 0 FOR n.clients
    FORK client (cli)
  ... do other things
```

The "other things", in the above code, may include waiting for events that trigger the forking of more clients — or, maybe, shutting some down. The code uses just forking to create its parallel process network. The parallelism is derived from the semantic model of the 'FORK', described in [16]. This involves an external parallel process that receives, from the forking process, arguments for the forked one and constructs an instance of the requested process, with those arguments, in parallel with a recursive instance of itself. Forking offers no semantic power over that available from parallel recursion, but for many applications it is more convenient to program and has important implementation benefits (such as no memory leakage and faster setup).

3   Mobile Processes

The main subject of this paper, mobile processes, combines aspects of both mobility and dynamic process creation. The model for mobile processes, used by occam-π, is summarised at the start of this paper (section 1.1).

Note that mobile processes, encapsulating data and code, exist in one of two meta-states: *active* and *passive* — see figure 8. The internal (computational) state of a mobile process is only relevant when the process is active and interacting with the rest of the system. Initially, a mobile process is passive. In its passive state, a mobile process may be *activated* or *moved*. Once active, a mobile process only becomes passive either by *suspending* or *terminating* — these are voluntary internal events, not imposed (though may be requested) by its environment. The internal computational state (of data values and code positions) is retained between suspension and reactivation, and moves with the process. When reactivated, a mobile process sees exactly the same computational state that it did when it suspended. Once terminated, the mobile process may not be reactivated. Any attempt to do so behaves as *Stop*.

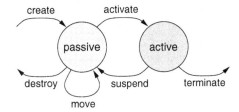

Fig. 8. Mobile process meta-state transitions

3.1   Process Types

The interface to a mobile process is defined through *process types*. For example, the `integrator.kill` processes (sections 2.1 and 2.2) match the type:

```
PROC TYPE IO.SUSPEND IS (CHAN INT in?, out!, suspend?):
```

where we have renamed the 'kill' property to 'suspend' for this context.

Activation arguments must conform to the parameter template defined by the mobile's process type — the activator process does not usually know, or care about, the actual process lying beneath that type. The activator sleeps while its activated process runs. The environment of the activator becomes the environment of the active mobile, interfaced through, and only through, the arguments supplied to the mobile.

Process types serve two purposes: the definition of the connection interface to a mobile process (section 3.2) and the declaration of mobile process variables (section 3.3).

Note that the process type is not itself explicitly mobile. This allows process types to be used for non-mobile mechanisms in the future (such as making classical, as well as mobile, processes first-class types so they may be passed through parameter lists — similar to 'function pointers' in C).

3.2   Defining Mobile Processes

Mobile processes are defined in a similar way to ordinary occam-π procedures, except that they must be explicitly declared 'MOBILE' and must indicate which process-type is implemented.

Different mobile processes may implement the same process-type, assuming that the code conforms to any *contract* (section 3.5) that may, in future, be specified for the process type. For this example, a contract may be that an 'in?' event triggers an 'out!', and that a 'suspend?' signal triggers suspension of the mobile. However, suspension must not occur until the number of 'in?' and 'out!' events are equal.

Figure 9 shows the design and implementation of a 'suspendable' serial integrator that honours such a contract. To suspend itself, a mobile process invokes the new 'SUSPEND' primitive process. This suspends the mobile process and returns control to the activator. When next activated, the 'SUSPEND' terminates and control resumes (on the line indicated) with its local state (in this case, total and s) unchanged. The environment on the other side of its interface will probably be different. Activation of a mobile is covered in the next section.

```
MOBILE PROC integrate.suspend (CHAN INT in?, out!, suspend?)
  IMPLEMENTS IO.SUSPEND
    INITIAL INT total IS 0:            -- local state
    WHILE TRUE
      PRI ALT
        INT s:
        suspend ? s
          SUSPEND        -- return control to activator
          -- control returns here when next activated
        INT x:
        in ? x
          SEQ
            total := total + x
            out ! total
  :
```

Fig. 9. A suspendable serial mobile integrator

The above mobile has a purely serial implementation. Suspending a mobile with a parallel implementation is presented in section 3.4.

3.3   Declaring, Allocating, Moving and Activating Mobile Processes

Mobile process variables are declared with reference to a process type. They hold instances of mobile processes, possibly many different ones during their lifetime.

Allocation of a mobile process is similar to the allocation of other mobiles — via a special assignment. For example, an instance of the 'integrate.suspend' mobile process (defined in the previous section) is allocated by:

```
MOBILE IO.SUSPEND x:
SEQ
  x := MOBILE integrate.suspend
  ... use 'x'
```

After allocation, the process in 'x' may be communicated, assigned or activated. Communication and assignment follow the semantics of other mobiles — which is that the mobile process *moves*, leaving the source undefined.

The 'CLONE' operator may be used to copy a mobile process, with a restriction that the mobile must not contain any state that cannot itself be cloned. For example, a mobile process containing an *unshared* mobile channel-end cannot be cloned. Any attempt to do so results in a compiler (or run-time) error.

Activation of a mobile process connects its interface to a local environment and transfers control to it. Control is returned when the mobile process either terminates or suspends.

Figure 10 shows a network of two processes, 'A' and 'B'. The 'A' process simply creates a new mobile process then outputs it. 'B' inputs a mobile process, activates it using channels from its own environment, waits for the activation to suspend (or terminate), before passing on the mobile.

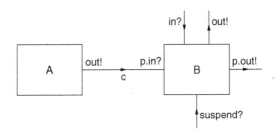

Fig. 10. A communicating mobile process network

The implementation of these examples are trivial:

```
PROC A (CHAN MOBILE IO.SUSPEND out!)
  MOBILE IO.SUSPEND x:
  SEQ
    x := MOBILE integrate.suspend
    out ! x
    -- 'x' is no longer defined
  :
```

```
PROC B (CHAN MOBILE IO.SUSPEND p.in?, p.out!,
        CHAN INT in?, out!, suspend?)
  MOBILE IO.SUSPEND v:
  SEQ
    p.in ? v
    v (in?, out!, suspend?)
    -- control returns here when 'v' terminates or suspends
    p.out ! v
:
```

Note that the 'B' process is unaware what mobile process it is activating —
only that it carries the 'IO.SUSPEND' interface. Note also the strong synchronisation between an activated mobile and its host. There is no way the host can
operate on the mobile while it is active — it has to wait for the mobile to suspend
or terminate. The parallel usage checker (implemented by the occam-π compiler)
views an activated process variable as *writable* — i.e. it may change state. This
means that that variable may not be *observed* in parallel with that activation —
i.e. it may not be activated, moved, cloned or overwritten. Any attempt to do
so is a language violation and will not be compiled.

The code implementing the portion of the network shown in figure 10 is:

```
CHAN MOBILE IO.SUSPEND c:
PAR
  A (c!)
  B (c?, p.out!, in?, out!, suspend?)
```

3.4   Suspending Mobile Networks

So far we have shown how a serial mobile process may be activated, suspended
and moved. We are grateful to Tony Hoare for providing insight into how a
mobile process, that has gone parallel internally, may be safely suspended and
efficiently re-activated. An earlier proposal for mobile processes in occam-π [4]
required the mobile to *terminate* before it could be moved. For parallel mobiles,
such termination is just the multi-way synchronisation of all sub-processes on the
termination event. So for each mobile process, introduce a hidden '*suspension*'
event for all its sub-processes to synchronise upon — this, then, is the meaning
of the new 'SUSPEND' primitive.

The suspension event barrier on which processes synchronise when executing
'SUSPEND' is internal to the mobile process and follows a similar implementation
to that described in [17] for multiway events. The main difference being that
whichever process completes the synchronisation must then arrange for control
to be returned to the activator. Barrier completion may also be triggered when
processes internally *resign* from the event (e.g. when terminating). The use of
this barrier synchronisation enables very efficient re-activation — since all suspended sub-processes are on the queue (implemented by the barrier), they can
be instantly located and rescheduled together in a constant-time operation (by
appending the barrier queue to the kernel run-queue).

Parallel Suspension. As an example we consider a suspendable version of the parallel integrator. The design of this integrator is similar to the earlier 'killable' parallel integrator and is shown in figure 11. As with the suspendable serial integrator, the process is declared as implementing the 'IO.SUSPEND' interface.

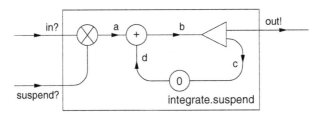

Fig. 11. A suspendable mobile parallel integrator

The top-level implementation of this mobile network is:

```
MOBILE PROC integrate.suspend (CHAN INT in?, out!, suspend?)
 IMPLEMENTS IO.SUSPEND
  CHAN TAGGED.INT a, b, c, d:
  PAR
    freeze (in?, suspend?, a!)
    plus.suspend (a?, d?, b!)
    delta.suspend (b?, c!, out!)
    prefix.suspend (0, c?, d!)
 :
```

Note that the internal channels carry a boolean tag:

```
PROTOCOL TAGGED.INT IS BOOL; INT:
```

where a 'TRUE' tag means that the INT part carried 'live' data (compute as normal) and a 'FALSE' tag indicates 'suspended' data (forward and suspend). The '**freeze**' process is implemented:

```
PROC freeze (CHAN INT in?, suspend?, CHAN TAGGED.INT out!)
  WHILE TRUE
    INT x:
    PRI ALT
      suspend ? x
        SEQ
          out ! FALSE; 0    -- suspend signal
          SUSPEND
      in ? x
        out ! TRUE; x       -- live data
 :
```

For structuring reasons and general reusability, we allow mobile processes to invoke 'ordinary' PROCs (which is what is happening between integrate.suspend and freeze). There is, therefore, the possibility some other application may invoke freeze by a chain of calls from a top-level process that is not itself mobile! If that happens, 'SUSPEND' behaves as 'STOP'.

The 'graceful' protocol safely distributes the suspend signal to all processes that need it. The implementation of 'plus.suspend' and 'delta.suspend', therefor, become:

```
PROC plus.suspend                      PROC delta.suspend
   (CHAN TAGGED.INT in.0?,                (CHAN TAGGED.INT in?,
    in.1?, out!)                           out.0!, CHAN INT out.1!)
  WHILE TRUE                           WHILE TRUE
    BOOL b.0, b.1:                       BOOL b:
    INT x.0, x.1:                        INT x:
    SEQ                                  SEQ
      PAR                                  in ? b; x
        in.0 ? b.0; x.0                   IF
        in.1 ? b.1; x.1                     b          -- live data
      IF                                      PAR
        b.0      -- live data                 out.0 ! TRUE; x
          out ! TRUE; x.0 + x.1               out.1 ! x
        TRUE     -- suspend signal          TRUE     -- suspend signal
          SEQ                                 SEQ
            out ! FALSE; x.1                    out.0 ! FALSE; x
            SUSPEND                             SUSPEND
  :                                      :
```

Unlike the other two '.suspend' components, 'prefix.suspend' executes its 'SUSPEND' *between* input and output. It is the last process in the network that receives the suspend signal and someone has to hold the suspended data. The implementation is:

```
PROC prefix.suspend (VAL INT n, CHAN TAGGED.INT in?, out!)
  SEQ
    out ! FALSE; n
    WHILE TRUE
      BOOL b:
      INT x:
      SEQ
        in ? b; x
        IF
          b                  -- input was live data
            SKIP
          TRUE               -- input was a suspend signal
            SUSPEND
        out ! TRUE; x        -- output is always live data
  :
```

The way in which the 'integrate.suspend' network suspends is as follows. A communication made on the external 'suspend?' channel is intercepted by the 'freeze' process, which reacts by outputting a suspend signal before suspending itself. The 'plus.suspend' component inputs this, in parallel with the current running-sum, and outputs a suspend carrying the current running-sum before suspending itself. 'delta.suspend' reacts to the suspend by forwarding the suspend (and associated running-sum) on the feedback channel only, and then suspending itself — no output is made to the external (integer) channel. 'prefix.suspend' is the final process to receive the suspend signal and reacts by immediately suspending. At this point, all sub-processes have suspended and the network, therefore, suspends, returning control to its activator.

When the network is reactivated (elsewhere), the sub-processes resume execution from their respective 'SUSPENDs. The 'prefix.suspend' component returns the saved running-sum to 'plus.suspend' and the network state is restored (as though the suspend never happened).

So, this parallel mobile 'integrate.suspend' promptly suspends when its environment offers the 'suspend?' signal. It does this without deadlocking, without accepting any further data from 'in?' and flushing on 'out!' any data owed to its environment — i.e. it honours the contract that we intend to associate with the 'IO.SUSPEND' process-type (section 3.5).

Care must be taken to implement this "graceful suspension" protocol correctly to avoid deadlock. If the sequence of output and suspension were reversed in any of the internal components, deadlock would occur. In fact, the output and suspension could be run in parallel by all components *except* for 'prefix.suspend' (where deadlock would result, since its output would never be accepted). For the moment, responsibility for getting this right lies with the application engineer.

Note that the request for a suspend need not come from the environment — it could be a unilateral decision taken by the mobile process itself, provided that it conforms to any specified behavioural contract for the process (e.g. that the number of 'in?''s equals the number of 'out!''s. In general, the decision to trigger suspension in a mobile process network may happen in several places independently. The protocol for managing safely the deadlock-free distribution of the multiple suspend signals so generated is described in [13].

Finally, although the 'integrate.suspend' mobile behaves as a 'server', responding only to ('in?' and 'suspend?') communications from its environment, this need not be the case. A mobile could behave as a 'client', gathering data from its various environments (which behave as 'servers'). Indeed, the relationship between mobile and its environment could follow any pattern — but it would help to formalise that into a *contract*.

3.5   Mobile Contracts

A "PROC TYPE" only defines a connection interface — a set of abstract events that are bound to actual events each time its implementing mobile is activated.

Such an interface is necessary. It prevents arriving mobiles from accessing resources the host is unwilling to provide. Activation is entirely under the control of the accepting host, who must set up all connections to the mobile (as well as actually activate it). An occam-π process cannot simply make "system calls" (e.g. to access a file), unless it has been given the means to make them (e.g. the file server channels). So, the host is in charge. If suspicious, the host may still provide resource access channels, but route them via a monitoring "fire-wall" process with whatever level of security it chooses. This is in marked contrast to conventional mobile platforms (e.g. web browsers and common office tools), which execute arriving code with the authority and permissions granted to the platform. Various "sand-boxing" techniques are available to counter the worst behaviour the mobile might throw, but these are foreign to the normal execution model. For the *process-oriented* model around which occam-π is centered, such "sand-boxing" is the way things are arranged anyway — and the security is automatic[2].

However, process type interfaces are not sufficient to guarantee safety. The host environment needs further assurance of good behaviour from an arriving mobile that it will use its given channels properly — e.g. that it will not cause deadlock or livelock, and will not starve processes in the host environment of attention (including a request to suspend). Conversely, a mobile process requires similar guarantees of good behaviour from whatever environment activates it.

We are currently investigating ways to augment process-types with a contract that makes some level of CSP specification about process behaviour. Initially we are considering methods of specifying traces for a mobile process, that the compiler can verify against an implementing mobile and any (potential) host environment. Such contracts would be burnt into an extended definition of the process type. We have not yet made proposals for a syntax for these contracts.

For the 'IO.SUSPEND' process type, a contract might specify that implementing mobiles are a 'server' on the 'in?' and 'suspend?' channels, responding to an 'in?' with an 'out!', and to 'suspend?' with suspension. This could be strengthened to indicate priorities for service, or weakened to allow some level of internal buffering.

A particular behaviour that a contract may wish to prohibit (for the example considered here) is that of suspension with an output outstanding on 'out!' — i.e. that suspension may only occur when the number of 'in?' and 'out!' events are equal. Without such a contract, a mobile could arrive that activates with an 'out!' to an environment that offers only an 'in?'.

4 Performance

4.1 Basics

The implementation of the various concurrency mechanisms in occam-π are very lightweight compared with other software technologies (e.g. threads in Java or

---

[2] Like any software system, it is ultimately possible to circumvent guarantees such as this — but not if all codes are compiled from source by a certified occam-π compiler.

C), while providing substantial guarantees about the integrity of concurrent systems (an attribute preserved from classical occam and CSP).

The memory overhead for a parallel process is less-than or equal to 32 bytes, depending on what kinds of synchronisation it may choose to perform (e.g. ALTing and/or timeouts). The memory overhead for setting up a network of parallel process is approximately 16 bytes.

Table 1 shows the times for a number of "micro-benchmarks", measured on an 800 MHz Pentium-3 and a 3.4 GHz Pentium-4. These measure the minimum time to perform an operation, where the code and data required by a process is in the processor cache. Both machines have 512 Kbytes of fast cache. All times derive from multiple runs on an otherwise quiet Linux machine and are rounded to the nearest 10 nanoseconds.

Table 1. occam-π micro-benchmarks

Benchmark	Time (nanoseconds) P3 (0.8)	P4 (3.4)
process startup + shutdown (no priorities)	30	0
process startup + shutdown (priorities)	70	50
priority change (up and down)	160	140
channel communication (INTs, no priorities)	60	50
channel communication (INTs, priorities)	60	40
channel communication (mobile fixed-size data, priorities)	120	150
channel communication (mobile runtime-sized data, priorities)	120	110
channel communication (mobile channel-ends, priorities)	120	110

The time for starting up and shutting down a process on the P4 running the occam-π kernel, with no support for priorities, was too small to measure accurately. The P4 (integer) channel communication costs were lower using the kernel *with* priorities than *without*. This shows the problems of relying too much on micro-benchmarks and we present them only as a guide.

4.2   Missing the Cache

A separate benchmark measures the penalty resulting from cache misses. This communicates integer messages between pairs of processes, with the number of pairs ranging from 1 to 1 million, increasing in factors of 10. The results from this benchmark are shown in figure 12. Graphs are drawn showing the effect of setting (and not setting) relevant optimisation flags to the compiler that in-line certain kernel operations.

Up to 1000 pairs of processes, the total memory footprint for the benchmark fits into cache. For 10,000 pairs and above, it does not. (In the case of a million pairs, the footprint is around 100 Mbytes.) Each cycle of the benchmark exercises all the data. Between each communication by any one process, all other (20,000+) processes will have been scheduled once and cached state will have been lost. There are ways of managing scheduling that attempt to minimise cache displacement that might work for this benchmark. However, the KRoC runtime for occam-π simply uses *round-robin* scheduling on each priority queue of runnable processes. This benchmark uses no priorities, but it was run on the standard KRoC system build supporting them.

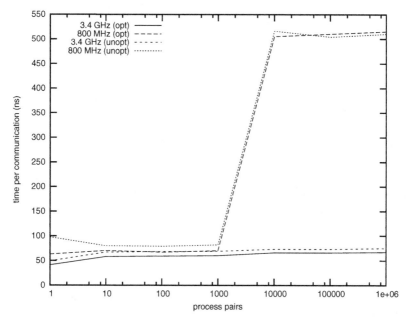

Fig. 12. Results for the communicating process pairs benchmark

As can be seen, the difference between optimised and unoptimised compiled codes is minor and consistent (except where very small numbers of processes are concerned). For the 800 MHz Pentium-3, the channel communication costs ceiling out at (a still respectable) 520ns for 10,000 pairs (20,000 processes) and above — measured up to 2M processes. The extra cost (over the minimum 80ns, when all process state is permanently cached) results from the relatively slow memory bus on that machine. The 3.4 GHz Pentium-4 machine has a more modern and much faster memory — even so, the results are remarkable! The costs start around 40ns and ceiling out at 70ns. Cache behaviour is not always what we expect; but whatever it is that the P4 is doing (and it may involve parallel operations from its *Hyperthreading* mechanism [18]), it is very well-suited to the operation of our occam-π kernel. The figures for large numbers of processes do reflect the worst-case memory behaviour that a large application might exhibit.

4.3   Mobile Process Basics

Table 2 shows micro-benchmark results for mobile process operations. All are well under 1 micro-second. Even so, they are still slightly higher than we eventually hope to achieve, due to the relative immaturity of the implementation. The figures given for suspension and re-activation only apply to a serial mobile process (i.e. just *one* process synchronising on the hidden implementation barrier). Note that mobile process activation and termination costs are similar to those for ordinary procedure call and return.

Table 2. Micro-benchmarks for mobile process operations

Benchmark	Time per visit (nanoseconds)	
	P3 (0.8 GHz)	P4 (3.4 GHz)
Mobile process allocation and deallocation	450	210
Mobile process activation and termination	100	20
Mobile process suspend and re-activate	630	260

For a more application-oriented scenario, two further benchmarks have been created that stress the memory cache and exercise mechanisms for mobility that are relevant for large-scale modelling. The first, "tarzan", provides mobility using mobile channels; the second, "mole", provides mobility using mobile processes. Both do similar work and show a sense of *duality* between mobile channels and mobile processes. This duality is considered further in section 4.6.

4.4   The Tarzan Benchmark

This benchmark measures the time taken to "swing" a process down a chain of a million 'server' processes, using mobile channels. The process network is shown in figure 13.

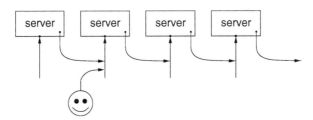

Fig. 13. Process network for the 'tarzan' benchmark

Starting with a connection to the first process in the pipeline, the `tarzan` process does some 'business' with the server and, then, receives from it the *shared* mobile channel-end of the next server. `tarzan` overwrites its connection to the current server (a shared mobile channel-end variable) with the connection to the next server, and loops. In this way, `tarzan` 'moves' (swings) down the chain. In fact, `tarzan` is actually fixed in memory and continuously running — only its connection to the individual servers changes as it swings down the line.

Note that if each server had connections to both its neighbours, it would be trivial for `tarzan` to move in both directions along the chain — in response to run-time decisions based on his communications with the chain nodes. Step this up one or two dimensions, add millions of other tarzans (and, maybe, some janes) and we are into serious application modelling — see section 5.

The channel type that defines the service channels in this benchmark is:

```
RECURSIVE CHAN TYPE SERVE
  MOBILE RECORD
    ...  business channels
    CHAN SHARED SERVE! next!:
  :
```

The 'RECURSIVE' keyword causes the name 'SERVE' to be brought into scope early, instead of at the end of the declaration. This allows a channel-type to contain channels that communicate ends of its own channel-type (they may be 'client' or 'server' ends, shared or unshared). This is useful for many situations — e.g. having some client give up its (typically unshared) connection to a server, by communicating the client-end back to the server (for distribution to, and reuse by, some other client not known to the original one). For this benchmark, the feature enables a server to communicate (to its visiting tarzan) a 'client'-end connection to the next server in the pipeline.

The main loop of the tarzan process, for example, is implemented:

```
SEQ i = 0 FOR 1000000
  SHARED SERVE! next.server:
  SEQ
    CLAIM current.server
      SEQ
        ...  do business using 'current.server' channels
        current.server[next] ? next.server
    current.server := next.server
```

The tarzan client measures the time it takes to swing through 1 million server processes, and then reports. Table 3 shows the results for a client that just swings through the servers, doing no business (other than getting the link to the next server); and a client that asks each server a question (represented by an integer) and receives a reply (another integer), which it uses on the next server. Each visit by the tarzan client causes a cache miss as the service channel is accessed and the corresponding server is scheduled. tarzan's own state will remain in cache (since it is repeatedly scheduled for each visit).

Table 3. Results for the 'tarzan' benchmark

Benchmark	Time per visit (nanoseconds)	
	P3 (0.8 GHz)	P4 (3.4 GHz)
'just visiting' client	450	120
'question and answer' client	770	280

These results show over 3.5 million interacting visits per second are possible with this mechanism.

4.5   The Mole Benchmark

This benchmark is similar to the above in its basic operation (a visitor process interacting with and moving down a chain of servers), but is implemented using mobile processes rather than mobile channel-ends. Instead of moving a server connection to the visitor, the visitor suspends itself and is moved by its environment to the next server.

Figure 14 shows the process network for this 'mole' benchmark, with an activated visitor, our `mole`, connected to one of the servers. When a visitor arrives at the `butler` process, the latter forks a `host` platform and passes to it the visitor, the local server connection and the connection to the next butler. This host activates the `mole`, giving it the server connection. When the `mole` suspends, the host sends it on its way to the next butler and terminates.

This protocol is complicated by the fact that we wish to allow multiple visitors to connect to any single server at the same time. Our benchmark runs only one such visitor, so the butler could have done the work of the host platform itself without any extra concurrency (the forked host) — but then it could only service one visitor at a time. This would reduce the overheads measured by the benchmark, but also the realism of the scenario.

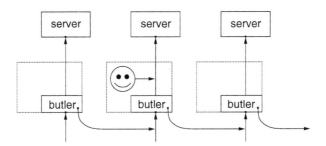

Fig. 14. Process network for the 'mole' benchmark

The channel-types servicing, respectively, the server and butler processes are:

```
CHAN TYPE SERVE.2                    CHAN TYPE BUTLER.2
  MOBILE RECORD                        MOBILE RECORD
    ...  business channels               CHAN MOBILE VISITOR c?:
  :                                    :
```

where the process type of the mobile visitors is:

```
PROC TYPE VISITOR (SHARED SERVE.2! client, CHAN INT in?, out!):
```

The extra 'in?' and 'out!' channels in the 'VISITOR' type allow initial state to be loaded into the mobile and results to be downloaded upon completion of the benchmark. This is not an happy situation since those channels are not used during server visits (and, therefore, dummies must be supplied by the activating host platform). Our previous model for mobile processes, [4], allowed them to implement many process types. That would let us activate our visitor with one interface for initialisation, another for server visits and a third for debriefing. We are considering ways to combine the two models robustly.

The host and butler processes are rather trivial, apart from the current awkwardness with the dummy channels:

```
PROC host (MOBILE VISITOR mole,
           SHARED SERVE.2! my.server,
           SHARED BUTLER.2! next.butler)
  CHAN INT dummy.in, dummy.out:
  SEQ
    mole (my.server, dummy.in, dummy.out!)   -- dummy chans not used
    CLAIM next.butler
      next.butler[c] ! mole
:

PROC butler (CHAN MOBILE VISITOR in?,
             SHARED SERVE.2! my.server,
             SHARED BUTLER.2! next.butler)
  WHILE TRUE
    MOBILE VISITOR mole:
    SEQ
      in ? mole
      FORK host (mole, my.server, next.butler)
:
```

The main loop of the mole process is very similar to that for tarzan, except that it *suspends* and lets its environment move it to the next server:

```
SEQ i = 0 FOR 1000000
  SEQ
    CLAIM current.server
      ...  do business using 'current.server' channels
    SUSPEND
```

Table 4 shows the results for a mole that does no business with servers (other than claim their service channels) and one that does the same 'question and answer' interaction described for tarzan.

Table 4. Results for the 'mole' benchmark

Benchmark	Time per visit (nanoseconds)	
	P3 (0.8 GHz)	P4 (3.4 GHz)
'just visiting' client	1340	470
'question and answer' client	1590	620

The results show that the time per visit for this 'mole' benchmark is more than double the time per visit for the 'tarzan' benchmark. Some of the extra overhead comes from the mobile process suspension and re-activation in between visits — `tarzan` never stopped running! The rest comes from the forking of a new host platform to activate the mobile process. Nevertheless, more than 1.5 interacting visits per second are achieved with this mechanism.

4.6   Mobile Channels and Mobile Processes — a Duality

The two benchmark programs show how similar functionality can be implemented either using mobile channels or mobile processes. In both cases, a 'client' process moves down a line of 'server' processes, interacting with each in turn.

The main difference between the benchmarks involves the *locality* of processes. In the 'tarzan' benchmark, the visitor remains 'alive' throughout: channels are moved, 'stretching' across the network to provide mobility to the visitor (that sees itself serially connected to different servers). In the 'mole' benchmark, the visitor suspends its execution and is moved to the locality of the server — before being plugged in, re-activated and interacting over local channels. Putting aside the mechanism-specific code (for communicating a mobile channel-end in one and suspending in the other), the visitors and servers have identical logic.

On individual shared-memory systems (e.g. a typical workstation), the cost of communicating a mobile channel-end and the cost of communicating a passive mobile process are approximately the same — in the order of tens of nanoseconds. As we have seen, however, the mobile process cost has to be supplemented with the cost of suspension, forking and re-activation. Once connected, however, the costs of doing business in the new environment are the same, regardless of the mechanism used to achieve mobility.

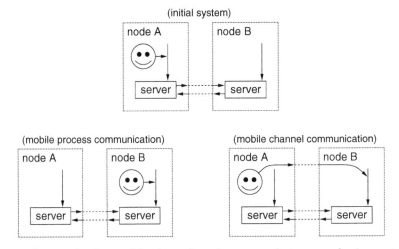

Fig. 15. Communicating mobile channels and processes between nodes in a network

If the system is distributed over a network of processors operating in separate memory spaces, the costs of doing business if a network link is involved differ significantly. Communicating a mobile process between nodes in a network has a relatively constant cost. Communicating mobile channel-ends between nodes in a network has a similar constant cost, but the 'stretching' of that channel between the nodes incurs a network overhead for each subsequent communication on the channel. Figure 15 illustrates this difference.

For optimal performance on distributed systems, the two techniques can be combined. Mobile processes are *moved* only when they need to connect to a new environment across the network. Otherwise, only channel-ends are moved. This reduces the level of transparency, however, since processes will need to be aware of where they are currently placed in the *physical distribution* of the system.

5   Application Outlines

5.1   Grand Challenges

"in Vivo ⇔ in Silico" (iViS) is one of the UK *'Grand Challenges in Computer Science'* project areas [19, 20, 21]. Its aims are to move the application of computing in the life sciences beyond cataloguing and pattern discovery and into modelling and prediction. An exemplar challenge is to model the development of a Nematode worm, one of the simplest multicellular forms of animal life, from fertilised cell to adult — allowing *virtual* experiments to be performed on its reactions to various stimuli, physical or chemical, and on interactions between organisms. It is hoped that success will lead to better understanding of the basic science and the processes involved, followed by improved treatment of disease and environmental dangers. One particular dream is the conduction of drug trials within the computer (*in silico*) that are trustable in real life (*in vivo*).

For the necessary modelling technologies, dynamic communicating process networks are a good fit. The fundamental ideas of *process, communication, concurrency* and *mobility* are uniformly applicable at any level of granularity and those levels build on each other seamlessly. They enable the expression of controlled, but not specifically planned, self-evolving topologies reflecting natural growth and decay. This uniformity of concept could contribute to simplicity of structure and understanding of multi-level simulation programs applied in biology. Furthermore, the semantics are independent of the actual distribution of systems on to different computer architectures and network configurations, allowing them to take quick advantage of all technological improvements to the hardware.

The mechanisms and implementation of occam-π, described in this paper, offer one way to make a start in these experiments. They are lightweight and robust and have good theoretical foundations — though we are aware that there is a lot more work to be done. To investigate emergent properties of such networks, self-constructed from low level processes with explicitly programmed behaviour, will require very large numbers of mobiles. Fortunately, current low cost architectures (e.g. PC networks) let us build systems with millions of processes per processor, yielding useful work in useful run-times.

5.2   Locality, Environment and the Matrix

Our models need to capture a sense of *location*, so that free-ranging processes become aware of who else is in their neighbourhood and do business with them (or, maybe, run away!). Processes may also be influenced by pervasive forces in their *environment* — these may be widely dispersed (e.g. gravitational) or highly localised (e.g. chemical).

Figure 16 illustrates some ideas for meeting these requirements. Space is modelled by the *'Matrix'* — a network of (usually passive and non-mobile) server processes representing locations. The figure shows a portion of a regular 2-dimensional grid. Other spaces may have higher dimensions, or distortions (e.g. wormholes), or the ability to change shape (reflecting dramatic changes in the modelled world, such as physical damage).

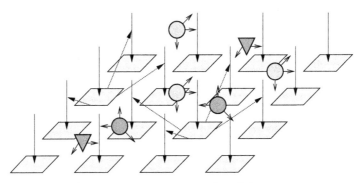

Fig. 16. Process matrix with mobile agents

Each matrix node services a channel bundle, shown in the figure as a vertical downward pointing arrow ending at the node. The 'server-end' of each bundle is exclusive to the node. The 'client-end', however, is SHARED and MOBILE (i.e. freely useable by, and communicable to, any number of clients).

Locality is realised by each node having access to the 'client-ends' of each of its neighbours' service channels, where we have free choice in deciding who are those neighbours. (In figure 16, only two sets of these connections are shown, but all nodes have them.) Once the connections are established, there are no run-time costs associated with locating neighbourhoods — even in the most twisted of topologies.

Organisms, or parts of organisms, living in this space are modelled by mobile processes — *'Agents'*. (These are shown by the shaded circles and triangles in figure 16.) An agent attaches to one matrix node (location) at a time, by acquiring the 'client-end' of its service channel bundle. It interacts with the server node, first to register its arrival and any connections to itself it cares to share with the locality. Then, it enquires about the local *environment* (e.g. electrostatic or chemical forces) and connections to other agents currently present. It may pick up compatible connections and transact business directly with those other agents. This may include combining with them to form larger agent structures or to reproduce. It may also pick up connections to neighbouring locations and decide to move.

Agent-matrix interactions must follow matrix-defined protocols ('contracts', section 3.5) for the avoidance of deadlock. Agent-agent communication protocols will be specific to the types of agent involved. The extent of these interactions will vary, along with the computations provoked by them. Model simulation time may need to be maintained by global (or, maybe, local) event barriers.

occam-π provides all the mechanisms needed to express such designs directly and execute them. Its overheads are sufficiently low so that the very large numbers of processes required for modelling realism will not be a show stopper. Formal verification of the systems, at least for the absence of deadlock and race hazards, also becomes possible.

Serial implementations of these designs, that iterate through collections of passive objects representing the locations and agents, may run (a little) faster. Unfortunately, the logic expressing object behaviour has to be inverted to the point of view of the (single) thread executing them all — there can be no *direct* expression. This introduces complexity, making formal and informal reasoning much harder. It will be necessary to experiment with many rules of behaviour, changing them quickly and often. The direct reflection of behaviour in the programming of active processes, together with the compositional semantics of the underlying algebra, simplifies this.

Finally, we note that the 'tarzan' and 'mole' benchmarks (sections 4.4 and 4.5) are stripped down versions of this scheme — where the matrix has one dimension, neighbourhoods are connected one-way only and there is just one agent. The discussion of *duality* between the use of mobile channels and mobile processes in these benchmarks (section 4.6) is directly relevant to this grander vision, especially for large scale models that need to be distributed over many machines.

5.3   Agents in Distributed Systems — and Security

The most commonly understood meaning of the term "mobile agent" is that of code and data mobility, as described by White in [22]. The main focus is on mobility between nodes in a distributed system. *Agents* are stateful mobile units of execution and *agent platforms* are the environments in which those agents operate. Supporting infrastructure is provided by the applications and by libraries, not by the programming model or language.

occam-π provides a simple model and language for agents: agents are mobile processes and agent platforms are processes that *activate* a mobile. Mobile processes may also activate other mobiles, becoming agent platforms themselves — i.e. nested hierarchies of agent are naturally expressed.

Agent platforms exist for two purposes: to allow agents to interact with the host system providing the platform; and to allow agents to interact with each other. occam-π supports both types of interaction, as outlined in the previous section.

Within the wider mobile-agent community, there is a good deal of concern for the security of mobile agents and agent based systems, as discussed in [23, 24, 25].

Broadly, these security considerations fall into two categories: those affecting the integrity of the overall system; and those affecting the integrity of individual agents and agent-platforms.

Integrity of the overall system is outside the scope of this paper. Here, we assume that arriving mobile agents are *valid* — because that agent was either created locally or came from another part of the system that we trust over secure links. Correspondingly, an agent may assume that whatever activates it was meant to do so.

In an insecure networked environment (such as the Internet), the part of the system that manages network connections would need to be responsible for ensuring the integrity of data communicated over networked channels (where that data may be 'serialised' mobile processes). This may involve proper (public/private key) authentication and encryption.

Of course, we could create a system that freely admits mobile processes from open network connections. Such a system would be open to many of the potential abuses that afflict mobile-agent systems in general. The use of occam-π in the construction of agents allows some of this threat to be eliminated. Instead of communicating serialised agent object code, source (or byte) code could be sent, along with the saved state of the agent, and used to re-create the agent locally. The occam-π compiler makes certain guarantees about the systems it compiles. For example, agents (processes) cannot access resources without being given specific connections (channels) to those resources and that giving is entirely at the discretion of the activating host — see section 3.5.

The mandated use of a synchronisation-only interface to mobile processes further limits the threats associated with existing agent systems. It separates the activation of an agent from its interaction with the local resources granted to it, by safely modelling the *concurrency* between the agent and those resources (which existed before the agent arrived and will continue to exist after it departs). There can be no unsynchronised actions between the agent and its host environment that can lead to race hazards.

Further, the concept of 'contract' (also described in section 3.5) would enforce safe patterns of synchronisation, eliminating the dangers of the agent deadlocking its host — or vice-versa. Such contracts are not yet defined for occam-π, although some preliminary investigations have been completed (see the 'TRACES' extension described in [16]).

6   Conclusions and Future Research

This paper has given an introduction to the occam-π language, concentrating on mobile processes and channels. occam-π combines process and channel mobility (from the π-calculus) with the disciplines of classical occam (whose semantics follow CSP). Mobile processes complement mobile channels to provide the occam-π programmer with powerful new tools for directly, safely and efficiently capturing the dynamic aspects of complex large-scale systems. Applications for the multi-layer modelling of micro-organisms and their environments (the *'in Vivo ⇔ in*

Silico' Grand Challenge [20, 21]) and process migration (agents) in distributed systems have been outlined. Performance benchmarks have been reported.

The occam-π language is implemented by recent releases of KRoC (the Kent Retargetable occam Compiler) [3]. Current versions of the system support all aspects of mobility described here, with the exception of support for 'serialisation' (and de-serialisation) of mobile processes — needed for their movement between distinct memory spaces.

At this time of writing, no *distributed* version of occam-π has been released (although library processes providing non-blocking low-level support for socket communication have long been included in the release). The *distributed* version, KRoC.net, will provide for the stretching of channels across network fabric (with no change in semantics), automatic multiplexing and de-multiplexing of channels over limited network resource (with no change in semantics), brokers for the discovery and run-time connection of processes between network nodes and full support for the networked communication of mobile data, channel-ends and processes [15].

Also under investigation are ways of formally specifying behaviours for process types ('contracts'), in ways that allow the compiler to verify that a mobile process conforms. In cases where this is too complex, the compiler may generate information suitable for use with a separate model checker (e.g. FDR [26]).

We emphasise that this work is still an *experiment* in language design and implementation. The abstractions and semantics captured are not settled and may change — especially in the light of new theory and experience with (large) applications. Certain elements of the language are incomplete. For example, we need *static* channel-bundle types as well as the *mobile* ones implemented so far; we need *arrays* of shared classical channels as well as the scalar ones currently available. However, such developments are largely routine and are a matter of (finding the) time.

occam-π is built upon classical occam and very little has been discarded. Classical occam was very compact, powerful and elegant. A key principle underlying the extensions is that the original semantics are not disturbed, so that the ultra-low overheads for process management and all the safety guarantees are preserved — despite the introduction of the new dynamics. For example, although there is now plenty of dynamic memory allocation (for run-time sized arrays, parallel process replication, recursion, forking, mobile channels and mobile processes), there is no need for any garbage collection — the system deallocates immediately when final references are lost (thanks to the strong policing of aliases, carried over from classical occam). Such properties are crucial for its continued relevance to real-time applications.

Nevertheless, perhaps *Ockham's razor* needs to be wielded a little more aggressively — the removal of the 'OF' keyword is not very radical! For example, the syntax for declaring channel-bundle variables is not aligned with that for classical channels — maybe one of these versions should go? Could the compiler decide whether elements should be implemented as *mobile* or *shared* so that the programmer does not have to make this explicit — or would that require extra run-time cost and reduce system clarity? The duality noted between mobile processes and (some ways of working with) mobile channels may indicate that there is some simpler abstraction out there, from which these are special projections.

A formal denotational semantics, supporting refinement, needs completing. This is necessary both as a sanity check on the new ideas and to enable formal design and development. Such a semantics, based on Hoare and Jifeng's *Unified Theories of Programming* [27] has been built by Woodcock and Tang [28] for our earlier proposal for mobile processes [4]. That model allowed *multiple* interfaces for mobile processes but did not support *suspension* — they had to *terminate* before they could be moved and that required extra syntax to define persistent state (that moved with them). However, suspension should not be a major problem for that semantics to capture. In any case, it seems possible (and may be necessary) to merge that proposal with the one reported in this paper — the awkwardness of only having a single interface for mobile processes, discussed in section 4.5, needs addressing. It is also important for the semantics to address the issues raised by mobile channels, since the events bound to a process (mobile or static) will change as channel-ends are moved — section 2.4.

We welcome all feedback on this work. We shall be working towards the applications outlined in section 5, plus a few others — including RMoX [29], which is experimenting with occam-π for the design and implementation of real-time operating/embedded systems with low memory footprint, very fast reaction times and high-level (occam-π) programmability. The latest occam-π release, supported by the KRoC system, may be downloaded from [3].

Acknowledgements

We are grateful to Tony Hoare for his insights and advice, especially on how to suspend parallel process networks safely and efficiently [30]. We also wish to thank colleagues and other members of the concurrency research group at Kent — in particular David Wood, Christian Jacobsen and Mario Schweigler for their advice and associated work; and Jim Woodcock and Xinbei Tang, who produced the denotational semantics for our earlier model of mobile processes [4, 28].

References

1. May, D.: occam. ACM SIGPLAN Notices **18** (1983) 69–79
2. Inmos Limited: occam2 Reference Manual. Prentice Hall (1988) ISBN: 0-13-629312-3.
3. Welch, P., Moores, J., Barnes, F., Wood, D.: The KRoC Home Page (2000) Available at: http://www.cs.kent.ac.uk/projects/ofa/kroc/.
4. Barnes, F., Welch, P.: Prioritised dynamic communicating and mobile processes. IEE Proceedings – Software **150** (2003) 121–136
5. Barnes, F., Welch, P.: Mobile Data Types for Communicating Processes. In: Proceedings of the 2001 International Conference on Parallel and Distributed Processing Techniques and Applications (PDPTA'2001). Volume 1., CSREA press (2001) 20–26 ISBN: 1-892512-66-1.

6. Schweigler, M., Barnes, F., Welch, P.: Flexible, Transparent and Dynamic occam Networking with KRoC.net. In Broenink, J., Hilderink, G., eds.: Communicating Process Architectures 2003. WoTUG-26, Concurrent Systems Engineering,
   ISSN 1383-7575, Amsterdam, The Netherlands, IOS Press (2003) 199–224 ISBN:
   1-58603-381-6.
7. Barnes, F., Welch, P.: Communicating Mobile Processes. In East, I., Martin,
   J., Welch, P., Duce, D., Green, M., eds.: Communicating Process Architectures
   2004. Volume 62 of WoTUG-27, Concurrent Systems Engineering, ISSN 1383-
   7575., Amsterdam, The Netherlands, IOS Press (2004) 201–218 ISBN: 1-58603-
   458-8.
8. Milner, R., Parrow, J., Walker, D.: A Calculus of Mobile Processes – parts I and II.
   Journal of Information and Computation **100** (1992) 1–77 Available as technical
   report: ECS-LFCS-89-85/86, University of Edinburgh, UK.
9. Muller, H., Walrath, K.: Threads and Swing (2000) Available from: http://java.
   sun.com/products/jfc/tsc/articles/threads/threads1.html.
10. Barrett, G.: occam 3 Reference Manual. Technical report, Inmos Limited (1992)
    Available at: http://wotug.org/parallel/occam/documentation/.
11. Moores, J.: The Design and Implementation of occam/CSP Support for a Range
    of Languages and Platforms. PhD thesis, The University of Kent at Canterbury,
    Canterbury, Kent. CT2 7NF (2000)
12. Boosten, M.: Formal Contracts: Enabling Component Composition. In Broenink,
    J., Hilderink, G., eds.: Communicating Process Architectures 2003. WoTUG-26,
    Concurrent Systems Engineering, ISSN 1383-7575, Amsterdam, The Netherlands,
    IOS Press (2003) 185–197 ISBN: 1-58603-381-6.
13. Welch, P.: Graceful Termination – Graceful Resetting. In: Applying Transputer-
    Based Parallel Machines, Proceedings of OUG 10, Enschede, Netherlands, occam
    User Group, IOS Press, Netherlands (1989) 310–317 ISBN 90 5199 007 3.
14. Brinch Hansen, P.: Efficient Parallel Recursion. ACM SIGPLAN Notices **30** (1995)
    9–16 Reprinted in: *The Origin of Concurrent Programming*, edited by Per Brinch
    Hansen, pp. 525-534, Springer, ISBN 0-387-95401-5. 2002.
15. Schweigler, M.: Adding Mobility to Networked Channel-Types. In East, I., Martin,
    J., Welch, P., Duce, D., Green, M., eds.: Communicating Process Architectures
    2004. Volume 62 of WoTUG-27, Concurrent Systems Engineering, ISSN 1383-
    7575., Amsterdam, The Netherlands, IOS Press (2004) 107–126 ISBN: 1-58603-
    458-8.
16. Barnes, F.R.: Dynamics and Pragmatics for High Performance Concurrency. PhD
    thesis, University of Kent (2003)
17. Welch, P.H., Wood, D.C.: Higher Levels of Process Synchronisation. In Bakkers,
    A., ed.: Parallel Programming and Java, Proceedings of WoTUG 20. Volume 50
    of Concurrent Systems Engineering., Amsterdam, The Netherlands, World occam
    and Transputer User Group (WoTUG), IOS Press (1997) 104–129 ISBN: 90-5199-
    336-6.
18. Lin Chao et al.: Hyper-Threading Technology. Intel Technology Journal **6** (2002)
    ISSN: 1535-766X.
19. UKCRC: Grand Challenges for Computing Research (2004) http://www.nesc.
    ac.uk/esi/events/Grand_Challenges/.
20. Sleep, R.: In Vivo ⇔ In Silico: High fidelity reactive modelling of develop-
    ment and behaviour in plants and animals (2003) Available from: http://www.
    nesc.ac.uk/esi/events/Grand_Challenges/proposals/ViSoGCWebv2.pdf.

21. Welch, P.: Infrastructure for Multi-Level Simulation of Organisms (2004) Available from: `http://www.nesc.ac.uk/esi/events/Grand_Challenges/gcconf04/submissions/42.pdf`.
22. White, J.: Mobile agents white paper (1996) General Magic. `http://citeseer.ist.psu.edu/white96mobile.html`.
23. Jansen, W., Karygiannis, T.: NIST special publication 800-19 – mobile agent security. Technical report, National Institute of Standards and Technology, Computer Security Division, Gaithersburg, MD 20899. U.S. (2000) `http://citeseer.ist.psu.edu/jansen00nist.html`.
24. Jansen, W.A.: Countermeasures for Mobile Agent Security. Computer Communications, Special Issue on Advances in Research and Application of Network Security (2000)
25. Chess, D., Harrison, C., Kershenbaum, A.: Mobile agents: Are they a good idea? In Vitek, J., Tschudin, C., eds.: Mobile Object Systems: Towards the Programmable Internet. Volume 1222 of Lecture Notes in Computer Science., Springer-Verlag (1997) 25–45
26. Formal Systems (Europe) Ltd. 3, Alfred Street, Oxford. OX1 4EH, UK.: FDR2 User Manual. (2000)
27. Hoare, T., Jifeng, H.: Unified Theories of Programming. Prentice Hall (1998) ISBN: 0-134-58761-8.
28. Tang, X., Woodcock, J.: Travelling processes. In Kozen, D., ed.: The 7the International Conference on Mathematics of Program Construction. Lecture Notes in Computer Science, Stirling, Scotland, UK, Springer-Verlag (2004) To Appear.
29. Barnes, F., Jacobsen, C., Vinter, B.: RMoX: a Raw Metal occam Experiment. In Broenink, J., Hilderink, G., eds.: Communicating Process Architectures 2003. WoTUG-26, Concurrent Systems Engineering, ISSN 1383-7575, Amsterdam, The Netherlands, IOS Press (2003) 269–288 ISBN: 1-58603-381-6.
30. Welch, P.: UKC-CRG-01-04-2004: Suspending Networks of Parallel Processes. Technical report, Computing Laboratory, University of Kent at Canterbury, UK (2004)

Model-Based Design of Concurrent Programs

Jeff Magee and Jeff Kramer

Department of Computing, Imperial College London,
South Kensington campus, London SW7 2AZ, UK
{j.magee, j.kramer}@imperial.ac.uk

Abstract. A model is a simplified representation of the real world and, as such, includes only those aspects of the real-world system relevant to the problem at hand. The paper reviews a modelling approach to the design of concurrent programs in which models represent the behaviour of concurrent Java programs. A notation based on CSP is used to model behaviour. Tool support enables both interactive model exploration and the mechanical verification of required safety and liveness properties. Models are systematically translated into Java programs. The approach, supported by a textbook, forms the basis of a course at the authors' institution and has also been widely adopted elsewhere. With the benefit of five years hindsight, we examine the strengths and weaknesses of the approach and look at some of the subsequent remedies and directions.

1 Introduction

A model is a simplified representation of the real world. Engineers use models to focus on some aspects of a problem while deferring the consideration of others. For example, the models of aircraft used in wind-tunnels are used to focus on aerodynamic properties while ignoring considerations such as the power of the engines and the number of seats. In the book [1], we presented a modelling approach to the design of concurrent programs. We used Labelled Transition Systems (LTSs) to model the interaction behaviour of real concurrent programs written in Java and model-checking to mechanically verify safety and liveness properties. We quickly discovered that LTSs described in graphical form can be used only to model small programs and as a result used a process algebra notation F̲inite S̲tate P̲rocesses (FSP) which owes much to CSP[2]. This short paper is an attempt to review the strengths and weaknesses of the approach from the benefit of five years of hindsight. Along the way, we look at some of the differences with CSP.

In the following, section 2 describes our approach to model-based design of concurrent programs through the medium of a small example – the Single-lane Bridge. Section 3 present some observations and assessment of the approach while section 4 concludes.

A.E. Abdallah, C.B. Jones, and J.W. Sanders (Eds.): CSP25, LNCS 3525, pp. 211–219, 2005.

2 Single-Lane Bridge

The problem is depicted in Figure 1. A bridge over a river is only wide enough to permit a single lane of traffic. Consequently, cars can only move concurrently if they are moving in the same direction. A safety violation occurs if two cars moving in different directions enter the bridge at the same time.

To clarify discussion, we will refer to cars moving from left to right as red cars and cars moving from right to left as blue cars. In our concurrent programming model, each car is a process and the problem is to ensure that cars moving in different directions cannot concurrently access the shared resource that is the bridge. To be more precise, the *safety* property we require of the bridge is that blue cars and red cars must not be on the bridge at the same time, and the *liveness* property we require is that all cars eventually get to cross the bridge. To make the model realistic, we must also ensure that cars moving in the same direction cannot pass each other.

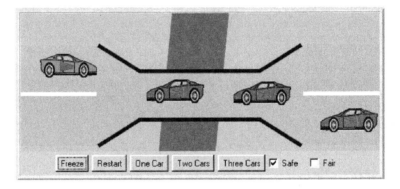

Fig. 1. Single-lane Bridge

2.1 FSP Model

The model of interaction for the Single-lane bridge consists of a set of CAR processes and a BRIDGE process that constrains the access of cars to the bridge. In addition, the processes NOPASS1 and NOPASS2 prohibit cars moving in the same direction from passing each other. Essentially, NOPASS1 preserves entry order and NOPASS2 preserves exit order. A CONVOY of cars is formed from the parallel composition of a set of cars and the no passing constraints. The entire model is formed from the parallel composition of a convoy of red cars, a convoy of blue cars and the process controlling access to the bridge. The syntax of FSP is nearly exactly that presented for CSP in [2]:- "->" is action prefix, "|" action choice and "| |" parallel composition. The only extension here is the addition of Boolean guards on actions denoted by the keyword **when** and used here in the definition of the BRIDGE process. As we will see in the following, these facilitate the translation of models into Java programs. The full model is listed in Figure 2 below and should be understandable with little effort by those familiar with CSP. More explanation may of course be found in[1].

```
const N = 3
range Id  = 1..N
range Int = 0..N

CAR = (enter -> exit -> CAR).

NOPASS1  = C[1], //preserves entry order
C[i:Id]  = ([i].enter-> C[i%N+1]).

NOPASS2  = C[1], //preserves exit order
C[i:Id]  = ([i].exit-> C[i%N+1]).

||CONVOY = ([Id]:CAR||NOPASS1||NOPASS2).

BRIDGE = BRIDGE[0][0],
BRIDGE[nr:Int][nb:Int]
       = (when nr==0
           blue[Id].enter -> BRIDGE[nr][nb+1]
          |blue[Id].exit  -> BRIDGE[nr][nb-1]
          |when nb==0
           red[Id].enter  -> BRIDGE[nr+1][nb]
          |red[Id].exit   -> BRIDGE[nr-1][nb]
          ).

||SingleLane = (red:CONVOY || blue:CONVOY || BRIDGE).
```

Fig. 2. FSP Model of Single-lane Bridge

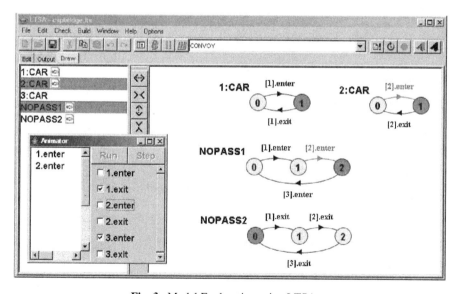

Fig. 3. Model Exploration using LTSA

2.2 Model Exploration and Analysis

A screenshot of the Labelled Transition System Analyser tool is depicted in Figure 3.
This tool is fundamentally a model checker; however, it also graphically depicts the

LTSs for the constituent processes of a model and in addition, permits the user to step through the model by selecting which enabled actions to execute. The figure depicts the animation of part of the single-lane bridge model – the CONVOY composition. Two of the CAR processes and the NOPASS processes are drawn as LTSs. The popup Animator window shows the actions enabled in the current state; these are 1.exit and 3.enter. The LTSA depicts the current state of a process by darker shading of one of its LTS states.

Graphical depiction of LTSs is satisfactory only for small processes. However, it serves an extremely useful pedagogic purpose in depicting precisely the meaning of FSP process definitions for small examples. The ability to step through a model and produce an example execution trace has proved useful for both small and large models. It is very much in the spirit of the LISP implementations described in [2] which supported the execution of CSP programs. CSP programs can of course now be exercised using the Probe tool [3].

In addition to exploring a model as described above, we also need to demonstrate that it exhibits the required safety and liveness properties. Here we use what is fundamentally a check for trace refinement; however, as outlined below, this check is implemented somewhat differently from the check found in FDR. Safety properties are specified in FSP by processes. The example asserts that either the red car numbered R is on the bridge or the blue car numbered B is on the bridge, but not both i.e. these cars have mutually exclusive access. Figure 4 depicts the property and the LTS generated for it.

```
property SAFE(R=1,B=1)
    = (red[R].enter  -> red[R].exit  -> SAFE
      |blue[B].enter -> blue[B].exit -> SAFE
      ).
```

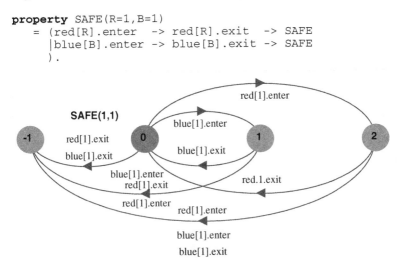

Fig. 4. Safety property LTS for SAFE(1,1)

It can be seen that any trace in which red car 1 and blue car 1 try to enter the bridge simultaneously leads to a transition to the ERROR state – labelled -1. In addition, it can be seen that each state of the LTS has outgoing actions for all actions in the alphabet of the property. This means that a safety property can be composed with a set of processes without affecting their correct behaviour (see [4]) for further details).

The property that no blue car can be on the bridge at the same time as any read car and vice-versa, is specified:

```
||SafeCheck = (forall[r:Id][b:Id] SAFE(r,b)
               || SingleLane
              ).
```

The advantages of checking safety in this way are twofold. Firstly, it is compositional in that property automata can be combined hierarchically with the components to which they apply. Secondly, multiple properties can be checked at the same time. The check is implemented as a search for reachability of the ERROR state.

Liveness or progress properties, as described more fully in [5], assert that is always eventually the case that an action occurs. In checking liveness properties, we assume fair choice and then specify adverse scheduling conditions using action priority. In the bridge example, this means building a system in which exit actions have lower priority than enter actions. This creates a congested or high load situation since, if given the choice between a car entering and leaving the bridge, the model will always choose an enter action. For the example model, the required liveness properties and the congested bridge are specified by:

```
progress LIVE_RED[r:Id]  = {red[r].enter}
progress LIVE_BLUE[b:Id] = {blue[b].enter}

||LiveCheck = SingleLane >> {{red,blue}[Id].exit}.
```

This gives rise to the following counter-example in which a continuous stream of blue cars leads to red car starvation:

```
Progress violation: LIVE_RED.1 LIVE_RED.2
Trace to terminal set of states:
        blue.1.enter
Cycle in terminal set:
        blue.2.enter
        blue.1.exit
        blue.1.enter
        blue.2.exit
Actions in terminal set:
        blue[1..2].{enter, exit}
Progress Check in: 10ms
```

The book[1] goes on to describe how the model may be modified to remedy the problem. Instead, we will illustrate how the model can be systematically transformed into a Java program, which will of course also exhibit the liveness problem. Indeed we have found that the ability to exhibit the same problems in models as in implementations is a great motivator for studying formal approaches to modelling concurrent systems.

2.3 Translation to Java

Since models by their nature capture only some aspects of a program, we do not attempt to automatically generate entire concurrent programs from FSP models. Instead we adopt a systematic translation of the FSP model into Java. The first step is to identify which of the processes in the model will be active entities in the Java program i.e. Java threads, and which will be passive entities i.e. Java monitors. In our example, cars are clearly active entities and the bridge a passive entity. We will focus here on translating the BRIDGE process, since the CAR processes simply become threads that repetitively call bridge enter followed by bridge exit methods. The key step is the translation of guarded actions in the model of the form:

```
when condition action -> NEWSTATE
```

into Java synchronized methods of the form:

```
public synchronized void action() throws InterruptedException
{
    while (!condition) wait();
    // modify monitor data
    notifyAll();
}
```

Using this on the BRIDGE process of Figure 2 yields the Java Bridge class of Figure 5 below.

```
class Bridge {
    private int nr = 0; //number of red cars on bridge
    private int nb = 0; //number of blue cars on bridge

    //when nb==0 red[Id].enter -> BRIDGE[nr+1][nb]
    synchronized void redEnter()throws InterruptedException {
        while (nb>0) wait();
        ++nr;
    }

    //red[Id].exit -> BRIDGE[nr-1][nb]
    synchronized void redExit(){
        --nr;
        notifyAll();
    }

    // blueEnter & blueExit are as above with nb & nr transpose
}
```

Fig. 5. Java monitor – class Bridge

Figure 1 is the applet display for the Single-lane bridge program. When the "Three Cars" button is pressed a convoy of three cars circulates in each direction. However, since with three cars, there is always a car from one colour on the bridge, starvation of the other coloured cars results. This is the liveness violation that was predicted by the model.

3   Evaluation

The book includes twenty-nine complete programs. With the help of our readers, we have discovered four bugs. Two of these bugs resulted from optimizing notifyAll() to notify() and ignoring our own systematic translation rules for doing so! One bug resulted from an ad-hoc translation from a model and the last bug is a liveness bug in a bounded allocator program for which we did not build a model. This last bug has since been corrected by producing the model and performing the translation.

Interestingly, none of the above bugs are exhibited by the Java implementations using the standard JVM and all four of them can be found using the modelling approach we advocate. In mitigation for publishing these erroneous programs, we have also found bugs in programs published in existing textbooks on concurrent programming.

3.1 Finite State Processes (FSP)

FSP is really a subset of CSP designed to facilitate tool support. In this section, we discuss some of the differences from CSP and the machine readable version of CSP used in FDR [3].

As mentioned, the main design influence on FSP was the need to facilitate tool support. For example, to simplify the display of the meaning of FSP processes as LTSs, there is a strict separation between basic processes defined using action prefix and choice, and composite processes defined using parallel composition, relabelling and hiding. In practice, we have not found this limiting when applying FSP to either educational or industrial examples.

For FSP we adopted the approach to alphabets outlined in [2] rather than [3]. Each process P has an alphabet P as in[2, 3]. However, alphabets are not explicitly declared but may be explicitly extended as in:

```
P = STOP + {never}.
```

The advantage is a simple parallel composition operator. FSP does not have an interleaving operator, so we can always associate an action in a trace with a specific process or a set of processes that share that action. This has considerable advantages in exploring and debugging models. Regrettably, alphabets are the biggest source of both student confusion and errors in models.

FSP does not include the signature output (!) and input (?) operators of CSP. This was motivated by a desire to avoid the preconception that the modelling notation is best suited to specifying message passing systems. Our main use of action synchronization is to model method invocation. The benefit is a more flexible interpretation of the domain significance of action labels. In practice, the omission of ! and ? does not seem to cause a problem for users even when models are of message passing systems.

3.2 Properties

Our approach to dealing with safety and liveness properties has proved limiting in a number of respects. Firstly, for simple models, the safety property is sometimes very similar to the model. Secondly, we cannot specify some common liveness properties such as the response property i.e. [](request $\Rightarrow$ <> reply). Consequently, we have augmented the LTSA tool with a Linear Temporal Logic model checking facility. The particular form of LTL we use is termed FLTL for Fluent LTL[6]. Fluents are used to describe the abstract states of a model and simplify the specification of logical properties. A fluent is defined by stating the (set of) events that make it true, and the (set of) events that make it false. For example, the following fluent RED_ON[r] is true when car r is on the bridge and is otherwise false.

```
fluent RED_ON[r:Id]  = <red[r].enter, red[r].exit>
fluent BLUE_ON[b:Id] = <blue[b].enter, blue[b].exit>
```

The safety property for the bridge is now:

```
assert NOCOLLISION
          = []!(exists[r:Id] RED_ON[r]
              && exists[b:Id] BLUE_ON[b])
```

which asserts that its is always not the case that there exists a red car on the bridge and a blue car on the bridge. A further major advantage of this sort of property specification is that we can easily generate witness executions by asserting the negation of the property. This is non-trivial with properties specified as processes or automata.

The liveness properties that are exactly equivalent to the progress properties we defined earlier are:

```
assert RED_ACCESS   = forall[r:Id] []<>red[r].enter
assert BLUE_ACCESS  = forall[b:Id] []<>blue[b].enter
```

4 Conclusion

The approach we have briefly outlined in the foregoing combines clear models in a notation based on CSP with tool support and a systematic path to implementation. It has proved attractive to students and practitioners. We sincerely hope that, as intended, it has played a part in overcoming resistance to formal development methods by providing some real benefits in building correct and robust concurrent programs.

In addition, the LTSA tool has proved a flexible platform for both our research and that of others. Its plugin architecture [7] has enabled a range of experimental tools to be added. Examples of these are tools to support model synthesis from scenarios [8], graphic animation of models [9] and verification of Web services implementations[10].

In conclusion, it remains only to acknowledge the huge debt that this work owes to that of Tony Hoare. We can do this best by reiterating the words of Edsger Dijksta in his preface to [2] in expressing our gratitude for "the scientific wisdom, the notational intrepidity, and the manipulative agility of Charles Antony Richard Hoare." Nowhere is this more in evidence than in Communicating Sequential Processes.

References

1. Magee, J. and Kramer, J., *Concurrency: State Models & Java Programs*: John Wiley & Sons, 1999.
2. Hoare, C.A.R., *Communicating Sequential Processes*: Prentice-Hall, 1985.
3. Roscoe, A.W., *The Theory and Practice of Concurrency*: Prentice Hall, 1998.
4. Cheung, S.C. and Kramer, J., *Checking Safety Properties Using Compositional Reachability Analysis*. ACM Transactions on Software Engineering and Methodology, Vol. **8**(1), January 1999: pp. 49-78.

5. Giannakopoulou, D., Magee, J., and Kramer, J. "Checking Progress with Action Priority: Is it Fair?" in *Proc. of the 7th European Software Engineering Conference held jointly with the 7th ACM SIGSOFT Symposium on the Foundations of Software Engineering (ESEC/FSE'99).* September 1999, Toulouse, France. Springer, Lecture Notes in Computer Science 1687, pp. 511-527. O. Nierstrasz and M. Lemoine, Eds.

6. Giannakopoulou, D. and Magee, J. "Fluent Model Checking for Event-Based Systems", in *Proc. of the 4th joint meeting of the European Software Engineering Conference and ACM SIGSOFT Symposium on the Foundations of Software Engineering (ESEC/FSE 2003),* Helsinki.

7. Chatley, R., Eisenbach, S., Kramer, J., Magee, J., and Uchitel, S. "Predictable Dynamic Plugin Systems", in *Proc. of the Fundamental Approaches to Software Engineering, Joint Conferences on Theory and Practice of Software,* Barcelona. Springer, Lecture Notes in Computer Science 2984.

8. Uchitel, S., Kramer, J., and Magee, J., *Incremental Elaboration of Scenario-Based Specifications and Behaviour Models using Implied Scenarios.* Transactions on Software Engineering and Methodology (TOSEM), Vol. **13**(1), Association of Computing Machinery Press: pp. 37-85.

9. Magee, J., Kramer, J., Giannakopoulou, D., and Pryce, N. "Graphical Animation of Behavior Models", in *Proc. of the 22nd International Conference on Software Engineering (ICSE'00).* June 2000, Limerick, pp. 499-508.

10. Foster, H., Kramer, J., Magee, J., and Uchitel, S. "Model-based Verification of Web Service Compositions", in *Proc. of the Automated Software Engineering,* Montreal. IEEE CS Press.

Of Probabilistic *wp* and *CSP*
—and Compositionality *

Carroll Morgan**

Dept. Comp. Sci. & Eng., University of New South Wales,
NSW 2052 Australia
`carrollm@cse.unsw.edu.au`

Abstract. We connect *probabilistic Action Systems* and *probabilistic
CSP*, inducing healthiness conditions for the probabilistic traces, failures and divergences of the latter.

A probabilistic sequential semantics for *pGCL* [31] is "inserted un-
derneath" an existing but non-probabilistic link between action systems
and *CSP*. Thus the link, which earlier yielded the classic *CSP* healthiness conditions [34], is induced to produce probabilistic versions of them
"for free".

Although probabilistic concurrency has enjoyed the attentions of
a very large number of researchers over many years—including ourselves [37]—we nevertheless hope to gain new insights by combining the
two approaches *CSP* and *pGCL*. In the meantime, however, we probably raise more questions than we answer: in particular, the issue of
compositionality—for the moment—remains as delicate as ever.

1   Introduction

A typical *state-based* approach to concurrency is the *Action System* formalism
of Back and Kurki-Suonio [3], in which the effects of transitions are described in
some simple programming language such as Dijkstra's *Guarded-Command Language GCL* [10]; the transitions' enabling conditions are given by the commands'
guards, which are predicates over the variables of some state space. By labelling
the transitions we determine a labelled transition system.

That is, a state space is shared between a number of *actions*, each of which
is enabled or not depending on the current state. The execution of an (enabled)
action changes the state, which consequentially changes the set of enabled actions
available for the very next step. *UNITY* [7] and *Event-B* [1] have essentially the
same structure (although the former makes assumptions of scheduling fairness).

In contrast, a typical *event-based* formalisation of concurrency is the *Communicating Sequential Processes* approach due to C.A.R. Hoare [17]. There the

---

* We retrace the path of an earlier work [34].
** The author is supported by a Fellowship from the Australian Research Council under
  its Discovery Grant *DP0345457*.

A.E. Abdallah, C.B. Jones, and J.W. Sanders (Eds.): CSP 2004, LNCS 3525, pp. 220–241, 2005.
© Springer-Verlag Berlin Heidelberg 2005

actions are called *events*, have no internal structure, and affect no explicit state. The behaviour of a process is understood in terms of the sequences of events in which it might engage, called *traces* and, for finer distinctions, in terms of its *failures* (modelling deadlock) and its *divergences* (for livelock and other chaotic misbehaviour).

Linking state- and event-based approaches is attractive because there are so many real systems whose behaviour is partly controlled by state changes and partly by sequencing, and for that reason a great number of researchers have brought them together before.[1] For example, the contents of a buffer is probably best described by a state, *i.e.* the value(s) it contains; but the exchange of request- and confirm messages necessary to set up the communication channel, which the buffer serves, could well be best described by explicit sequencing.

In our earlier work [34] we linked *standard*, that is non-probabilistic, *GCL*-style action systems and *CSP* by giving three simple formulae for the traces, failures, and divergences of any action system; our approach differed from *e.g.* He's [12] and Josephs' [22] in its use of predicate transformers [10] rather than relations; we felt that the benefit of the predicate transformers was firstly a simpler formulation that included divergence naturally and automatically, and secondly the access to source-level reasoning afforded by predicate-transformer based (*i.e. wp*-style) programming logic. That *wp*-approach has led to further research [45, 4, 6].

In our work here we replace standard predicate transformers by the *probabilistic* predicate transformers [24, 36] that have been developed and extended since our earlier visit to this topic [37]: we (re-)construct and then explore a link between "probabilistic action systems" and what will be, in effect, part of a synthesised "probabilistic *CSP*".[2]

We present probabilistic Action Systems first—they will be action systems written in the probabilistic version *pGCL* of Dijkstra's *guarded-command language* [35, 31, 10]; the "*p*" in the name indicates that we have extended *GCL* with an explicit operator "$_p\oplus$" for the probabilistic choice between two commands.

Then we recall the details of *CSP* very briefly.

Finally, we use *pGCL*'s probabilistic relational model [23, 13] to make a link between probabilistic Action Systems and probabilistic *CSP*, resulting in a synthesis of probabilistic traces, failures and divergences. In the appendix we go on to show how the probabilistic program logic [36, 35, 31], accompanying that model, facilitates algebraic reasoning.

We conclude by discussing *compositionality*, which we regard as the key issue in any exercise of this kind.

---

[1] They have used both *CSP* and other styles of concurrency.

[2] It differs significantly from the probabilistic *CSP* we constructed via the probabilistic powerdomains of Jones and Plotkin [37, 19, 20, 32], and from other probabilistic *CSP*'s as well [25, 44, 32].

System $\mathcal{H}$:

$$\begin{array}{lcl}
\mathsf{hic} & \widehat{=} & \mathsf{n} \neq 0 \;\rightarrow\; \mathsf{n}\colon= 0 \\
\mathsf{haec} & \widehat{=} & \mathsf{n} = 0 \;\rightarrow\; \mathsf{n}\colon= -1\,{}_{1/3}\!\oplus 0 \\
\mathsf{hoc} & \widehat{=} & \mathsf{n} < 0 \;\rightarrow\; \mathsf{n}\colon= \pm 1
\end{array}$$

initially $\mathsf{n}\colon= 0\ {}_{1/2}\!\oplus\ \pm 1$

The program variable is just n of type integer (*i.e.* $\mathbb{Z}$).

The initial state is chosen by flipping an unbiased coin: if it comes up heads, then n is set to 0; if it is tails, then a demonic choice is made between setting n to $+1$ or to -1.

When n is $+1$, only hic is enabled; if it is 0, only haec is enabled; if it is -1, both hic and hoc are enabled and an external choice is offered between them.

Action hic is neither probabilistic nor demonic; the haec action is purely probabilistic, without demonic choice; and hoc is purely demonic, without probabilistic choice.

Note we are using the given names (*e.g.* hic) both to refer to *actions*, which can have internal structure (*e.g.* can be demonic or probabilistic, and can include a guard), and to refer to *events* which are simply the *labels* of actions and have no structure in themselves.

Fig. 1. A probabilistic action system $\mathcal{H}$

2   Probabilistic Action Systems: *pAS*

A *probabilistic action system*—or *pAS*—is a set of labelled actions and an initialisation; an *action* is a guard and a command; a *guard* is a predicate; and a *command* is a program fragment in the probabilistic extension *pGCL* of Dijkstra's language of guarded commands [35, 31]. An *initialisation* is a command with no guard. We assume all of the above are given in the context of a collection of program variables over which the meanings of the commands and predicates are defined. Figure 1 is an example of a probabilistic action system in which the actions have been labelled hic, haec and hoc.

Execution of a probabilistic action system proceeds as follows:

1. First, the initialisation is executed; then
2. Repeatedly an enabled action is selected then executed.

An action is *enabled* if its guard is true; it is *executed* by carrying out its command as determined by the semantics of *pGCL*; at the same time, its associated event is deemed to have occurred.

If the repetition in Step 2 fails—because no action is enabled—then the system is *deadlocked*.

One of the possible behaviours of the probabilistic action system in Fig. 1 is to execute hic,haec,hoc repeatedly and forever. But—thankfully—there are many other possibilities: which one actually occurs depends on the outcomes of probabilistic and demonic choices made as the *pAS* evolves.

$$\mathcal{H} \quad \stackrel{\frown}{=} \quad \mathcal{H}_0 \; {}_{1/2}\oplus (\mathcal{H}_{-1} \sqcap \mathcal{H}_1)$$

$$\mathcal{H}_1 \quad \stackrel{\frown}{=} \quad \mathsf{hic} \to \mathcal{H}_0$$
$$\mathcal{H}_0 \quad \stackrel{\frown}{=} \quad \mathsf{haec} \to (\mathcal{H}_{-1} \; {}_{1/3}\oplus \mathcal{H}_0)$$
$$\mathcal{H}_{-1} \quad \stackrel{\frown}{=} \quad \mathsf{hic} \to \mathcal{H}_0 \; \square \; \mathsf{hoc} \to (\mathcal{H}_{-1} \sqcap \mathcal{H}_1)$$

Process $\mathcal{H}$ is the entire system of Fig. 1 initially. Process $\mathcal{H}_1$ is then the system as it would behave when n is +1; and the processes $\mathcal{H}_0, \mathcal{H}_{-1}$ correspond to values $0, -1$ respectively.

Fig. 2. A "plausible" *pCSP*-style encoding of the system $\mathcal{H}$ from Fig. 1

---

3   Probabilistic Communicating Sequential Processes: *pCSP*

Probabilistic CSP is standard *CSP* extended with a ${}_p\oplus$ operator between processes: there are many versions, distinguished usually by the way in which internal choice, probabilistic choice and external choice interact, and by whether other features (*e.g.* priorities [25]) are included. When we say "*pCSP*" we mean "as defined here".[3]

Written in *pCSP*, the *pAS* in Fig. 1 would probably be as in Fig. 2: a set of mutually recursive process equations in which we have "coded up" the *pAS* by inventing one process term for each possible state.

The semantics of *CSP*–in its simplest form—includes a set of traces in which processes can engage, where a *trace* is a finite sequence of events and an *event* (as for a *pAS*) is the name of some action; we will see, however, that for *pCSP* we must also consider the *probability* that those traces can occur. Some of the possible traces for the *pAS* of Fig. 1, or equivalently (but informally) the *pCSP* process of Fig. 2, are set out in Fig. 3.

After the next section we will give a formula for the traces of a *pAS*, and for their associated probabilities. Subsequent sections introduce probabilistic failures and divergences.

4   Relational Semantics of *pGCL*

The *pGCL* we use for probabilistic action systems has both a relational semantics [23, 13] and a transformer semantics [24, 36]; they are consistent with each other [36, 31] in the same way that conventional relational semantics is consistent with Dijkstra's original predicate-transformer semantics [14, 10]. In this section we concentrate on relational semantics, because it is more intuitive (than transformer semantics, at least at first); we develop the associated probabilistic predicate transformers in the appendix.

---

[3] We do not mean "*the*" probabilistic *CSP*, since there are many.

$$\{ \ \langle \rangle,$$

$$\langle \mathsf{hic} \rangle, \ \langle \mathsf{haec} \rangle, \ \langle \mathsf{hoc} \rangle,$$

$$\langle \mathsf{hic}, \quad \mathsf{haec} \rangle,$$

$$\langle \mathsf{haec}, \mathsf{hic} \rangle,$$
$$\langle \mathsf{haec}, \mathsf{haec} \rangle,$$
$$\langle \mathsf{haec}, \mathsf{hoc} \rangle,$$

$$\langle \mathsf{hoc}, \mathsf{hic} \rangle,$$
$$\langle \mathsf{hoc}, \mathsf{hoc} \rangle,$$

$$\langle \mathsf{hic}, \mathsf{haec}, \mathsf{hic} \rangle,$$
$$\langle \mathsf{hic}, \mathsf{haec}, \mathsf{haec} \rangle,$$
$$\langle \mathsf{hic}, \mathsf{haec}, \mathsf{hoc} \rangle,$$

$$\vdots$$

$$\}$$

If the left alternative n: = 0 is taken in the *pAS* initialisation of $\mathcal{H}$–with probability 1/2—then only haec is offered initially in the associated *pCSP* process. If the right alternative n: = ±1 is taken—also probability 1/2—then the choice between setting n to −1 or to +1 is made demonically. If n is set to −1, then an external choice between hic and hoc is offered initially. In this case we thus have probabilistic, then internal (demonic), then finally external (angelic) choice in succession. If n is set to +1, then only hic is offered.

After hic, only haec can be offered.

After haec, with probability 1/3 an external choice hic/hoc is offered; with probability 2/3, only haec is offered (again).

After hoc, the choice between the offers hic and hic/hoc is demonic.

Fig. 3. A partial *pCSP* view of $\mathcal{H}$ from Figs. 1 and 2: its set of traces

---

Let the state space be S; we assume it is countable. A *sub-distribution* over S is a function Δ from S into the unit interval $[0, 1]$ such that $(\sum_{s:S} \Delta.s) \leq 1$, that is such that the total probability over all states s of the individual probabilities $\Delta.s$ is no more than one.[4] A sub-distribution that sums to one may be called a *distribution* (*i.e.* dropping the "sub-").

The set of all sub-distributions over S is written $\overline{S}$, and as a special case we write $\overline{s}$ for the element of $\overline{S}$ that is one at s and zero elsewhere, *i.e.* is the *point distribution* on s. We say that a distribution is *standard* if it is $\overline{s}$ for some s.

Non-demonic—but possibly probabilistic—programs are functions from S to $\overline{S}$, so that program f takes initial state s to the final sub-distribution $f.s$.

---

[4] In general for function f and argument x we write $f.x$ for the application of f to x, and the operator associates to the left: thus $f.g.x$ is $(f(g))(x)$.

Equivalently, the probability that f takes s to s' is just $f.s.s'$. If some program f is such that $f.s.s'$ is either zero or one for all s, s', then we say that f itself is *standard*; clearly such f's are the representatives of traditional deterministic programs.

Demonic probabilistic programs are functions from S to *subsets* rather than to simple elements of $\overline{S}$, that is they are of type $S \to \mathbb{P}\overline{S}$, so that program r can take initial state s to final sub-distribution Δ' just when $\Delta' \in r.s$. (In this multi-valued case we are writing "r"—instead of "f"—as a mnemonic for "relation".) Thus for example the possible probabilities that program r can take initial s to some final s' ranges (demonically) between the minimum and the maximum of $\Delta'.s'$ over all Δ' in $r.s$.

4.1   Examples of Simple Programs

Let the state space again be $\mathbb{Z}$, and for *pGCL* program *prog* (*i.e.*, given syntactically), let $[\![prog]\!]$ be its relational interpretation as described above. We use n for the program variable and n for the whole state.

We begin with atomic programs, and then introduce simple compounds.

identity — $[\![\mathbf{skip}]\!].n = \{\overline{n}\}$

The "do-nothing" program **skip** takes any state to itself. Because of our demonic/probabilistic type for programs, however, the result is not just n again, nor even the set $\{n\}$, but rather is the singleton set containing just the point distribution on n.

assignment — $[\![\mathsf{n}:= \mathsf{n}+1]\!].n = \{\overline{n+1}\}$

Non-demonic and non-probabilistic assignments deliver singleton sets of point distributions: singleton sets because there is no demonic choice; point distributions because there is no (non-trivial) probabilistic choice.

probabilistic choice — $[\![\mathsf{n}:= \mathsf{n}+1 \ {}_{1/3}\oplus \ \mathsf{n}:= \mathsf{n}+2]\!].n$
$$= \{\Delta'\}$$
$$\text{where } \Delta'.(n+1) = 1/3$$
$$\Delta'.(n+2) = 2/3$$
$$\Delta'.n' = 0 \quad \text{for other values } n'$$

Non-demonic but probabilistic assignments deliver singleton sets of non-trivial sub-distributions: again the sets are singleton because there is no demonic choice; but the single element of the set is a proper sub-distribution.

demonic choice — $[\![\mathsf{n}:= \mathsf{n}+1 \ \sqcap \ \mathsf{n}:= \mathsf{n}+2]\!].n$
$$= \{\overline{n+1}, \overline{n+2}\}$$

A purely demonic (and non-probabilistic) binary choice delivers the sub-distributions contributed by each of its operands.

demonic probabilistic choice — $[\![\mathsf{n}\!:=\,\mathsf{n}+1\ \ _{1/3}\oplus_{1/3}\ \mathsf{n}\!:=\,\mathsf{n}+2]\!].n$

$$= \{\varDelta'_{1/3},\,\varDelta'_{2/3}\}$$

$$\text{where } \begin{array}{rcll} \varDelta'_p.(n+1) &=& p \\ \varDelta'_p.(n+2) &=& 1-p \\ \varDelta'_p.n' &=& 0 & \text{for other values } n' \end{array}$$

The notation $_p\oplus_q$, for $p+q \le 1$, abbreviates the demonic choice between the two probabilistic choices $_p\oplus$ and $_{1-q}\oplus$: it executes the left branch with probability *at least* p, the right with probability *at least* q and—in any case—it is certain to execute one or the other.

4.2   "Naked" Guarded Commands and Miracles

The *pGCL* commands in probabilistic action systems are equipped with a guard that controls whether or not they are enabled in the current state. We build that in to the relational semantics of *pGCL* by "erasing" the parts of transitions that the guard does not enable: if a state does not make the guard true, then its result set is empty from that state. That is, for predicate gd we define

$$\varDelta' \in [\![gd \to prog]\!].s \quad \widehat{=} \quad s \in [\![gd]\!] \;\wedge\; \varDelta' \in [\![prog]\!].s \;,$$

where by $[\![gd]\!]$ we mean the subset of S denoted by the guard gd.

This is of course the "normal" way of dealing with *miracles* when considered relationally: because a miraculous command has no final states at all, every final state it produces satisfies false–and therefore we imagine that its execution cannot even be started [41, 33, 40, 18].

The enabling/disabling property of a guard is very convenient when moving between action systems and *CSP* [34, 45, 22] —whether probabilistic or not— since it automatically excludes the traces which the action system cannot produce.

4.3   Sequential Composition in *pGCL*

As an action system executes, it carries out one (guarded) command after another; the overall effect is the sequential composition of all the (finitely many) commands concerned. Given two commands $prog_1$ and $prog_2$, we therefore want to construct the relational semantics of their composition.

We begin with non-demonic programs f (*i.e.* with their meanings). If we are given some sub-distribution $\varDelta$ of *initial* states from which f will repeatedly be run, the overall effect can be obtained by averaging f's output sub-distributions for each initial state over the known "incoming" sub-distribution $\varDelta$ for them: thus we define

$$f^*.\varDelta.s' \quad \widehat{=} \quad \left(\sum_{s:S} \varDelta.s * f.s.s'\right), \qquad\qquad (1)$$

where we distinguish the f-over-sub-distributions from the original f by writing f^* for the former. Note that the original can be recovered, since $f.s = f^*.\overline{s}$.

Now to determine the effect of a possibly demonic r on an initial sub-distribution Δ, we construct the collection of its non-demonic "refinements" f and then refer to (1) above: that is, we say that "r is refined by f" just when f satisfies $(\forall s: S \cdot r.s \ni f.s)$, and we write it $r \sqsubseteq f$. Then we define

$$r^*.\Delta \quad \widehat{=} \quad \{f: S \to \overline{S} \mid r^+ \sqsubseteq f \cdot f^*.\Delta\} , \quad 5$$

where again we use $(\cdot)^*$ to indicate "lifting" a function to act over sub-distributions rather than individual states, and where the relation r^+ is the "down closure" of r obtained by adding the everywhere-zero sub-distribution to $r.s$ whenever $r.s$ is empty.

Finally, we describe sequential composition simply by applying the "lifted" semantics of the second component to every final sub-distribution the first component could produce: that is, for initial state s we define

$$[\![prog_1; prog_2]\!].s \quad \widehat{=} \quad \{\Delta: [\![prog_1]\!].s \cdot [\![prog_2]\!]^*.\Delta\} . \quad 6$$

5   Traces of a *pAS*

We now use the sequential composition of Sec. 4.3 to determine the traces of a *pAS*. Let its initialisation be command *ini* and let its events be $e_1, e_2, \cdots$. The *alphabet* of the action system *pAS* is the set of all its events (whether or not they actually can be executed).

We write subsets of the state space in three different ways, as convenient: as *sets of states* directly (whether enumerated or given as a comprehension); as *predicates* over program variables, denoting sets whose variables' values satisfy the predicate; and as *sets of events*, in which case we will mean the set of states corresponding to the disjunction of the events' guards. Note that the empty set $\emptyset$, whether of states or of events, corresponds to the predicate false.

When we write events or sequences of events between semantic brackets $[\![\cdot]\!]$, we mean the relational semantics of the corresponding actions, with their guards, sequentially composed if appropriate.

In standard *CSP*, a trace is a finite sequence of events drawn from the alphabet; and the *traces* model of a process is the set of all the traces it could carry out [17]. Because a particular trace is included in the trace-semantics of a processes if it *can* occur, our probabilistic view will be that we are interested in the *maximum probability* of that occurrence. For example, the sets of traces for the two standard processes

---

[5] This set comprehension is read "vary bound variable f over its type $S \to \overline{S}$; select those values satisfying the condition $r^+ \sqsubseteq f$; form set elements from them according to the expression $f^*.\Delta$."

[6] In this comprehension the omitted condition defaults to *true*; refer Footnote 5 immediately above.

System $\mathcal{A}$:	**initially** n: = 0	hic $\hat{=}$ n ≥ 0 $\rightarrow$ n: = +1	
		hoc $\hat{=}$ n ≤ 0 $\rightarrow$ n: = -1	
System $\mathcal{D}$:	**initially** n: = ±1	hic $\hat{=}$ n ≥ 0 $\rightarrow$ n: = +1	
		hoc $\hat{=}$ n ≤ 0 $\rightarrow$ n: = -1	
System $\mathcal{P}$:	**initially** n: = $-1\,_{1/2}\oplus +1$	hic $\hat{=}$ n ≥ 0 $\rightarrow$ n: = +1	
		hoc $\hat{=}$ n ≤ 0 $\rightarrow$ n: = -1	

All three systems exhibit the same potential traces, *i.e.* any trace comprising either all hic's or all hoc's; but in System $\mathcal{P}$ the associated probabilities can be included by giving a set of trace-probability pairs

$$\{ \ (\langle\rangle, 1), \quad (\langle\mathsf{hic}\rangle, 1/2), \ (\langle\mathsf{hic},\mathsf{hic}\rangle, 1/2), \ (\langle\mathsf{hic},\mathsf{hic},\mathsf{hic}\rangle, 1/2), \cdots$$
$$(\langle\mathsf{hoc}\rangle, 1/2), \ (\langle\mathsf{hoc},\mathsf{hoc}\rangle, 1/2), \ (\langle\mathsf{hoc},\mathsf{hoc},\mathsf{hoc}\rangle, 1/2), \cdots \ \} \ ,$$

where the second element of each pair is the (maximum) probability with which the first element can occur.

In Systems $\mathcal{A}$ and $\mathcal{D}$ the "trace-probability" would be just one when a trace can occur, and zero when it cannot. The standard trace semantics in those cases is obtained by removing the probability-zero pairs, and then "projecting away" the probability-one information from those that remain.

Fig. 4. Three action systems: angelic, demonic, probabilistic

---

	hic $\rightarrow STOP$ $\square$ hoc $\rightarrow STOP$	—external choice
and	hic $\rightarrow STOP$ $\sqcap$ hoc $\rightarrow STOP$	—internal choice

are the same, being just $\{\langle\rangle, \langle\mathsf{hic}\rangle, \langle\mathsf{hoc}\rangle\}$ in each case and not taking account of the fact that the second process—with its "demon" $\sqcap$ representing the internal choice—cannot be forced to produce either of the non-empty traces separately.

Accordingly, in our probabilistic view, we will associate *probability one* with all three traces, for both processes, with the same caveat about ignoring the demon (for now).

Action systems for two similar processes $\mathcal{A}$ (for angelic) and $\mathcal{D}$ (for demonic) are given in Fig. 4, together with a third system $\mathcal{P}$ which chooses probabilistically between the two events. As we are about to see, it exhibits proper probabilities.

We begin by considering System $\mathcal{P}$. By (informal) inspection, the probability that hic will occur is just the probability that the initialisation *ini* establishes the guard n ≥ 0 of that event. From our relational semantics of Sec. 4 we know that the initialisation produces the single distribution

$$\Delta_{ini} \quad \hat{=} \quad \{-1 \mapsto 1/2, \ +1 \mapsto 1/2\} \tag{2}$$

which assigns probability $1/2$ to the subset $\{0, 1, \cdots\}$ of $\mathbb{Z}$ in which hic is enabled.[7] We could also write that as the singleton set of guards "{hic}".

That probability is in fact the *expected value* of the characteristic function of the set concerned, taken over the distribution (2) above that the initialisation produces. However that set is written, whether explicitly or as a predicate or as a set of events (*i.e.* as the disjunction of their guards, in the last case), we use the notation $[\cdot]$ to form the associated characteristic function: thus we would write $[0, 1, \cdots]$ or $[n \geq 0]$ or $[\text{hic}]$ here, meaning in each case the function over the integers that takes non-negative arguments to one and negative arguments to zero.

In general, for the expected value over a sub-distribution Δ of some random variable B (itself a function from the state space into the reals), we write

$$\int_{\Delta} B \quad \widehat{=} \quad \left(\sum_{s:S} \Delta.s * B.s \right) , \tag{3}$$

so that the probability $1/2$ we calculated above is just $\int_{\Delta_{ini}} [\text{hic}]$.

We now form a combined notation for all the above operations, that is of determining the relational semantics of a non-demonic command, applying it to an initial state, and then taking the expected value of some function: we define

$$\text{Exp.}[\![prog]\!].B.s \quad \widehat{=} \quad \int_{\Delta'} B \qquad \text{given that } [\![prog]\!].s = \{\Delta'\} .$$

As a result, we know that when B is some standard $[Q]$ for predicate Q, the expression $\text{Exp.}[\![prog]\!].[Q].s$ is the probability that the non-demonic *prog* will reach Q from s.[8]

If we now look at the *action* associated with hic, we see that its relational semantics is given by

$$[\![n \geq 0 \rightarrow n := +1]\!] \quad = \quad \{ n: \mathbb{Z} \mid n \geq 0 \cdot \{ n \mapsto \{ \overline{+1} \} \} \} ,$$

the partial function defined only on non-negative arguments which produces the singleton result set of sub-distributions $\{ \overline{+1} \}$ for each one of them. If we ask "what is the *maximum* possible expected value of random variable [true] after executing hic?" from initial state n—for which we could invent the notation

$$\overline{\text{Exp.}}[\![n \geq 0 \rightarrow n := +1]\!].[\text{true}].n \qquad {}^{9} \tag{4}$$

by incorporating the "maximum" as an overbar— we find it is just the random variable [hic] itself, since whenever n does not satisfy hic's guard $n \geq 0$ we

---

[7] In the usual terminology of probability theory we would speak of the probabilistic *event* $\{0, 1, \cdots\}$ rather than subset; but we must avoid confusion with the "events" of *CSP*.

[8] We will deal with the demonic-*prog* case shortly.

[9] We are defining $\overline{\text{Exp.}}[\![prog]\!].B.s \ \widehat{=} \ (\sqcup \Delta' : [\![prog]\!].s \cdot \int_{\Delta'} B)$.

are taking the maximum over an *empty* set of non-negative reals, yielding zero. When n does satisfy hic's guard, the expression (4) gives one, the probability assigned by the distribution $\overline{+1}$ to the whole state space (of which [true] is the characteristic function). That is, we find that

$$[\text{hic}] \quad = \quad \overline{\text{Exp}}.[\![\text{hic}]\!].[\text{true}] \ , \tag{5}$$

where we recall that "hic" between semantic brackets refers to the corresponding action, including its guard.

We can now put our two experiments with hic together: since the initialisation is unguarded, terminating and purely probabilistic, it produces a single distribution from every initial state and so is unaffected if we use $\overline{\text{Exp}}.[\![\cdot]\!]$ rather than $\text{Exp}.[\![\cdot]\!]$. Thus we have that the (maximum) probability of the occurrence of the trace $\langle\text{hic}\rangle$ in System $\mathcal{P}$ can be written

$$\overline{\text{Exp}}.[\![ini]\!].[\text{hic}].n \ , \quad \text{that is} \quad \overline{\text{Exp}}.[\![ini]\!].(\overline{\text{Exp}}.[\![\text{hic}]\!].[\text{true}]).n \ , \tag{6}$$

where on the right we have appealed to (5). But, as we prove later in Fig. 7 of App. A, the "cascaded" use of expectations at (6) on the right can be simplified to just

$$\overline{\text{Exp}}.[\![ini; \ \text{hic}]\!].[\text{true}].n \tag{7}$$

because $\overline{\text{Exp}}.[\![\cdot]\!]$ distributes over sequential composition, becoming functional composition.

From our operational intuition, we believe that the expression (7) will equal $1/2$ for any initial n, as will the further extended $\overline{\text{Exp}}.[\![ini; \ \text{hic}; \ \text{hic}]\!].[\text{true}].n$, and so on.

Now to give the "trace semantics" of a probabilistic action system we can use the above to map every potential trace (finite sequence of events) to the maximum probability of its occurrence.

Let the *pAS* be $\mathcal{S}$ over a state space S. As before, for a given finite trace say es $= \langle\text{e}_1, \text{e}_2, \cdots, \text{e}_n\rangle$ of events from $\mathcal{S}$ we mean the sequential composition $\text{e}_1; \text{e}_2; \cdots; \text{e}_n$ of the events' corresponding actions whenever es appears within semantic brackets $[\![\cdot]\!]$. Also, we continue to use $[\cdot]$ to form characteristic functions, and we let *ini* be the initialisation of $\mathcal{S}$. Then for any predicate Q over the state space S we define

$$\mathcal{S}.\langle\!\langle\text{es}\rangle\!\rangle.Q \quad \widehat{=} \quad (\sqcup s: S \cdot \overline{\text{Exp}}.[\![ini; \ \text{es}]\!].[Q].s) \ , \tag{8}$$

where on the right the terms S, ini, es, Q are to be interpreted within the system $\mathcal{S}$ mentioned on the left. When $\mathcal{S}$ is clear from context, however, we omit it and write just $\langle\!\langle\text{es}\rangle\!\rangle.Q$ on the left.

Thus Eqns. (6) and (7)—the maximum probability that trace $\langle\text{hic}\rangle$ can occur in $\mathcal{P}$—would be written simply $\mathcal{P}.\langle\!\langle\text{hic}\rangle\!\rangle.\text{true}$. What the notation of (8) has done is simply to bundle up the choice of action system, the inclusion of the initialisation, and the maximising over all initial states.[10]

---

[10] Maximising over *initial* states is usually unnecessary: since the initialisation rarely depends on *its* initial state, the effect of the quantification is merely to replace some constant *function* (of the initial s) by the constant itself.

We can now give the probabilistic trace-semantics of $\mathcal{S}$: it is a function from finite sequences of the events of $\mathcal{S}$ into the real interval $[0, 1]$, giving for each sequence es the maximum probability of its occurrence. We call the function $\text{pTr}_{\mathcal{S}}$, and define

$$\text{pTr}_{\mathcal{S}}.\text{es} \quad \widehat{=} \quad \mathcal{S}.\langle\!\langle\text{es}\rangle\!\rangle.\text{true} . \tag{9}$$

Again, we omit the $\mathcal{S}$ when it is obvious, so that $\text{pTr}.\text{es} = \langle\!\langle\text{es}\rangle\!\rangle.\text{true}$.

6   Failures

The traces of *CSP* are sufficient only for describing deterministic behaviour: when describing (internal) nondeterminism as well, *CSP* makes more detailed observations. A *failure* is a pair comprising a trace and a refusal; a *refusal* is a set of events in which the system can "refuse" to engage.

Let es be a trace and E a refusal. The behaviour (es, E) is observed whenever the process first engages in all the events in es and then refuses to extend the trace with any event in E.

Systems $\mathcal{A}$, $\mathcal{D}$ and $\mathcal{P}$ from Fig. 4 have the same standard traces, as we have already seen; and the first two agree even for probabilistic traces, mapping each possible trace to probability one and all others to zero. But $\mathcal{A}$ and $\mathcal{D}$ are distinguished by their failures, since for example $(\langle\rangle, \{\text{hic}\})$ is a failure of $\mathcal{D}$ but not of $\mathcal{A}$. Operationally we see this by noting that after initialisation of $\mathcal{A}$ the event hic cannot fail to be enabled; but if the initialisation of $\mathcal{D}$ sets n to -1, then hic will be disabled, and so can be refused.

In the previous section we considered expressions $\overline{\text{Exp}}.[\![prog]\!].[\text{true}].s$, for trace semantics; but we know more generally that for standard $[Q]$ (*i.e.* for predicate Q not necessarily true), the expression $\overline{\text{Exp}}.[\![prog]\!].[Q].s$ is the *maximum* probability that *prog* will reach Q from s; and again that maximum is zero whenever the guard of *prog* is false, since in that case *prog* cannot reach anything.

Now the "failure semantics" of an action system should give for each potential failure (es, E) the maximum probability that it will be observed. Since this is the maximum probability that the system can engage in es and reach a state *not* enabling any event in E, we define

$$\text{pFail}.(\text{es}, \text{E}) \quad \widehat{=} \quad \langle\!\langle\text{es}\rangle\!\rangle.(\neg\text{E}) , \tag{10}$$

where $\neg\text{E}$ is the complement of E, that is the subset of S in which no event of E is enabled. Thus, as in standard *CSP*, we have

$$\text{pTr}.\text{es} \quad = \quad \text{pFail}.(\text{es}, \emptyset) .$$

7   Divergences

A *divergence* of a *CSP* process is a trace after which the process behaves chaotically. In a *pAS* that behaviour is deemed to result from a potentially "aborting" command, one which we will model by adding a special element $\bot$ to our state space, to represent non-termination. Sub-distributions are now taken over $S_\perp = S \cup \{\perp\}$, with the value they assign to $\perp$ itself being the probability that the command fails to terminate normally.

Sequential composition is handled (in the usual way) by insisting that every command preserves "having failed to terminate"; that is, in extending our relational semantics we insist that for all programs $prog$ we have $[\![prog]\!].\perp = \{\overline{\perp}\}$. And we add to our earlier list of relational semantics examples (Sec. 4.1) the item

abort — $[\![\textbf{abort}]\!].n = \{\overline{\perp}\}$

> The diverging program **abort** takes every state to the special "bottom" state $\perp$.

We need not extend our random variables, however, which remain functions of S alone; instead, we adjust the definition of $\overline{\text{Exp}}.[\![\cdot]\!]$ (from (4) and its Footnote 9), which becomes

$$\overline{\text{Exp}}.[\![prog]\!].B.s \quad \widehat{=} \quad (\sqcup\Delta' : [\![prog]\!].s \cdot \Delta'.\perp + \int_{\Delta'} B) , \tag{11}$$

where the $\int$ notation continues to denote a summation over proper (*i.e.* non-$\perp$) values of S only, as at (3). This reflects our interest in the traces and failures a process *might* do (as opposed to "can be forced to do"): the maximum probability of *any* behaviour, after divergence, is one; and that is why we introduce the extra additive term $\Delta'.\perp$, which assigns a value of one to a command's reaching $\perp$. (Recall that B itself is not defined for $\perp$.)

With this new apparatus, we now define

$$\text{pDiv.es} \quad \widehat{=} \quad \langle\!\langle \text{es} \rangle\!\rangle.\text{false} ,$$

giving for any sequence of events es the maximum probability that executing the corresponding actions can achieve the predicate false–because the only way an action can "achieve" false is to diverge, and that is precisely the behaviour we are trying to quantify.

In Fig. 5 we give several examples of potentially diverging probabilistic action systems, all with alphabet $\{\text{hic}, \text{hoc}\}$. System $\mathcal{X}_1$ aborts immediately, and is equivalent to the *CSP* process *CHAOS*; for example (writing the $\mathcal{X}_1$ explicitly) we have $\text{pDiv}_{\mathcal{X}_1}.\text{es} = 1$ for all traces es, including the empty trace.[11]

System $\mathcal{X}_2$ literally (but informally) translated into *CSP* appears to be the process that can execute (and indeed can be forced to execute) any number of hic's; but as soon as it does a hoc, it diverges. As in System $\mathcal{X}_1$, all traces have probability one; but we have $\text{pDiv}_{\mathcal{X}_2}.\langle\rangle = 0$ whereas we have seen that $\text{pDiv}_{\mathcal{X}_1}.\langle\rangle = 1$. The shortest nonzero-probability divergence for $\mathcal{X}_2$ is $\langle\text{hoc}\rangle$; it and all its extensions have (maximum) probability one of divergence.

---

[11] Divergence has implications for the failures of a system as well, as we see in Sec. 7 below: any trace or failure extending a divergence has probability at least as great as the divergence.

System $\mathcal{X}_1$	**initially abort**	hic	$\widehat{=}$	false	$\rightarrow$	**skip**	[12]
		hoc	$\widehat{=}$	false	$\rightarrow$	**skip**	
System $\mathcal{X}_2$	**initially** n: = 0	hic	$\widehat{=}$	n ≥ 0	$\rightarrow$	**skip**	
		hoc	$\widehat{=}$	n ≤ 0	$\rightarrow$	**abort**	
System $\mathcal{X}_3$	**initially** n: = ±1	hic	$\widehat{=}$	n ≥ 0	$\rightarrow$	**skip**	
		hoc	$\widehat{=}$	n ≤ 0	$\rightarrow$	**abort**	
System $\mathcal{X}_4$	**initially** n: = $-1_{1/2}\oplus +1$	hic	$\widehat{=}$	n ≥ 0	$\rightarrow$	**skip**	
		hoc	$\widehat{=}$	n ≤ 0	$\rightarrow$	**abort**	

Fig. 5. Action systems that can diverge

System $\mathcal{X}_3$ contains demonic choice in its initialisation, and so the process decides internally whether to begin with hic or with hoc. If the former, it must continue with hic's forever (and cannot diverge); if the latter, it can execute hoc and then diverge, continuing after that with hic's, hoc's or deadlock *ad lib.*

System $\mathcal{X}_4$ is like $\mathcal{X}_3$ except that the initial choice —still not accessible externally—is at least predictable to the extent that it is made with the probability shown; after that, it behaves like $\mathcal{X}_3$. We give the complete traces, failures and divergences of $\mathcal{X}_4$ in App. B.

8 Healthiness Conditions for Probabilistic Action Systems

The failures and divergences of standard *CSP* satisfy the conditions listed in Fig. 6. We discuss the probabilistic version for each one in turn; they all have straightforward proofs in the program logic of *pGCL*, and as an example of that the proof of **pC3** below is given in App. A.1. Throughout, by "probability" we mean "maximum probability".

pC0 —   pFail.$(\langle\rangle, \emptyset)$ = 1

It is always possible for a system to start, since its initialisation is unguarded.

pC1 —   pFail.(es ++ es', E) $\leq$ pFail.(es, $\emptyset$)

The probability of continuing a trace is no more than the probability of achieving the trace itself.

---

[12] Events with guard false are in the alphabet of the system but can never be explicitly enabled.

C0 $(\langle\rangle, \emptyset) \in F$
C1 $(\mathsf{es} + \mathsf{es}', \mathsf{E}) \in F \;\Rightarrow\; (\mathsf{es}, \emptyset) \in F$ [13]
C2 $(\mathsf{es}, \mathsf{E}) \in F \;\wedge\; \mathsf{E}' \subseteq \mathsf{E} \;\Rightarrow\; (\mathsf{es}, \mathsf{E}') \in F$
C3 $(\mathsf{es}, \mathsf{E}) \in F \;\Rightarrow\; (\mathsf{es} + \langle \mathsf{e}\rangle, \emptyset) \in F \;\vee\; (\mathsf{es}, \mathsf{E} \cup \{\mathsf{e}\}) \in F$
C4 $\mathsf{es} \in D \;\Rightarrow\; \mathsf{es} + \mathsf{es}' \in D$
C5 $\mathsf{es} \in D \;\Rightarrow\; (\mathsf{es}, \mathsf{E}) \in F$

For any set of failures F and divergences D of a standard CSP process, the above conditions hold for any event e, traces $\mathsf{es}, \mathsf{es}'$ and sets of events E, E' over the alphabet of the process.

Fig. 6. Healthiness conditions for standard CSP over a finite alphabet

---

pC2 —
$$\mathrm{pFail}.(\mathsf{es}, \mathsf{E}) \;\geq\; \mathrm{pFail}.(\mathsf{es}, \mathsf{E} \cup \mathsf{E}')$$
The probability of refusing a set of events is no less than the probability of refusing a superset of it.

pC3 —
$$\mathrm{pFail}.(\mathsf{es}, \mathsf{E}) \;\leq\; \begin{aligned}&\mathrm{pFail}.(\mathsf{es} + \langle \mathsf{e}\rangle, \emptyset) \\ +\; &\mathrm{pFail}.(\mathsf{es}, \mathsf{E} \cup \{\mathsf{e}\})\end{aligned}$$
If an event cannot be refused, then it must be accepted.

pC4 —
$$\mathrm{pDiv}.\mathsf{es} \;\leq\; \mathrm{pDiv}.(\mathsf{es} + \mathsf{es}')$$
Any event is possible after divergence.

pC5 —
$$\mathrm{pDiv}.\mathsf{es} \;\leq\; \mathrm{pFail}.(\mathsf{es}, \mathsf{E})$$
Any refusal is possible after divergence.

Recall that **pC3** is proved in App. A.1.

9   What Now?

In fact almost everything still remains to be done.

- The *refinement* order for $pCSP$—when one process can be said to be implemented by another—is suggested by the refinement order for $pGCL$ that we describe briefly in App. A, provided care is taken with the guards of the generating pAS. This has been shown already by a number of authors for the standard case [22, 11, 12, 45, 4], and it should be checked for the probabilistic case.

---

[13] We use $+$ for concatenation of traces.

- Because there is a *pGCL* construction [36, 31] taking transformer semantics (as in App. A) back to relational semantics (as in Sec. 4), we should expect that there is a canonical mapping from *pCSP* back to a *pAS* in what we would consider a "normal form", using the technique earlier employed in the standard case [22, 11] where the normal-form state space is the set of *CSP*-style refusals over the alphabet of the process. This induces an equivalence relation on the *pAS*'s directly, and it should be verified that it is intuitively reasonable.

- The combining operations between *pAS*, especially their parallel composition but also prefixing, internal and external choice, probabilistic choice, hiding... are suggested by the corresponding operations defined for standard action systems [4, 5]: it must be checked that they respect the normal-form equivalence. But parallel composition raises interesting problems, since it must in turn be based on the parallel composition *of commands* (*e.g.* [2]), which operation requires great care when those commands include both probabilistic and demonic choice. (In fact parallel composition of initialisation commands is necessary for external choice also.)

- Most important of all—and subsuming much of the above—is that once the *pAS* operations have been defined, there should be *pCSP* operations corresponding to them that are expressed only in terms of our semantic observations pFail and pDiv. This would be *compositionality*.

9.1   Compositionality

Unfortunately, it has been known for some time that compositionality is not possible in terms of observations like pFail and pDiv alone [26]; indeed, we know that "probability-of-attaining-a-postcondition" -style semantics is not compositional even for *sequential* demonic/probabilistic programs [29].

The *expectation-transformer* semantics of *pGCL* however uses a generalised form of postcondition in which states are associated with non-negative reals (the states' "value") rather than simply with a Boolean (whether the state is "acceptable" or not); and *pGCL* semantics is compositional for sequential programs, even when demonic- and probabilistic choice appear together [36, 35, 31].

The corresponding extension which that suggests for *pCSP* is that a refusal should be a function from event to $\mathbb{R}^{\geq}$ (the "cost" of refusing the event?) rather than simply a function from event to Boolean (whether it can or cannot be refused). A failure pFail.(es, E) would then be the (maximum possible) expected value of the real-valued function E after observations of the trace es.

Unfortunately (again), it has already been shown that this does not offer an easy road to compositionality [21, 15]: and so there probably will be even further extensions required, for example a form of "may/must" testing but with respect to testing *trees* (rather than the simpler "broom-like" shapes offered by failures [42]), *together with* delivering quantitive rewards rather than only "yes" or "no" [9, 21].

Compositionality of course is the key to a successful abstraction. We take our favourite example—and it is probabilistic—from genetics.

Knowing parents' eye colour, on its own, cannot be used to predict distribution of eye colour among their children: some brown-eyed parents are virtually certain to produce brown-eyed children, *i.e.* with probability one; other brown-eyed parents may produce blue-eyed children with a predictable probability of one in four. Since the distribution of children's eye colour cannot be predicted from their parents' eye colour alone, the eye-colour abstraction (of a person) is not compositional for the binary operation "having children" between people: it is too severe. This is in effect where we find ourselves with pFail and pDiv.

At the other extreme, we have the full genetic profile of both parents; though still an abstraction, since it ignores phenotype, it may be sufficient *in principle* to predict the distribution of genotype in their children: as such it would be compositional. But it is far too costly a method if eye colour is all that interests us. This is where we might be if we worked with *pAS* directly, or (equivalently) probabilistic labelled transition systems or even probabilistic nondeterministic automata.

Thus "eye colour" alone is economical but not reliable; and "full genetic profile" is reliable but not economical. The right level of abstraction—the crucial breakthrough of Mendel—came from understanding the role of dominant and recessive characteristics (*alleles*), and led to a method of analysis which is both accurate and cheap to perform. Although very difficult to find, once discovered the abstraction "eye colour *together with* its dominant/recessive characteristic" turned out to be economical, reliable and easy to understand. Most importantly, it is compositional.

This is what we seek: the "alleles" for probabilistic, nondeterministic concurrent systems.

10   Conclusion

We are aware that many *CSP*-researchers—not to mention the even more numerous membership of the *CCS*-based community—have "thought long and hard" about how to introduce probability and nondeterminism together into a concurrent setting.

Clearly that has not stopped us from trying again, even using a very simple approach. In the ten years since our earlier encounter with "*pCSP*" [37], we have learned a great deal about the subtleties of probabilistic *vs.* demonic choice from having worked extensively on probabilistic semantics [36, 31]—both for sequential programs (and abstraction/nondeterminism), and for two-player games with probabilistic, demonic and angelic choice treated together [27, 28].

Treating concurrency in the "behavioural" style seems to be an inescapable point of view for anyone who has ever seriously been exposed to "the *CSP* effect" [43]. Its astonishing conceptual power and beauty—that it can express such subtle concepts with such simple means—is undiminished, even twenty-five years later. Nothing less elegant can ever suffice.

Acknowledgements

We thank the *Australian Research Council* for their support under their *Discovery Grants* Programme, and Christine Paulin-Mohring and the Laboratoire de Recherche en Informatique (*LRI*) at Orsay for their hospitality during the period March–June 2004.

We are grateful also to the organisers of the *25 Years of* CSP *Meeting* at which this work was first presented, and to the referee who advised us on the preparation of the final version of the article.

References

1. J.-R. Abrial. Extending *B* without changing it (for developing distributed systems). In H. Habrias, editor, *First Conference on the B Method*, pages 169–190. Laboratoire LIANA, L'Institut Universitaire de Technologie (IUT) de Nantes, November 1996.

2. R.-J.R. Back and M.J. Butler. Fusion and simultaneous execution in the refinement calculus. *Acta Informatica*, 35(11):921–949, 1998.

3. R.-J.R. Back and R. Kurki-Suonio. Decentralisation of process nets with centralised control. In *2nd ACM SIGACT-SIGOPS Symp. Principles of Distributed Computing*, pages 131–142, 1983.

4. M.J. Butler. A CSP approach to action systems. Technical report, Oxford University, 1992. (DPhil Thesis).

5. M.J. Butler. *csp2B*: A practical approach to combining CSP and B. *Formal Aspects of Computing*, pages 182–196, 2000.

6. M.J. Butler and C.C. Morgan. Action systems, unbounded nondeterminism and infinite traces. *Formal Aspects of Computing*, 7(1):37–53, 1995.

7. K.M. Chandy and J. Misra. *Parallel Program Design: A Foundation*. Addison-Wesley, Reading, Mass., 1988.

8. J.W. Davies, A.W. Roscoe, and J.C.P. Woodcock, editors. *Millennial Perspectives in Computer Science*. Cornerstones of Computing. Palgrave, 2000.

9. M. de Nicola and M. Hennessy. Testing equivalence for processes. *Theoretical Computer Science*, 34, 1984.

10. E.W. Dijkstra. *A Discipline of Programming*. Prentice Hall International, Englewood Cliffs, N.J., 1976.

11. Jifeng He. Process refinement. In J. McDermid, editor, *The Theory and Practice of Refinement*. Butterworths, 1989.

12. Jifeng He. Process simulation and refinement. *Formal Aspects of Computing*, 1(3):229–241, 1989.

13. Jifeng He, K. Seidel, and A.K. McIver. Probabilistic models for the guarded command language. *Science of Computer Programming*, 28:171–192, 1997. Available at [30–key HSM95].

14. Wim H. Hesselink. *Programs, Recursion and Unbounded Choice*. Number 27 in Cambridge Tracts in Theoretical Computer Science. Cambridge University Press, Cambridge, U.K., 1992.

15. Chris Ho-Stuart. Private communication. 1996.

16. C.A.R. Hoare. An axiomatic basis for computer programming. *Communications of the ACM*, 12(10):576–580, 583, October 1969.

17. C.A.R. Hoare. *Communicating Sequential Processes*. Prentice-Hall International, 1985.

18. C.A.R. Hoare and Jifeng He. *Unifying Theories of Programming*. Prentice-Hall, 1998.

19. C. Jones. Probabilistic nondeterminism. Monograph ECS-LFCS-90-105, Edinburgh University, 1990. (Ph.D. Thesis).

20. C. Jones and G. Plotkin. A probabilistic powerdomain of evaluations. In *Proceedings of the IEEE 4th Annual Symposium on Logic in Computer Science*, pages 186–195, Los Alamitos, Calif., 1989. Computer Society Press.

21. B. Jonsson, C. Ho-Stuart, and W. Yi. Testing and refinement for nondeterministic and probabilistic processes. In Langmaack, de Roever, and Vytopil, editors, *Formal Techniques in Real-Time and Fault-Tolerant Systems*, volume 863 of *LNCS*, pages 418–430. Springer Verlag, 1994.

22. M.B. Josephs. A state-based approach to communicating processes. *Distributed Computing*, 3(1):9–18, December 1988.

23. D. Kozen. Semantics of probabilistic programs. *Jnl. Comp. Sys. Sciences*, 22:328–350, 1981.

24. D. Kozen. A probabilistic PDL. *Jnl. Comp. Sys. Sciences*, 30(2):162–178, 1985.

25. G. Lowe. Probabilities and priorities in timed CSP. Technical Monograph PRG-111, Oxford University Computing Laboratory, 1993. (DPhil Thesis).

26. G. Lowe. Representing nondeterministic and probabilistic behaviour in reactive processes.
web.comlab.ox.ac.uk/oucl/work/gavin.lowe/Papers/prob.html, 1993.

27. A.K McIver and C.C. Morgan. Games, probability and the quantitative μ-calculus qMu. In *Proc. LPAR*, volume 2514 of *LNAI*, pages 292–310. Springer-Verlag, 2002. Revised and expanded at [28].

28. A.K. McIver and C.C. Morgan. Results on the quantitative μ-calculus $qM\mu$. *ACM Trans. Comp. Logic*, provisionally accepted, 2004.

29. A.K. McIver, C.C. Morgan, and J.W. Sanders. Probably Hoare? Hoare probably! In Davies et al. [8], pages 271–282.

30. A.K. McIver, C.C. Morgan, J.W. Sanders, and K. Seidel. Probabilistic Systems Group: Collected reports.
web.comlab.ox.ac.uk/oucl/research/areas/probs/bibliography.html.

31. Annabelle McIver and Carroll Morgan. *Abstraction, Refinement and Proof for Probabilistic Systems*. Technical Monographs in Computer Science. Springer Verlag, 2004.

32. M. Mislove. Nondeterminism and probabilistic choice: Obeying the laws.
math.tulane.edu/~mwm/.

33. C.C. Morgan. The specification statement. *ACM Transactions on Programming Languages and Systems*, 10(3):403–419, July 1988. Reprinted in [39].

34. C.C. Morgan. Of wp and CSP. In W.H.G. Feijen, A.J.M. van Gasteren, D. Gries, and J. Misra, editors, *Beauty is Our Business*. Springer Verlag, 1990.

35. C.C. Morgan and A.K. McIver. *pGCL*: Formal reasoning for random algorithms. *South African Computer Journal*, 22, March 1999. Available at [30–key PGCL].

36. C.C. Morgan, A.K. McIver, and K. Seidel. Probabilistic predicate transformers. *ACM Transactions on Programming Languages and Systems*, 18(3):325–353, May 1996. doi.acm.org/10.1145/229542.229547.

37. C.C. Morgan, A.K. McIver, K. Seidel, and J.W. Sanders. Refinement-oriented probability for CSP. *Formal Aspects of Computing*, 8(6):617–647, 1996.

38. C.C. Morgan and A.K. McIver. Cost analysis of games using program logic. Proc. 8th Asia-Pacific Software Engineering Conference (APSEC 2001), December 2001. Abstract only: full text available at [30–key MDP01].
39. C.C. Morgan and T.N. Vickers, editors. *On the Refinement Calculus*. FACIT Series in Computer Science. Springer Verlag, Berlin, 1994.
40. J.M. Morris. A theoretical basis for stepwise refinement and the programming calculus. *Science of Computer Programming*, 9(3):287–306, December 1987.
41. G. Nelson. A generalization of Dijkstra's calculus. *ACM Transactions on Programming Languages and Systems*, 11(4):517–561, October 1989.
42. Amir Pnueli. Linear and branching structures in the semantics and logics of reactive systems. In *Proc. 12th Colloq. on Automata, Languages and Programming*, pages 15–32. Springer Verlag, 1985.
43. A.W. Roscoe, G.M. Reed, and R. Forster. The successes and failures of behavioural models. In Davies et al. [8].
44. K. Seidel. Probabilistic communicating processes. Technical Monograph PRG-102, Oxford University, 1992. (DPhil Thesis).
45. J.C.P. Woodcock and C.C. Morgan. Refinement of state-based concurrent systems. In *Proc. VDM-90*, volume 428 of *LNCS*, 1990.

A   Probabilistic Program Logic for *pAS*

The sequential probabilistic/demonic relational semantics for *pAS* that we gave in Sec. 4 is based on the work of Jifeng He and his colleagues [13]—however we have simplified the presentation here by omitting the closure conditions they defined for their relations and, for reasons we explained in Sec. 5, we have taken an angelic (maximum) rather than their demonic (minimum) view.

Noting that our explicitly given random variables are all standard (*i.e.* they are characteristic functions of some enabling predicate of an action), we restrict *all* the random variables we use to the real interval $[0, 1]$ throughout. This is possible due to the probabilistic *feasibility* [31–Def. 1.6.2] that is the quantitative version of Dijkstra's *Law of the Excluded Miracle* [10–Property 1 p. 18]. In our case, it says that the random variables we generate via $\overline{\text{Exp}}.[\![\cdot]\!]$ are pointwise dominated by the characteristic functions we started with.

Then we define the dual

$$\overline{\text{Exp}}.[\![prog]\!].B.s \quad = \quad 1 - \overline{\text{Exp}}.[\![prog]\!].(1 - B).s \; , \tag{12}$$

made possible by the fact that, by the remarks above, we can assume $B \leq 1$. The 1-bounded demonic behaviour defined by $\overline{\text{Exp}}.[\![\cdot]\!]$, including miracle-producing guards, is isomorphic to our *Lamington model* [38], obtained by extending our original demonic/probabilistic but miracle-free model [36] with a miraculous command **magic** satisfying $\overline{\text{Exp}}.[\![\textbf{magic}]\!].B.s = 1$ for all B and s.

From the Lamington semantics for *pGCL* we can induce a sequential $\overline{\text{Exp}}.[\![\cdot]\!]$-style semantics for the commands of our *pAS*, as in Fig. 7, and we note crucially that it includes the sequential-composition property appealed to at (6) in Sec. 5 above. That is, it need not be proved from the relational semantics directly—duality has given it to us for free.

$$\overline{\text{Exp.}}[\![\textbf{abort}]\!].B \quad \hat{=} \quad 1$$

$$\overline{\text{Exp.}}[\![\textbf{skip}]\!].B \quad \hat{=} \quad B$$

$$\overline{\text{Exp.}}[\![\textsf{n}:= expr]\!].B \quad \hat{=} \quad B_\textsf{n}^{expr} \quad {}^{14}$$

$$\overline{\text{Exp.}}[\![G \to prog]\!].B \quad \hat{=} \quad [G] * \overline{\text{Exp.}}[\![prog]\!].B$$

$$\overline{\text{Exp.}}[\![prog;\ prog']\!].B \quad \hat{=} \quad \overline{\text{Exp.}}[\![prog]\!].(\overline{\text{Exp.}}[\![prog']\!].B)$$

$$\overline{\text{Exp.}}[\![prog \sqcap prog']\!].B \quad \hat{=} \quad \overline{\text{Exp.}}[\![prog]\!].B \ \textbf{max} \ \overline{\text{Exp.}}[\![prog']\!].B$$

$$\overline{\text{Exp.}}[\![prog\ {}_p\!\oplus prog']\!].B \quad \hat{=} \quad p * \overline{\text{Exp.}}[\![prog]\!].B + (1-p) * \overline{\text{Exp.}}[\![prog']\!].B\ .$$

Fig. 7. Structurally inductive definition of $\overline{\text{Exp.}}[\![\cdot]\!]$ for pAS

A.1   Super-Disjunctivity for $\overline{\text{Exp.}}[\![\cdot]\!]$

A second spinoff of duality relates to the algebra of $\overline{\text{Exp.}}[\![\cdot]\!]$.

The Lamington transformers, with their **magic**, do not satisfy the sublinearity property of our original demonic/probabilistic transformers—for example, **magic** itself is clearly not scaling. Nevertheless they do satisfy *sub-conjunctivity*, that is that for all programs *prog* and $[0,1]$-valued random variables B, B' we have

$$\underline{\text{Exp.}}[\![prog]\!].B \ \& \ \underline{\text{Exp.}}[\![prog]\!].B' \quad \leq \quad \underline{\text{Exp.}}[\![prog]\!].(B \& B')\ , \qquad (13)$$

where for $0 \leq x, y \leq 1$ we define $x \& y \ \hat{=}\ (x + y - 1) \ \textbf{max} \ 0$. From the duality (12) we then have immediately that

$$\overline{\text{Exp.}}[\![prog]\!].B \ [\!]\ \overline{\text{Exp.}}[\![prog]\!].B' \quad \geq \quad \overline{\text{Exp.}}[\![prog]\!].(B \,[\!]\, B')\ , \qquad (14)$$

where the duality has induced a definition $x \,[\!]\, y \ \hat{=}\ (x+y) \ \textbf{min} \ 1$ of a "probabilistic disjunction". We call this *super-disjunctivity*.

This important inequality—which is fully general, applying even when *prog* is both probabilistic and angelic[15]—can be used for example to prove the healthiness condition **pC3** for probabilistic action systems that we gave in Sec. 8. Thus we have for trace es, event e and set of events E the calculation

$$
\begin{array}{lll}
& \text{pFail.}(\textsf{es} \mathbin{+\!\!+} \langle\textsf{e}\rangle, \emptyset) \ + \ \text{pFail.}(\textsf{es}, \textsf{E} \cup \{\textsf{e}\}) & \\
\geq & \text{pFail.}(\textsf{es} \mathbin{+\!\!+} \langle\textsf{e}\rangle, \emptyset) \ [\!]\ \text{pFail.}(\textsf{es}, \textsf{E} \cup \{\textsf{e}\}) & \text{arithmetic} \\
= & \langle\!\langle \textsf{es} \mathbin{+\!\!+} \langle\textsf{e}\rangle \rangle\!\rangle.(\neg\emptyset) \ [\!]\ \langle\!\langle\textsf{es}\rangle\!\rangle.(\neg(\textsf{E} \cup \{\textsf{e}\})) & \text{definition pFail at (10)} \\
= & \langle\!\langle\textsf{es}\rangle\!\rangle.\{\textsf{e}\} \ [\!]\ \langle\!\langle\textsf{es}\rangle\!\rangle.(\neg(\textsf{E} \cup \{\textsf{e}\})) & \text{sequential composition} \\
\geq & \langle\!\langle\textsf{es}\rangle\!\rangle.(\{\textsf{e}\} \,[\!]\, (\neg\textsf{E} \cup \{\textsf{e}\})) & \text{definition } \langle\!\langle\textsf{es}\rangle\!\rangle \text{ at (8); Property (14)} \\
= & \langle\!\langle\textsf{es}\rangle\!\rangle.(\neg(\textsf{E} - \{\textsf{e}\})) & \text{set algebra} \\
= & \text{pFail.}(\textsf{es}, \ \textsf{E} - \{\textsf{e}\}) & \text{definition pFail} \\
\geq & \text{pFail.}(\textsf{es}, \ \textsf{E})\ . & \text{Condition } \textbf{pC2}
\end{array}
$$

---

[14] By $B_\textsf{n}^{expr}$ we mean syntactic replacement of $\textsf{n}$ by *expr* in B, respecting bound variables.

[15] Neither sub-conjunctivity nor super-disjunctivity applies however if the probabilistic programs are *both* demonic and angelic.

B   Complete Traces *etc.* for System $\mathcal{X}_4$ of Fig. 5

Trace	Associated maximum probability	
$\langle\rangle$	1	Empty trace always gives 1.
$\langle$hic$\rangle$	1/2	Initialisation sets n to +1.
$\langle$hoc$\rangle$	1/2	Initialisation sets n to −1.
$\langle$hic, hic$\rangle$	1/2	Variable n remains +1 . . .
$\langle$hic, hoc$\rangle$	0	. . . so that hoc is never enabled;
$\langle$hoc, hic$\rangle$	1/2	but divergence after hoc . . .
$\langle$hoc, hoc$\rangle$	1/2	. . . allows anything.

Any non-empty trace comprising only hic's :   Probability 1/2.
Any trace beginning hic but containing a hoc :   Probability 0.
Any trace beginning hoc :   Probability 1/2.

Fig. 8. Complete traces for System $\mathcal{X}_4$ of Fig. 5

Failure	Associated maximum probability	
$(\langle\rangle, \{\})$	1	Empty offer is always refused.
$(\langle\rangle, \{$hoc$\})$	1/2	Initialisation sets n to +1.
$(\langle\rangle, \{$hic$\})$	1/2	Initialisation sets n to −1.
$(\langle\rangle, \{$hic, hoc$\})$	0	Initialisation does not diverge or deadlock.
$(\langle$hic$\rangle, \{\})$	1/2	Empty offer refused. . . *if* we get this far.
$(\langle$hic$\rangle, \{$hic$\})$	0	Event hic must follow hic . . .
$(\langle$hic$\rangle, \{$hoc$\})$	1/2	. . . but hoc cannot.
$(\langle$hic$\rangle, \{$hic, hoc$\})$	0	Action *hic* does not diverge or deadlock.
$(\langle$hoc$\rangle, \mathsf{E})$	1/2	Anything can be refused after divergence, including the entire alphabet.

Any failure whose non-empty trace comprises only hic's :   *As for trace* $\langle hic\rangle$.
Any failure whose trace begins hic but contains a hoc :   Probability 0.
Any failure whose trace begins hoc, no matter what refusal :   Probability 1/2.

Fig. 9. Complete failures for System $\mathcal{X}_4$ of Fig. 5

Divergence	Associated maximum probability
Any trace beginning hoc	Probability 1/2.
Any other trace	Probability 0.

Fig. 10. Complete divergences for System $\mathcal{X}_4$ of Fig. 5

Order, Topology, and Recursion Induction in *CSP*

Mike Reed

Oxford University Computing Laboratory

Abstract. Recursion induction is a method for proving that *CSP* processes which are defined as the least fixed points of some Scott-continuous function from a complete partial order on the set of all processes to itself meet a given behavioural specification. The Scott (order version) requires that (1) the specification S is closed via the least upper bound of directed sets in the complete partial order, (2) $S(bottom)$, and (3) if $S(P$ then $S(F(P)$. It is then concluded that $S(fix(F))$, where $fix(F)$ is the least fixed point of F. This version uses the Tarski fixed point theorem. The Roscoe (topology version) assumes not only the complete partial order on the set of all processes, but also a complete metric on the set of all processes. This version requires that the recursive function F be a contraction function with respect to the complete metric. It requires (1) S is closed with respect to limits in the complete metric, (2) there exists a P such that $S(P)$, and (3) if $S(P)$ then $S(F(P))$. Again, it is then concluded that $S(fix(F))$, where $fix(F)$ is the unique fixed point of F. This version uses the Banach fixed point theorem. The Scott version is sufficient in the traces model for *CSP*, since most useful predicates are satisfied by $(bottom = STOP)$. However in the failures-divergences model, the Roscoe version is required, since few useful predicates are satisfied by $(bottom = CHAOS)$. The usual model for the failures-divergences model is a Scott domain (i.e., an algebraic, bounded-complete, complete partial order), where the maximal elements are exactly the non-deterministic processes. The complete metric used for the Roscoe fixed point version agrees with the Scott topology on the set of maximal elements. In this talk we develop a general theory for recursion induction based on the Scott topology of the maximal elements in a domain. The theory assumes no other information, hence it is only applicable for functions which have their least fixed point as a maximal element. It includes all complete metric spaces. It covers spaces which are not metrizable. It covers the existing examples for recursion induction in *CSP*. As a result of our topological analysis, we answer several open questions in the literature about the topology of the set of maximal elements in a domain. One interesting example is showing that one proposition is independent and consistent with ZFC.

A.E. Abdallah, C.B. Jones, and J.W. Sanders (Eds.): CSP25, LNCS 3525, p. 242, 2005.

Verifying Security Protocols:
An Application of CSP

Steve Schneider and Rob Delicata

Department of Computing, University of Surrey

Abstract. The field of protocol analysis is one area in which CSP has proven particularly successful, and several techniques have been proposed that use CSP to reason about security properties such as confidentiality and authentication. In this paper we describe one such approach, based on theorem-proving, that uses the idea of a rank function to establish the correctness of protocols. This description is motivated by the consideration of a simple, but flawed, authentication protocol. We show how a rank function analysis can be used to locate this flaw and prove that a modified version of the protocol is correct.

1   Introduction

In their seminal paper [NS78], Needham and Schroeder proposed a way of using cryptographic mechanisms, such as public-key and shared-key encryption, in order to establish authentication guarantees across networks. Such mechanisms typically involve an exchange of messages between participants, and are known as authentication protocols. Participants carry out cryptographic operations particular to them (such as encrypting with a specific secret key) which are intended to provide guarantees as to their identity. Such protocols are designed to provide authentication even in insecure environments, where other parties can potentially interfere with messages over the network in various ways. For example, messages can be overheard, copied, blocked, replayed, diverted, duplicated, and spoofed.

As a motivating and running example, we will consider the following exchange of messages, which appears as a simple (flawed) authentication protocol in the Handbook of Applied Cryptography [MVV96]:

$$A \rightarrow B : n_A$$
$$B \rightarrow A : \{n_A, n_B\}_{K_{AB}}$$
$$A \rightarrow B : n_B$$

The aim of this protocol is for each of the participants to authenticate themselves to the other. In other words, each participant should know, by the end of the protocol, the identity of the other participant.

This protocol involves two participants, A and B, who share a symmetric cryptographic key K_{AB} (which can also be written K_{BA}) which is used by each

A.E. Abdallah, C.B. Jones, and J.W. Sanders (Eds.): **CSP25**, LNCS 3525, pp. 243–263, 2005.

of A and B to encrypt and decrypt messages to and from the other. The protocol relies on the assumption that no party other than A or B knows this key. The protocol begins with A, acting as *initiator*, who invents a new random number (or *nonce*), n_A, and transmits it to B. This nonce is sent unencrypted, so any other agent could potentially eavesdrop and learn its value, or spoof some arbitrary nonce n_I to B as if it came from A. (As a result, B's receipt of the nonce does not carry any assurance that it originated from A.)

On receipt of the nonce n_A, B, as *responder*, performs a cryptographic operation that no other party can perform: by encrypting the nonce with K_{AB}. This message is then sent to A, who decrypts it using K_{AB}. If this decryption contains the nonce n_A then this provides a guarantee that n_A must have been received and encrypted by B, since B is the only other party that knows K_{AB}. This results in the authentication of B to A: A knows that she has been communicating with B, and not some malicious party pretending to be B. In order to achieve authentication in the other direction (A to B), B also includes a freshly generated nonce n_B in the encryption of the second message. A is able to decrypt this nonce and send it back, unencrypted, to B. On receipt of n_B, B has an assurance that it was A who received and returned the nonce, and hence was the other party involved in the protocol run.

The assurances are obtained by virtue of the fact that K_{AB} is known only to A and B, and hence evidence of its use provides evidence that A or B were involved in carrying out the encryption or decryption. Indeed, if A and B are only ever involved in one protocol run, then the protocol does provide the authentication required of it: A cannot reach the end of the run unless B is involved; and B cannot reach the end of the run unless A is involved.

However, agents can generally be involved in multiple protocol runs, possibly simultaneously, potentially with a variety of other participants, and in each case may assume the role of either initiator or responder (or, indeed, both). Under such circumstances, the protocol is susceptible to an *attack*: an exchange of messages after which one agent has reached a state where authentication appears to have been established, and yet where the party supposedly authenticated has not in fact been involved.

The attack (also given in [MVV96]) involves two runs, where A assumes the role of initiator in one run and responder in the other. In both runs A intends B to be the other party, but in fact the messages are being processed by some other agent $E(B)$, who A considers to be B. The runs, labelled α and β, are interspersed as follows:

$$\alpha: \quad A \rightarrow E(B): n_A$$
$$\beta: \quad E(B) \rightarrow A: n_A$$
$$\beta: \quad A \rightarrow E(B): \{n_A, n_A'\}_{K_{AB}}$$
$$\alpha: \quad E(B) \rightarrow A: \{n_A, n_A\}_{K_{AB}}$$
$$\alpha: \quad A \rightarrow E(B): n_A$$

The steps of the attack are as follows:

1. A initiates a run using nonce n_A, apparently with B; but the nonce is intercepted by $E(B)$.
2. $E(B)$ initiates a separate run with A (who thus takes the role of responder), apparently with B, using the same nonce n_A.
3. On receipt of the nonce n_A, A invents a responder's nonce n'_A and then returns it, together with n_A, encrypted under K_{AB}.
4. $E(B)$ intercepts this message and sends back exactly the same message to A as the response to the original nonce challenge n_A of the first run. A accepts the nonce n'_A as the nonce n_B provided by B.
5. A responds with the nonce n_A just received.

After this exchange of messages, A has reached the end of the protocol run, apparently with B, and hence the protocol is intended to provide an assurance that B was indeed the other participant. However, B has not been involved at all. Hence the protocol does not provide the assurances required of it.

Having identified the attack, it is possible to suggest corrections which will prevent it. In this example the attack was possible because the second message is symmetric in terms of initiator and responder, and contains no information about which participant created it. This allowed a situation in which A generated such a message and was later persuaded to accept it as if it came from the other party. Introducing the name of the participant who encrypted the message would prevent the attack above. This results in the revised protocol:

$$A \to B : n_A$$
$$B \to A : \{B, n_A, n_B\}_{K_{AB}}$$
$$A \to B : n_B$$

However, can we be confident that no other attacks are possible on the corrected protocol?

In order to obtain such confidence, it is necessary first to clarify several issues around the protocol:

- What kind of environment is the protocol designed for? In other words, what are the kinds of attacks that the protocol is designed to be resistant to? For example, on a broadcast network an attacker may be able to overhear and spoof messages, but be unable to block them.
- What level of authentication is the protocol designed to provide? For example, is it simply intended to establish that the authenticated agent is present (e.g. that a server is up), or that the authenticated agent knows who he is communicating with.
- Are the other participants assumed to be honest (i.e. attacks can only originate from outside the collection of protocol participants) or can they be dishonest?
- Can participants run arbitrarily many concurrent protocol sessions, or are there restrictions?

This kind of information should be included with any protocol description: the correctness of a protocol consists not only in the sequence of messages it describes, but also the environment it is designed for.

There have been a variety of approaches proposed for analysing and verifying security protocols [Mea92, Mil95, THG99, Low98, Pau98, CDL$^+$99b, AG98, DFG00]. Such approaches do indeed incorporate such information into the models that they describe and analyse.

This paper is concerned with the application of CSP [Hoa85, Ros97, Sch99] to the verification of security protocols, and in particular with the *rank function* approach. There has already been significant experience of the application of CSP to communications protocols, and that experience provides a framework for the application of CSP to authentication protocols. Broadly speaking, there are three components of the approach:

- The requirements on the protocol are expressed either as a CSP process (to be refined by the implementation), or as **sat** specifications on the observable behaviours of the overall system: traces, failures, divergences. Such specifications describe the appropriate behaviour, and provide a basis for judging whether protocols exhibit correct behaviour or not.
- A protocol, although initially described in terms of message exchanges, is captured in CSP in terms of the behaviour of each participating agent, leading to an *agent-oriented* rather than a *message-oriented* viewpoint. Each participant in the protocol is described as a CSP process. This shift in viewpoint, away from message transmission and reception, and towards the individual agents considered in terms of their interactions with the rest of the system, is a key feature in the success of the approach when applied to authentication protocols, since it naturally focuses on where attacks might come from and hence how they should be prevented.
- Finally, the environment is also described as a CSP process. In communications protocols, this is generally an unreliable medium which might lose, reorder, or duplicate messages. The particular behaviour captured within the medium is precisely that behaviour that the protocol has been designed to overcome. For example, the traditional alternating bit protocol (see e.g. [Sch99]) is designed to provide reliable communication over a medium which can lose messages, and so the analysis of the protocol includes a CSP description of exactly such a medium (which non-deterministically either reliably communicates a message or else loses it). In the case of security protocols, we need to include the capabilities of possible attackers.

When all three components are in place: specification, environment, and protocol description, then the mature tools and techniques that CSP has to offer can be brought to bear on particular protocols, and whether or not they meet a particular specification.

This paper assumes a knowledge of CSP and, in particular, the notations of [Sch99].

The next section elaborates a theory for verifying authentication protocols based on this approach.

2   Verifying Authentication Protocols in CSP

Any authentication protocol is intended to run over a network which can be subject to particular kinds of attack. We take the approach of considering an attacker (synonymous terms include 'intruder', 'enemy', 'spy', and 'penetrator') in terms of *capabilities*, such as being able to intercept messages on the network, create new messages for passing on the network, redirecting messages, and so on. We will assume a single attacker, though in fact the attacker we will describe has the ability to behave as a collection of attackers.

2.1   The Attacker

Since the aim is to prove that protocols are correct, we take a pessimistic point of view and assume an attacker with maximal capabilities. In the worst case, the attacker has complete control over all the messages in the network. If a protocol is secure even in such an environment, then it will be secure in any weaker, perhaps more realistic, environment. The only capabilities the attacker should not have are the ability to encrypt or decrypt messages without the appropriate keys. As a consequence, we assume there is enough redundancy in the cryptosystem so that each ciphertext can be produced in exactly one way. This restriction has become known as the *perfect encryption* assumption [PQ00].

We use the Dolev-Yao model, first proposed in [DY83], in which the attacker has complete control of the network and, to all intents and purposes, replaces the network. Thus, messages that are sent are automatically intercepted and held by the attacker. Messages that are received from the network must have come from the attacker. This simple model allows for the kinds of attacker behaviour described earlier. It allows for messages to be delivered normally, since one action the attacker can take is to deliver messages to the intended recipient unaltered. However, it also allows for messages to be misdirected, blocked, spoofed, reordered, and duplicated. Furthermore, the attacker can himself be in possession of some agent identities (names and associated cryptographic keys) and so appear to other agents on the network as a potential communication partner. In this way, dishonest agents are encapsulated within the model. Any message that can be generated by the attacker, from what he has already observed and what he originally knows, can potentially be delivered to any other agent on the network, as if it came from any other agent.

The details of the CSP description of the attacker model will reflect the kind of environment the protocol is designed for. For example, if the protocol is intended to operate between two known honest participants, then the attacker might not itself control any agent identities. Furthermore, the precise cryptographic capabilities of the attacker will also be incorporated into the model, and this might be protocol-specific.

The overall network consists of a number of users connected to the communications medium, which is under the control of the attacker. The users will be modelled as CSP processes $USER_i$, where i is the agent's name. We will use a channel $trans.i$ for agent i to transmit messages intended for other users onto

PAIRING
$$\dfrac{S \vdash m_1 \qquad S \vdash m_2}{S \vdash m_1 \cdot m_2}$$

UNPAIRING
$$\dfrac{S \vdash m_1 \cdot m_2}{S \vdash m_1 \qquad S \vdash m_2}$$

MEMBER
$$\dfrac{}{S \vdash m} \ [m \in S]$$

SUBSET
$$\dfrac{S' \vdash m}{S \vdash m} \ [S' \subseteq S]$$

TRANSITIVE CLOSURE
$$\dfrac{\forall\, s' \in S'.\, S \vdash s' \qquad S' \vdash m}{S \vdash m}$$

ENCRYPTION
$$\dfrac{S \vdash m \qquad S \vdash k}{S \vdash \{m\}_k}$$

DECRYPTION
$$\dfrac{S \vdash \{m\}_k \qquad S \vdash k}{S \vdash m}$$

Fig. 1. Attacker inference rules

the network. An event $trans.i.j.m$ will correspond to agent i sending message m, intended for agent j. We will use a channel $rec.j$ for agent j to receive messages from the network. An event $rec.j.i.m$ corresponds to agent j receiving message m from the network, apparently from i. All message exchanges between protocol participants will use channels and events of this form.

We also need to define the kind of messages that can be passed around the network. This will depend on the protocol under analysis, since different protocols use different message constructions. For the example protocol introduced earlier, we will have three pairwise disjoint sets, *USER*, *NONCE*, *KEY*, which give the agent identities, nonces, and keys respectively. Furthermore, for each pair of distinct users i and j, there will be a shared key $k_{ij} = k_{ji}$ such that different pairs of agents have different shared keys. We will use the following space of messages, defined using BNF as the set *MESSAGE*:

$M_1, M_2 ::=$		messages
I	($\in$ *USER*)	agent identities
N	($\in$ *NONCE*)	nonces
K	($\in$ *KEY*)	keys
$M_1.M_2$		concatenation of messages
$\{M\}_K$		encryption of message M by key K

For this space of messages, we can define the attacker's capabilities in terms of the generation of new messages from those already possessed. We introduce a 'generates' relation $\vdash$, which relates a set of messages S to a message m that can be generated from S. It is defined to be the least relation closed under the inference rules of Figure 1. We are now in a position to describe the CSP model of the Dolev-Yao style attacker. It is given as the process *ENEMY*, defined as follows:

$$ENEMY(S) = trans?i?j?m \rightarrow ENEMY(S \cup \{m\})$$

$$\square$$

$$\underset{\substack{i \in USER \\ j \in USER \\ m \mid S \vdash m}}{\square} \ rec!i!j!m \rightarrow ENEMY(S)$$

The process $ENEMY(S)$ describes the possibilities available to an attacker in possession of the set of messages S. The first branch of the choice models the situation that a new message m can always be transmitted from any user to any other user, and this will be intercepted and added to the set of messages possessed by the attacker. The second branch of the choice describes that the attacker can provide any message m that can be generated from S to any user i, as if it came from any other user j. In this case the attacker's store of known messages S does not change.

The enemy will have some initial knowledge, including some nonces he can use, agents' identities, and cryptographic keys of agents that he controls. If the initial knowledge is given as the set IK, then $ENEMY$ — the environment that the protocol runs over — is given by

$$ENEMY = ENEMY(IK)$$

2.2   Specifying Authentication

When two parties engage in a protocol run aimed at authenticating one to the other, the intention is that completion of the run by the authenticating party provides a guarantee that the other party had also participated in the run. Since specifications in CSP are defined in terms of events, we will introduce special signal events into the protocol runs at the points we wish to mark: completion of a protocol run, and participation in a run. The approach of introducing matching signals to specify authentication was introduced (not in the CSP context) by Woo and Lam [WL93]. These signals are introduced purely for the purposes of specification, to describe stages that protocol participants have reached, and they are used in the analysis and verification of the protocol. They are not events that the attacker can engage in.

In our example, we will introduce only two signals. Generally, others could be introduced depending on the authentication properties of interest.

Here we consider the property of the initiator authenticating the responder. This can be specified by introducing the following signals:

- $initdone.i.j.n$, which i performs after a protocol run as initiator involving j, and using n as the nonce.
- $respgo.j.i.n$, which j performs during a protocol run as responder apparently initiated by i with nonce n.

The set of all possible signals for this protocol and property is defined as follows:

$$SIGNAL = \{initdone.i.j.n \mid i \in USER \wedge j \in USER \wedge n \in NONCE\}$$
$$\cup \{respgo.i.j.n \mid i \in USER \wedge j \in USER \wedge n \in NONCE\}$$

These signals will be inserted into the protocol runs. The intention is that an occurrence of the signal $initdone.A.B.n_A$ guarantees that (elsewhere in the network, at B's location) the event $respgo.B.A.n_A$ has previously occurred, at least once. Thus the $respgo$ signal must be inserted *before* the responder transmits his response to the first message, since it must be placed causally prior to

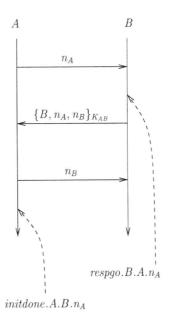

Fig. 2. Introducing matching signals

the *initdone* message. The placing of the signals into the protocol is illustrated in Figure 2.

The inclusion of a specific nonce with the signal means that the agents must agree on the particular protocol run: A does not only authenticate B's presence, but also that B was engaged in the same protocol run.

The use of signals enables authentication to be expressed as a trace specification: that any occurrence of *initdone.A.B.n_A* in any trace of the overall network must be preceded by some occurrence of *respgo.B.A.n_A*. This can be defined formally on traces, as:

$$respgo.B.A.n_A \text{ precedes } initdone.A.B.n_A$$

where

$$a \text{ precedes } b \,\widehat{=}\, tr \upharpoonright a = \langle\rangle \Rightarrow tr \upharpoonright b = \langle\rangle$$

Observe that this specification allows arbitrarily many b events in response to a single a event. This has been termed *non-injective agreement* [Low97].

The inclusion of different information in the signals can give rise to different authentication requirements. For example, the removal of the nonce from the signals would allow interactions in which A's run could correspond to a different run from B (i.e. one with a different nonce). However, there would still be a guarantee that B has been involved in some run apparently with A. An even weaker authentication would simply allow the signal *respgo.B*, not even requiring that B is engaged in a run apparently with A. This form of authentication might be appropriate if A simply requires some guarantee that B is alive. In practice different notions of authentication are appropriate to different situations, and the use of signals containing appropriate levels of detail allow these differences to be expressed. The various flavours of authentication are discussed in [Sch98, Low97].

2.3   Protocol Participants

The protocol participants are also described as CSP processes. Here we will consider the modified version of the protocol where the responder's identity is included in the encryption of the second message. There are two possible roles in the protocol, and each of these will be described as a process.

An initiator run is parameterised by the identity of the initiating agent, the identity of the agent she wishes to authenticate, and the nonce used in the run. Thus we define $INIT_i(j, n)$ as a run of agent i using nonce n to authenticate j:

$$INIT_i(j, n) = trans.i.j.n \rightarrow$$
$$rec.j.i?\{j.n.y\}_{k_{ij}} \rightarrow$$
$$trans.i.j.y \rightarrow$$
$$initdone.i.j.n \rightarrow Stop$$

Observe the use of pattern matching in the input of the second message: n, j, and k_{ij} are already fixed, and the input message must match these. However, any value for y can be accepted.

Similarly, $RESP_j(n')$ is a responder run for agent j, using nonce n' for the nonce that he generates. This is defined as follows:

$$RESP_j(n') = rec.j?i?x \rightarrow$$
$$respgo.j.i.x \rightarrow$$
$$trans.j.i.\{j.x.n'\}_{k_{ij}} \rightarrow$$
$$rec.j.i.n' \rightarrow Stop$$

Observe that $RESP_j(n')$ is ready to run the protocol with anyone who requests.

In the most general case, an agent will be prepared to participate in any number of concurrent protocol runs in either role, which is expressible as an interleaving of runs. Our model must incorporate the fact that each run uses a different nonce, so we will use a collection of pairwise disjoint sets of nonces: N_j^I will be an infinite set of nonces that j can use on initiator runs; and N_j^R will be an infinite set of nonces that j can use on responder runs. A general agent is then given as:

$$USER_j = (|||_{n \in N_j^I} \square_i INIT_j(i, n))$$
$$|||$$
$$(|||_{n \in N_j^R} RESP_j(n))$$

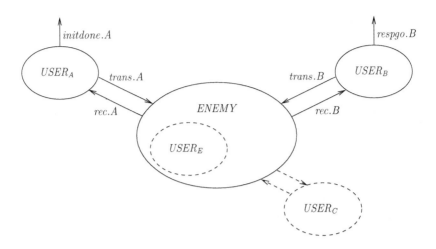

Fig. 3. The Dolev-Yao model in CSP

The resulting system is given by

$$SYSTEM = (\left|\left|\right|_i USER_i) \left|[\{\!|\ trans, rec\ |\!\}]\right| ENEMY$$

This architecture is pictured in Figure 3.

To show that the protocol ensures that A authenticates B, we aim to establish that the following specification holds:

$$SYSTEM \textbf{ sat } respgo.B.A.n_A \textsf{ precedes } initdone.A.B.n_A$$

3   A Theorem for Verifying Authentication

We will now introduce the *rank function* approach to verifying authentication protocols. In this approach we consider a restriction to the process $SYSTEM$ which prevents the occurrence of $respgo.B.A.n_A$, and then aim to establish that $initdone.A.B.n_A$ cannot occur. This approach is valid because

$$SYSTEM \textbf{ sat } respgo.B.A.n_A \textsf{ precedes } initdone.A.B.n_A$$
$$\Leftrightarrow SYSTEM \left|[\ respgo.B.A.n_A\ ]\right| Stop \textbf{ sat } tr \upharpoonright \{initdone.A.B.n_A\} = \langle\rangle$$

We will associate a value, or *rank*, with each message that might occur in the restricted system, and aim to establish an invariant based on the message values: that only those with positive ranks can circulate in the restricted system. We aim to define a rank function $\rho : MESSAGE \cup SIGNAL \rightarrow \mathbb{Z}$ with properties that enable us to do this.

Our required result will follow if we can establish the following properties for the rank function:

1. The attacker should not initially possess any messages of non-positive rank;
2. If the attacker only possesses messages of positive rank, then any messages he can generate should also be of positive rank;
3. The signal $initdone.A.B.n_A$ has non-positive rank;
4. Any agent, when restricted on $respgo.B.A.n_A$, does not introduce messages or signals of non-positive rank if it has not previously received any such messages.

The first two conditions between them ensure that the attacker cannot introduce any non-positive rank messages; and the fourth condition ensures that the protocol agents cannot do this either. Together these conditions ensure that no message or signal of non-positive rank can occur in the restricted system. Since the third condition requires that the signal we are concerned about should have non-positive rank, we can conclude that this signal indeed cannot occur.

These conditions are formalised in the rank function theorem, which is the heart of the approach:

Theorem 1. *If* $\rho : MESSAGE \cup SIGNAL \rightarrow \mathbb{Z}$ *is such that:*

1. $\forall\, m \in IK . \rho(m) > 0$
2. $\forall\, S \subseteq MESSAGE.(\rho(S) > 0 \wedge S \vdash m) \Rightarrow \rho(m) > 0$
3. $\rho(b) \leqslant 0$
4. $\forall\, i.(USER_i \,\|[\, a \,]\| \, Stop)$ **sat** $\rho(tr \upharpoonright rec) > 0 \Rightarrow \rho(tr) > 0$

then $(\,\|\|_i\, USER_i) \,\|[\, trans, rec \,]\| \, ENEMY$ **sat** a precedes b.

Here we have abused notation, and extended ρ to apply not only to messages and signals, but also to events, traces, and sets:

- $\rho(c.m) = \rho(m)$
- $\rho(tr) = \min\{\rho(s) \mid s \text{ in } tr\}$
- $\rho(S) = \min\{\rho(s) \mid s \in S\}$

Thus, if we can find a rank function ρ which meets the four conditions above, then we will have established that the system as described meets the corresponding authentication property expressed as a precedes b.

3.1   Preserving Rank

The first three conditions of the rank function theorem can be checked independently of any CSP protocol description. However, the fourth condition requires verification of CSP processes against a specification. The benefits of using the CSP traces model is that a number of application-specific rules can be identified, and applied in this particular kind of verification. We are interested in the property maintains ρ:

$$\text{maintains } \rho \,\widehat{=}\, \rho(tr \upharpoonright rec) > 0 \Rightarrow \rho(tr) > 0$$

Figure 4 identifies some compositional rules which are useful for establishing this property.

$$\text{INTERLEAVING} \qquad \frac{\forall\, i.(P_i \text{ sat maintains } \rho)}{\left|\left|\right|\right._i P_i \text{ sat maintains } \rho}$$

$$\text{EXTERNAL CHOICE} \qquad \frac{\forall\, i.(P_i \text{ sat maintains } \rho)}{\square_i P_i \text{ sat maintains } \rho}$$

$$\text{PREFIXING} \qquad \frac{P \text{ sat maintains } \rho \qquad \rho(e) > 0}{e \rightarrow P \text{ sat maintains } \rho}$$

$$\text{STOP} \qquad \frac{}{Stop \text{ sat maintains } \rho}$$

$$\text{INPUT} \qquad \frac{\forall\, x.(\rho(f(x)) > 0 \Rightarrow P(x) \text{ sat maintains } \rho)}{rec.i?j?f(x) \rightarrow P(x) \text{ sat maintains } \rho}$$

Fig. 4. Composition rules for maintains ρ

The last rule in this figure requires some explanation. It concerns input of a message which matches a particular pattern $f(x)$, with subsequent behaviour $P(x)$. If we can show that $P(x)$ **sat** maintains ρ whenever the input has positive rank, then we can conclude that the inputting process $rec.i.j?f(x) \rightarrow P(x)$ also maintains positive rank. We are not concerned with $P(x)$ for which $\rho(f(x)) \leqslant 0$, since in such cases the non-positive-rank message must have been introduced externally to the process, and so we do not need to consider whether $P(x)$ maintains positive rank.

3.2 Verifying the Modified Protocol

We aim to identify a rank function which meets the four conditions of the rank function theorem. In devising a rank function it is helpful to consider the sorts of messages that can legitimately pass on the network. Furthermore, the nature of the generates relation $\vdash$, and the CSP protocol descriptions, impose constraints on any putative function ρ.

For the fourth condition, we are required to show, for an arbitrary user C, that:

$$USER_C \,||\, [\, respgo.B.A.n_A \,]\,||\, Stop \text{ sat maintains } \rho$$

We have that:

$$USER_C \,||\, [\, respgo.B.A.n_A \,]\,||\, Stop$$
$$= \left|\left|\right|\right._n \square_i (INIT_C(i, n) \,||\, [\, respgo.B.A.n_A \,]\,||\, Stop)$$
$$\left|\left|\right|\right. \left|\left|\right|\right._n (RESP_C(n) \,||\, [\, respgo.B.A.n_A \,]\,||\, Stop)$$

In order to show that this combination satisfies maintains ρ, the inference rules for interleaving and choice in Figure 4 mean that we have only to establish that each component separately maintains ρ. In other words, for each C, i, and n, we have to establish:

$$INIT_C(i, n) \,\|[\, respgo.B.A.n_A \,]\| \, Stop \text{ \textbf{sat} maintains } \rho$$
$$RESP_C(n) \,\|[\, respgo.B.A.n_A \,]\| \, Stop \text{ \textbf{sat} maintains } \rho$$

There are a number of cases to consider:

Case $INIT_C$, $C = A$, $i = B$, $n = n_A$ In this case we have

$$INIT_A(B, n_A) \,\|[\, respgo.B.A.n_A \,]\| \, Stop =$$
$$trans.A.B.n_A \rightarrow rec.A.B?\{B.n_A.y\}_{K_{AB}}$$
$$\rightarrow trans.A.B.y \rightarrow initdone.A.B.n_A \rightarrow Stop$$

We know from condition 3 that $initdone.A.B.n_A$ must have non-positive rank, since this is the signal whose non-occurrence we wish to establish. If we are to apply the rules for prefixing to establish that this process satisfies maintains ρ, then we require that the message input in step 2 of the protocol must have non-positive rank. This follows because the behaviour following a positive rank input must itself satisfy maintains ρ—and this is not possible because $initdone.A.B.n_A$ (necessarily non-positive rank) is performed.

Thus we obtain a constraint on the rank function we are searching for to establish correctness: that any message of the form $\{B.n_A.y\}_{K_{AB}}$ must have non-positive rank.

Case $RESP_B$ A second case which is of interest is that of agent B as responder. In this case we have that

$$RESP_B(y) \,\|[\, respgo.B.A.n_A \,]\| \, Stop =$$
$$rec.B?i?x \rightarrow$$
$$\left\{ \begin{array}{ll} respgo.B.i.x \rightarrow trans.B.i.\{B.x.y\}_{K_{Bi}} & \\ \quad \rightarrow rec.B.i.y \rightarrow Stop & \text{if } i \neq A \text{ or } x \neq n_A \\ Stop & \text{if } i = A \text{ and } x = n_A \end{array} \right.$$

The particular run with A and nonce n_A is blocked, but all other runs are allowed.

If the input message x has positive rank, and the first branch of the condition is followed, then we have that either $i \neq A$, or $x \neq n_A$. In this case the transmitted message $\{B.x.y\}_{K_{Bi}}$ should also have positive rank, since this protocol run should not introduce non-positive-rank messages.

A Candidate Rank Function. The constraints arising from the two cases above give rise to the first attempt at a rank function. This is given in Figure 5. In this rank function, we give a rank of 0 to those messages and signals identified above as requiring non-positive rank, and also the shared key K_{AB}, which

$$\rho(i) = 1$$
$$\rho(n) = 1$$
$$\rho(k) = \begin{cases} 0 \text{ if } k = k_{AB} \\ 1 \text{ otherwise} \end{cases}$$
$$\rho(m_1.m_2) = \min\{\rho(m_1).\rho(m_2)\}$$
$$\rho(\{m\}_k) = \begin{cases} 0 & \text{if } m = B.n_A.y \text{ and } k = k_{AB} \\ \rho(m) \text{ otherwise} \end{cases}$$
$$\rho(sig) = \begin{cases} 0 \text{ if } sig = initdone.A.B.n_A \\ 1 \text{ otherwise} \end{cases}$$

Fig. 5. A rank function for authentication

must remain out of the hands of the attacker to prevent him from constructing messages that should not circulate. Other atomic messages (nonces, agent identities, other keys) can have rank 1. Other compound messages essentially have the ranks dictated by their components: if a message's content has rank 0, then any encryption or concatenation of that message will likewise have a rank of 0.

It is straightforward to check that condition 2 holds for this rank function, and it is entirely reasonable to state that in the model the attacker does not start with any message of rank 0, as required by condition 1.

Lastly, we are required to show that condition 4 holds for all other cases. However, since these cases do not involve the important signals or protocol messages their proofs are all straightforward:

- $RESP_A$: only generates messages $\{A.x.n\}_{K_{Ai}}$, which are of positive rank;
- $INIT_A(i, n)$, where $i \neq B$ or $n \neq n_A$. In this case, the signal provided at the end of the run will have rank 1, so no message or signal of non-positive rank is produced;
- $INIT_B(i, n)$: only produces messages and signals of positive rank;
- $INIT_C$, $RESP_C$ ($C \neq A, B$): only produce messages and signals of positive rank.

Thus the rank function is sufficient to establish that the corrected protocol indeed provides authentication of B to A.

It is instructive to see where this approach fails on the original flawed protocol. In that protocol there is no agent name included in the second message. When considering the case $INIT_C$, $C = A$, $i = B$, $n = n_A$, we will obtain the requirement that $\{n_A.y\}_{K_{AB}}$ must have non-positive rank for any y, since it is the input of such a message that leads to the performance of the non-positive-rank signal $initdone.A.B.n_A$[1]. However, consideration of the case $RESP_A(n)$ finds that messages of the form $\{x.n\}_{K_{Ai}}$ are output, and so these will need to

---

[1] In the proof of the correct protocol, the corresponding requirement was that $\{B.n_A.y\}_{K_{AB}}$ must have non-positive rank.

have positive rank, for any x and i^2. But now there is a conflict on the message $\{n_A.n\}_{K_{AB}}$, which from the first case must have non-positive rank, but from the second case must have positive rank. Hence there can be no rank function for this version of the protocol: the constraints on any rank function are contradictory. The contradiction is avoided by introducing the name of the agent generating the message.

4   Discussion

4.1   Theorem-Proving

In practice, of course, protocols tend to be more complicated than our running example, in a variety of ways. For example: the messages used in the protocol might be more complex, or simply much larger; there may be more messages involved in the protocol; the protocol could involve additional protocol agents, such as trusted third parties, or even entire groups of communicating agents; more complex combinations of cryptographic mechanisms might be used. All of these possibilities make the CSP modelling of the protocol a more difficult task, and the verification of candidate rank functions becomes more intricate and error-prone. Tool support is of great benefit in keeping track of the housekeeping involved in consideration of numerous cases, and in assisting in the construction of rank functions.

The constraints introduced by the rank function theorem can generally be used to derive a candidate rank function. Firstly, every message in IK must have positive rank. Secondly, any message derivable from a set of positive rank messages must also have positive rank. Thirdly, any output (message or signal) from a protocol step which follows only positive rank inputs must also be of positive rank. These three conditions allow the identification of a set S of messages and signals which must have positive rank. However, the signal required in condition 3 of the rank function theorem is required to have non-positive rank. If that signal is in the set S then no rank function can exist. Otherwise the function ρ which gives a rank of 1 to all messages in S, and a rank of 0 to all other messages, will be a suitable rank function.

The *RankAnalyser* tool [HS00, Hea00, HS04] provides a way of computing this rank function automatically for standard cases (where the protocol uses public-key or shared-key cryptography, nonces, agent names, and concatenation). The (infinite) message space is partitioned to a finite set of equivalence classes, and the set of messages and signals of positive rank is obtained by repeatedly applying protocol steps and generates rules (on the equivalence classes), starting from the attacker's initial knowledge IK.

More generally, the PVS theorem prover [OSR93] has also been used to support rank function proofs of protocol correctness. Theorem provers such as PVS are well-suited to keeping track of all the unavoidable detailed housekeeping involved in the nuts and bolts of a protocol correctness proof. The traces model for

---

[2] Previously, it was required that $\{A.x.n\}_{K_{AB}}$ had positive rank.

CSP has been embedded in PVS, together with much of the consequent theory, including proof rules such as those of Figure 4 and the rank function theorem has been proved for this embedding [DS97]. Specific protocols can be modelled and verified, for example the recursive authentication protocol analysed in [BS97], demonstrating that this approach supports the full generality of an infinite message space, and arbitrary numbers of runs and protocol agents. More recently the CSP hierarchy of theories within PVS has been restructured [Eva03, ES04] to more easily allow extensions within the rank function framework, such as the introduction of (discrete) time [ES00], as well as consideration of other properties such as non-repudiation [Eva03].

The rank function approach has also been extended in other ways. It is able to incorporate algebraic properties of the cryptographic mechanisms into the analysis, provided they can be expressed appropriately within the model [Sch02]. For example, if Vernam encryption (exclusive-or) is used explicitly within a protocol, then the algebraic properties of exclusive-or should be taken into account in the analysis. This can be achieved by giving the algebraic identities that encapsulate exclusive-or on the message space, and checking that whenever two messages are equivalent then they should have the same rank. This approach is clearly limited since only *known* algebraic properties can be included in the model. Nonetheless their inclusion allows the protocol analyser to reason about the properties which a cryptosystem must satisfy if the protocol is to be implemented correctly.

Another extension concerns the verification of secrecy properties of protocols, particularly in situations where keys can be leaked to an attacker without compromising the security of past protocol runs. Such keys are temporary secrets: components of messages that are required to be unknown to the attacker at a particular point of the protocol, but can be disclosed later. The standard rank function approach cannot handle temporary secrets, because their rank should be non-positive at the point they are used, but positive because of the fact that the attacker learns them during the protocol run [DS04]. Temporal rank functions are a generalisation that take into account the time at which a message can first be learned by the attacker, enabling a finer way of analysing the relationships between messages. Use of temporal rank functions requires a generalisation of the rank function theorem, but they allow analysis of an additional class of secrecy properties not covered by the standard approach.

4.2   Model-Checking

The use of CSP to describe and specify protocols naturally enables the use of model-checking for verification, and there has been a significant body of work using FDR [For03] in this area which began a decade ago [Low95, Ros95, LR96]. The approach constructs a CSP description of the protocol agents interacting over a Dolev-Yao style attacker as described earlier, and refinement-checks it against authentication and secrecy properties expressed as CSP trace specifications in terms of the signal events which are inserted judiciously into the protocol runs. If the refinement check fails then FDR produces a (minimal-length) counterexample trace which corresponds to an attack on the protocol: a sequence of messages which lead to a failure of the authentication or secrecy property under consideration.

Since the construction of the model of the protocol is routine from the message-passing protocol description, Lowe has developed a tool, Casper [Low98], which translates a high-level protocol description into the corresponding CSP model, ready for FDR to analyse. The ease of use of this tool, together with the speed of the FDR analysis, means that the model-checking analysis should generally be the first to be carried out when considering a new protocol: simple flaws can be identified and corrected quickly, before too much effort is put into carrying out a rank function proof.

Of course, any CSP model which can be completely checked by FDR must have a finite number of states. This means that the number of protocol runs in the model, the number of agents, and the size of the message space, must necessarily be finite. Refinement failures will always correspond to attacks, but a successful refinement check on a finite model does not guarantee correctness in the presence of arbitrary concurrent runs—it may be that an attack requires more possibilities than have been included in the analysis. However, a collection of sophisticated techniques have been developed for enabling more general conclusions to be drawn from finite model-checking. For example, Lowe [Low99] has presented, for secrecy specifications, a list of conditions under which the correctness of just a single run of a protocol is sufficient to conclude the correctness of an unbounded number of runs of the same protocol. Hui and Lowe have shown how protocol messages in CSP models can be simplified without losing attacks (fault-preserving transformations) [HL01], thus enabling complex protocols to be reduced to a point where they can be analysed by FDR. Broadfoot and Roscoe have applied data independence techniques [BR99, BR02] which allow results about a finite number of runs to be lifted to arbitrary runs.

An extensive coverage of the use of CSP for modelling protocols, and both the model-checking and the rank function approaches to protocol analysis, is provided in [RSG+00].

4.3   Related Approaches

In addition to the CSP approaches discussed above, a wide variety of formal techniques have been developed for protocol specification and analysis. These include approaches based on graph theory, induction, multiset rewriting, type-checking, and non-interference. Here we give a flavour of each.

In the strand space approach [THG99], a strand is a trace that represents either the execution of a legitimate protocol participant (an 'honest' strand) or the action of an attacker (a 'penetrator' strand). A strand space is a collection of strands equipped with a graph structure that represents both consecutive operations on the same strand (the behaviour of a single user) and the interaction between strands (communication between users). Theorems have been developed on strand spaces which enable proofs that a protocol is correct, and tool support for the approach has been provided by Athena [SBP01], a program that is part model-checker and part theorem-prover. Some relationships have been identified

[Hea02] between the rank functions used to verify protocols, and the structures (ideals) used in the strand spaces approach, and there are some similarities in the philosophies of the two approaches.

The inductive approach [Pau98] uses the theorem-prover Isabelle/HOL to support a theorem-proving approach to protocol verification. Protocols are coded directly in terms of event traces and rules that participants apply to 'received' messages in order to produce new messages. The possible actions of a 'Spy' are also specified by rules. A theory concerning the possible traces of the overall system is developed and the protocol is verified by establishing inductively that no trace violating the specification can ever occur. A particular achievement of this approach is its use in the verification of SET [Pau02], an electronic commerce protocol whose description runs to nearly 1000 pages.

Cervesato et al. [CDL+99a] have developed a way of specifying protocols using first-order multiset rewriting. This has become known as the MSR approach. Using MSR, protocols are specified by *roles* which represent the behaviour of protocol participants. Each role constitutes a series of rewrite rules which represent the actions of that particular user. The attacker, typically in the style of Dolev and Yao, is also defined via rewrite rules. Each rewrite rule that an attacker can apply corresponds to a deduction of the form ⊢ in the rank function approach. Recent work has sought to establish a correspondence between MSR and the strand space [CDM+00] and process algebraic approaches [BCLM03].

Abadi and Gordon have proposed the spi-calculus [AG98] as an extension to the π-calculus which includes cryptographic primitives. Protocols in the spi-calculus are modelled as processes—but the similarity with CSP ends here. The fundamental differences between CSP and nominal calculi mean that, in the spi-calculus, communication of secrets between parties is achieved via restriction and scope extrusion, and the nature of testing equivalence removes the need for an explicit attacker process. However, proving correctness via equivalence can be difficult. Abadi [Aba97] and, more recently, Gordon and Jeffrey [GJ01, GJ04] have therefore developed type-systems that enable authentication properties—expressed using signals—to be statically checked for a spi-calculus protocol model. The use of correspondence assertions (in the spirit of the *initdone* and *respgo* events) suggests a similarity between this approach and the rank function approach, and it is also interesting to consider that the 'trusted' and 'untrusted' secrecy types may be interpreted as non-positive and positive ranks, respectively.

The concept of non-interference has also formed the basis of protocol analysis techniques. These approaches generally impose a partition on protocol agents, with a group of 'high-level' privileged users distinguished from other 'low-level' users. Non-interference is achieved if the behaviour of a high-level user has no effect on what a low-level user can observe. For the purposes of protocol analysis this corresponds to the inability of an attacker (a high-level user) to induce bad behaviour in the legitimate participants (the low-level users). A suite of tools have been developed that enable protocols to be reasoned about using non-interference. A high-level protocol description can be translated into the notation of the Security Process Algebra (SPA) using the CVS compiler [DFG00].

This SPA script is then amenable for analysis using the CoSec tool [FG97] which checks for the presence of non-interference. Similarities between non-interference and the concept of process equivalence in CSP have been established [RS00].

The above techniques, along with the CSP-based approaches, have much in common, most notably their basic assumption about the capabilities of the attacker. Indeed, in many cases it will be feasible to reason about a protocol using any one of these methods, and the results obtained from each will be broadly similar. As alluded to above, there is a growing body of research which aims to demonstrate fundamental similarities between these different approaches. In the end the choice of which technique to use will be guided by the previous experience of the protocol analyser. The advantage of applying CSP in this domain lies in the simplicity of the notation and the transparency with which protocols can be modelled. This transparency is essential for a model to be shown as an appropriate abstraction of a real protocol. Furthermore, the maturity of the language backs this up by allowing well-understood and powerful techniques to be brought to bear on the problem of verifying whether a given protocol model meets its intended goal.

References

[Aba97]   M. Abadi. Secrecy by typing in security protocols. In *Proceedings of the Third International Symposium on Theortical Aspects on Computer Software*, number 1281 in Lecture Notes in Computer Science, pages 611–638, September 1997.

[AG98]   M. Abadi and A.D. Gordon. A calculus for cryptographic protocols: the spi calculus. *Information and Computation*, 1998. also DEC Research Report 149, 1998.

[BCLM03]   S. Bistarelli, I. Cervesato, G. Lenzini, and F. Martinelli. Relating process algebras and multiset rewriting for security protocol analysis. In *WITS '03: Workshop on Issues in the Theory of Security*, 2003.

[BR99]   P.J. Broadfoot and A.W. Roscoe. Proving security protocols with model checkers by data independence techniques. *Journal of Computer Security*, 7(2/3), 1999.

[BR02]   P.J. Broadfoot and A.W. Roscoe. Capturing parallel attacks within the data independence framework. In *Proceedings of the 15th Computer Security Foundations Workshop*. IEEE Computer Society Press, 2002.

[BS97]   J.W. Bryans and S.A. Schneider. CSP, PVS, and a recursive authentication protocol. In *DIMACS Workshop on Design and Formal Verification of Crypto Protocols*, 1997.

[CDL+99a]   I. Cervesato, N.A. Durgin, P. Lincoln, J.C. Mitchell, and A. Scedrov. A meta-notation for protocol analysis. In *Proceedings of the 12th Computer Security Foundations Workshop*. IEEE Computer Society Press, 1999.

[CDL+99b]   I. Cervesato, N.A. Durgin, P.D. Lincoln, J.C. Mitchell, and A. Scedrov. A meta-notation for protocol analysis. In *12th IEEE Computer Security Foundations Workshop*, 1999.

[CDM+00]   I. Cervesato, N. Durgin, J.C. Mitchell, P. Lincoln, and A. Scedrov. Relating strands and multiset rewriting for security protocol analysis. In *Proceedings of The 13th Computer Security Foundations Workshop*. IEEE Computer Society Press, 2000.

[DFG00]   A. Durante, R. Focardi, , and R. Gorrieri. A compiler for analyzing crypto-graphic protocols using non-interference. *ACM Transactions on Software Engineering and Methodology*, 9(4), 2000.

[DS97]   B. Dutertre and S.A. Schneider. Embedding CSP in PVS: an application to authentication protocols. In *tpHOL*, 1997.

[DS04]   R. Delicata and S.A. Schneider. Towards the rank function verification of protocols with temporary secrets. In *WITS '04: Workshop on Issues in the Theory of Security*, 2004.

[DY83]   D. Dolev and A.C. Yao. On the security of public key protocols. *IEEE Transactions on Information Theory*, 29(2), 1983.

[ES00]   N. Evans and S.A. Schneider. Analysing time dependent security proper-ties in CSP using PVS. In *ESORICS*, volume 1895 of *LNCS*, 2000.

[ES04]   N. Evans and S.A. Schneider. Verifying security protocols with PVS: Widening the rank function approach. *Journal of Logic and Algebraic Programming*, in press

[Eva03]   N. Evans. *Investigating Security Through proof*. PhD thesis, Royal Hol-loway, University of London, 2003.

[FG97]   R. Focardi, , and R. Gorrieri. The compositional security checker: A tool for the verification of information flow security properties. *IEEE Trans-actions on Software Engineering*, 23(9), 1997.

[For03]   Formal Systems (Europe) Ltd. FDR2 user manual, 2003.

[GJ01]   A.D. Gordon and A. Jeffrey. Authenticity by typing for security proto-cols. In *Proceedings of the 14th Computer Security Foundations Workshop*. IEEE Computer Society Press, 2001.

[GJ04]   A.D. Gordon and A. Jeffrey. Types and effects for asymmetric crypto-graphic protocols. *Journal of Computer Security*, 12(3/4), 2004. Also in Proceedings of the 15th Computer Security Foundations Workshop. IEEE Computer Society Press, 2002.

[Hea00]   J.A. Heather. *"Oh! Is it really you?"—Using rank functions to verify au-thentication protocols*. PhD thesis, Royal Holloway, University of London, 2000.

[Hea02]   J.A. Heather. Strand spaces and rank functions: More than distant cousins. In *Proceedings of The 15th Computer Security Foundations Workshop*. IEEE Computer Society Press, 2002.

[HL01]   M.L. Hui and G. Lowe. Fault-preserving simplifying transformations for security protocols. *Journal of Computer Security*, 9(1/2), 2001.

[Hoa85]   C.A.R. Hoare. *Communicating Sequential Processes*. Prentice-Hall, 1985.

[HS00]   J.A. Heather and S.A. Schneider. Towards automatic verification of au-thentication protocols on unbounded networks. In *Proceedings of the 13th Computer Security Foundations Workshop*. IEEE Computer Society Press, 2000.

[HS04]   J.A. Heather and S.A. Schneider. A decision procedure for the existence of a rank function. *Journal of Computer Security*, in press.

[Low95]   G. Lowe. An attack on the Needham-Schroeder public-key authentication protocol. *Information Processing Letters, 56,*, 56, 1995.

[Low97]   G. Lowe. A hierarchy of authentication specifications. In *Proceedings of the 10th Computer Security Foundations Workshop*. IEEE Computer Society Press, 1997.

[Low98]   G. Lowe. Casper: A compiler for the analysis of security protocols. *Journal of Computer Security*, 6(1/2), 1998.

[Low99]   G. Lowe. Towards a completeness result for model checking of security protocols. *Journal of Computer Security*, 7(2/3), 1999.

[LR96]   G. Lowe and A.W. Roscoe. Using CSP to detect errors in the TMN protocol. *IEEE Transactions on Software Engineering*, 1996.

[Mea92]   C. Meadows. Applying formal methods to the analysis of a key management protocol. *Journal of Computer Security*, 1(1), 1992.

[Mil95]   J. Millen. The interrogator model. In *IEEE Computer Society Symposium on Research in Security and Privacy*, 1995.

[MVV96]   A.J. Menezes, P.C. Van Oorschott, and S.A. Vanstone. *Handbook of Applied Cryptography*. CRC Press, 1996.

[NS78]   R. Needham and M. Schroeder. Using encryption for authentication in large networks of computers. *Communications of the ACM*, 21(12), 1978.

[OSR93]   S. Owre, N. Shankar, and J. Rushby. The PVS specification language. Technical report, Computer Science Lab, SRI International, 1993.

[Pau98]   L.C. Paulson. The inductive approach to verifying cryptographic protocols. *Journal of Computer Security*, 6(1/2), 1998.

[Pau02]   L. Paulson. Verifying the SET protocol: Overview. In *FASec 2002: Formal Aspects of Security*, 2002.

[PQ00]   O. Pereira and J-J. Quisquater. On the perfect encryption assumption. In *WITS '00: Workshop on Issues in the Theory of Security*, 2000.

[Ros95]   A.W. Roscoe. Modeling and verifying key-exchange protocols using CSP and FDR. In *Proceedings of the 8th Computer Security Foundations Workshop*. IEEE Computer Society Press, 1995.

[Ros97]   A.W. Roscoe. *The Theory and Practice of Concurrency*. Prentice-Hall, 1997.

[RS00]   P.Y.A. Ryan and S.A. Schneider. Process algebra and non-interference. *Journal of Computer Security*, 9(1/2), 2000. Also in Proceedings of the 12th Computer Security Foundations Workshop. IEEE Computer Society Press, 1999.

[RSG+00]   P.Y.A. Ryan, S.A. Schneider, M.H. Goldsmith, G. Lowe, and A.W. Roscoe. *Modelling and Analysis of Security Protocols*. Addison-Wesley, 2000.

[SBP01]   D.X. Song, S. Berezin, and A. Perrig. Athena: A novel approach to efficient automatic security protocol analysis. *Journal of Computer Security*, 9(1/2), 2001.

[Sch98]   S.A. Schneider. Verifying authentication protocols in CSP. *IEEE Transactions on Software Engineering*, 1998.

[Sch99]   S.A. Schneider. *Concurrent and Real-time Systems: the CSP Approach*. Addison-Wesley, 1999.

[Sch02]   S.A. Schneider. Verifying security protocol implementations. In *FMOODS'02: Formal Methods for Open Object-based Distributed Systems*, 2002.

[THG99]   F.J. Thayer Fábrega, J.C. Herzog, and J.D. Guttman. Strand spaces: proving security protocols correct. *Journal of Computer Security*, 7(1), 1999.

[WL93]   T. Woo and S. Lam. A semantic model for authentication protocols. In *IEEE Computer Society Symposium on Research in Security and Privacy*, 1993.

Shedding Light on Haunted Corners of Information Security

Peter Ryan

University of Newcastle, UK

Abstract. Characterising the fundamental concepts of information security, such as confidentiality and authentication, has proved problematic from the outset and remains controversial to this day. Non-interference was proposed some 25 years ago to give a precise, formal characterisation of the absence of information flows through a system, motivated in large part by the discovery of covert channels in access control models such as Bell-LaPadula. Intuitively, it asserts that altering Highs interactions with a system should not result in any observable difference in Lows interactions with the system. Superficially it appears to be a very natural and compelling concept but it turns out to harbor some surprising subtleties.

Over the years various models of computation have been used to formalise non-interference. Typically these floundered on non-determinism, "input/output" distinctions, input totality and so forth. In the late 80's and early 90's, process algebras, in particular CSP, were applied to information security. In this talk I will briefly overview this approach and discuss how the concepts and results from process algebra shed light on these haunted corners of non-interference, including the role of non-determinism, unwinding results, composition, refinement and input/output distinctions. In particular, we argue that the absence of information flow can be characterised in terms of process equivalence, itself a delicate and fundamental concept.

References

1. J. A. Goguen and J. Meseguer: Security policies and security models, IEEE Symposium on Security and Privacy (1982).
2. Goguen, J., Meseguer, J: Inference Control and Unwinding, Proceedings of the IEEE Symposium on Research in Security and Privacy (1984)
3. Lowe, G.: Defining Information Flow University of Leicester tech report (1999).
4. A. W. Roscoe and J. Woodcock and L. Wulf: Non-interference through determinism, Proceedings of ESORICS (1994).
5. P. Y. A. Ryan: A CSP formulation of non-interference and unwinding, Presented at CSFW 1990 and published in Cipher, Winter 1990/2000
6. P.Y.A. Ryan and S.A. Schneider: Process Algebra and Non-interference, JCS 2001.
7. S. A. Schneider and A. Sidiropoulos: CSP and anonymity, Proceedings of ESORICS (2000)

A.E. Abdallah, C.B. Jones, and J.W. Sanders (Eds.): **CSP25**, LNCS 3525, p. 264, 2005.

Operational Semantics for Fun and Profit

Michael Goldsmith[1,2]

[1] Formal Systems (Europe) Ltd
michael@fsel.com
http://www.fsel.com
[2] Worcester College, University of Oxford

Abstract. The FDR refinement-checking tool[1] [5] relies fundamentally upon the congruences between operational and denotational semantics for CSP, in order to determine a denotational property by exploring an operationally presented system. But the calculation of the standard structured operational semantics of complex systems proves a bottleneck in the performance of the tool, and so we compile a custom inference system for each case, optimised for facilitating execution of the relevant queries. Recent developments have revealed how these calculations can be re-used in restructuring systems to maximise the potential for hierarchical compression and for export to a related probabilistic formalism.

1 Introduction: FDR – Refinement Checking CSP

The essential function of the FDR tool is to compare two CSP processes to determine whether refinement holds. This may be a useful fact to know in a variety of situations, whether the refinement be:

- between an ideal system and a more complex implementation
- between an encoding of some property and a process meant to satisfy it
- between a denial of solubility and a model of a game or problem – in this situation a counterexample gives a solution, which is typically optimal due to the broadly breadth-first exploration strategy

Refinement is strictly a denotational property: it holds iff every behaviour of the candidate implementation process is a possible behaviour of the specification process, where a 'behaviour' is an element of one of the semantic models:

- *traces*: $\mathcal{T}[\![P]\!]$
- *traces* and *stable failures*: $\mathcal{T}[\![P]\!]$ and $\mathcal{S}[\![P]\!]$
- *failures/divergences*: $\mathcal{F}[\![P]\!]$ and $\mathcal{D}[\![P]\!]$

But denotational values are infinite sets rather ill-suited to direct mechanical manipulation.

---

[1] FDR is a commercial product of Formal Systems (Europe) Ltd, available free for academic purposes.

A.E. Abdallah, C.B. Jones, and J.W. Sanders (Eds.): **CSP25**, LNCS 3525, pp. 265–274, 2005.
© Springer-Verlag Berlin Heidelberg 2005

FDR works by exhaustive state enumeration, so it is not unreasonable to insist that the processes involved must be finite-state! Denotationally, 'finite-state' means that the set

$$\{P/s \mid s \in \mathcal{T}[\![P]\!]\}$$

is finite, but recognising this requires in general the identification of infinite numbers of infinite values as being equal.

Fortunately this property is implied by being operationally finite-state: that the process always eventually evolves to a syntax (or more generally a closure) that has been seen before, so that the labelled transition system (LTS) yielded by the operational semantics is a finite graph. In practice we encounter few processes which are denotationally but not operationally finite-state, and it is usually straightforward to recode one that is in order to bring it within the more restrictive class.

But how can we check refinement from an operational presentation?

2   The Operational-Denotational Congruence and FDR

The full operational semantics for CSP did not see the light of day until relatively late [2], although much of the research dates back to the time when Roscoe and Brookes were students of Hoare [8]. Its congruence with each of the standard denotational models is established through the medium of synchronisation trees, but boils down to the two equations:

$$\mathcal{F}[\![P]\!] = \{\langle s, X \rangle \mid \exists Q \bullet P \stackrel{s}{\Rightarrow} Q \wedge Q \ ref \ X\}$$
$$\cup$$
$$\{\langle s ^\frown t, X \rangle \mid \exists Q \bullet P \stackrel{s}{\Rightarrow} Q \wedge Q{\uparrow}\}$$

$$\mathcal{D}[\![P]\!] = \{s ^\frown t \mid \exists Q \bullet P \stackrel{s}{\Rightarrow} Q \wedge Q{\uparrow}\}$$

where an operational state Q *ref*uses X iff it cannot perform an internal action τ nor any of the events in X

$$\forall x \in X \cup \{\tau\} \bullet Q \stackrel{x}{\not\rightarrow}$$

and where $Q{\uparrow}$ means that Q is operationally divergent, in that there exists an infinite τ-path from Q:

$$\langle Q_n \mid n \in \omega \rangle \quad \text{such that} \quad Q_0 = Q \wedge \forall n \in \omega \bullet Q_n \stackrel{\tau}{\rightarrow} Q_{n+1}$$

The closure under divergence is a feature of the 'improved' failures-divergences model [1], and does not apply to the (later) stable-failures model [9] or the simpler traces model. Here the equations reduce to one or both of:

$$\mathcal{T}[\![P]\!] = \{s \mid \exists Q \bullet P \stackrel{s}{\Rightarrow} Q\}$$

$$\mathcal{S}[\![P]\!] = \{\langle s, X \rangle \mid \exists Q \bullet P \stackrel{s}{\Rightarrow} Q \wedge Q \ ref \ X\}$$

But, in all these cases, the existential form of the right-hand side

$$\{\ldots s \ldots \mid \exists\, Q \bullet P \overset{s}{\Rightarrow} Q \wedge \ldots\}$$

means that the denotational behaviour of a process relating to a trace is the union of the corresponding operational behaviours from all operational states reachable on that trace. For example, it can be extended by any event in the initials of any such state:

$$\{a \mid s ^\frown \langle a \rangle \in \mathcal{T}[\![P]\!]\} = \bigcup_{P \overset{s}{\Rightarrow} Q} \{a \mid Q \overset{a}{\rightarrow} \}$$

and it can form a stable refusal with a set of events iff some stable operational state is unable to perform every element of it:

$$s \in \mathcal{T}[\![P]\!] \Rightarrow \{X \mid (s, X) \in \mathcal{S}[\![P]\!]\} = \bigcup_{P \overset{s}{\Rightarrow} Q \overset{\tau}{\nrightarrow}} \mathbb{P}\{a \mid Q \overset{a}{\nrightarrow} \}$$

Refinement in any of the models is simply (pointwise) reverse inclusion of the appropriate semantic components. But

$$V \supseteq \bigcup \mathcal{U} \quad \text{iff} \quad \forall\, U \in \mathcal{U} \bullet V \supseteq U$$

If we are trying to check refinement, as we do in FDR, then this is incredibly convenient. We need to check that the behaviours of the purported implementation process are a subset of those of the specification, but this observation means that we can check this piecemeal, at least as far as the implementation is concerned: if the implementation has an unacceptable denotational behaviour, then that will manifest as an unacceptable operational behaviour of one of its states. (The situation with the specification is more problematic: we need to know if *any* of its states admits some behaviour, all at once, since there is no corresponding decomposition for $V = \bigcup \mathcal{V}$ on the left-hand side of the inequation; the solution is *normalisation* [9, 11].)

The final ingredient of the theoretical cocktail underpinning FDR is a little recursion induction: if we fail to find a counterexample exploring the relation between a particular specification normal-form state and a given implementation state along some path that leads back to the same pair, then we can be certain that there is no point in exploring any further around the loop. So given finite-state representations of the two processes, we can guarantee to determine whether refinement holds after exploring at most the product of their sizes. In practice it is relatively rare for an implementation state to correspond to more than one state of the normalised specification, and we only visit the parts of the product that are reachable by performing the same trace in both processes, so the number of state-pairs visited is typically few more than the number of implementation states.

3   Leaping to Conclusions – Supercompilation

The modern style of presenting operational semantics is as 'Plotkin-style' inference rules. Thus the semantics of the 'communicating'-parallel operator can be captured by:

$$\frac{P \xrightarrow{x} P'}{P \parallel_A Q \xrightarrow{x} P' \parallel_A Q} \quad [\, x \notin A \,] \qquad \frac{P \xrightarrow{\alpha} P' \quad Q \xrightarrow{\alpha} Q'}{P \parallel_A Q \xrightarrow{\alpha} P' \parallel_A Q} \quad [\, \alpha \in A \,]$$

together with a symmetric variant of the first (where x may include τ).
In the same way, FDR-style relational renaming[2] is captured by:

$$\frac{P \xrightarrow{x} P'}{P[[R]] \xrightarrow{y} P'[[R]]} \quad [\, x \,(1 \oplus R)\, y \,]$$

In order to calculate the operational semantics of a more complex process term, for example

$$T \mathrel{\hat{=}} (P[[a \leftarrow a, a \leftarrow b]] \parallel_{\{b\}} Q)[[c \leftarrow b]],$$

repeated applications of these rules will be required.

FDR implements a compromise between completely precalculating the transition systems that correspond to the processes in a refinement check, and a fully 'on-the-fly' approach: some components (essentially those which are purely sequential or recursive) are compiled down to a labelled transition system, while the overall structure of the process syntax is retained as an operator tree, and its operational semantics is calculated according to such rules. The repeated application of the canonical rules proved a significant bottleneck in the execution speed, however, in large part due to the expense (and memory turnover) of generating the intermediate results, the conclusions of lower rules that feed in as antecedents to ones higher in the tree.

One may remark (and Roscoe did) that the pattern of inference is repeated for every query to such a process, and thus a significant optimisation can be achieved by collapsing the possible inference trees to leave only their conclusion and their leaves as antecedents. This can be calculated by considering each way that each top-level event can arise as a result of the operational semantics of the outermost operator in terms of the actions of its argument processes, and recursively investigating how each of these can arise, until we reach a leaf LTS,

---

[2] Here the relationship is given by 'maplets' $x \leftarrow y$: an event x in the argument relates to any y on the right-hand side of such a term where it is the left-hand side, or to itself if there is none such. Channels can be renamed wholesale, corresponding to the pointwise pairing of events arising from their respective extension by any valid common suffix.

which can produce an event in at most one way: by being able to perform it. This *supercompilation* procedure thus identifies zero or more derived rules for each event, which collectively capture the operational semantics of the process.

Thus for our example process T, above, supposing we know (as a result of the compilation) that P can perform only a, while Q is limited to $\{b, c\}$, then (writing R_{ab} for $[a \leftarrow a, a \leftarrow b]$) the semantics are fully captured by five rules. First, there are two deriving from single leaf actions:

$$\frac{P \xrightarrow{a} P'}{T \xrightarrow{a} (P'[[R_{ab}]] \; \underset{\{b\}}{\|} \; Q)[[c \leftarrow b]]} \qquad \frac{Q \xrightarrow{c} Q'}{T \xrightarrow{b} (P[[R_{ab}]] \; \underset{\{b\}}{\|} \; Q')[[c \leftarrow b]]}$$

each arising through one application of the first rule for communicating parallel and two or one (respectively) of the renaming rule, thus:

$$\frac{\dfrac{\dfrac{P \xrightarrow{a} P'}{P[R_{ab}] \xrightarrow{a} P'[R_{ab}]}}{P[R_{ab}] \; \underset{\{b\}}{\|} \; Q \xrightarrow{a} P'[R_{ab}] \; \underset{\{b\}}{\|} \; Q}}{(P[R_{ab}] \; \underset{\{b\}}{\|} \; Q)[[c \leftarrow b]] \xrightarrow{a} (P'[R_{ab}] \; \underset{\{b\}}{\|} \; Q)[[c \leftarrow b]]} \begin{array}{l} [\, a \,(1 \oplus R_{ab})\, a \,] \\[8pt] [\, a \notin \{b\} \,] \\[8pt] [\, a \,(1 \oplus [c \leftarrow b])\, a \,] \end{array}$$

$$\frac{\dfrac{Q \xrightarrow{c} Q'}{P \; \underset{\{b\}}{\|} \; Q \xrightarrow{c} P \; \underset{\{b\}}{\|} \; Q'}}{(P[R_{ab}] \; \underset{\{b\}}{\|} \; Q)[[c \leftarrow b]] \xrightarrow{b} (P[R_{ab}] \; \underset{\{b\}}{\|} \; Q')[[c \leftarrow b]]} \begin{array}{l} [\, c \notin \{b\} \,] \\[8pt] [\, c \,(1 \oplus [c \leftarrow b])\, b \,] \end{array}$$

Similarly, we may calculate a derived rule:

$$\frac{P \xrightarrow{a} P' \qquad Q \xrightarrow{b} Q'}{T \xrightarrow{b} (P'[[R_{ab}]] \; \underset{\{b\}}{\|} \; Q')[[c \leftarrow b]]}$$

arising from the second rule for parallel, and two appeals to renaming:

$$\frac{\dfrac{\dfrac{P \xrightarrow{a} P'}{P[R_{ab}] \xrightarrow{b} P'[R_{ab}]} \; [\, a \,(1 \oplus R_{ab})\, b \,] \qquad Q \xrightarrow{b} Q'}{P[R_{ab}] \; \underset{\{b\}}{\|} \; Q \xrightarrow{b} P'[R_{ab}] \; \underset{\{b\}}{\|} \; Q'}}{(P[R_{ab}] \; \underset{\{b\}}{\|} \; Q)[[c \leftarrow b]] \xrightarrow{b} (P'[R_{ab}] \; \underset{\{b\}}{\|} \; Q')[[c \leftarrow b]]} \begin{array}{l} \\ [\, b \in \{b\} \,] \\[8pt] [\, b \,(1 \oplus [c \leftarrow b])\, b \,] \end{array}$$

and finally two more, both involving τ:

$$\frac{P \xrightarrow{\tau} P'}{T \xrightarrow{\tau} (P'[[R_{ab}]] \underset{\{b\}}{\|} Q)[[c \leftarrow b]]} \qquad \frac{Q \xrightarrow{\tau} Q'}{T \xrightarrow{\tau} (P[[R_{ab}]] \underset{\{b\}}{\|} Q')[[c \leftarrow b]]}$$

which again come from the first rule for parallel, passing through the renamings unchanged, since a renaming relation such as R cannot mention τ. (In fact, every CSP operator has the property that it allows its (currently active[3]) components to perform τ without modification or hindrance, and such rules are dealt with implicitly as a special case in FDR.)

Now we can tabulate the effect of each state of each leaf process on each rule:

- either the leaf is not involved, in which case we record *true*
- or else we record whether the given state is able to perform the event listed in the relevant antecedent[4].

Then to determine the initial events of a state of the system, represented as a vector of states of its leaves, we look up a vector of booleans for each leaf, and form the pointwise conjunction[5] to determine which rules can fire; the initials are simply the set of resultant events of those rules.

FDR works with the complements of refusals, partly because empirically minimal acceptances tend to be smaller (and so faster to compare) than maximal refusals; but mostly because exactly the same inference system serves to calculate the composition of leaf acceptances into those of the process as a whole. Thus the benefits of the supercompilation procedure are also felt in the calculations of whether local liveness constraints are satisfied.

The one remaining wrinkle is how to calculate the successor states for each event. Here we may usefully separate the CSP operators into two classes: the communicating and the sequential!

What we may call the communicating operators, all forms of parallel, renaming and hiding, have the property that every rule in their operational semantics has an application of the operator on both sides of its resultant transition. That is, transitions do not change the 'shape' of the process[6]. In this case, it is quite straightforward to calculate the successor states arising from each rule which fires: we know the successor states of each leaf after performing the relevant event, and it is simply a matter of multiplying these possibilities together in

---

[3] The exception being the right-hand argument of $P \,;\, Q$.

[4] Each leaf can occur at most once among the antecedents.

[5] There is a τ due to an autonomous leaf transition iff any leaf can perform τ, so we need rather a disjunction here; so inverted logic is used to encode this eventuality in an additional bit in each vector.

[6] This would not be the case if we implemented Roscoe's Ω-semantics for termination directly; we don't.

place to form a new set of vectors; the set of all successors after an event is simply the union of these sets over all enabled rules which generate it.

The other operators all have the property that at least one of their rules has no mention of the operator in the destination state of its resultant transition: perhaps the canonical example being

$$\frac{P \xrightarrow{\checkmark} P'}{P \,;\, Q \xrightarrow{\tau} Q}$$

So the 'shape' of the process changes after such a transition, and different sets of rules must apply, before and after.

Often such operators will occur only in the parts of the process which are compiled down to labelled transition systems, but we do not want to insist that this always be the case. To cater for the possibility, we need to perform the same supercompilation for each 'shape', and provide each with its own set of supercombinator-style derived rules. Now the state of the system includes a format number, indicating which set is active, and some transitions are *dynamic*, changing format. In such circumstances the components of the successor state fall into one of three categories:

- they are leaves from the old configuration which were not involved in the transition, whose state is simply copied across;
- they are leaves which were involved, whose own successor states need to be multiplied in; or
- they are previously inactive leaves, which start in their initial state.

Thus the calculation of the resultant states is unpleasantly complicated, but perfectly well defined.

4   By-products of Supercompilation

The algorithm to calculate the supercompiled rule-base is coded quite efficiently, although a result of Valmari and Kervinen [12] taken together with Theorem 1 below implies that its worst-case performance must be quite poor. Nonetheless, the information about the system that is calculated in the process of supercompilation proves to have value in a rather unexpected facet of the tool.

4.1   Watchdog Transformations for Compression

It has long been known [10] that the hierarchical compression operators provided by FDR tend to work best when there is a lot of hidden activity that can be compressed away. One evident possible route towards maximising this is somehow to move the specification over to the right-hand-side of the refinement, in such a way that the resulting check is invariant under hiding; and then hide everything!

We have shown [13, 4] that this is indeed possible, and we have addressed the issue that it is not just hidden activity, but rather localised hidden activity, which is necessary in order to get real benefit from hierarchical compression. Unfortunately the simple execution of the watchdog transformation, where the specification is transformed into a monitor process which signals a failure of refinement either through an error-flag event or by deadlocking the system (in the traces and failures models respectively), yields a system where the hidden events are nearly all shared immediately below the outermost hiding, so that virtually no extra compression is obtained. We explain in the cited works how the syntax tree can be rebalanced to solve this problem, but CSP operators are generally not precisely associative and do not commute with one another, so the transformation is often quite intricate.

More recently, we have been able to take advantage of the supercompiler:

Theorem 1. *Any CSP communicating-operator tree can be transformed, leaving the leaf processes untouched, into an equivalent one (unique up to reordering and choice of new event names) that uses only outward (inverse-functional) renaming at the leaves, 'natural' alphabetised parallel, and functional renaming and hiding at the outermost level.*

Proof: We sketch the algorithm. Simply use the (identifiers of the) supercombinator rules as the intermediate events: include a rule as a target of the outward renaming of an event at a leaf iff that leaf's engaging in that event is one of the antecedents of the rule; and rename each rule back to the event in its conclusion at the outermost level (or hide those giving rise to τ). □

In the general case, a similar strategy applies, complicated by the need for a monitor process that switches between which sets of rules are active as the formats change. That is all that is necessary, if the operator tree is actually a tree; if it is a graph, then further mechanisms are required to allow leaf processes to be re-initialised, where appropriate, in their new incarnation.

Using this transformation allows the system to be expressed in a form which can be reordered and rebracketed at relatively little cost in either CPU cycles or, more importantly, intellectual effort.

4.2   Watchdogs for Analysis Elsewhere

In the interests of code re-use, as much as anything else, exactly the same approach has been followed in performing a watchdog transformation on the specification in order to export assertions in an experimental probabilistically-enhanced version of CSP_M [3] to the Birmingham University tool *PRISM* [6].

The only real difference is that the global visibility of *PRISM* variables and the fact that the actual specification property in the *PRISM* analysis is a PCTL formula which is expressed in terms of them together allow a slight simplification in detecting failure of refinement. In particular, the use of the interrupt operator in [4–§4] can be avoided. Some quite neat encodings have been found of, for instance, the slices through the minimal acceptances in the failures-model watchdog, and the resulting *PRISM* code is quite compact (if not much more readable than most autogenerated code). The reader is referred to [3] for details.

Acknowledgements

As in so many other areas of the work on CSP, much of the inspiration of this work, including the original concept of applying a supercombinator approach to the calculation of operational semantics within FDR, is due to Bill Roscoe. Many other talented individuals on the Formal Systems' staff have also contributed to the development of the algorithms and data-structures involved: (in purely chronological order) David Jackson, Paul Gardiner, Bryan Scattergood, Jason Hulance, Philip Armstrong, Paul Whittaker and Tim Whitworth.

Much of the work in Section 4 was carried out as part of the DTI Next Wave Technologies and Markets project *FORWARD* [7], building upon research undertaken for QinetiQ Trusted Information Management System Assurance Group. The assistance of the *PRISM* design team at Birmingham University, in particular Dave Parker, is gratefully acknowledged.

References

1. S.D. Brookes and A.W. Roscoe. An improved failures model for communicating processes. In *Proceedings of the Pittsburgh seminar on concurrency LNCS 197*, pages 281–305. Springer-Verlag, 1985.
2. Steve Brookes, Bill Roscoe, and David Walker. An operational semantics for CSP. Technical report, Oxford University Programming Resarch Group, 1986.
3. Michael Goldsmith. CSP: The best concurrent-system description language in the world – probably! (extended abstract). In Ian East, Jeremy Martin, Peter Welch, David Duce, and Mark Green, editors, *Communicating Process Architectures 2004*. IOS Press, 2004.
4. Michael Goldsmith, Nick Moffat, Bill Roscoe, Tim Whitworth, and Irfan Zakiuddin. Watchdog transformations for property-oriented model-checking. In Keijiro Araki, Stefania Gnesi, and Dino Mandrioli, editors, *FME 2003: Formal Methods*, pages 600–616, Pisa, September 2003. Formal Methods Europe.
5. Formal Systems (Europe) Ltd. *FDR2 manual*, 1998. http://www.formal.demon.co.uk/fdr2manual/.
6. PRobabilistIc Symbolic Model checker. http://www.cs.bham.ac.uk/~dxp/prism/.
7. QinetiQ, Birmingham University, Formal Systems, and Oxford University. *FORWARD: A Future of Reliable Wireless Ad-hoc networks of Roaming Devices*. http://www.forward-project.org.uk.
8. A.W. Roscoe. *A mathematical theory of communicating processes*. DPhil, Oxford University Programming Research Group, 1982.
9. A.W. Roscoe. *The Theory and Practice of Concurrency*. Prentice Hall, 1998. ISBN 0-13-6774409-5, pp. xv+565.
10. A.W. Roscoe, P.H.B. Gardiner, M.H. Goldsmith, J.R. Hulance, D.M. Jackson, and J.B. Scattergood. Hierarchical compression for model-checking CSP *or* How to check 10^{20} dining philosophers for deadlock. In *Proceedings of TACAS Symposium, Aarhus, Denmark*, 1995.
11. P.Y.A. Ryan, S.A.Schneider with M.H. Goldsmith, G. Lowe, and A.W. Roscoe. *The Modelling and Analysis of Security Protocols: the CSP Approach*. Addison-Wesley, 2000.

12. Antti Valmari and Antti Kervinen. Alphabet-based synchronisation is exponentially cheaper. In L. Brim, P. Janar, M. Ketínský, and A. Kuera, editors, *CONCUR 2002 – Concurrency Theory: 13th International Conference*, volume 2421 of *LNCS*, pages 161–176, Brno, Czech Republic, August 2002. Springer-Verlag Heidelberg.
13. Irfan Zakiuddin, Nick Moffat, Michael Goldsmith, and Tim Whitworth. Property based compression strategies. In *Proceedings of Second Workshop on Automated Verification of Critical Systems (AVoCS 2002)*. University of Birmingham, April 2002.

On Model Checking Data-Independent Systems with Arrays with Whole-Array Operations*

Ranko Lazić[1],[**], Tom Newcomb[2], and A.W. Roscoe[2]

[1] Department of Computer Science, University of Warwick, UK
[2] Computing Laboratory, University of Oxford, UK

Abstract. We consider programs which are data independent with respect to two type variables X and Y, and can in addition use arrays indexed by X and storing values from Y. We are interested in whether a program satisfies its control-state unreachability specification for all non-empty finite instances of X and Y. The decidability of this problem without whole-array operations is a corollary to earlier results.

We address the possible addition of two whole-array operations: an *array reset* instruction, which sets every element of an array to a particular value, and an *array assignment* or *copy* instruction. For programs with reset, we obtain decidability if there is only one array or if Y is fixed to be the boolean type, and we obtain undecidability otherwise. For programs with array assignment, we show that they are more expressive than programs with reset, which yields undecidability if there are at least three arrays. We also obtain undecidability for two arrays directly.

Keywords: Model checking, infinite-state systems, data independence, arrays.

1 Introduction

A system is *data independent* (DI) [17, 12] with respect to a type if it can only input, output, move values of that type around within its store, and test whether pairs of such values are equal. This has been exploited for the verification of communication networks [4], processors [14], and security protocols [2].

We consider programs DI with respect to two distinct types X and Y, which can in addition use *arrays* (or *memories*), indexed by X and storing values from Y. We have already shown that a particular class of programs that do not use whole-array operations (i.e. ones that can only read and write to individual

---

* We acknowledge support from the EPSRC grant GR/M32900. The first author was also supported by grants from the Intel Corporation and the EPSRC (GR/S52759/01), the second author by QinetiQ Malvern, and the third author by the US ONR.
** Also affiliated to the Mathematical Institute, Serbian Academy of Sciences and Arts, Belgrade.

A.E. Abdallah, C.B. Jones, and J.W. Sanders (Eds.): CSP 2004, LNCS 3525, pp. 275–291, 2005.

locations in the array) are amenable to model checking [11]. In this paper, we study what happens to these decidability results on the addition of whole-array operations.

One motivation for considering DI programs with arrays is cache and cache-coherence protocols [1]. Such protocols are DI with respect to the types of memory addresses and data values. Another application area is parameterised verification of network protocols by induction, where each node of the network is DI with respect to the type of node identities [4]. Arrays arise when each node is DI with respect to another type, and it stores values of that type.

The techniques which we used to establish decidability of parameterised model checking for DI programs with arrays cannot be used when whole-array operations are introduced. The *partial-functions semantics* used there relied on the fact that there could always be parts of the array that were 'untouched' by the program, and can therefore be assumed to hold any required value.

In order to investigate data independence with arrays, we introduce a programming framework inspired by UNITY [3], where programs have state and execute in discrete steps depending only on the current state. Although data independence has been characterised in many other languages, e.g. [17, 8, 10], our language is designed to be a simple framework for the study of data independence without the clutter of distracting language features.

Given a DI program with arrays and a specification for the program, the main question of interest is whether the program satisfies the specification *for all non-empty finite instances* of X and Y. The class of specifications we will be considering here is control-state unreachability, which can express any safety property. For such specifications, we observe that the answer to the above parameterised model-checking problem for finite instances reduces to a single check with X and Y instantiated to infinite sets.

We consider the *reset* (or *initialiser*) instruction, which sets every location in an array to a given value. This is useful for modelling distributed databases and protocols with broadcasts. We prove that such systems with exactly one array are well-structured [7], showing that unreachability model checking is decidable for them. However, we also show that for programs with just two arrays with reset, unreachability is not decidable: this result is acquired using an emulation by such systems of universal register machines (e.g. [5]). We further show that unreachability is decidable for programs with arbitrarily many arrays with reset when Y is *not* a type variable, but is fixed to be the boolean type. In such programs, any boolean operation can be used, since it can be expressed in terms of equality tests.

The study of cache protocols motivates an *array assignment* (or array *copy*) instruction, for moving blocks of data between memory and cache or setting up the initial condition that the contents of the cache accurately reflects the contents of the memory. For programs with array assignment, we show that they are more expressive than programs with reset, which yields undecidability if there are at least three arrays. We also obtain undecidability for two arrays by direct emulation of universal register machines.

Programs with arrays with reset are comparable to broadcast protocols [6]. The arrays can be used to map process identifiers to control states or data values, and the broadcasting of a message, which may put all processes into a particular state, might be mimicked by a reset instruction. In [6], it is shown that the model checking of safety properties is decidable for broadcast protocols. This result has technical similarities to the decidability results in this paper. However, arrays can contain data whose type is a parameter (i.e. an unboundedly large set), whereas the set of states of a process in a broadcast protocol is fixed.

Our decidability results are also related to decidability results for Petri Nets. The result for arrays storing booleans is related to the decidability of the Covering Problem for Petri Nets with transfer arcs [7]: the differences in formalisms, especially that we have state variables which can index the arrays, make our result interesting. Programs with an array storing data whose type is a parameter are related to Nested Petri Nets [13] with transfer arcs: in addition to formalism differences, decidability of the Covering Problem for Nested Petri Nets with transfer arcs has not been studied.

Another related technique is *symbolic indexing* [15], which is applicable to circuit designs with large memories. However, the procedure relies on a case split which must be specified manually, and only fixed (although large) sizes of arrays can be considered.

Some of the results in this paper were announced by the authors at the VCL 2001 workshop, whose proceedings were not formally published. This paper can be considered an abridged version of Chapters 3, 8 and 9 of [16], and readers are advised to consult this reference for further details and full proofs.

2   Preliminaries

A *well-quasi-ordering* $\preceq$ is a reflexive and transitive relation on a set Q which has the property that for any infinite sequence $q_0, q_1, \ldots \in Q$, there exist $i < j$ such that $q_i \preceq q_j$.

A *transition system* is a structure $(Q, Q^0, \rightarrow, P, \ulcorner \cdot \urcorner)$ where:

- Q is the *state space*,
- $Q^0 \subseteq Q$ is the set of *initial states*,
- $\rightarrow \subseteq Q \times Q$ is the *successor relation*, relating states with their possible next states,
- P is a finite set of *observables*,
- $\ulcorner \cdot \urcorner : P \rightarrow \mathcal{P}(Q)$ is the *extensions function*, so that $\ulcorner p \urcorner$ is the set of states in Q that have some observable property p.

Given two transition systems $\mathcal{S}_1 = (Q_1, Q_1^0, \rightarrow_1, P, \ulcorner \cdot \urcorner_1)$ and $\mathcal{S}_2 = (Q_2, Q_2^0, \rightarrow_2, P, \ulcorner \cdot \urcorner_2)$ over the same observables P, a relation $\approx \subseteq Q_1 \times Q_2$ is a *bisimulation* between $\mathcal{S}_1$ and $\mathcal{S}_2$ when the following five conditions hold:

1. If $s \approx t$, then for every $p \in P$, we have that $s \in \ulcorner p \urcorner_1$ iff $t \in \ulcorner p \urcorner_2$.
2. For all $s \in Q_1^0$, there exists $t \in Q_2^0$ such that $s \approx t$.

3. If $s \approx t$ and $s \rightarrow_1 s'$ then there exists $t' \in Q_2$ such that $s' \approx t'$ and $t \rightarrow_2 t'$.
4. For all $t \in Q_2^0$, there exists $s \in Q_1^0$ such that $s \approx t$.
5. If $s \approx t$ and $t \rightarrow_2 t'$ then there exists $s' \in Q_1$ such that $s' \approx t'$ and $s \rightarrow_1 s'$.

In this case, we can say that the transition systems $\mathcal{S}_1$ and $\mathcal{S}_2$ are *bisimilar*.

A state s is *reachable* in a transition system $\mathcal{S} = (Q, Q^0, \rightarrow, P, \ulcorner \cdot \urcorner)$ if there exists a sequence of states $s_0 \rightarrow s_1 \rightarrow \cdots \rightarrow s_n$ such that $s_0 \in Q_0$ and $s_n = s$.

3   Language

A *type* is one of the following: the booleans **Bool**, the natural numbers **Nat**, either of the *type variables* X or Y, and the *array types* $T_2[T_1]$ where T_1 and T_2 are non-array types.

A *type context* is a mapping from *variables* (which are just mathematical symbols) to types. For a type context Γ we will write $\Gamma \vdash x : T$ if Γ maps the variable x to the type T, and say that x *has type* or *is of type* T in Γ. We may omit Γ in these notations if the type context we are referring to is obvious or unambiguous.

A *type instance* for a type context Γ (or for a program with type context Γ) gives two countable non-empty sets as instances for X and Y. We may also talk of *(in)finite* type instances, which map only to (in)finite sets.

A *state* s of a type context Γ (or of a program with type context Γ) together with a type instance $\mathcal{I}$ for Γ is a function mapping each variable used in Γ to a concrete value in its type. The set of all states of a type context (or of a program) is called the *state space*. We may write $s(a[x])$ as a shorthand for $s(a)(s(x))$.

The *instructions* associated with a type context Γ are as displayed in Table 1, where T_1 and T_2 range over the non-array types.

The ? operator represents the selection (or input) of a value into a variable or location. There are also guarding (or blocking) instructions such as equality testing $x = x'$, that do not update the state but which can only proceed if true. The instructions b and $\bar{b}$ can proceed only if b is respectively true or false.

The instruction **reset**(a, y) will implement an array reset or initialiser operation, setting every location in an array a to a particular value y. There is also an array copy or assignment operation $a[\,] := a'[\,]$.

Table 1. Instructions

	Instruction	Type constraints on Γ
Boolean	$?b, b, \bar{b}$	$b : \textbf{Bool}$
Data	$?x, x = x', x \neq x'$	$x, x' : X$ or Y
Array	$?a[x], a[x] = y$	$a, a' : T_2[T_1]$,
	$\textbf{reset}(a, y), a[\,] := a'[\,]$	$x : T_1, \ y : T_2$
Counter	$\textbf{inc}(r), \textbf{dec}(r), \textbf{isZero}(r)$	$r : \textbf{Nat}$

Variables of type **Nat** can be increased by one, decreased if not zero, and compared to zero.

The *operations* of a type context Γ are generated by the grammar:

$$Op ::= Op; Op \mid Op + Op \mid Op^* \mid I$$

where I is any Γ-permitted instruction. The operator combinators are sequential composition $(;)$, choice or selection $(+)$, and finite repetition $(^*)$.

We may use syntactic abbreviations such as $x := x'$ for $?x; x = x'$ or **while** Op_1 **do** Op_2 **od** for $(Op_1; Op_2)^*; \neg Op_1$. We may use brackets $(\cdots)$ or indentations in programs to show precedence.

A *program* with type context Γ is syntax of the form **init** Op_I **repeat** Op_T, where the *initial operation* Op_I and the *transitional operation* Op_T are both Γ-operations.

Given a program $\mathcal{P} = $ **init** Op_I **repeat** Op_T and a type instance $\mathcal{I}$ for the program, the *semantics* of the program under $\mathcal{I}$ is the transition system $\langle\!\langle \mathcal{P} \rangle\!\rangle_{\mathcal{I}} = (Q, Q^0, \rightarrow, P, \ulcorner \cdot \urcorner)$, where

- Q (states) is the state space of the program $\mathcal{P}$ with the type instance $\mathcal{I}$,
- Q^0 (initial states) is the set of all states that can result from the execution of Op_I from any state in Q (i.e. the variables and all locations in the arrays can be considered arbitrarily initialised before the execution of Op_I),
- $\rightarrow$ is the relation induced by the operation Op_T,
- P (observables) is the set of boolean variables used in $\mathcal{P}$.
- $\ulcorner \cdot \urcorner$ is a mapping from P to sets in Q such that $\ulcorner b \urcorner = \{s \mid s(b) = \mathbf{true}\}$.

$\mathcal{P}$ can be thought of as executing Op_I once from any state to form the set of initial states of the transition system. Given any state, executing the transitional operation Op_T once from that state yields all its successors, i.e. all states which $\mathcal{P}$ can reach by one transition.

Note 1. A UNITY program over a set of variables consists of an initial condition, followed by a set of guarded multiple assignments [3]. A UNITY program can be expressed in our language quite naturally, although extra temporary variables may be needed to reproduce multiple simultaneous assignment. Conversely, any program in our language can be converted to a UNITY program which would have equivalent observational behaviour whenever a boolean signal is true.

Further discussion of motivation and application of the language, and example programs, can be found in [16].

$\square$

4   Model-Checking Problems

The *control-state unreachability problem* **CU** for a class of programs $\mathcal{C}$ is: 'Given any program $\mathcal{P}$ from the class $\mathcal{C}$, any boolean b from the program $\mathcal{P}$, and *any particular* type instance $\mathcal{I}$ for $\mathcal{P}$, are all states which map b to true unreachable in $\langle\!\langle \mathcal{P}\rangle\!\rangle_{\mathcal{I}}$?' We will write **FinCU** and **InfCU** to restrict the problem to just finite and infinite type instances respectively.

The *parameterised control-state unreachability problem* **PCU** for a class of programs $\mathcal{C}$ is: 'Given any program $\mathcal{P}$ from the class $\mathcal{C}$ and any boolean b from the program $\mathcal{P}$, are all states which map b to true unreachable in $\langle\!\langle \mathcal{P}\rangle\!\rangle_{\mathcal{I}}$ for *all possible* type instances $\mathcal{I}$ for $\mathcal{P}$?' We will write **FinPCU** to restrict the problem to just finite type instances.

The data independence of the data types means that systems with equinumerous type instances are isomorphic. Therefore, **InfPCU** is in fact the same problem as **InfCU**.

We can use the following theorem to deduce results about the parameterised model-checking problem for all finite types from checks using just one particular infinite type instance.

Theorem 1. *Suppose we have a program $\mathcal{P}$ without variables of type* **Nat***, a boolean variable b of $\mathcal{P}$, and an infinite type instance $\mathcal{I}^*$ for $\mathcal{P}$. Then,*

$$b \text{ reachable in } \langle\!\langle \mathcal{P}\rangle\!\rangle_{\mathcal{I}^*} \quad \Longleftrightarrow \quad \exists \mathcal{I} \cdot b \text{ reachable in } \langle\!\langle \mathcal{P}\rangle\!\rangle_{\mathcal{I}}.$$

where $\exists \mathcal{I}$ existentially quantifies only over finite *type instances for $\mathcal{P}$.*   □

Corollary 1. *For any class of programs without variables of type* **Nat***,* **InfCU** *is decidable if and only if* **FinPCU** *is decidable.*   □

A *DI system with arrays with reset* is a program with no variables of type **Nat**, which does not use array assignment, and which is of the form

$$\textbf{init} \quad (\,\overset{\circ}{,}_a ?y; \textbf{reset}(a, y)); Op_I$$
$$\textbf{repeat } Op_T,$$

where y is any variable with type Y. It is sensible to assume that the program has such a variable, otherwise it would be unable to read from or write to its arrays. The notation $(\,\overset{\circ}{,}_a \cdots)$ means repetition of syntax, as a ranges over all arrays.

In the above definition of DI systems with arrays with reset, the prefix of instructions ensures that all arrays are initialised (i.e. reset) to arbitrary values. This simplifies proofs a little.

A *universal register machine* (URM) is a program that may only use variables of type **Bool** or **Nat**. The program must be of the form

$$\textbf{init} \quad (\,\overset{\circ}{,}_r \textbf{isZero}(r)); Op_I$$
$$\textbf{repeat } Op_T.$$

where the operation before Op_I repeats **isZero**(r); for some complete enumeration of the variables of type **Nat**.

5   Reset

5.1   One Array Storing Data from a Variable Type

In this section we will prove that parameterised model checking of control-state unreachability properties for systems with one array of type $Y[X]$ with reset is decidable. We begin with the following crucial observation.

Note 2. Arrays are initialised at the beginning of the program, and at any reachable state there has been a finite number of instructions since the last reset on a particular array. Therefore every possible reachable state will have only a finite number of locations in each array that are different from the last reset value. □

Let $\mathcal{P}$ be a DI program with only one (resettable) array, and let $\mathcal{I}^*$ be an infinite type instance for $\mathcal{P}$. Let $\langle\!\langle \mathcal{P} \rangle\!\rangle_{\mathcal{I}^*} = (Q, Q^0, \rightarrow, P, \ulcorner \cdot \urcorner)$. To aid the following proof, we restrict Q to contain only states that conform to the observation made in Note 2—that there are only finitely many different values in the array at any time and only one of them occurs infinitely often—as other states can never be reachable. This simplifies the presentation, although it would be possible not to restrict Q and to just mention this at the required places in the proof.

We define some notation before giving the well-quasi-ordering on the states.

Definition 1. *For a state s, a subset V of $\mathcal{I}^*(X)$, and a value $w \in \mathcal{I}^*(Y)$, we will denote the number of occurrences of w in locations V in the array $s(a)$ as $C_s(V, w)$, which can be formally defined as follows:*

$$C_s(V, w) = |\{v \in V \mid s(a)(v) = w\}|.$$

Note that the answer will be ∞ if V is an infinite set and w is the value of the last reset, else it will be a natural number. □

We write $y :: Y$ to mean y is a term of type Y—that is, y is either a variable $y : Y$ or y is syntax of the form $a[x]$ where $x : X$. We will also use:

$$s(: X) = \{s(x) \mid x : X\} \quad \text{and} \quad s(:: Y) = \{s(y) \mid y :: Y\}.$$

For ease of presentation, we may also write X and Y to mean $\mathcal{I}^*(X)$ and $\mathcal{I}^*(Y)$ when it is clear that a set is required rather than a type symbol.

Definition 2. *The relation $\preceq \subseteq Q \times Q$ is defined as $s \preceq t$ iff there exist bijections:*

$$\alpha : s(: X) \rightarrow t(: X) \quad \text{and} \quad \beta : s(:: Y) \rightarrow t(:: Y)$$

such that all of the following hold:

1. *$s(b) = t(b)$ for all $b : \mathbf{Bool}$.*
2. *$\alpha(s(x)) = t(x)$ for all $x : X$.*
3. *$\beta(s(y)) = t(y)$ for all $y :: Y$.*

4. *For all $w \in s(:: Y)$, there are at least the same number of $\beta(w)$'s in the array $t(a)$ as there are w's in $s(a)$, excluding locations which are the terms. Formally:*

$$C_s(X \setminus s(:X), w) \leq C_t(X \setminus t(:X), \beta(w)).$$

5. *There exists an injection $\gamma : Y \setminus s(:: Y) \rightarrow Y \setminus t(:: Y)$ such that all other values from the type Y not dealt with above can be matched up from $s(a)$ to $t(a)$ in the manner of Condition 4 above, but with the injection γ instead of the bijection β. Formally: for all $w \in Y \setminus s(::Y)$,*

$$C_s(X \setminus s(:X), w) \leq C_t(X \setminus t(:X), \gamma(w)). \qquad \square$$

Example 1. We illustrate the definition of $\preceq$ on an example pair of states s and t. The first three conditions say that boolean variables must be equal and the terms must have the same equality relationship on them. We will focus of the final two conditions, which are used to compare the parts of the array that are not referenced by the current values of X-variables (i.e. locations that are not immediately accessible in the current state before doing a $?x$ instruction).

Condition 4 says that, for each term $y :: Y$, there must be at least as many $t(y)$'s in the rest of the array $t(a)$ (i.e. locations not referenced by X-variables) than there are $s(y)$'s in the rest of the array $s(a)$.

Suppose s has no other location in the array holding a value equal to the value of term y_0; similarly, suppose there are four, one, and three other locations containing the values $s(y_1), s(y_2)$ and $s(y_3)$ respectively. This is represented pictorially as a histogram: see Figure 1 (a). Condition 4 of $s \preceq' t$ holds for any t whose corresponding histogram 'covers' the histogram of s.

Condition 5 says that the same relationship holds for all the other Y-values (i.e. values not held in terms), except that we are allowed to arrange the columns of the histogram in any way we wish. In this example we use the fact that it is sufficient to consider the arrangement where they are sorted in reverse order, instead of having to consider every possible permutation.

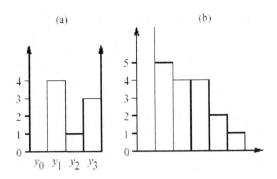

Fig. 1. Histogram representation of array with reset

Suppose the state s was last reset to a value v_0 which is not equal to a value held in any term: the array will therefore hold an infinite number of these values. The array may also hold a finite number of other values: suppose $s(a)$ also holds distinct values $v_1, \ldots, v_5$ (which are different from v_0 and the values of any terms) in cardinalities five, four, four, two, and one respectively. This can be represented as a histogram: see Figure 1 (b). Condition 5 requires that t's corresponding histogram covers that of s. □

The following two propositions tell us that $\langle\!\langle \mathcal{P} \rangle\!\rangle_{\mathcal{I}^*}$ is a well-structured transition system [7].

Proposition 1. *The relation $\preceq$ is a well-quasi-ordering on the state set Q.* □

Proposition 2. *The relation $\preceq$ is strongly upward compatible with $\rightarrow$, i.e. for all $s \preceq t$ and $s \rightarrow s'$ there exists $t' \in Q$ such that $t \rightarrow t'$ and $s' \preceq t'$.* □

Any state s can be represented finitely by a tuple with the following components:

- the values of the boolean variables;
- the equivalence relations on the variables of type X and on terms of type Y induced by the equality of values stored in them;
- for each $y :: Y$, the value $C_s(X \setminus s(:X), s(y))$;
- a bag (i.e. multiset) consisting of, for each $w \in Y \setminus s(::Y)$, the value

$$C_s(X \setminus s(:X), w)$$

if it is non-zero.[3]

This representation yields a quotient $\widehat{\langle\!\langle \mathcal{P} \rangle\!\rangle_{\mathcal{I}^*}}$ of the transition system $\langle\!\langle \mathcal{P} \rangle\!\rangle_{\mathcal{I}^*}$, which is a well-structured transition system with respect to the quotient $\hat{\preceq}$ of the quasi ordering $\preceq$. Moreover, for any state representation $\hat{s}$, a finite set of state representations whose upward closure is $\uparrow Pred(\uparrow \hat{s})$ is computable, and $\hat{\preceq}$ is decidable. Therefore, control-state unreachability can be decided by the backward set-saturation algorithm in [7].

Theorem 2. *The problems **InfCU** and **FinPCU** are decidable for the class of DI programs with reset with just one array of type $Y[X]$.* □

5.2   Multiple Arrays Storing Boolean Data

Here we consider DI programs that use multiple arrays all indexed by a type variable X and storing boolean values. Decidability of parameterised model checking of control-state unreachability properties for these systems follows similarly as for systems in Section 5.1.

---

[3] There are only finitely many w's for which this value is non-zero—see Note 2.

The following are the main differences in defining the quasi ordering:

- As the type Y used there is now the booleans, the program is no longer DI with respect to it. Therefore, the function β must be removed (i.e. replaced with the identity relation) from Definition 2.
- In Definition 1, redefine the C_s operator to take a vector of boolean values $\mathbf{w} = (w_1, \ldots, w_n)$ rather than a single value:

$$C_s(V, (w_1, \ldots, w_n)) = |\{v \in V \mid \forall i \cdot s(a_i)(v) = w_i\}|.$$

The finite representation of states is now as follows:

- the values of the boolean variables;
- the equivalence relation on the variables of type X induced by the equality of values stored in them;
- for each $\mathbf{w} \in \mathbb{B}^n$, the value $C_s(X \setminus s(:X), \mathbf{w})$.

Theorem 3. *The problems* **InfCU** *and* **FinPCU** *are decidable for the class of DI programs with arbitrarily many arrays only of type* **Bool**$[X]$ *with reset.* $\square$

5.3   Multiple Arrays Storing Data from a Variable Type

We now show that unreachability model checking is undecidable with more than one array of type $Y[X]$. We demonstrate that for any URM $\mathcal{P}$ there is a DI program $\mathcal{P}^\sharp$ with just two type variables X and Y and only two arrays with reset which has the same observable behaviour as $\mathcal{P}$. We can encode the values of the variables $r : \mathbf{Nat}$ as the length of a linked list in the arrays in $\mathcal{P}^\sharp$.

Definition 3. *The type context $\Gamma^\sharp$ of $\mathcal{P}^\sharp$ is defined as follows, where $\mathcal{P}$ has type context Γ. $\Gamma^\sharp$ has the same variables of type* **Bool** *as Γ and has two arrays $\Gamma^\sharp \vdash S, I : Y[X]$ to hold the linked lists. It also has variables $\Gamma^\sharp \vdash h_r : X$ for the heads of the linked lists representing each $\Gamma \vdash r : \mathbf{Nat}$, and a variable $\Gamma^\sharp \vdash e : X$ which marks the end of all the lists. A variable $\Gamma^\sharp \vdash y_0 : Y$ is used to hold a special value which marks a location in I as being unused. The program also makes use of temporary variables $\Gamma^\sharp \vdash x : X$ and $\Gamma^\sharp \vdash y, n : Y$.* $\square$

Example 2. Figure 2 shows an example state of the arrays S and I, representing a state in the URM where its counter variables are set as follows: $r_0 = 0$, $r_1 = 2$ and $r_2 = 3$.

The array I is used to give unique identifiers in Y to all of the finitely many locations in X that are currently being used to model the linked lists. It is set to y_0 (which happens to be the value 0 in this example) at all the unused locations. Where I is non-zero, the array S gives the identifier of that location's successor.

Checking a register r is zero becomes a simple matter of checking whether $h_r = e$. We can decrease a register r by updating h_r to the value x, where $I[x]$ is equal to $S[h_r]$, remembering to mark the old location as being now unused by doing $I[h_r] := y_0$.

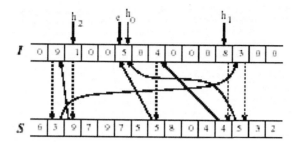

Fig. 2. Building a linked list using arrays with reset

To increase r by one, we must find a brand new identifier as well as an unused location for h_r and make it link to the old location. To ensure that a chosen identifier is new we must go through all the lists and check that it is not being used already. We can check whether a location is being used by testing if it is zero in I.

Notice that there are important invariants our emulator must maintain in addition to the requirement that the linked lists must have length equal to the appropriate URM register.

- The identifiers should be unique so that each head has exactly one list from it.
- Aside from the end marker e, the locations in any pair of lists are disjoint.
- I must have unused locations set to y_0, of which there must always be in-finitely many. □

Definition 4. *An instruction translator* $^\sharp$ *from instructions in* $\mathcal{P}$ *to operations in* $\mathcal{P}^\sharp$ *is shown in Table 2. The syntax* $(;_{r'} \cdots)$ *means the repetition of syntax, replacing* r' *with a different variable of type* **Nat** *each time, all conjoined with the ; operator.* □

Definition 5. *Given a URM* $\mathcal{P} = $ **init** o_I **repeat** o_T, *the corresponding DI program with arrays is*

$$\mathcal{P}^\sharp = \textbf{init} \quad \text{reset}(I, y_0); \quad y \neq y_0; \quad I[e] := y; \quad o_I^\sharp$$
$$\textbf{repeat} \quad o_T^\sharp.$$
□

Let $\langle\!\langle \mathcal{P} \rangle\!\rangle = (Q, Q_0, \rightarrow, P, \ulcorner \cdot \urcorner)$ and $\langle\!\langle \mathcal{P}^\sharp \rangle\!\rangle = (Q^\sharp, Q^{0\sharp}, \rightarrow^\sharp, P, \ulcorner \cdot \urcorner^\sharp)$. We will show there exists a bisimulation between $\langle\!\langle \mathcal{P} \rangle\!\rangle$ and $\langle\!\langle \mathcal{P}^\sharp \rangle\!\rangle_{\mathcal{I}^*}$ for any infinite type instance $\mathcal{I}^*$ for $\mathcal{P}^\sharp$.

First, some shorthands. Given a state t, we will say that the inverse function $t(I)^{-1} : \mathcal{I}^*(Y) \rightarrow \mathcal{I}^*(X)$ is defined at a value $w \in \mathcal{I}^*(Y)$ and is equal to the value v when there is exactly one value v in $\mathcal{I}^*(X)$ such that $t(I)(v) = w$. We will use notation to compose arrays as follows: $t(I)^{-1}(t(S)(v))$ may be written $t(I^{-1} \circ S)(v)$.

We now define our correspondence relationship between the two transition systems.

Table 2. Translating URM instructions to instructions on arrays with reset

I	$I^\sharp$
isZero(r)	$h_r = e$
dec(r)	$h_r \neq e; I[h_r] := y_0; y := S[h_r];$ $?h_r; I[h_r] = y$
inc(r)	$?n; n \neq y_0; n \neq I[e];$ $(;_{r'}\ x := h_{r'};$ $\quad$ **while** $x \neq e$ **do** $\qquad n \neq I[x]; y := S[x];$ $\qquad ?x; I[x] = y$ $\quad$ **od**); $?x; I[x] = y_0;$ $I[x] := n; y := I[h_r]; S[x] := y;$ $h_r := x$
other	no change

Definition 6. *Define a relation $\approx \subseteq Q \times Q^\sharp$ as $s \approx t$ iff*

- $s(b) = t(b)$ *for b : **Bool**.*
- *For every r : **Nat** there exists a finite sequence $v_0^r \cdots v_{s(r)}^r$ such that:*
  - *For each r : **Nat**:*
    - $v_{s(r)}^r = t(h_r)$,
    - $v_{i-1}^r = t(I^{-1} \circ S)(v_i^r)$ *for $i = 1, \ldots, s(r)$,*
    - $v_0^r = t(e)$.
  - *The values of each $t(I)(v_i^r)$ for r : **Nat** and $i = 1, \ldots, s(r)$ together with $t(e)$ are pairwise unequal. ('Uniqueness Invariant.')*
  - *For all $v \in \mathcal{I}^*(X)$, we have that $v_i^r \neq v$ for every r : **Nat** and $i = 0, \ldots, s(r)$ if and only if $t(I)(v) = t(y_0)$. ('Unused Invariant.')* □

Proposition 3. *The relation $\approx$ is a bisimulation between $\langle\!\langle \mathcal{P} \rangle\!\rangle$ and $\langle\!\langle \mathcal{P}^\sharp \rangle\!\rangle_{\mathcal{I}^*}$ for any infinite type instance $\mathcal{I}^*$ for $\mathcal{P}^\sharp$.* □

The following can be deduced from the undecidability of the Halting Problem for URM's and Corollary 1.

Theorem 4. *The problems **InfCU** and **FinPCU** for the class of DI programs with two arrays of type $Y[X]$ with reset are undecidable.* □

6   Array Assignment

6.1   Simulation of Arrays with Reset

We show that for any program $\mathcal{P}$ using arrays with reset, there exists a program $\mathcal{P}^\sharp$ using arrays with assignment which has bisimilar semantics. This shows that, in some sense, array assignment is at least as expressive as array reset.

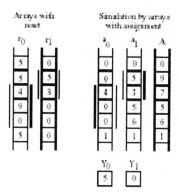

Fig. 3. Emulating array reset with array assignment

Definition 7. *The type context $\Gamma^\sharp$ of the program $\mathcal{P}^\sharp$ is defined as follows. If we assume the arrays used in $\mathcal{P}$ are $r_0, \ldots, r_{n-1}$, we have arrays $\Gamma^\sharp \vdash a_0, \ldots, a_{n-1} : Y[X]$ in $\mathcal{P}^\sharp$. We also have another array $\Gamma^\sharp \vdash A : Y[X]$ which we will use to check whether locations have changed since the last reset of that array. The type context $\Gamma^\sharp$ has all the same non-array variables as Γ except that it also has extra variables $\Gamma^\sharp \vdash Y_0, \ldots, Y_{n-1} : Y$ to store the last reset value to the corresponding array. There are also temporary variables $\Gamma^\sharp \vdash y_a, y_A, n : Y$.* □

Example 3. Here is an example state of a system using arrays with reset, together with an emulating state from the system using array assignment.

On the left of the figure, the arrays r_0 and r_1 from the system with the reset operation available are shown. It can be seen that r_0 was last reset to 5 and r_1 was last reset to 0. The locations where these arrays have been changed since their last update are emphasised with vertical bars.

On the right, the arrays a_0 and a_1 from the system with array assignment are shown to be identical to r_0 and r_1 respectively at these locations that have been changed (also shown within vertical bars). Places which have not been changed since the last reset of the array are instead equal to whatever is in the array A at those locations—the variables Y_0 and Y_1 can be used to find the value of the last resets. Now the instructions translate as follows:

- When we wish to read a location $r_i[x]$ in the abstract program $\mathcal{P}$, we return $a_i[x]$ when $a_i[x] \neq A[x]$, and Y_i when $a_i[x] = A[x]$.
- Resetting an array can be emulated by the array assignment $a_i[] := A[]$, while setting Y_i to the value of the reset.
- When writing to an abstract location $r_i[x]$, we write instead to $a_i[x]$. Furthermore we should make sure that $A[x]$ is not equal to $a_i[x]$; if it is not, we must change $A[x]$ and any other $a_j[x]$ which is marked as unchanged by being equal to $A[x]$. □

Table 3. Translating instructions for arrays with reset to instructions for arrays with assignment

I	$I^\sharp$

$y = r_i[x]$	$y_A := A[x]; y_a := a_i[x];$
	if $y_A = y_a$
	   then $y = Y_i$
	   else $y = y_a$
	fi

$\mathbf{reset}(r_i, y)$	$a_i[\,] := A[\,]; Y_i := y$

$?r_i[x]$	$?a_i[x]; y_A := A[x]; ?n; a_i[x] \neq n;$
	$(\underset{j \neq i}{\overset{\bullet}{,}} \quad y_a := a_j[x];$
	    if $y_a \neq y_A$
	      then $y_a \neq n$
	      else $a_j[x] := n$
	    fi);
	$A[x] := n$

other	no change

Definition 8. *An instruction translator $^\sharp$ from instructions in $\mathcal{P}$ to operations in $\mathcal{P}^\sharp$ is shown in Table 3. The notation $(\overset{\bullet}{,}_{j \neq i} \cdots)$ means repetition of syntax for every j from 0 to $n-1$ except i, all conjoined with ; in any order.* □

Definition 9. *Given a DI program with arrays with reset $\mathcal{P} = \mathbf{init}\ o_I\ \mathbf{repeat}\ o_T$, we can form a corresponding DI program with arrays with assignment $\mathcal{P}^\sharp = \mathbf{init}\ o_I^\sharp\ \mathbf{repeat}\ o_T^\sharp$ as described above.* □

Theorem 5. *Given a DI program $\mathcal{P}$ with n arrays of type $Y[X]$ with reset and a type instance $\mathcal{I}$ for $\mathcal{P}$, there exists a DI program $\mathcal{P}^\sharp$ with $n+1$ arrays of type $Y[X]$ with assignment such that there is a bisimulation between $\langle\!\langle \mathcal{P} \rangle\!\rangle_{\mathcal{I}}$ and $\langle\!\langle \mathcal{P}^\sharp \rangle\!\rangle_{\mathcal{I}}$.* □

6.2 Simulation of universal register machines

By Theorem 5, any program with two arrays with reset is bisimilar to a program with three arrays with assignment. Theorem 4 states that unreachability is undecidable for the former class, and so it also is for the latter.

It turns out that a stronger negative result is possible. We adapt the results from Section 5.3 about array reset to work instead with array assignment. We show that, for any universal register machine $\mathcal{P}$, there exists a DI program $\mathcal{P}^\sharp$ with only two arrays with array assignment which has the same observable behaviour as $\mathcal{P}$. The proof runs very similarly, so we present only the differences.

 – The variable $\Gamma^\sharp \vdash y_0 : Y$ from Definition 3 is unnecessary.
 – Figure 2 could be replaced by Figure 4.

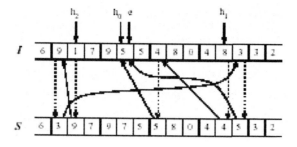

Fig. 4. Building a linked list using arrays with assignment

- The corresponding explanation from Example 2 would be altered as follows: Instead of $I[x]$ being set to y_0 at unused locations x, we have $I[x] = S[x]$ to mark a location as unused. Conversely, a location x must have $I[x] \neq S[x]$ if it is in use to prevent it being overwritten. This had to be the case anyway otherwise the successor of that location would be itself, and hence would be an infinite list—except at e, whose successor is never used, so we must be sure to have $I[e] \neq S[e]$.
- Table 2 is updated as follows:

  - Remove the instruction $n \neq y_0$ in $(\mathbf{inc}(r))^\sharp$. The role of y_0 has been replaced.
  - Replace $I[h_r] := y_0$ with $I[h_r] := S[h_r]$ in $(\mathbf{dec}(r))^\sharp$. This is the new way of marking a location as unused.
  - Replace $?h_r$ with $?h_r; I[h_r] \neq S[h_r]$ in $(\mathbf{dec}(r))^\sharp$, and replace the first occurrence of $?x$ (i.e. within the while-loop) with $?x; I[x] \neq S[x]$ in $(\mathbf{inc}(r))^\sharp$. This is the new check for a used location.
  - Replace $I[x] = y_0$ with $I[x] = S[x]$ in $(\mathbf{inc}(r))^\sharp$. This tests for an unused location.

- In Definition 5, the piece of code $\mathbf{reset}(I, y_0); ?y; y \neq y_0; I[e] := y$ is used to mark every location as unused, and to pick a non-y_0 value as the identifier for location e so it is marked as being used. This should be replaced by $I[] := S[]; ?y; y \neq S[e]; I[e] := y$ to mark every location as unused (because $I[x] = S[x]$ at every location x), and then to make $I[e] \neq S[e]$ so this location is marked as being used.
- We require a modification to the inverse function implied by an array as used in Section 5.3. We now say that $t(I)^{-1}$ is defined at a value w and is equal to v when there is exactly one v such that both $t(I)(v) = w$ and $t(I)(v) \neq t(S)(v)$.
- In the definition of $\approx$ (Definition 6), the last condition should be that $t(I)(v)$ is equal to $t(S)(v)$ instead of $t(y_0)$.

We can now state the following theorems.

Theorem 6. *Given a universal register machine $\mathcal{P}$ there exists a DI program $\mathcal{P}^\sharp$, and two arrays of type $Y[X]$ with array assignment, such that there is a bisimulation between $\langle\!\langle \mathcal{P} \rangle\!\rangle$ and $\langle\!\langle \mathcal{P}^\sharp \rangle\!\rangle_{\mathcal{I}^*}$ for any infinite type instances $\mathcal{I}^*$.*   □

Theorem 7. *The problems* **InfCU** *and* **FinPCU** *for the class of DI programs with just two arrays of type $Y[X]$ with array assignment is undecidable.*   □

Note that a program with only one array with array assignment is unable to make any use of the array assignment instruction: it can therefore be considered not to have this instruction.

7   Conclusions

This paper has extended previous work on DI systems with arrays without whole-array operations [9, 14, 11] by considering array reset and array assignment.

For programs with array reset, we showed that parameterised model checking of control-state unreachability properties is decidable when there is only one array, but undecidable if two arrays are allowed. If the arrays store booleans rather than values whose type is a parameter, we showed decidability for programs with any number of arrays. The decidability results are based on the theory of well-structured transition systems [7], whereas undecidability followed by reducing the Halting Problem for universal register machines.

Programs with array assignment were shown to be at least as expressive as programs with array reset. However, this yields a weaker undecidability result than for programs with reset, but undecidability for two arrays was obtainable directly.

Future work includes considering programs with array assignment in which the arrays store booleans. More generally, programs with more than two data-type parameters, multi-dimensional arrays, and array operations other than reset and assignment should be considered, as well as classes of correctness properties other than control-state unreachability.

We would like to thank Zhe Dang, Alain Finkel, and Kedar Namjoshi for useful discussions.

References

1. S. Adve and K. Gharachorloo. Shared memory consistency models: a tutorial. *Computer*, 29(12):66–76, December 1996.
2. P. J. Broadfoot, G. Lowe, and A. W. Roscoe. Automating data independence. In *Proceedings of the 6th European Symposium on Research on Computer Security*, pages 75–190, 2000.
3. K. M. Chandy and J. Misra. *Parallel Program Design: A Foundation*. Addison Wesley Publishing Company, Inc., Reading, Massachusetts, 1988.
4. S. J. Creese and A. W. Roscoe. Data independent induction over structured networks. In *International Conference on Parallel and Distributed Processing Techniques and Applications*. CSREA Press, June 2000.

5. N. Cutland. *Computability: An Introduction to Recursive Function Theory*. Cambridge University Press, 1980.
6. J. Esparza, A. Finkel, and R. Mayr. On the verification of broadcast protocols. In *Proceedings of the 14th IEEE Symposium on Logic in Computer Science*, pages 352–359. IEEE Comp. Soc. Press, 1999.
7. A. Finkel and P. Schnoebelen. Well-structured transition systems everywhere! *Theoretical Computer Science*, 256(1–2):63–92, 2001.
8. R. Hojati and R. K. Brayton. Automatic datapath abstraction in hardware systems. In *Proceedings of the 7th International Conference on Computer Aided Verification*, volume 939 of *Lecture Notes in Computer Science*, pages 98–113. Springer-Verlag, 1995.
9. R. Hojati, A. J. Isles, and R. K. Brayton. Automatic state reduction techniques for hardware systems modelled using uninterpreted functions and infinite memory. In *Proceedings of the IEEE International High Level Design Validation and Test Workshop*, November 1997.
10. R. S. Lazić. *A Semantic Study of Data Independence with Applications to Model Checking*. PhD thesis, Oxford University Computing Laboratory, 1999.
11. R. S. Lazić, T. C. Newcomb, and A. W. Roscoe. On model checking data-independent systems with arrays without reset. *Theory and Practice of Logic Programming*, 4(5–6):659–693, 2004.
12. R. S. Lazić and D. Nowak. A unifying approach to data independence. In *Proceedings of the 11th International Conference on Concurrency Theory*, volume 1877 of *Lecture Notes in Computer Science*, pages 581–595. Springer-Verlag, August 2000.
13. I. A. Lomazova. Nested petri nets: Multi-level and recursive systems. *Fundamenta Informaticae*, 47:283–294, 2001.
14. K. L. McMillan. Verification of infinite state systems by compositional model checking. In *Conference on Correct Hardware Design and Verification Methods*, pages 219–234, 1999.
15. T. Melham and R. Jones. Abstraction by symbolic indexing transformations. In *Proceedings of the Fourth International Conference on Formal Methods in Computer-Aided Design*, volume 2517 of *Lecture Notes in Computer Science*. Springer-Verlag, 2002.
16. T. C. Newcomb. *Model Checking Data-Independent Systems With Arrays*. PhD thesis, Oxford University Computing Laboratory, 2003.
17. P. Wolper. Expressing interesting properties of programs in propositional temporal logic. In *Proceedings of the 13th ACM Symposium on Principles of Programming Languages*, pages 184–193, 1986.

Industrial-Strength CSP: Opportunities and Challenges in Model-Checking

Sadie Creese

Qinetiq, UK

Abstract. The Systems Assurance Group within QinetiQ Trusted Information Management is concerned with the development of high integrity systems. Historically these have been military safety or security critical applications, more recently our focus includes customers with dependability concerns from the civil and commercial sectors. CSP has become a core capability of the group, and is widely applied throughout our work. Central to our use of CSP is the ability to verify automatically refinements using the FDR model checker. This talk will present an overview of our application of model-checking to industrial systems assurance, the technical challenges we face, the methods we employ to overcome them, the future technology landscape that we will be facing and the associated opportunities and challanges for application of CSP.

A.E. Abdallah, C.B. Jones, and J.W. Sanders (Eds.): **CSP25,** LNCS 3525, p. 292, 2005.
© Springer-Verlag Berlin Heidelberg 2005

Applied Formal Methods – From CSP to Executable Hybrid Specifications

Jan Peleska

University of Bremen, P.O. Box 330 440,
28334 Bremen, Germany and Verified Systems International GmbH
jp@verified.de

Abstract. Since 1985, CSP has been applied by the author, his research team at Bremen University and verification engineers at Verified Systems International to a variety of "real-world" projects. These include the verification of high-availability database servers, of fault-tolerant computers now operable in the International Space Station, hardware-in-the-loop tests for the novel Airbus A380 aircraft controller family and conformance tests for the European Train Control System. Illustrated by examples from these projects, we highlight important aspects of the CSP language design, its semantics and tool support, and describe the impact of these features on the quality and efficiency of verification and testing. New requirements with regard to the test of hybrid control systems, the demand for executable formal specifications, as well as the ongoing discussion about the practical applicability of formal methods have led to the development of new specification formalisms. We sketch some key decisions in the formalism design and indicate how some of the fundamental properties of CSP have been adopted, while others have been deliberately discarded in these new developments.

1   Introduction

Motivation. The objectives of this contribution are twofold. First, we wish to illustrate the usability of *Communicating Sequential Processes CSP* for specification, verification and testing in an industrial "real-world" context. Second, we are convinced that further research work on CSP and similar formalisms will benefit from the challenges which are posed by problems occurring in daily industrial verification practice.

Overview. In Section 2, an overview of industrial verification projects managed by the author is given. In each of these projects, CSP served as the underlying formalism for specification, verification and testing. We sketch how existing methods and theories contributed to the solution of each problem, and how the "feed-back loop" between research and industrial projects was closed by practical problems leading to novel research challenges. In the two sections to follow, more recent related research activities are described: Section 3 outlines recent results and ongoing research work in the field of automated testdata generation

A.E. Abdallah, C.B. Jones, and J.W. Sanders (Eds.): CSP25, LNCS 3525, pp. 293–320, 2005.
© Springer-Verlag Berlin Heidelberg 2005

from Timed CSP (TCSP) specifications. In Section 4 we introduce a framework for generating run-time environments for real-time execution of specifications written in "high-level" formalisms, such as TCSP, Statecharts, further diagram types of the Unified Modeling Language and Hybrid systems extensions thereof. The latter allow to describe both time-discrete changes and analog evolutions of physical observables. The framework, which is currently used for specification-based testing against various formalisms – TCSP is one of them – has been developed for the purpose of model-based development, test data generation and on-the-fly checking of system behaviour. Section 5 contains the conclusion.

Further Reading. Some basic knowledge about CSP in its untimed and timed variants is assumed in this article. For a detailed introduction readers are referred to [Hoa85, Ros98, Sch00]. References to further research results which are of interest within the scope of this paper are given in the sections below.

2   Practice Stimulates Theory – Applied CSP and Related Research Activities

2.1   Specification and Verification of Fault-Tolerant Systems

The Dual Computer System DCP. In 1985 the author and his team at Philips started the design and development of a fault-tolerant dual computer system *DCP* for a high-availability data base server. A design novelty at that time consisted in using a more symmetric concept than the usual master-standby technique: Both computers $CP_i, i = 0, 1$ of the *DCP* were active during normal operation without being strictly synchronised on instruction level. They both executed read-write transactions on their local data bases, but read-only transactions were executed by just one of them, while the other only stored the inputs from the client until the associated transaction had been completed. This strategy could be exploited for higher performance in comparison to a server consisting of only one computer. To minimise the number of synchronisation messages to be exchanged and processed between them, the two computers only synchronised their serialisation for conflicting read-write transactions[1], so that a consistent database state was maintained. As long as both computers were active only one of them returned transaction results back to the client. If CP_i failed, computer $CP_{(1-i)}$ only had to redo the open read-only transactions performed by CP_i – this was possible because $CP_{(1-i)}$ still kept the associated input data – and to transmit the results of all transactions which had not yet been sent to the client when failure occurred. This strategy avoided loss of transactions or messages from server to client, but it could lead to duplicate messages. These could be filtered by implementing an alternating bit protocol for client-server communication. After delivering the results of all open transactions to

---

[1] Two transactions $T_i, i = 0, 1$ are called *conflicting* if the write set of T_i has a non-empty intersection with the union of $T_{(1-i)}$'s read and write sets.

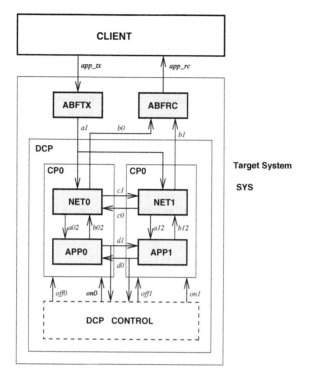

Fig. 1. Architecture of the dual computer system DCP

the clients, the remaining computer $CP_{(1-i)}$ could provide all database services since its local database was up-to-date. The only degradation visible to clients consisted in slower response time, since now all read-only transactions had to be performed on a single computer. Figure 1 sketches the DCP architecture; the fault-tolerance mechanisms are encapsulated in a separate layer denoted by $NET_i, i = 0, 1$. Specification details are available in [Pel97–pp. 59].

Verification Strategy for the DCP. The complexity of the fault-tolerance services which were needed to implement this type of behaviour suggested that a rigorous verification approach should complement the conventional testing activities planned for the DCP. At that time, Tony Hoare's book [Hoa85] on CSP became available, and later a joint publication with He Jifeng [JH87] described an elegant verification technique for fault-tolerant systems: Using purely algebraic reasoning within the CSP process algebra, the authors showed that the fault-tolerant implementation process and the associated requirements specification process both satisfied the same set of mutually recursive equations. Now equivalence between the two followed simply from fixed-point theory.

During initial formal verification attempts, however, it was realised that – rather than applying a single verification technique for all tasks – it would be more efficient to use a combination of specification and verification "styles", so that for each step within the verification suite the most promising technique could be selected:

1. The top-level requirements were formulated in implicit specification style, as a proof obligation on traces and refusals: SYS **sat** $S(tr, R)$.
2. Following a top-down decomposition of the system design sketched in Figure 1, each component was first associated with local proof obligations about its interface behaviour.
3. Using compositional reasoning for the parallel and hiding operators (see, for example, [Sch00–pp. 197]) it was shown in each decomposition step that the required behaviour of sub-components would imply the proof obligation specified for the higher-level component.
4. When the stepwise decomposition reached the level of sub-components to be implemented as sequential processes P_i, these processes were not only associated with their implicit specifications P_i **sat** $S_i(tr, R)$, but also with explicit representations in terms of the CSP process algebra.
5. If the explicitly defined processes were sufficiently simple to be implemented in a direct way, their compliance with the associated implicit proof obligations was shown using the proof rules [Sch00–pp. 197] for the satisfaction relation. If necessary, term re-writing based on the laws of the CSP process algebra was performed for the process, in order to reach a representation close enough to an implementation in the target programming language (Pascal) and operating system.
6. If the implementation of the sequential process P_i required more complex sequential algorithms the proof theories for nondeterministic sequential programs and distributed programs elaborated by Apt and Olderog [AO91] were applied, in order to show that the communication pattern used in the process, together with the sequential algorithms executed between communications, really implied the proof obligations P_i **sat** $S_i(tr, R)$.

The first five specification and verification techniques are all defined within the well-known denotational semantics and associated proof theories of "modern" CSP: Term re-writing based on the algebraic laws preserves failures equivalence, compositional proof rules about the satisfaction relation are defined for each CSP operator, and failures refinement preserves the satisfaction relation. The sixth technique, however, requires some explanation:

Verification of CSP With Sequential Imperative Program Parts. As is often the case in distributed systems design, the communication structure of the dual computer system and the sequential algorithms for queue management, serialisation of conflicting transactions, fault management and related activities were designed separately. Since Pascal was used as programming language, it was only natural to use a conventional operational semantics interpretation and Hoare logic for reasoning about pre- and postconditions, in order to prove the correctness of the sequential parts. This left us with the task to prove that the effect of the sequential algorithms as visible on local process variables also implied the proof obligations P_i **sat** $S(tr, R)$ specified for the visible communication behaviour of each sequential process P_i. Though Hoare had indicated in [Hoa85–pp. 185] how to integrate local variables, assignment and control structures of imperative programming languages into sequential CSP processes, the validity of combining proofs obtained for sequential program fragments interpreted in an operational semantics with CSP process behaviour interpreted in the denotational models did not seem quite as obvious to us to be applied without further consideration.

To this end, the *distributed programs* introduced by Apt and Olderog [AO91] proved to be helpful: The authors consider networks $X = (S_1 \parallel \ldots \parallel S_n)$ of sequential processes

$$S_i \equiv S_{i0}; \ \textbf{do} \ \square_{j=1}^{m_i} g_{ij} \rightarrow S_{ij} \ \textbf{od} \ \ (*)$$

In this representation, S_{i0}, S_{ij} are sequential nondeterministic program fragments written in an imperative style, operating on local variables [AO91–pp. 106]. Each g_{ij} is a communication construct of the form $g_{ij} \equiv B_{ij} \& c_{ij}!x$ or $g_{k\ell} \equiv B_{k\ell} \& c_{k\ell}?x$. The communication construct is structured into guards B_{ij} which are Boolean expressions over local variables and channels c_{ij} carrying messages $c_{ij}.x$. Channel outputs and inputs are denoted in the usual CSP style as $c_{ij}!x$ and $c_{k\ell}?x$. Communication between sequential processes S_i and S_k can take place over *matching* $g_{ij}, g_{k\ell}$ – that is, $g_{ij} = B_{ij} \& c_{ij}!x_{ij}$, $g_{k\ell} = B_{k\ell} \& c_{k\ell}?x_{k\ell}$ and $c_{ij} = c_{k\ell} = c$ – whenever both B_{ij} and $B_{k\ell}$ evaluate to *true* in the actual process states of S_i and S_k. The *effect* of the communication is equivalent to an assignment $x_{k\ell} := x_{ij}$ of the output variable value to the input variable.

The communication structure of the sequential processes S_i matched exactly with the communication pattern applied for the sequential processes of the dual computer system. Moreover, Apt and Olderog introduced an operational semantics for distributed programs which was identical with (nondeterministic) sequential program semantics for the sequential process parts S_{ij}. Indeed, it is shown in [AO91–pp. 334] that distributed programs X can be transformed into equivalent nondeterministic sequential programs $\nu(X)$, so that proofs about distributed programs can be performed using the rules for nondeterministic sequential program verification. Program $\nu(X)$ is given by

$$\nu(X) \equiv S_{10}; \ \ldots; \ S_{n0};$$
$$\textbf{do} \ \square_{(i,j,k,\ell)\in\Gamma} B_{ij} \wedge B_{k\ell} \rightarrow x_{k\ell} := x_{ij}; \ S_{ij}; \ S_{k\ell}; \ \textbf{od}$$

where the set Γ contains index quadruples of matching communication constructs $g_{ij} = B_{ij} \& c_{ij}!x_{ij}$ and $g_{k\ell} = B_{k\ell} \& c_{k\ell}?x_{k\ell}$ with $c_{ij} = c_{k\ell}$. For a channel c_{ij} let $\alpha(c_{ij})$ (the *channel alphabet*) denote the set of all pairs $c_{ij}.x$ with correctly typed channel messages x. For distributed program X the alphabet $A = \alpha(X)$ is the union over all alphabets of channels referenced in X plus event $\checkmark$ indicating termination of X (if X terminates at all). Using abbreviation

$$r_\Gamma = A - \{c_{ij}.x_{ij} \mid (i,j,k,\ell) \in \Gamma \wedge B_{ij} \wedge B_{k\ell}\}$$

and augmenting $\nu(X)$ by fresh variables $tr_v : A^*$ and $R_v : \mathbb{P}(A)$ and corresponding assignments, we construct a new nondeterministic sequential program

$$X' \equiv S_{10}; \ \ldots; \ S_{n0}; \ tr_v :=<>; \ R_v := r_\Gamma;$$
    do
$$\square_{(i,j,k,\ell)\in\Gamma} B_{ij} \wedge B_{k\ell} \rightarrow$$
$$x_{k\ell} := x_{ij}; \ tr_v := tr_v{}^\frown < c_{ij}.x_{ij} >; \ S_{ij}; \ S_{k\ell}; \ R_v := r_\Gamma;$$
    od

which still has the same behaviour with respect to the local variables of $\nu(X)$
since the fresh variables tr_v, R_v are nowhere referenced within the sequential
fragments S_{ij}. In [Pel97–pp. 87] we have constructed a syntactic mapping from
the set of CSP processes X following the communication pattern (*) into the set
of nondeterministic sequential programs structured like X'. Furthermore it has
been shown that proof obligation X **sat** $S(tr, R)$ holds if and only if

$$\forall U : \mathbb{P}(R_v) \bullet S(tr_v, U)$$

is a **do . . . od** loop invariant of the associated sequential program X' and
holds in case of termination. Intuitively speaking, the pair (tr_v, R_v) represents a
failure of X, when interpreted in the denotational model, and R_v is a maximal
refusal applicable in the current process state X/tr_v.

With this correspondence between CSP processes and nondeterministic sequential programs at hand, proof obligations X **sat** $S(tr, R)$ can be derived for
the process by reasoning about its sequential program parts and local variables,
using the operational semantics and Hoare logic.

Remarks and Related Publications. In [Pel91, Pel97, BCOP98] it is illustrated
how this combination of sequential reasoning with algebraic, assertional and
refinement verification methods can be applied, so that also projects of a larger
scale, where a single verification technique would not suffice to discharge every
type of proof obligation, can be effectively handled.

Observe that the necessity to embed description techniques for sequential algorithms into CSP has been realised by several authors, so that a variety of solutions is now available, allowing to pick the ones which are most appropriate for
the description of each verification problem or for transformation of specifications
into executable code: When using machine-readable CSP with the FDR tool, algorithms are specified using a functional programming language [Ros98–pp. 495].
The combined use of the functional programming paradigm and CSP has been
investigated extensively by several authors; we name Abdallah's work [Abd94]
on the development of parallel algorithms based on functional specifications as
an example. As an alternative to imperative and functional descriptions, the implicit specification of data manipulations has been made available by embedding
Z or one of its object-oriented variants into CSP. For this combination, we refer
to Fischer and Smith [FG97] and the literature cited there.

2.2   Formal Methods for the International Space Station

The International Space Station. The *International Space Station ISS*, launched in July 2000 and today still in its construction phase in orbit, is a joint venture between the United States, Russia, Japan, Canada and Europe. Managed through the European Space Agency ESA, Europe contributes to this huge international project by

- The Colombus Orbital Facility, a research laboratory to specialise in research into fluid physics, materials science and life sciences,
- The Automated Transfer Vehicle (ATV) to be used for carrying cargo from the earth to the ISS and – once docked at the ISS – for boosting the station higher in its orbit.

Moreover, Europe has developed and delivered several smaller sub-systems for the ISS. One of these is the *Data Management System DMS-R* for the Russian segment of the ISS. The main responsibilities of the DMS-R are guidance, navigation and control for the entire ISS, on-board system control, failure management and recovery, data acquisition and control for on-board systems and experiments. The DMS-R has been developed by ESA with an industrial team led by EADS ASTRIUM in Bremen, Germany.

The Fault-Tolerant Computer. The computing platform for the DMS-R is the *FTC*, a fault-tolerant computer system. Various fault-tolerant configurations can be selected for the FTC; the most reliable and at the same time the most complex one consists of a four-times redundant setting, where the four computer nodes cooperate according to Lamport's Byzantine Agreement Protocol [LSP82]. The corresponding FTC architecture is sketched in Figure 2.

The FTC communicates with other components in the ISS using a strictly synchronised frame protocol over redundant MIL-STD 1553 busses. Each FTC

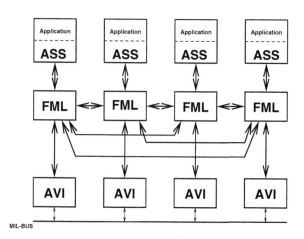

Fig. 2. FTC architecture

node has a layered hardware and software architecture: Applications are programmed in C and run on a ruggedised variant of the SUN Sparc CPU board developed by Matra in France. The application layer makes use of the Application Service Layer ASS for communication, time management and other services. The fault-tolerant mechanisms are encapsulated in the fault management layer FML. On each node, the FML is implemented on a separate hardware board equipped with transputer technology, with software programmed in occam. Transputer links connect all FTC nodes with each other, in order to provide the communication infrastructure for the Byzantine Agreement Protocol. Data bus access is managed through the avionics interface layer AVI, which again resides on a transputer board of its own and is also driven by occam software.

Between 1995 and 1998 the author and his research team at the University of Bremen performed a variety of verification and testing activities for the FTC. Two major objectives from a wider list of correctness goals consisted in proving the absence of potential deadlocks or livelocks in the occam code of the FML and AVI.

Verification Strategy for the FTC. The close relationship between occam and CSP and the availability of the FDR model checker [For01], [Ros98–pp. 517] suggested an *abstract interpretation* approach for these tasks: occam code P was mapped to a CSP abstraction $\mathcal{A}(P)$, thereby dropping all coding details of P without impact on communication behaviour. Then deadlock or livelock freedom was verified for $\mathcal{A}(P)$ by means of model checking with FDR. It soon became clear that model checking on CSP abstractions could only be used to verify small portions of occam code; it would have been infeasible to map the approximately 24,000 lines of code as "one chunk" to CSP and then perform model checking on the complete system abstraction. Instead, a verification strategy combining several techniques had to be designed:

1. Abstraction methods were only used on small portions $P_1, \ldots, P_n$ of occam code, resulting in a collection of CSP abstractions $\mathcal{A}(P_1), \ldots, \mathcal{A}(P_n)$.
2. Verification sub-goals were specified for the $\mathcal{A}(P_i)$ as refinement relations $SPEC_i \sqsubseteq \mathcal{A}(P_i)$ and verified via model checking for trace-, failures- or failures-divergence refinement. The choice of the semantic model depended on the sub-goal to be proved.
3. Compositional reasoning was used to derive the global verification goals from sub-goals verified for the $\mathcal{A}(P_1), \ldots, \mathcal{A}(P_n)$.
4. Generic theories were applied to re-use correctness results which only depend on generic characteristics of (sub-)systems: By showing that a CSP process $\mathcal{A}(P_i)$ complied with a specific communication design pattern (this proof was again performed by model checking) it was possible to use an instance of the generic theory, in order to prove that $\mathcal{A}(P_i)$ satisfied a desired property.

While the techniques 2. and 3. were just routine tasks, the abstraction techniques and the elaboration and application of generic theories required additional investigations.

Abstraction Techniques. The verification strategy sketched above implied that a variety of verification sub-goals would be investigated for **occam** code portions $P_1, \ldots, P_n$. Furthermore, taking into account that verification goals on occam level were expressed on a different syntactic level than the associated goals for CSP abstractions, a more formal definition of abstractions was required:

Definition 1. *Let P be an* **occam** *or CSP process and p a property of P to be verified. Let $\mathcal{A}(P)$ denote a CSP process and $\mathcal{A}^*(p)$ a property defined on CSP level. Then the pair $(\mathcal{A}(P), \mathcal{A}^*(p))$ is called a valid abstraction for (P, p), if*

$$\mathcal{A}(P) \text{ satisfies } \mathcal{A}^*(p) \text{ implies } P \text{ satisfies } p. \qquad \square$$

The most important abstraction technique applied was *abstraction through data independence*. Using this technique, the data ranges T of all occam channel protocols and local process variables are partitioned into the minimal number of subsets $T_1 \cup \ldots \cup T_k = T$ which have to be distinguished in order to prove a given property p for an **occam** process P. The CSP abstraction $\mathcal{A}(P)$ then operates on channels whose alphabet contains as many elements as partitions for T have to be distinguished; these can always be encoded as integral numbers $\{1, \ldots, k\}$. Control commands in P which are relevant for p and involve variables of type T are then abstracted to decisions on CSP level, where only the membership in a partition T_i is distinguished, but not the actual variable values itself.

Example 1. Suppose that channels c, d range over the natural numbers. We wish to prove that process system

$$channel\ c, d : \mathbf{N}$$
$$SYSTEM = (P \underset{\{|c|\}}{\|} Q)$$
$$P = c!0 \to STOP \sqcap c!1 \to STOP$$
$$Q = c?x \to (\mathbf{if}\ (x < 10)\ \mathbf{then}\ (d!0 \to STOP)\ \mathbf{else}\ (d!10 \to STOP))$$

is free of livelocks and always produces event $d.0$ before blocking. Formally, this property p can be expressed as $p \equiv ((d.0 \to STOP) \sqsubseteq_{FD} SYSTEM \setminus \{|\ c\ |\})$, $\sqsubseteq_{FD}$ denoting the failures-divergence refinement relation. Since the condition in Q only depends on the two situations $x < 10$ and $x \geq 10$, it suffices to analyse the abstracted process system

$$channel\ c', d' : \{1, 2\}$$
$$\mathcal{A}(SYSTEM) = (P' \underset{\{|c'|\}}{\|} Q')$$
$$P' = c'!1 \to STOP$$
$$Q' = c'?x \to (\mathbf{if}\ (x == 1)\ \mathbf{then}\ (d'!1 \to STOP)\ \mathbf{else}\ (d'!2 \to STOP))$$

where channels c', d' are defined with the finite alphabet $\{1, 2\}$ instead of the infinite set $\mathbf{N}$; value 1 representing the partition $\{x < 10\}$, value 2 partition $\{10 \leq x\}$ of the original channels c, d. The abstracted property $\mathcal{A}^*(p)$ to be verified for $\mathcal{A}(SYSTEM)$ is

$$\mathcal{A}^*(p) \equiv ((d'.1 \rightarrow STOP) \sqsubseteq_{FD} \mathcal{A}(SYSTEM) \setminus \{| \ c' \ |\})$$

referring to abstracted channels c', d'.   □

With a CSP process $\mathcal{A}(P)$ generated from the original **occam** process P by abstraction through data independence at hand, further simplifications could be made by constructing even more abstract CSP processes P' satisfying a refinement relation $P' \sqsubseteq \mathcal{A}(P)$ such that the desired property $\mathcal{A}^*(p)$ was preserved by this type of refinement. Then it sufficed to establish $\mathcal{A}^*(p)$ for P'. This technique is called *abstraction through refinement* and is less powerful, but considerably simpler than the abstraction through data independence, since it does not allow to further reduce the alphabet of the abstraction process P'.

Generic Theories. The local properties established for **occam** processes $P_1, \ldots, P_n$ via abstraction and model checking had to be combined by compositional reasoning, in order to establish overall verification goals like deadlock and livelock freedom over given sets of input and output channels. In order to simplify this compositional reasoning process, *generic theories* were elaborated and applied in various situations, where different process sub-systems followed the same communication pattern, as required by the generic theory. For FTC verification, the generic parameters of each theory were

- number of processes involved,
- number and names of channels involved,
- specific parameters referring to re-occurring patterns in the communication behaviour.

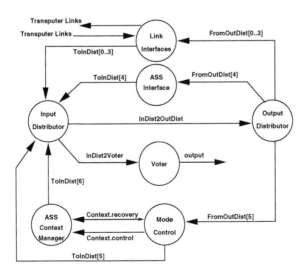

Fig. 3. Top-level processes of the fault management layer FML

Example 2. In the compositional reasoning process performed to prove deadlock freedom of the FML, it could be shown by model checking that each of the process sub-systems depicted in Figure 3 is a refinement of a process instance of type "multiplexer/concentrator" specified as *MUXCON* below. The definition of *MUXCON* is generic in the number N specifying how many outputs must be produced before the next input can be accepted and the number, names and alphabet of input channels $\{in_1, \ldots, in_n\}$ and output channels $\{out_1, \ldots, out_m\}$. Observe that an instance of *MUXCON* defined with $N = 0$ never refuses an input.

$$MUXCON[N, \{in_1, \ldots, in_n\}, \{out_1, \ldots, out_m\}] =$$
$$MC[N, \{in_1, \ldots, in_\ell\}, \{out_1, \ldots, out_m\}](0)$$

$$MC[N, \{in_1, \ldots, in_\ell\}, \{out_1, \ldots, out_m\}](n) =$$
$$\textbf{if } (n = 0)$$
$$\textbf{then } (GET[N, \{in_1, \ldots, in_\ell\}, \{out_1, \ldots, out_m\}]$$
$$\square (STOP \sqcap PUT[N, \{in_1, \ldots, in_\ell\}, \{out_1, \ldots, out_m\}](1)))$$
$$\textbf{else } PUT[N, \{in_1, \ldots, in_\ell\}, \{out_1, \ldots, out_m\}](n)$$

$$GET[N, \{in_1, \ldots, in_\ell\}, \{out_1, \ldots, out_m\}] =$$
$$(\square e : \{| \ in_1, \ldots, in_\ell \ |\} \bullet$$
$$e \rightarrow MC[N, \{in_1, \ldots, in_\ell\}, \{out_1, \ldots, out_m\}](N))$$

$$PUT[N, \{in_1, \ldots, in_\ell\}, \{out_1, \ldots, out_m\}](n) =$$
$$(\sqcap e : \{| \ out_1, \ldots, out_m \ |\} \bullet$$
$$e \rightarrow MC[N, \{in_1, \ldots, in_\ell\}, \{out_1, \ldots, out_m\}](n - 1))$$

The following generic theory is associated with the above process class:

Theorem 1. *A network of process instances $P_1, \ldots, P_q$ from class $MUXCON[N, \{in_1, \ldots, in_n\}, \{out_1, \ldots, out_m\}]$ is free of deadlocks, if every communication cycle*

$$\boxed{P_{j_1}} \xrightarrow{c_{j_1}} \boxed{P_{j_2}} \xrightarrow{c_{j_2}} \ldots \xrightarrow{c_{j_k - 1}} \boxed{P_{j_k}} \xrightarrow{c_{j_k}} \boxed{P_{j_1}}$$

contains at least one process instance P_{j_ℓ} defined with $N = 0$.

It could be shown by model checking that for each communication cycle in the network of sub-systems shown in Figure 3, at least one sub-system is a refinement of a *MUXCON* instance with $N = 0$. Since deadlock freedom is preserved under refinement and refinement distributes through the parallel operator, this established deadlock freedom for the full FML layer.   □

Remarks and Related Publications. The operation of the DMS-R system and its fault-tolerant computing platform has started with the launch of the Russian Service Module in July 2000 and is working nominally since then.

For more details about the ISS, the reader is referred to the web sites of the European Space Agency (http://www.esa.int) and of EADS (http://www.eads.net). A more comprehensive description of the verification activities[2] performed by the author and his research team for the International Space Station is given in [PB99]. Details about the fault-tolerant computer system FTC have been published in [UKP98]. The technical aspects of the FTC deadlock and livelock analysis are described in [BKPS97, BPS98]. The systematic application of generic theories and their mechanised verification with the HOL theorem prover has been sketched in [BCOP98]. Roscoe presents a detailed introduction and analysis of CSP abstraction concepts in [Ros98].

It should be noted that the abstractions from **occam** to CSP which were required to prove absence of deadlocks or livelocks by model checking have been constructed in a manual way, relying on the verification engineers' expertise with respect to the decision whether an **occam** code detail was relevant for communication behaviour or could be removed in the abstraction. Of course, this approach introduced the risk of inadvertently "losing" relevant code during the abstraction process. However, the activity of code abstraction differs considerably from the activity of code development itself. Moreover, the verification team was completely independent from the development team. Therefore we consider it as justified to assume that the probability of producing an abstraction error which exactly masks a programmed deadlock or livelock situation is low enough to be neglected. Observe finally, that the undecidability results presented by [LNR05] indicate that a mechanised abstraction may be generally infeasible, as soon as more complex data structures are involved.

2.3   Embedded Systems Testing for Airbus Avionic Systems

Testautomation Requirements Defined by Airbus. When Verified Systems International GmbH was founded as a spin-off company of the University of Bremen in 1998, the company received the first contract from Airbus for testing an avionics controller of the Airbus A340 aircraft.

The crucial requirements defined by Airbus in 1998 for the testing environment and its automation capabilities were

- Test data generation should be highly automated with respect to choices of data on individual interfaces, combinational patterns of input/output traces and their timing.
- All output interfaces of the system under test (SUT) should be continuously monitored, so that also transient output errors could be detected.
- Automated test oracles, that is, checkers of SUT responses against expected (i. e., specified) SUT behaviour should be simple to program and capable of detecting behavioural discrepancies with respect to interface data, causal chains of inputs and outputs, as well as timing.
- Regression testing should be fully automated.

---

[2] These activities also included hardware-in-the-loop tests and statistical throughput analysis which have not been mentioned in the present contribution.

Conventional Testing, as of 1998. At the time when Airbus defined the test automation requirements listed above, most conventional testing approaches used
sequential test scripts: Each test execution consisted of an alternating sequence of

- inputs to the SUT,
- explicitly programmed checks of SUT responses against expected results.

This technique had considerable disadvantages with respect to the above mentioned test automation goals defined by Airbus: First, the simulation of components in the operational environment which interacted in parallel with the
SUT were hard to express in sequential scripts, since all relevant interleavings
of the parallel systems had to be programmed explicitly. This often led to over-
simplified test scripts where SUT failures occurring only for special input/output
sequences were overlooked. Second, illegal SUT outputs at event-based interfaces
or illegal state changes at state-based interfaces were not detected if they occurred during the phase were the testing environment sent new inputs to the
SUT: Checking was only performed at specific points in time, and often only at
a subset of SUT output interfaces. Third, regression tests often failed though the
SUT behaved correctly: This was caused by not considering all legal SUT output
sequences in the test scripts. Instead, only one sequence was accepted as correct,
which corresponded to the observed SUT behaviour in a certain revision. After
changes in the SUT software, this output order changed slightly, but still legally.
However, since the test script could only handle one sequence, the regression tests
failed. Last, but not least, the effort for developing programmed test scripts was
somewhat proportional to the length of the test execution: If different behaviours
should be exercised on the SUT over a long period, all behavioural patterns had
to be explicitly programmed, leading either to long and complex scripts or to
over-simplified ones where the same pattern was executed over and over.

Specification-Based Testing With CSP and RT-Tester. Based on the experiences
with embedded systems testing for the International Space Station, Verified Sys-

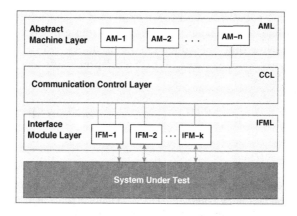

Fig. 4. Generic architecture of the RT-Tester test automation system

tems' test automation tool RT-Tester had matured to a commercial product in 1998. In contrast to other approaches, test configurations were always designed as distributed systems, as indicated in Figure 4: The test automation tool offers the possibility to run an arbitrary number of concurrent *abstract machines (AM)* on the test engine, each machine performing one or more testing tasks like

- simulation of components in the operational environment of the SUT,
- stimulation of specific input sequences, in order to test a special test objective which can only be checked in a certain pre-state, that is, after a specific input trace starting with SUT initialisation,
- checking SUT outputs against expected results specifications.

The execution of abstract machines in hard real-time and the efficient communication between them is supported by multi threading mechanisms and a *communication control layer (CCL)* allowing to exchange data within a multi CPU/multi node cluster architecture for test engines (see Section 4). The CCL implements an abstract notion of communication channels. In the RT-Tester version available in 1998, this notion corresponded to the CSP channel concept implemented by the FDR tool, [Sch00–pp. 469]. Channels were used as the only means of communication between abstract machines[3]. In order to map the channel abstraction onto concrete SUT interfaces, *interface modules (IFM)* refined data from abstract channel events to concrete hardware driver calls or software interfaces and abstracted SUT outputs back to channel events. This abstraction concept allowed to re-use test specifications implemented as networks of AMs on different integration levels: If a software integration test accessed software interfaces $s_1, \ldots, s_n$ of the SUT software, and these mapped directly to hardware interfaces $h_1, \ldots, h_n$ in the integrated HW/SW system, then the abstract machines used in software the integration test could be re-used on HW/SW integration level, just by exchanging the interface modules.

The behaviour of abstract machines could either be programmed in C or – and this was considered as a major advantage when compared to other testing tools – specified in Timed CSP (TCSP). In order to use the syntax which is accepted by FDR, TCSP timing constructs had to be expressed as special events expressing the setting of a timer – that is, a clock counting from a given value $\delta > 0$ down to 0 – and indicating that the timer has elapsed: As shown by Meyer in his dissertation [Mey01], each network P of TCSP processes may be decomposed into parallel processes

$$P' = (P_U \underset{\{| s_0, \ldots, s_k, e_0, \ldots, e_k |\}}{\|} TIM) \setminus \{| s_0, \ldots, s_k, e_0, \ldots, e_k |\} \qquad (**)$$

such that

---

[3] The current version of RT-Tester supports a broader variety of communication mechanisms: Test designers may combine the CSP channel concept described here with channels transporting structured C/C++ data and with shared memory data exchange.

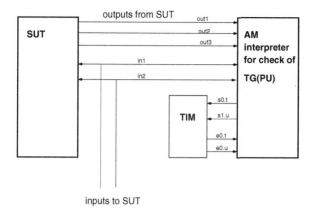

Fig. 5. Abstract machine acting as on-the-fly checker during a test execution

- P_U does not contain any timing operator like $WAIT\ t$ or $\overset{t}{\rhd}$,
- $TIM = \|\|\,i : \{\,0,\dots,k\,\} \bullet T_i$ with timer processes

$$T_i = s_i?t \to ((WAIT\ t;\ e_i.t \to T_i)\,\square\,T_i)$$

- P and P' are equivalent in the Timed Failures Model of TCSP.

Example 3. Consider the TCSP process network SYS with alphabet $A = \{\,in, out, a\,\}$,

$$SYS = (P \underset{\{\,a\,\}}{\|} Q) \setminus \{\,a\,\}$$
$$P = WAIT\ t;\ a \to in \to P$$
$$Q = (a \to Q) \overset{u}{\rhd} (out \to Q)$$

This can be equivalently tranformed into

$$SYS' = (((P' \underset{\{\,a\,\}}{\|} Q') \setminus \{\,a\,\}) \underset{\{|s_0,s_1,e_0,e_1|\}}{\|} (T_0 \,\|\|\, T_1)) \setminus \{|\,s_0, s_1, e_0, e_1\,|\}$$
$$P' = s_0!t \to e_0.t \to a \to in \to P'$$
$$Q' = s_1!u \to ((a \to Q')\,\square\,(e_1.u \to out \to Q'))$$

with T_0, T_1 as defined above.   □

With this equivalence transformation at hand, the FDR tool can be used to translate TCSP specifications written with timer events s_i, e_i into transition graphs. In fact, only the P_U component of equation (**) has to be transformed: A transition graph interpreter which is part of RT-Tester and controls the AM execution handles the s_i, e_i events in real-time by setting timers of duration $s_i.t$ when this event is generated by the abstract machine and simulating an $e_i.t$-event as soon as time interval t has elapsed (Figure 5). This approach immediately solves the automated checking problem for timed traces by using an

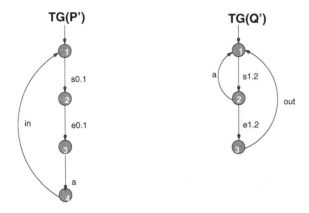

Fig. 6. Transition graphs of processes P', Q' from Example 3

abstract machine performing a *back-to-back test* in parallel with the SUT during the test execution: The AM tracks every SUT input and output by navigating through the transition graph TG representing the CSP specification of the required SUT behaviour. Whenever an outgoing transition of the current state is labelled by a timer event $s_i.t$, the AM sets the corresponding timer for duration t. Whenever the timer signals an $e_i.t$-event and such a transition exists in the current state, it is taken by the AM. If the SUT produces an output *out* for which no transition exists in the TG-state marked by the AM as current, an output failure has been produced. The failure may be caused by a erroneous calculation of output data within the SUT or by generating an output too early. Since TCSP specification semantics assumes maximal progress, outputs which cannot be refused by the SUT must occur immediately, if not blocked by the environment.

Example 4. Suppose the requirements for an SUT are expressed by TCSP process SYS as given in Example 3, with $t = 1$ and $u = 2$. Suppose further that *in* is an input to the SUT and *out* an SUT output, while a cannot be observed during the test execution. The checking abstract machine interprets the transition graph depicted in Figure 7, which is the product graph generated from the representations for P' and Q' shown in Figure 6. Suppose the checker observes trace

$$< (3, in), (3, out), (4, out) >$$

Then a failure is detected at timed event $(4, out)$ because the checking AM assumes transition graph state 42 in Figure 7, after internally tracing

$$< (0, s_0.1), (0, s_1.2), (1, e_0.1), (1, \tau), (1, s_1.2), (3, e_1.2),$$
$$(3, in), (3, s_0.1), (3, out), (3, s_1.2), (4, e_0.1), (4, \tau), (4, s_1.2) >$$

and the *out*-event is not legal in this state.   □

Observe that the checking technique sketched above only requires to specify SUT behaviour. If such a formal TCSP specification exists, no additional comparisons of observed test executions against expected results have to be programmed: Every SUT discrepancy is revealed by events for which no transitions exist in the current state of the checking AM.

On-the-fly checking has the further advantage that legal but nondeterministic SUT behaviour is not rejected by the checker, if the transition graph corresponds to a complete specification of legal SUT behaviour. If unnormalised transition graphs are used as in Figure 7, the checker has to mark several possible states as current. The SUT behaviour is accepted as long as at least one possible state exists. This procedure only allows checking in soft real-time, since the decision whether SUT behaviour is legal now not only depends on the maximal number of outgoing transitions to be compared against the observed behaviour but also on the number of possible states. Therefore, if hard real-time checking is required, normalised transition graphs should be used. These can also be generated by FDR.

The transition graph interpretation technique sketched above is obviously also suitable for real-time simulation: Abstract machines now operate on transition graphs representing environment specifications and generate events which are inputs to other AMs or to the SUT and choose different paths through the

TG((P' [| { a } |] Q') \ { a })

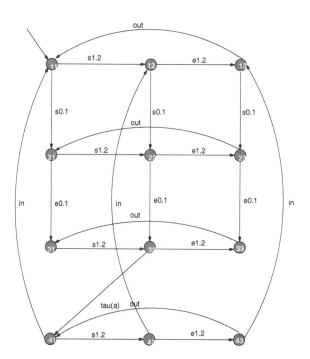

Fig. 7. Transition graph for parallel composition of P', Q' from Example 3

transition graph in places where several events are possible. This technique is also the starting point for systematic test data generation which will be discussed in more detail in Section 3.

Remarks and Related Publications. The testing activities performed by Verified Systems for Airbus could be extended since the first contract in 1998, so that today our testing projects comprise the A318, A340-500/600 and A380 aircrafts. The tested controllers are

- the Cabin Communication Data System CIDS developed by Airbus KID-Systeme,
- the Smoke Detection Controller SDF, also developed by Airbus KID-Systeme,
- the Integrated Modular Avionics (IMA) Modules, a new type of controllers which is first used for the Airbus A380 and has been developed by Diehl Avionics (Germany) in cooperation with Thales (France).

The testing activities comprise

- hardware/software integration tests for one or more controllers with integrated system and application software,
- so-called bare-module tests, where controller hardware, firmware, operating system and configuration data are tested before integration of the application software,
- software integration tests performed both on PC host simulation environments and on target hardware,
- module tests.

The same CSP-based testing technology has been applied by the author, his research group at Bremen University and by Verified Systems in several other projects: (1) Tests for a tramway crossing control system developed by EL-PRO in Berlin, (2) Tests for an aerospace satellite controller developed by OHB in Bremen [SMH99], (3) tests for interlocking system components developed by Siemens Transportation Systems in Braunschweig, (4) UNISIG conformance tests for radio-based train control systems developed by Siemens Transportation Systems in Berlin[4] and (5) tests of automotive controllers for DaimlerChrysler in Sindelfingen.

For untimed process algebras, the relationship between semantic equivalence (or refinement) and testing has first been observed by Hennessy and De Nicola [DNH84], within the context of Hennessy's Acceptance Tree semantics which corresponds to the failures model of CSP. Brinksma observed that these theoretic results could be applied in practice and developed techniques for automated conformance testing based on LOTOS specifications; an extensive

---

[4] The UNISIG standard has been defined for train control and communication within the European Train Control Systems (ETCS) initiative. The test automation concept has been published in [Ken04].

bibliography is given in [BT00]. The analogous concepts and further improvements have been elaborated for the untimed CSP world by the author in collaboration with Michael Siegel in [PS96, Pel96, PS97, Pel97].

During the period 2000—2004, our research activities related to real-time testing of avionics systems have been performed within the European research project VICTORIA[5] which focused on novel architectures, development and verification technologies for aircraft electronic systems. The test concepts developed for tests of integrated modular avionics have been described in more detail in [Pel03, MTB+04]. The advantages of interface abstraction and the resulting possibility to re-use test specifications on different integration levels have been discussed in more detail in [PT02]. The algorithm implemented in the RT-Tester system for automated checking of timed traces observed during test executions against SUT specifications has been published in [Pel02]. Further details about automated testing against Timed CSP specifications, in particular automated test data generation, are described below in Section 3.

3   Specification-Based Hard Real-Time Testing – Test Automation for Timed CSP

Solved Problems. It has already been sketched in Section 2.3 how the *test oracle* problem – that is, automated checking of SUT behaviour against expected results – and the simulation problem are solved for specification-based testing in a TCSP context: Using Meyer's structural decomposition of TCSP process networks, checking can be performed in back-to-back manner on transition graphs as the one depicted in Figure 7, and simulation can be performed by abstract machines deriving their behaviour from paths through these graphs.

Test Data Generation. For automated test data generation, that is, generation of timed traces containing inputs to the SUT, the evaluation of transition graphs has to be further refined. The reason for this is that graphs like the one depicted in Figure 7 do not encode information about the relative durations when several active timers will elapse. As a consequence, the graph suggests elapsed-timer transitions $e_i.t_i$ which cannot occur in a certain state, because another timer $e_k.t_k$ will elapse before.

Example 5. When initially entering state 22 in Figure 7, transition $e_1.2$ cannot occur, since timer $e_0.1$ will elapse before.

To solve this problem, we analyse an extended class of transition graphs, where each state is also annotated by the vector $(u_0, \ldots, u_k) \in (\mathbb{R}_0^+)^k$ of time durations left for each timer until it elapses.

---

[5] Detailed project descriptions are available under web links http://www.informatik.uni-bremen.de/agbs/projects/victoria/ and http://www.euproject-victoria.org/.

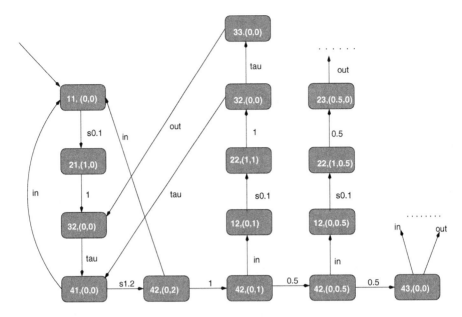

Fig. 8. Partial structure of graph G_A transformed from Figure 7

Example 6. When initially entering state 22 in Figure 7, the extended transition graph has encoding $(22, (1, 2))$ for the corresponding state, since the $e_0.1$ event will occur after 1 time unit, and it would take 2 time units to elapse, before the $e_1.2$ event could occur.

The transition system represented by these extended transition graphs has un-countably many states, but – adapting the concept of *regions* which has been introduced for Timed Automata [SVD01] – it can be abstracted to another graph G_A which only shows the finitely many different timer constellations which influence whether visible transitions are enabled or not. Graph G_A is generated from the original graph as the one shown in Figure 7 by repeated transformations with the goal to identify all nodes which are equivalent in this sense.

Example 7. To illustrate this process Figure 8 shows the initial part of G_A, as it results from this transformation applied to the graph from Figure 7.

In Figure 8, states like $(22, (1, 2))$ are identified with $(21, (1, 0))$, because in any case timer $e_0.1$ will elapse first. Original state 42 is now partitioned into 4 regions, each determining a different class of future behaviour: In $(42, (0, 2))$ only an *in* event can occur and after that, the future behaviour is determined by node $(11, (0, 0))^6$. This behaviour does not change until 1 time unit has passed after entering $(42, (0, 2))$, which is marked by the transition 1 to state $(42, (0, 1))$: If an *in* event occurs exactly in this state, both timers will elapse simultaneously in

---

[6] Note that in our notation $(42, (0, 2))$ identifies all nodes $(42, (0, 2 - d))$ with $0 \leq d < 1$. The analogous applies to $(42, (0, 1))$ and $(42, (0, 0.5))$.

state $(32, (0, 0))$, leading to a new type of behaviour, because a nondeterministic decision to engage into *out* instead of the hidden a event is possible. When state $(42, (0, 0.5))$ is reached, the hidden a transition can never occur in the next execution round, because the $e_1.2$ timer always elapses before $e_0.1$. Finally, when state $(43, (0, 0))$ is reached, both *in* and *out* become enabled.

For the resulting region graphs G_A it is possible to adapt a result by Chow [Cho78] which was established for testing untimed automata: Using a specific strategy to cover the graph by test traces and by checking that the SUT really reaches the intended target states in each test it is possible to *prove* (or disprove) a failures refinement relation between TCSP specification and SUT by executing a finite number of test traces. To this end, a *finite variability assumption* has to be stated for the SUT, saying that transient error states must be stable for at least a minimal time duration $\delta > 0$. This assumption is realistic from a practical point of view, since controllers cannot act arbitrarily fast.

Remarks and Related Publications. The simpler nature of the TCSP test data generation problem, when compared to the solution for Timed Automata has an important practical implication: In [SVD01] the authors emphasise that the number of traces to be generated for exhaustive testing of Timed Automata will be so large for non-trivial problems, that a complete execution of the corresponding tests would be infeasible. Moreover, this also indicates that a heuristic selection of "useful" test cases from the complete set might be equally infeasible, or at least extremely complicated, since there are too few known criteria for distinguishing "important" test traces from "less important" ones. We expect that for the TCSP approach a much smaller number of test traces will be required for exhaustive testing of non-trivial systems whose behaviour is required to be a timed trace refinement of a TCSP specification. The main reason for this assumption lies in the fact that TCSP does not allow to refer to clock values and durations in an explicit way within boolean expressions: Time is only "experienced" by observing that certain events occur before or after timers have elapsed.

It is interesting to note that Schneider has introduced a new operator in [Sch00–p. 272], the *timed event prefix* $a@u \to Q(u)$. This operator allows to measure the time u which has passed between offering an event a to its environment and the actual occurrence of the event. The measurement u may be used as free variable in CSP process terms, in particular, it may appear in communication guards. This operator is not allowed in our solution, where the timeout $\overset{t}{\rhd}$ and related syntactic abbreviations like *WAIT* t are the only admissible time-related operators. Since the timed prefix offers the possibility to access duration values explicitly within a TCSP specification, we expect that the TCSP test data generation problem will become as complex as the one for Timed Automata, if this operator is also admitted.

Further references related to specification-based testing have already been given in Section 2.3.

4   Executable Formal Specifications: The Hybrid Low-Level Language Framework

From Timed CSP to Specification Formalisms for Hybrid Systems. The application domains where most of our verification activities described in Section 2 were performed typically evaluated and acted on physical parameters of discrete (e. g., states of signals and points) and time-continuous (e. g., temperature, speed, thrust) nature. This led to the investigation of hybrid specification formalisms, where not only time-discrete changes of variables, but also time-continuous evolutions of "analog" parameters could be described.

After the successful applications of TCSP a natural candidate for such a formalism was He Jifeng's *Hybrid CSP (HCSP)* extension [Jif94]. Therefore its applicability was investigated by Amthor [Amt99] with respect to test automation problems. However, it turned out that the restriction of time-continuous evolutions to local CSP process variables was too severe to be used above software design level: In physicals, global time-continuous observables occur naturally as variables of physical laws and models. In contrast to this, HCSP already operates on a discretised level: The actual state of time-continuous evolutions specified in for local HCSP process variables can only be communicated to other observers by using CSP channels at discrete points in time. Therefore, according to our assessment, HCSP is well-suited for the software design of hybrid systems, but less usable for physical modelling.

As an alternative to HCSP, Henzinger's Hybrid Automata [Hen96] combine synchronous CSP-style communication with global time-continuous variables. Each sequential automaton concurrently acts on these analog parameters according to flow equations, that is, differential equations describing the continuous evolution of global parameters. Discrete changes can be triggered during transitions between control states. While offering the basic tools for physical modelling, Hybrid Automata are designed as flat networks, so that their practical application for large systems leads to specifications which are not sufficiently structured and therefore unmanageable. The hierarchic extension of Hybrid Automata developed by Alur et. al. [ADE+01] does not incorporate events in their semantic model; communication between parallel components is only performed via shared variables. Moreover, the syntactic representation is rather specialised, so that the chance for wider acceptance in an industrial application context seems rather low.

Inspired by Hierarchical Hybrid Automata and with the intention to reach a wider industrial community, we therefore decided to design a hybrid extension of the UML. To this end, the UML2.0 profile mechanism offers a rather well-defined means to extend the existing UML formalisms by new features and assign meaning to them. The resulting *HybridUML* profile has been published in [BBHP03], further description of its semantics can be found in [BBHP04]. HybridUML extends UML Statecharts [RJB99] by description mechanisms for invariants and flow conditions which hold for the complete hierarchy of states subordinate to the one where they have been defined (Figure 9). Additionally, class diagrams

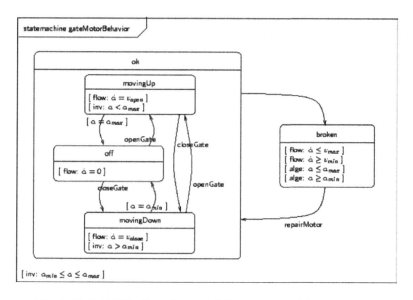

Fig. 9. HybridUML Statechart with invariants and flow conditions

are used to model state and sequential operations, and architectural aspects can be specified using the structure diagrams.

The Hybrid Low-Level Language Framework. Apart from formal verification of HybridUML specifications, a major research objective is to provide the means to execute the specifications in hard real-time, for the purpose of application development, simulation and testing. To this end, the HL^3 framework developed within our research group in cooperation with Verified Systems consists of a reusable hard real-time runtime environment R and a design pattern P for compilation targets of arbitrary hybrid specifications. Given a high-level formalism H – such as HybridUML – for the description of hybrid systems, transformations Φ_H from high-level specifications S into instances $\Phi_H(S)$ of the HL^3 pattern P can be developed. For $(\Phi_H(S), R)$, a formal semantics $\mathcal{S}(\Phi_H(S), R)$ based on timed state-transition systems is defined so that the transformation both provides a semantic definition of S and an executable program whose behavior will be consistent with $\mathcal{S}(\Phi_H(S), R)$. Similar to machine code, HL^3 should not be used for manual programming, but as a target language for automated transformations. In contrast to machine code, the real-time semantics of HL^3 program can be determined in a direct way, thereby assigning formal meaning to the high-level specification used as the transformation source. This is achieved by using a very limited range of instructions for multi-threading, timing control, and consistent handling of global state in presence of concurrency.

Remarks and Related Publications. The transition from CSP-based formalisms to hybrid systems has been performed since 1999 within the research project

HYBRIS[7] Currently, our main research focus lies on the elaboration of a testing theory for HybridUML. An instance of the HL^3 framework is already used in the latest version of the RT-Tester tool, and test support for specification-based testing against HybridUML is currently developed. On a more application-oriented level, the HL^3 framework is instantiated for novel application domains, in particular for railway control systems [HP03].

The importance of semantically well-defined real-time execution environments has also been noted by other authors: For the Duration Calculus [ZRH93], implementable subsets have been investigated by several authors, see Ravn [Rav95] and further references given there. Our HL^3 framework competes with Henzinger's Giotto [HHK03] which can be used for implementing executable Hybrid Automata and similar high-level formalisms. Giotto and HL^3 are similar with respect to the time-triggered scheduling of discretised time-continuous control functions. Our approach is slightly broader than Giotto, since it aims at creating both executable target applications and/or the corresponding testing environments, allows to distinguish between discretised time-continuous and discrete control functions in an explicit way and offers the mechanisms for implementing both CSP-style interleaving semantics and synchronous "true parallelism" semantics as required for executable Statecharts and synchronous languages.

5   Conclusion

In this article, the application of CSP in industrial projects has been described. The projects focused on verification and test of embedded real-time systems in the avionics and space application domains. References to further projects from these and other domains were given. The challenge of large-scale project verification and test led to numerous research activities – some of which have been sketched in this article – which were motivated by the need to combine various methods in order to cope with the size and complexity of the problems involved.

Since 1998, more than twenty verification engineers from Verified Systems International GmbH, the University of Bremen and from our customers have been involved in the CSP-based verification activities mentioned in this article. From our point of view this is a sufficient proof for the applicability of Formal Methods in general and, in particular, CSP. The other, even more important, benchmark for the success of verification efforts is certainly the number of problems identified in the analysed systems. Readers will understand that an explicit mentioning of "interesting" errors and their severity is not in the interest of our cooperation partners. However, it can be said that the databases managed by Verified Systems to document discrepancies uncovered during verification and

---

[7] Efficient Analysis of Hybrid Systems HYBRIS. Research project within the priority programme *Software Specification – Integration of Software Specification Techniques for Applications in Engineering* initiated by the Deutsche Forschungsgemeinschaft DFG. Information available under http://tfs.cs.tu-berlin.de/projekte/indspec/SPP.

testing projects since 1998 contain about 2000 entries. About one third of these findings are a direct consequence of Formal Methods applications in verifications or automated tests.

On the other hand, the search for novel formal description techniques which might appeal to a wider group of software or system developers is certainly not completed and still sub-divided into many competing and sometimes incompatible approaches.

According to our experience, the acceptance of a formal specification technique is considerably increased when specifications can be executed at least on simulation or prototyping level. The return of investment gained by uncovered bugs and discrepancies during verification, validation and testing does not seem to be a sufficient motivation to learn and use a formal description technique and associated methods and techniques in addition to the programming languages used to implement the executable system. We are therefore convinced that the most promising strategies for formal methods in industry are based on model-based development, where specifications can be directly transformed into efficient executable code. These observations have led to the research work on low-level formalisms which are suitable compilation targets for various more abstract specification languages and can be executed in hard real-time, as described in Section 4.

Finally, we would like to emphasise that the application of Formal Methods – in particular in the field of safety-critical systems – should always be considered as one means in a collection of several others which together ensure the quality and dependability of the products we develop. This collection also comprises techniques, tools and skills which are far less challenging from a scientific perspective (think of reliable configuration management, error reporting, project budget management, . . .) but contribute to the overall product quality, just as our latest advances in formal verification.

Acknowledgements. I would like to express my gratitude to the organisers and speakers of the *25 Years of CSP* event at the London South Bank University, for creating a stimulating conference with numerous interesting – sometimes even exciting – contributions and discussions. My special thanks go to Ali Abdallah for organising this outstanding event and for expertly compiling the conference proceedings.

References

[Abd94]   A.E. Abdallah. Derivation of Parallel Algorithms: From Functional Specifications to csp Processes. In B. Moller, editor, *Proceedings of Mathematics of Program Construction*, volume 947 of *Lecture Notes in Computer Science*, pages 67–96. Springer-Verlag, August 1994.

[ADE+01] R. Alur, T. Dang, J. Esposito, R. Fierro, Y. Hur, F. Ivančić, V. Kumar, I. Lee, P. Mishra, G. Pappas, and O. Sokolsky. Hierarchical hybrid modeling of embedded systems. *Lecture Notes in Computer Science*, 2211:14–31, 2001.

[Amt99]   P. Amthor. *Structural Decomposition of Hybrid Systems – Test Automation for Hybrid Reactive Systems*. Monographs of the Bremen Institute of Safe Systems (BISS) No. 13, University of Bremen, October 1999.

[AO91]   K. R. Apt and E.-R. Olderog. *Verification of sequential and concurrent programs*. Texts and monographs in computer science. Springer, 1991.

[BBHP03]   Kirsten Berkenkötter, Stefan Bisanz, Ulrich Hannemann, and Jan Peleska.   HybridUML Profile for UML 2.0.   SVERTS Workshop at the ⟨⟨ UML ⟩⟩ 2003 Conference, October 2003. http://www.verimag.imag.fr/EVENTS/2003/SVERTS/.

[BBHP04]   K. Berkenkötter, S. Bisanz, U. Hannemann, and J. Peleska. Executable HybridUML and its application to train control systems. In H. Ehrig, W. Damm, J. Desel, M. Große-Rhode, W. Reif, E. Schnieder, and E. Westkämper, editors, *Integration of Software Specification Techniques for Applications in Engineering*, volume 3147 of *LNCS*, pages 145–173. German Research Foundation DFG, Springer, 2004.

[BCOP98]   B. Buth, R. Cardell-Oliver, and J. Peleska. Combining tools for the verification of fault-tolerant systems. In B. Buth, R. Berghammer, and J. Peleska, editors, *Tools for System Development and Verification*, volume 1 of *Monographs of the Bremen Institute of Safe Systems*, pages 41–69. Shaker, 1998.

[BKPS97]   B. Buth, M. Kouvaras, J. Peleska, and H. Shi. Deadlock analysis for a fault-tolerant system. In M. Johnson, editor, *Algebraic Methodology and Software Technology. Proceedings of the AMAST'97, Sidney, Australia, December 1997*, volume 1349 of *LNCS*, pages 60–75. Springer, December 1997.

[BPS98]   B. Buth, J. Peleska, and H. Shi.   Combining methods for the livelock analysis of a fault-tolerant system. In A. M. Haeberer, editor, *Algebraic Methodology and Software Technology. Proceedings of the 7th International Conference, AMAST 98, Amazonia, Brazil, January 1999*, volume 1548 of *LNCS*, pages 124–139. Springer, January 1998.

[BT00]   E. Brinksma and J. Tretmans. Testing transition systems: An annotated bibliography. In F. Cassez, C. Jard, B. Rozoy, and M. Ryan, editors, *Proceedings of Summer School MOVEP'2k Modelling and Verification of Parallel Processes*, pages 44–50, Nantes, July 2000.

[Cho78]   Tsun S. Chow. Testing software design modeled by finite-state machines. *IEEE Transactions on Software Engineering*, SE-4(3):178–186, March 1978.

[DNH84]   R. De Nicola and M. Hennessy. Testing Equivalences for Processes. *Theoretical Computer Science*, 34:83–133, 1984.

[FG97]   C. Fischer and Smith G. Combining CSP and Object-Z: Finite trace or infinite trace semantics? In T. Mizuno, N. Shiratori, T. Higashino, and A. Togashi, editors, *Formal Description Techniques and Protocol Specification, Verification, and Testing (FORTE/PSTV'97)*, pages 503–518. Chapman & Hall, 1997.

[For01]   Formal Systems (Europe) Ltd. *Failures–Divergence Refinement – FDR2 User Manual*, 2001. http://www.formal.demon.co.uk/FDR2.html.

[Hen96]   Thomas A. Henzinger. The theory of hybrid automata. In *Proceedings of the 11th Annual Symposium on Logic in Computer Science (LICS)*, pages 278–292. IEEE Computer Society Press, 1996.

[HHK03]   Th. A. Henzinger, B. Horowitz, and Chr. M. Kirsch. Giotto: A time-triggered language for embedded programming. *Proceedings of the IEEE*, 91:84–99, 2003.

[Hoa85]   C.A.R. Hoare. *Communicating Sequential Processes*. International Series in Computer Science. Prentice Hall, 1985.

[HP03]   A. E. Haxthausen and J. Peleska. Generation of executable railway con-
           trol components from domain-specific descriptions. In G. Tarnai and
           E. Schnieder, editors, *Formal Methods for Railway Operation and Con-
           trol Systems: Proceedings of Symposium FORMS*, pages 83–90, Budapest,
           May 2003. L'Harmattan Hongrie.

[JH87]   He Jifeng and C. A. R. Hoare. Algebraic specification and proof of a
           distributed recovery algorithm. *Distributed Computing*, 2:1–12, 1987.

[Jif94]   He Jifeng. From CSP to hybrid systems. In A.W. Roscoe, editor, *A Classical
           Mind, Essays in Honour of C.A.R. Hoare*, International Series in Computer
           Science, pages 171–189. Prentice Hall, 1994.

[Ken04]   D. Kendelbacher. *Architekturkonzept und Designaspekte einer signal-
           technisch nichtsicheren Kommunikationsplattform für sicherheitsrele-
           vante Bahnanwendungen.* PhD thesis, University of Bremen, De-
           partment of Mathematics and Computer Science, 2004. Avail-
           able under http://elib.suub.uni-bremen.de/publications/dissertations/
           E Diss835_dis_50b.pdf.

[LNR05]   R. Lazic, T. Newcomb, and B. Roscoe. On model checking data-
           independent systems with arrays with whole-array operations. In A. Ab-
           dallah, C. B. Jones, and J. W. Sanders, editors, *Twenty-five Years of Com-
           municating Sequential Processes*, LNCS. To appear, Springer, 2005.

[LSP82]   L. Lamport, R. Shostak, and M. Pease. The byzantine generals problem.
           ACM Transactions on Programming Languages and Systems, 4(3), 1982.

[Mey01]   O. Meyer. *Structural Decomposition of Timed-CSP and its Application in
           Real-Time Testing*. PhD thesis, TZI Center for Computing Technologies,
           University of Bremen, Germany, 2001.

[MTB+04]   O. Meyer, A. Tsiolakis, S.-O. Berkhahn, J. Kruse, and D. Marti-
           nen. Automated testing of aircraft controller modules. In *Proceeding
           s of the 5th International Conference on Software Testing ICSTEST*,
           Düsseldorf, April 2004. SQS. Extended abstract and slides available under
           http://www.informatik.uni-bremen.de/~tsio/papers/.

[PB99]   J. Peleska and B. Buth. Formal Methods for the International Space Sta-
           tion ISS. In E.-R. Olderog and B. Steffen, editors, *Correct System Design
           – Recent Insights and Avances*, number 1710 in LNCS State–of–the–Art
           Survey, pages 363–389. Springer, 1999.

[Pel91]   Jan Peleska. Design and verification of fault tolerant systems with csp.
           Distributed Computing, 5(1):95–106, 1991.

[Pel96]   J. Peleska. Test automation for safety-critical systems: Industrial applica-
           tion and future developments. In M.-C. Gaudel and J. Woodcock, editors,
           FME '96: Industrial Benefit and Advances in Formal Methods, volume 1051
           of *LNCS*, pages 39–59, Berlin, Heidelberg, New York, 1996. Springer-Verlag.

[Pel97]   J. Peleska. *Formal Methods and the Development of Dependable Systems*.
           Bericht Nr. 9612. Christian-Albrechts-Universität Kiel, Institut für Infor-
           matik und praktische Mathematik, 1997. Habilitation thesis, available un-
           der http://www.informatik.uni-bremen.de/agbs/jp.

[Pel02]   Jan Peleska. Formal methods for test automation - hard real-time test-
           ing of controllers for the airbus aircraft family. In *Proc. of the Sixth
           Biennial World Conference on Integrated Design & Process Technology
           (IDPT2002)*. Society for Design and Process Science, June 2002. Avail-
           able under http://www.informatik.uni-bremen.de/agbs/jp/papers.

[Pel03]   J. Peleska. Automated testsuites for modern aircraft controllers. In R. Drechsler, editor, *Methoden und Beschreibungssprachen zur Modellierung und Verifikation von Schaltungen und Systemen*, pages 1–10, Aachen, 2003. Shaker.

[PS96]   J. Peleska and M. Siegel. From Testing Theory to Test Driver Implementation. In M.-C. Gaudel and J. Woodcock, editors, *FME '96: Industrial Benefit and Advances in Formal Methods*, volume 1051 of *LNCS*, pages 538–556, Berlin, Heidelberg, New York, 1996. Springer-Verlag.

[PS97]   J. Peleska and M. Siegel. Test automation of safety-critical reactive systems. *South African Computer Jounal*, 19:53–77, 1997.

[PT02]   J. Peleska and A. Tsiolakis. Automated Integration Testing for Avionics Systems. In *Proceedings of the 3rd ICSTEST – International Conference on Software Testing*, April 2002. Extended abstract and slides available under http://www.informatik.uni-bremen.de/agbs/jp/papers/ftrtft98.ps.

[Rav95]   A. P. Ravn. Design of embedded real-time computing systems. Technical Report ID-TR 1995-170, ID/DTU, Lyngby, Denmark, October 1995. dr. techn. dissertation.

[RJB99]   James Rumbaugh, Ivar Jacobson, and Grady Booch. *The Unified Modeling Language – Reference Manual*. Addison-Wesley, 1999.

[Ros98]   A. W. Roscoe. *The Theory and Practice of Concurrency*. Prentice-Hall, 1998.

[Sch00]   S. Schneider. *Concurrent and Real-time Systems – The CSP Approach*. Wiley and Sons Ltd., 2000.

[SMH99]   H. Schlingloff, O. Meyer, and Th. Hülsing. Correctness Analysis of an Embedded Controller. In *Proceedings of DASIA (Data Systems in Aerospace) '99 Conference*, volume ESA SP-447, Lisbon, Portugal, 1999.

[SVD01]   Jan Springintveld, Frits W. Vaandrager, and Pedro R. D'Argenio. Testing timed automata. *Theoretical Computer Science*, 254(1-2):225–257, 2001.

[UKP98]   G. Urban, H.-J. Kolinowitz, and J. Peleska. A survivable avionics system for space applications. In *The Twenty-Eighth Annual International Symposium on Fault-Tolerant Computing, FTCS-28, Munich, Germany, June 23-25, 1998*, pages 372–379. IEEE Computer Society, June 1998.

[ZRH93]   Chaochen Zhou, A. P. Ravn, and M. R. Hansen. An extended duration calculus for hybrid real-time systems. In *Hybrid Systems*, pages 36–59. The Computer Society of the IEEE, 1993. Extended abstract.

Author Index

Lecture Notes in Computer Science

For information about Vols. 1–3362

please contact your bookseller or Springer

Vol. 3414: M. Morari, L. Thiele (Eds.), Hybrid Systems: Computation and Control. XII, 684 pages. 2005.

Vol. 3412: X. Franch, D. Port (Eds.), COTS-Based Software Systems. XVI, 312 pages. 2005.

Vol. 3411: S.H. Myaeng, M. Zhou, K.-F. Wong, H.-J. Zhang (Eds.), Information Retrieval Technology. XIII, 337 pages. 2005.

Vol. 3410: C.A. Coello Coello, A. Hernández Aguirre, E. Zitzler (Eds.), Evolutionary Multi-Criterion Optimization. XVI, 912 pages. 2005.

Vol. 3409: N. Guelfi, G. Reggio, A. Romanovsky (Eds.), Scientific Engineering of Distributed Java Applications. X, 127 pages. 2005.

Vol. 3408: D.E. Losada, J.M. Fernández-Luna (Eds.), Advances in Information Retrieval. XVII, 572 pages. 2005.

Vol. 3407: Z. Liu, K. Araki (Eds.), Theoretical Aspects of Computing - ICTAC 2004. XIV, 562 pages. 2005.

Vol. 3406: A. Gelbukh (Ed.), Computational Linguistics and Intelligent Text Processing. XVII, 829 pages. 2005.

Vol. 3404: V. Diekert, B. Durand (Eds.), STACS 2005. XVI, 706 pages. 2005.

Vol. 3403: B. Ganter, R. Godin (Eds.), Formal Concept Analysis. XI, 419 pages. 2005. (Subseries LNAI).

Vol. 3401: Z. Li, L.G. Vulkov, J. Waśniewski (Eds.), Numerical Analysis and Its Applications. XIII, 630 pages. 2005.

Vol. 3399: Y. Zhang, K. Tanaka, J.X. Yu, S. Wang, M. Li (Eds.), Web Technologies Research and Development - APWeb 2005. XXII, 1082 pages. 2005.

Vol. 3398: D.-K. Baik (Ed.), Systems Modeling and Simulation: Theory and Applications. XIV, 733 pages. 2005. (Subseries LNAI).

Vol. 3397: T.G. Kim (Ed.), Artificial Intelligence and Simulation. XV, 711 pages. 2005. (Subseries LNAI).

Vol. 3396: R.M. van Eijk, M.-P. Huget, F. Dignum (Eds.), Agent Communication. X, 261 pages. 2005. (Subseries LNAI).

Vol. 3395: J. Grabowski, B. Nielsen (Eds.), Formal Approaches to Software Testing. X, 225 pages. 2005.

Vol. 3394: D. Kudenko, D. Kazakov, E. Alonso (Eds.), Adaptive Agents and Multi-Agent Systems II. VIII, 313 pages. 2005. (Subseries LNAI).

Vol. 3393: H.-J. Kreowski, U. Montanari, F. Orejas, G. Rozenberg, G. Taentzer (Eds.), Formal Methods in Software and Systems Modeling. XXVII, 413 pages. 2005.

Vol. 3392: D. Seipel, M. Hanus, U. Geske, O. Bartenstein (Eds.), Applications of Declarative Programming and Knowledge Management. X, 309 pages. 2005. (Subseries LNAI).

Vol. 3391: C. Kim (Ed.), Information Networking. XVII, 936 pages. 2005.

Vol. 3390: R. Choren, A. Garcia, C. Lucena, A. Romanovsky (Eds.), Software Engineering for Multi-Agent Systems III. XII, 291 pages. 2005.

Vol. 3389: P. Van Roy (Ed.), Multiparadigm Programming in Mozart/Oz. XV, 329 pages. 2005.

Vol. 3388: J. Lagergren (Ed.), Comparative Genomics. VII, 133 pages. 2005. (Subseries LNBI).

Vol. 3387: J. Cardoso, A. Sheth (Eds.), Semantic Web Services and Web Process Composition. VIII, 147 pages. 2005.

Vol. 3386: S. Vaudenay (Ed.), Public Key Cryptography - PKC 2005. IX, 436 pages. 2005.

Vol. 3385: R. Cousot (Ed.), Verification, Model Checking, and Abstract Interpretation. XII, 483 pages. 2005.

Vol. 3383: J. Pach (Ed.), Graph Drawing. XII, 536 pages. 2005.

Vol. 3382: J. Odell, P. Giorgini, J.P. Müller (Eds.), Agent-Oriented Software Engineering V. X, 239 pages. 2005.

Vol. 3381: P. Vojtáš, M. Bieliková, B. Charron-Bost, O. Sýkora (Eds.), SOFSEM 2005: Theory and Practice of Computer Science. XV, 448 pages. 2005.

Vol. 3380: C. Priami (Ed.), Transactions on Computational Systems Biology I. IX, 111 pages. 2005. (Subseries LNBI).

Vol. 3379: M. Hemmje, C. Niederee, T. Risse (Eds.), From Integrated Publication and Information Systems to Information and Knowledge Environments. XXIV, 321 pages. 2005.

Vol. 3378: J. Kilian (Ed.), Theory of Cryptography. XII, 621 pages. 2005.

Vol. 3377: B. Goethals, A. Siebes (Eds.), Knowledge Discovery in Inductive Databases. VII, 190 pages. 2005.

Vol. 3376: A. Menezes (Ed.), Topics in Cryptology – CT-RSA 2005. X, 385 pages. 2005.

Vol. 3375: M.A. Marsan, G. Bianchi, M. Listanti, M. Meo (Eds.), Quality of Service in Multiservice IP Networks. XIII, 656 pages. 2005.

Vol. 3374: D. Weyns, H.V.D. Parunak, F. Michel (Eds.), Environments for Multi-Agent Systems. X, 279 pages. 2005. (Subseries LNAI).

Vol. 3372: C. Bussler, V. Tannen, I. Fundulaki (Eds.), Semantic Web and Databases. X, 227 pages. 2005.

Vol. 3371: M.W. Barley, N. Kasabov (Eds.), Intelligent Agents and Multi-Agent Systems. X, 329 pages. 2005. (Subseries LNAI).

Vol. 3370: A. Konagaya, K. Satou (Eds.), Grid Computing in Life Science. X, 188 pages. 2005. (Subseries LNBI).

Vol. 3369: V.R. Benjamins, P. Casanovas, J. Breuker, A. Gangemi (Eds.), Law and the Semantic Web. XII, 249 pages. 2005. (Subseries LNAI).

Vol. 3368: L. Paletta, J.K. Tsotsos, E. Rome, G.W. Humphreys (Eds.), Attention and Performance in Computational Vision. VIII, 231 pages. 2005.

Vol. 3367: W.S. Ng, B.C. Ooi, A. Ouksel, C. Sartori (Eds.), Databases, Information Systems, and Peer-to-Peer Computing. X, 231 pages. 2005.

Vol. 3366: I. Rahwan, P. Moraitis, C. Reed (Eds.), Argumentation in Multi-Agent Systems. XII, 263 pages. 2005. (Subseries LNAI).

Vol. 3365: G. Mauri, G. Păun, M.J. Pérez-Jiménez, G. Rozenberg, A. Salomaa (Eds.), Membrane Computing. IX, 415 pages. 2005.

Vol. 3363: T. Eiter, L. Libkin (Eds.), Database Theory - ICDT 2005. XI, 413 pages. 2004.